American Foreign Policy: Aspirations and Reality

American Foreign Policy: Aspirations and Reality

Werner J. Feld
University of New Orleans

John Wiley & Sons
New York · Chichester · Brisbane · Toronto · Singapore

Library of Congress Cataloging in Publication Data:

Werner J. Feld
American Foreign Policy: Aspirations and Reality
   Includes index.
    1. United States—Foreign relations—1945–
2. United States—Foreign relations administration.
I. Title.
JX1417.F44   1984   327.73   83-23274
ISBN 0-471-87391-8

Printed in the United States.

10 9 8 7 6 5 4 3 2 1

Preface

American foreign policy is recognized as a very powerful force in shaping international relations. Although the United States' rise to globalism began before World War II, it was only after the conclusion of the war that the impact of American policy on the distribution of power in the world became fully apparent. For example, the containment policy, initiated by President Truman in 1947 to restrain Soviet expansionary designs in Europe, has broadened in scope over the years and has served as a governing principle for U.S. policies to halt communism in Korea, Vietnam, and more recently in the Middle East.

Important collateral policy instruments of containment such as the Marshall Plan and the establishment of NATO also shaped the course of world events. Western Europe was revived from the traumatic results of World War II and was able to stage an extraordinary economic recovery that altered the global and regional patterns of international economics and politics. NATO has created new relationships across the Atlantic that have helped to maintain peace between the superpowers.

American policy has also had important effects on the developing countries. Although U.S. responses to the demands of Third World leadership have often been perceived as less than satisfactory, they nevertheless have affected the development process in those countries where at present three-quarters of the world's population live, with a higher percentage likely by the year 2000.

The main purpose of this book is to provide analytical tools for explaining how and why particular American foreign policies have been formulated, how successfully these policies have been implemented, and how well the attainment of American policy aspirations has fared in the harsh reality of world politics. Admittedly, this is a tall order. But there is a clear need to provide students with a systematic and comprehensive introduction to understanding American foreign policy that links an examination of the policy-making process with an assessment of major U.S. policies since 1945. This book seeks to fill this need.

A number of individuals who helped in putting this book together deserve my deepest gratitude. Janet Davis typed the various drafts of the manuscript with her usual, superior expertise and, in addition, provided valuable counsel on organization and substance. S. Shivakumar was a very capable research assistant and helped immeasurably with the *Instructor's Guide* and the Index. Margaret Klemm and Frederick Dashner assisted in a very competent manner with the early research for the book. Judy Perkins was a very skillful copy editor and last, but certainly not least, Mark Mochary furnished the necessary, yet gentle, editorial guidance for the book's completion.

Again, I would like to extend my warmest and sincere thanks to all those named as well as those unnamed in the Wiley organization who have contributed to this endeavor. My gratitude also goes to the three "readers" of the manuscript who made many excellent suggestions for the improvement of the book. Finally, I would like to acknowledge the numerous thoughtful and useful arguments put forth by my students in American foreign policy classes and seminars from which this book has been able to benefit. Of course, only I am responsible for errors and omissions.

WERNER J. FELD

Contents

PART B   THE IMPLEMENTATION OF FOREIGN POLICY   **135**

PART C   THE CONTENT OF AMERICAN FOREIGN POLICIES   179

CHAPTER 1

Conceptualizations and Study Approaches

It is commonplace today to say that the world has been shrinking as the result of the tremendous technological advances made in transportation and telecommunications. Events in Vietnam, Afghanistan, El Salvador, Lebanon, and the Falkland Islands were flashed every day on the TV screen during either the evening or morning news. Not only are you continually exposed to the events of the world day after day, you are often also personally affected by them. Depending on your government's reactions to what happens in various parts of the world, and depending on how much the United States can influence the course of world affairs, you may be called on to fight on foreign soil or to be part of a "peacekeeping" force in the trouble spots of the globe. You may be compelled to wait in long lines to fill your gas tank, and your living standard may be lowered if future oil embargoes again raise the price of energy and increase the rate of inflation. If you are a farmer, the embargo of wheat shipments to the Soviet Union, which was imposed by the United States in 1980 but lifted later, hurt your income, and future embargoes and sanctions may harm the incomes not only of farmers but of other segments of the population as well. Thus, you can see that what your government does in managing U.S. relations with other countries, either on a day-to-day basis or in long-range terms, plays a crucial role in your life.

Considering the pervasive impact of U.S. foreign policy on the everyday life of Americans, it is not surprising that many complaints have been voiced outside and inside the American government about the conduct of our foreign affairs. One of the most strident criticisms came in the spring of 1982 from the U.S. ambassador to the United Nations, Jeane Kirkpatrick. In a speech before the conservative Heritage Foundation, she declared:

- The lack of influence of the United States in the United Nations does not represent some sort of worldwide revulsion against the Reagan Administration or even against me. The fact is that we have been virtually powerless in the United Nations for more than a decade.

- We have one vote; Vanatu [in the South Pacific] has one vote. That kind of principle creates a disjunction between power and responsibility because some of the nations who have . . . the resources to implement decisions are not identical with those who have the power to vote to make them.

- My tentative conclusion is that the lack of U.S. influence at the United Nations is due to our lack of skill in practicing international politics. It is also part and parcel of the decline of U.S. influence in the world.[1]

Obviously, these comments raise many questions that are highly pertinent to your present and future life and in particular to your physical security, your economic well-being, and the maintenance of your way of life. How effective is the U.S. governmental apparatus in dealing with our friends and foes throughout the world? How coherent and consistent are American policies that govern international relations? Indeed, what is meant by the term "foreign policy," and how does this policy relate to and interact with other public policies of the U.S. government? This chapter provides answers to the last two questions and prepares the foundation for answering later the other questions posed in this paragraph. Various approaches to the study of foreign policy will also be examined.

WHAT IS FOREIGN POLICY?

Definitions of foreign policy range from rather short, yet broad statements to more detailed propositions. For example, Cecil V. Crabb, Jr., considers foreign policy to consist fundamentally of two elements: "national objectives to be achieved and means for achieving them."[2] Marian Irish and Elke Frank, focusing specifically on American policy, offer the following definition:

> The foreign policy of the United States refers to the courses of action which official U.S. policymakers determine to take, beyond the territorial jurisdiction of the United States, in order to secure and advance the national interests of the American people, and to enhance the power and prestige of the United States in world affairs.[3]

A third view, perhaps the most appropriate in our interdependent world, is to regard foreign policy as that segment of public policy of a state that is concerned with the relations to other states and international organizations as well as with changes in the international environment.* This definition recognizes the essential interaction between different public policy sectors and indicates the multitude of activities and events with which a state's foreign policy must deal. There is no doubt many linkages exist between foreign and domestic sectors of public policy and that these linkages are often crucial in the making of foreign policy. An excellent example is the grain embargo mentioned earlier. The embargo was imposed by President Carter following the Soviet invasion of Afghanistan, which occurred in December 1979. It was lifted by President Reagan in the spring of 1981 because of political pressures by the American grain farmers who perceived themselves as bearing the brunt of economic warfare measures taken to induce the Soviet Union to withdraw its forces from Afghanistan. This shift in American policy toward the Soviet Union demonstrates the influential and sometimes inextricable economic and political interplay between domestic and foreign policy interests. It also means that foreign policy analysis cannot ignore domestic public policies and their political underpinnings.

In some cases, American domestic policies may have a direct impact on U.S. foreign relations. For example, a deliberate policy of deficit spending practiced by President Lyndon B. Johnson stimulated long-term inflation that proved to be contagious to the economies of other countries. United States fiscal policies that create or maintain large deficits (as has been the case under the Reagan administration) keep American interest rates high. The inflow of abundant private funds from other countries to take advantage of these high rates tends to undermine the stability of the foreign currencies. This is one of the reasons French President Mitterand wanted to move toward fixed exchange rates during the Williamsburg, Virginia, summit of the "Big Seven."* Other examples of what could be called "inadvertent foreign policy effects" are the consequences of U.S. immigration policies and laws, especially for Mexico, as well as the foreign impact of U.S. agricultural crop control measures, which are likely to influence the prices of agricultural commodities worldwide and could adversely affect the battle against famine in some of the less developed countries of Africa and Asia.

The United States, more than most other countries, has very extensive relations in the international arena. Not only do we have diplomatic missions in nearly every capital of the world, such missions and other contacts have also been established with many international governmental organizations ("inter-

---

* See also Joseph Frankel's definition according to which "foreign policy consists of decisions and actions which involve to some appreciable extent relations between one state and others."[4] Kegley and Wittkopf define foreign policy more in line with the Irish-Frank concept and emphasize goals and instruments.[5]

* United States, Canada, Japan, Great Britain, France, West Germany, and Italy.

governmental" for short, or IGOs) such as the United Nations, NATO, the European Communities (EC, better known as the European Common Market), and the Organization of American States (OAS). These organizations can be distinguished from international nongovernmental organizations (NGOs) such as the International Chamber of Commerce and the International Red Cross.

Another object of foreign policy mentioned in our definition is the international "environment" and, specifically, changes in this environment. This is a very important issue area and refers primarily to the exhaustion of raw materials such as crude oil or manganese. The United States is less dependent on oil for the smooth functioning of its economy than Western Europe; nevertheless, an interruption of oil imports would create a major calamity in the country. Equally serious, if not more so, is the need of the United States to import certain strategic raw materials including, besides manganese, cobalt and chromium. American foreign policy must address this problem and find solutions for the uninterrupted supply of these materials.

Another environmental issue with international implications is air and water pollution in different parts of the world. Pollution from neighboring countries might harm U.S. territory, and the lack of antipollution regulations in Third World countries may distort international trade, since it could lower substantially the cost of producing goods in comparison with production costs in the United States.

In light of the foregoing discussion, a refined definition of foreign policy may be desirable. *Foreign policy* is that segment of public policy of a state that either seeks to affect purposely or affects inadvertently the relations with other states, intergovernmental organizations, and international nongovernmental organizations as well as the international environment.

Policy Formulation and Implementation

It is important to distinguish analytically between the formulation and implementation of U.S. foreign policy. The formulation process for foreign policy is generally more complex than for purely domestic policies, because external participants and events may contribute to shaping American foreign policies. Border-crossing coordination may therefore be essential for the formulation of effective policies; moreover, the difficulty of this process is directly proportional to the number of states, IGOs, and even one or two international NGOs that might be involved. For example, the formulation of U.S. policies regarding NATO, which has a membership of sixteen states, is much more difficult than for policies vis-à-vis *one* other state.

In the implementation of foreign policies, the level of complexity also exceeds that in the exclusively domestic policy field. Not only must there be careful coordination and cooperation among American executive departments and agencies, but in some cases also agencies in foreign countries. This would be the case in foreign aid to Third World countries or when policy implementation needs the help of an IGO in the economic field such as GATT (the General Agreement on Tariffs and Trade, which supervises the operation of global international trade). The coordination of implementing actions may necessitate the use of diplomacy. Since intra- and extranational lines of authority are often discontinuous and difficult to trace, the task of policy implementation is compounded.

Another problem affecting foreign policy implementation (as well as that of any other policy) is the well-known phenomenon that the intended purpose of the policy (the *output*) and the actual consequences of its implementation (the *outcome*) may be at considerable variance. Consequently, foreign policy analysis requires careful evaluation of the policy outcome; this means that we must examine all phases of implementation for their effectiveness if the outcome differs substantially from policy intent.

Finally, whatever the outcome of a particular foreign policy implementation process, it is likely to have a feedback effect on the policy initiators and formulators who, in turn, may seek policy modification or may be exposed to new policy demands. As the result, policy-formulating and implementing processes may be changed, which might also result in different behavior by bureaucrats or even by nongovernmental participants involved in the complexities of foreign policymaking.

Foreign Policy Goals and Actions

In the analysis of foreign policy it is helpful to distinguish between foreign policy goals and foreign policy courses of action. The former are usually long-range, major national objectives, often closely intertwined with what the people in the United States regard as national purposes. These may include the retention and assurance of the democratic way of life in our country, the furtherance of American prestige in the world, and the achievement of an international order based on justice and fairness. However, foreign policy goals are also directed toward maintaining the territorial integrity of the United States and promoting the economic well-being of its people.

Foreign policy courses of action are normally means to achieve foreign policy goals. They basically serve as implementing instruments. In fast-moving situations, short-range objectives may have to be formulated that then will have to be attained by quickly devised and executed courses of action. Because the U.S. government must frequently react to current situations, a greater degree of flexibility is inherent in the formulation and execution of short-range policy actions than in the establishment of long-range policy goals. In such circumstances, very little time may elapse between policy formulation and implementation. An example of such circumstances is the U.S. decision to send military forces to the Dominican Republic in late April 1965. Fearful that communists and other left-wing elements had embarked on an insurrection against the government in the Dominican Republic, the American Ambassador W. Tapley Bennet, Jr., reportedly sitting under his desk to protect himself against rifle fire, telephoned President Johnson on April 25 and urged him to send troops to Santo Domingo to quell the insurrection. Following additional pleas from the embassy during the next 2 days, President Johnson responded affirmatively, and U.S. marines began landing in the Dominican Republic on April 28 as the advance guard for 25,000 American troops. Whether this rapidly made decision was a judicious foreign policy has been and continues to be the subject of heated controversy.[6] Regardless of its merit, the case illustrates the difficult circumstances under which government officials sometimes must make foreign policy decisions.

Long-range foreign policy goals and short-range policy objectives may be compatible or incompatible. They are *compatible* when the attainment of one goal reinforces the attainment of other goals. They are *incompatible* if one goal or objective can be attained only at the expense of the other. The difficulty for decision makers at times is to know precisely whether U.S. goals and objectives are compatible in particular situations, especially when events move rapidly. This may well have been the case in the U.S. intervention in the Dominican Republic when President Johnson was worried about another country falling into the Communist orbit as had happened with Cuba in the late 1950s. However, the application of hindsight leaves little doubt that the objective of suppressing the potential insurrection in the Dominican Republic was incompatible with the long-range foreign policy goal of the United States to improve its relations with Latin America.

APPROACHES TO THE STUDY OF FOREIGN POLICY

To gain an understanding of American foreign policy and in fact the foreign policy of any state and perhaps to make judgments about the future course of such policies, a number of study approaches have been used. In the pages to follow, we will briefly review five major approaches: historical description and analysis, legal analysis, structural-functional analysis, the "distribution of international power" approach, and decision-making analysis.

Historical Description and Analysis

During the early 1900s, the most common approach to the study of foreign policy was in the form of diplomatic history. Students reconstructed the diplomacy of a particular period, paying careful attention to details. They accomplished this and continue to do so by carefully researching governmental documents, the personal accounts of events by high-ranking participants such as secretaries of state or influential ambassadors, and newspaper stories dealing with diplomatic endeavors. Analysts describe the origins and causes of major American foreign policies and attempt to discover recurring patterns of foreign policymaking and foreign policy successes and failures. For example, in his *Short History of American Foreign Policy and Diplomacy*, Samuel F. Bemis offers a comprehensive account of America's varying involvement and interests in world trade from 1776 to 1959.[7]

Legal Analysis

Scholars espousing legal analysis as the proper approach to the study of American foreign policy focus on the relevant provisions of the Constitution, the particular laws passed by Congress in support of various foreign policies, especially their implementation, and bilateral and multilateral treaties concluded by the United States with other countries and with IGOs. Obviously, careful analysis of constitutional provisions dealing with foreign relations and of pertinent U.S. court decisions applying and interpreting these decisions offer important insights into the thrust and limitation of American foreign policy over long periods of time.

Equally important in this respect is the analysis of relevant federal laws that often provide the legal underpinnings of foreign policy initiatives by the U.S. government and furnish guidance for their execution. The thorough inspection of international bilateral and multilateral treaty provisions also is likely to yield fruitful insights into American policy objectives. For example, it is significant that none of the treaties establishing U.S. membership in multilateral alliances such as NATO or the Inter-American defense system (the Rio Treaty of Reciprocal Assistance) authorizes automatic military aid in the event our alliance partners are victims of aggression.[8] Bilateral commercial treaties with individual states define policy objectives and implementation with respect to economic intercourse between the United States and these countries.

There is no question that the legal approach to the study of foreign policy aids in comprehending the complexities of policy formulation and implementation. In fact, the actual role legal norms play in policy operation is substantial, if not crucial in some circumstances. However, legal scholars also tend not to fully appreciate the economic, social, and political environments in which foreign policy is initiated and carried out, with the result that they often overestimate the role of law in the world of international politics. Illustrative of this are the recommendations by Grenvill Clark and Louis B. Sohn that world peace can be achieved through a world of law and order,[9] including a reallocation of authority to existing bodies or the creation of new institutions. Unfortunately, the stark realities of interactions between states are at harsh variance with such hopes and aspirations.

Structural-Functional Analysis

The structural-functional approach to the study of foreign policy focuses on the U.S. institutional apparatus involved in foreign policy formulation and implementation, and on the formal and informal manners in which pertinent structures of this apparatus perform their functions in the policy processes. In a broad sense, as one scholar suggests, functions refer to "what must be done," while structures refer to "how must what must be done, be done?"* [10]

Analysts using the structural-functional approach evaluate the appropriateness of U.S. institutions and agencies that prepare policymaking decisions and execute them. In addition to the Department of State, which plays the central role, other executive departments—in particular Defense, the Treasury, and Commerce, as well as the Central Intelligence Agency—may also be involved to varying degrees. Scholars also analyze actions and forces triggering the performance of function by different institutions and structures, at times viewing them as inputs into policymaking systems that are often highly politicized. The end products of the function performance process may be viewed as outputs, and therefore the whole organizational sequence is similar to the input-output patterns developed by several political scientists for explaining the operation of the political system. [12]

The effectiveness of the performance of functions in the foreign policymaking process is also an important target of structural-functional analysis. This includes an assessment of the proper staffing of institutions and agencies, the skill and expertise of their civil services, their political acumen, and relations with influential clienteles.

The "Distribution of International Power" Approach

Another approach to the study of foreign policy emphasizes the distribution of power in the international arena as most significant. This approach does not completely ignore factors and motivations arising from the domestic environment in the United States but considers events and conditions in the international system, including foreign policy goals of other countries and the pursuit of these goals, to be the most influential elements in shaping American foreign policymaking.

This method of analysis has its intellectual roots in the *realist* interpretation of international politics, and therefore, like the realists, it emphasizes the relative power position of states in the world. [13] American foreign policy should

---

* According to Levy, structure means a *pattern*, that is, observable uniformity of action and operation. The purpose of functions is the maintenance of the unit with which it is associated. [11]

be based on assessments of its power and interests as they relate to other states. International sources set the directions and the issues of foreign policy, which is seen as a device to protect, defend, and if possible enrich the United States. Domestic matters are only crucial as modifiers or amplifiers of this policy.

An important aspect of this approach is the *proper* assessment of the power distribution between the United States and other states. This assessment must include not only military power but also financial resources and sociopsychological factors. Adherents of the realist school have argued that the basic cause of the U.S. defeat in Vietnam was the failure of American decision makers to define accurately the power of the United States and the failure to distinguish between what they wanted to happen and what could be achieved.

Consideration of the relative power positions of states in the formulation of foreign policy leads inevitably to the concept of the *balance of power*. The concept can be understood to mean an objective description of a situation in which the power of one state may be balanced by the more or less equal power of another state or in which the collective power of several states allied to each other is balanced by the collective power of an alliance of a number of other states. The first constellation is a bipolar balance-of-power system, exemplified essentially by the U.S. - Soviet relationship. The second is a multipolar system such as existed at the turn of the nineteenth century in Europe. The Triple Alliance of Germany, Austria-Hungary, and Italy was balanced by the Triple Entente Great Britain, France, and Russia formed in 1904.[14]

Another conception of the balance of power is as a guide for foreign policy matters. As such, it can be used to strengthen the American power position through formal alliances such as NATO or the establishment of less formal, close, friendly relations with countries occupying key geographical locations and/or possessing resources essential to America's economic and strategic interests. Egypt and Mexico might fall into the latter category. Balance-of-power considerations may also play a role in achieving a measure of regional stability, especially in the less-developed world. The successful search for peace in the Middle East may well depend on achieving such a balance of power among the states of the region.

Decision-Making Analysis

The most frequently used approach to the study of American foreign policy is decision-making analysis regarding foreign policymaking. The early works adhering to this approach are Richard C. Snyder and Edgar S. Furniss, Jr., in their book *American Foreign Policy*[15] and Joseph Frankel, *The Making of Foreign Policy*.[16]

Decision-making analysis focuses attention on official decision makers and their activities in the making of U.S. foreign policy. The term "official decision maker" is understood in a broad sense and includes Congress and even the Supreme Court.

According to Frankel, various influences on the decision makers come under the heading of environment. He considers the environment of foreign policy decisions as theoretically "limitless."* [17] Any domestic matter may impinge on foreign policy and may require adjustment, and any problem anywhere in the world or even outer space may call for urgent attention.

What do we mean by decision making? Fundamentally, we talk about the act of choosing among available alternatives about which a certain amount of uncertainty exists.[18] However, this simple statement conceals the difficulty of analysis. The many problems include the sufficiency of information available to decision makers, uncertainty about alternatives and their consequences, and the manifold pressures exerted on policymakers to accommodate special interests of domestic groups and foreign governments. Labor unions urging a higher level of protectionism are a good example of pressure from a domestic group that affects U.S. international trade policy; Israel is a prime example of a foreign government pushing to influence American security policy.

These problems make it very difficult to reach a *rational decision*, one directed toward the attainment of a clearly defined goal reflecting the highest preference of the decision makers, with the assumptions that, (a) for the choice of alternatives, comprehensive, relevant information was available *and* used, (b) the consequences of all alternative courses were fully established, and (c) the selected alternative has the highest utility in reaching the goal desired. Social scientists must assume, nevertheless, that in all human relations, rational elements predominate over the irrational.[19] These elements must be discovered rather than taken for granted, and their discovery requires an assessment of the various influences bearing on every decision made. They include the social and economic backgrounds of the decision makers, their personal values, moral standards, goals, interests, and aspirations, their prior commitments, and specific motivations that may stem from the bureaucratic position they hold.

Despite the many factors that affect the making of governmental decisions in the field of U.S. foreign policy and the recognition that action in this area involves not a single decision to be analyzed but a continuum of interrelated decisions, the decision-making approach provides significant insights into the dynamics of international politics and the strategies needed to attain U.S. objectives in the international arena. Indeed, movement in the international arena flows from hundreds of decisions made in the governmental and non-governmental institutions and enterprises around the world. It is on the basis of their analysis of how these decisions affect the American foreign policymaking process that scholars can make some predictions for the future; however, there are always the hazards that goals may change as the policymaking process

---

* This definition is broader than the one used earlier in this chapter, which referred primarily to the physical environment in the international arena

progresses, decision makers may not be aware of discrepancies between antici-pated and actual consequences of alternatives, and new information may become available.

It is important to note that significant constraints limit the final foreign policy decision. One of these constraints consists of the framework of foreign policy goals and particular transnational policies already existing in an individ-ual country. Unless a definite change is intended, the decision makers must work within this framework to assure that new objectives and policies are compatible with former ones. Three other constraints on foreign policy choices are even more binding: (1) the overrriding, paramount security and economic needs, and the political aspirations of the people of a country that may find expression in part or wholly in the national interest of this country, (2) the extent of the capabilities and vulnerabilities of a country, mainly in the military, economic, financial, and political fields determining the limits of support for a specific policy or goal, and (3) the extent of capabilities and vulnerabilities of other countries permitting the latter to obviate, interpose, or perhaps support the desired policy depending on the foreign policy goals of individual countries affected by the policy. Even the United States is not all-powerful, and American foreign policymakers must never ignore this fact. The fiasco of Vietnam has been a bitter lesson in this respect.

THE APPROACH OF THIS BOOK

In the examination and assessment of American foreign policy, this book will draw on several approaches. The core will be *decision-making analysis*, but whenever some of the other approaches will aid in the explanation of the policy formulation and implementation processes or help to illuminate certain aspects of these processes, we may resort to *structural-functional analysis* or *legal analysis*. As already indicated, foreign policy decision making must take into consideration the power positions of various states with which the United States has relations, and therefore the analysis for the international distribu-tion of power is likely to become an essential part of decision-making analysis. Finally, since historical background and assessment is needed for you to appreciate fully the significance and effect of individual American foreign policies in the different regions of the world, we may draw on relevant histori-cal descriptions and analyses to aid you in understanding particular foreign policy issues.

One of the main concerns of this book will be the presentation and discussion of sources of explanation relevant for the foreign policy decision-making process. Here we must keep in mind that the processes are crucial not only for the formulation of policies but also for the implementation of those policies, something that at times is overlooked or underestimated.

Sources of explanation refer to those factors that are primarily responsible for the formulation of individual policies and for the choice of instruments used in the implementation of these policies. They are key variables in the policy decision-making process, giving decisions their specific content and offering explanations why a particular policy has been adopted and why a particular manner for its execution was chosen. These variables cannot always be identified with ease in concrete situations, because the number of factors that tend to influence the decision makers is usually large.

To gain an understanding of the policy implementation process, we will also examine the available instruments and evaluate the implementation of particular U.S. policies, including a determination of how effectively these policies have attained their intended objectives and whether perhaps the use of different implementation instruments might have produced more favorable outcomes. This will require an overview of contemporary U.S. foreign policies designed to attain various American aspirations. This overview will be divided into policies toward the Communist countries, the Western advanced countries, and the Third World. A concluding chapter will examine to what degree the aspirations of American foreign policy have been fulfilled and to what degree they have been blocked by the economic, political, and strategic realities of this world. What are the prospects for overcoming the obstacles to American aspirations, and what contributions can improved foreign policy-making processes make toward this goal?

SUMMARY

This chapter has three purposes:

1. To acquaint you with basic terms and concepts useful for the understanding and analysis of American foreign policy.
2. To introduce you to a number of approaches to the study of foreign policy.
3. To give you an overview of the plan of this book.

Foreign policy is considered to be that segment of public policy of a state that either seeks to affect purposely or affects inadvertently the relation with other states, intergovernmental organizations, and international nongovernmental organizations as well as the international environment. In the making of foreign policy, an analytical distinction must be made between policy formulation and implementation. In the implementing phase, the intended objective and purpose of the policy (the *output*) may not be achieved, and the *outcome* of implementation may be quite different from that originally intended. This raises the question of implementation effectiveness when policy objectives abort and give rise to feedback flows to policy formulators who may want to modify the content of the original policy.

In this analysis of foreign policy, a distinction must be made between *policy goals* and *courses of action*. The former are long-range in nature and may be major national objectives. Courses of actions are usually short-range in nature;

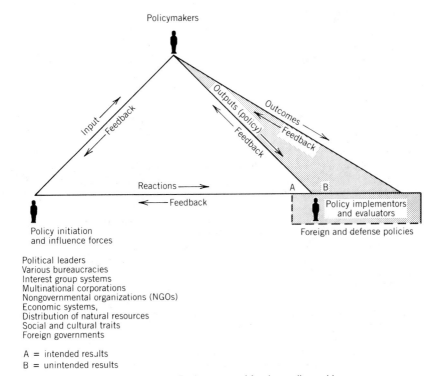

Policymakers

Input — Feedback

Outputs (policy) — Feedback

Outcomes — Feedback

Reactions →

← Feedback

A   B

Policy implementors and evaluators

Policy initiation and influence forces

Foreign and defense policies

Political leaders
Various bureaucracies
Interest group systems
Multinational corporations
Nongovernmental organizations (NGOs)
Economic systems,
Distribution of natural resources
Social and cultural traits
Foreign governments

A = intended results
B = unintended results

Figure 1.1   The Environment of foreign policymaking.

they may be means to achieve important foreign policy goals, and in fast-moving situations they must be formulated quickly.

The core approach used in this book for foreign policy assessment is *decision-making analysis*, but *historical accounts, legal analysis, structural-functional analysis*, and especially *distribution of international power analysis* are employed when these approaches help in shedding light on the complexities of the decision-making processes in the foreign policy arena. A great variety of domestic and external forces as well as institutional and psychological elements have a bearing on and influence these processes. In many instances, these processes have been and continue to be in permanent motion. Figure 1.1 provides a graphic illustration of the basic parts and dynamics of this process.

To evaluate how far the aspirations of American foreign policymakers (as reflected in contemporary U.S. policies) have been fulfilled and to what degree they have been obviated by economic, political, and strategic realities of the international system, the book strives to identify *key variables* that have affected or are likely to influence the foreign policy decision-making process with respect to different policies. These variables will help to provide sources of explanation when these policies are examined and assessed and, thereby, will enable you to obtain a better appreciation of American foreign policy of the past and the future.

NOTES

1. *Time*, June 21, 1982, p. 36.
2. Cecil V. Crabb, Jr., *American Foreign Policy in the Nuclear Age*, 3rd ed. (New York: Harper & Row, 1972), p. 1.
3. Marian D. Irish and Elke Frank, *U.S. Foreign Policy* (New York: Harcourt Brace Jovanovich, 1975), p. 1.
4. Joseph Frankel, *The Making of Foreign Policy* (New York: Oxford University Press, 1963), p. 1.
5. Charles W. Kegley and Eugene R. Wittkopf, *American Foreign Policy*, 2nd ed. (New York: St. Martin's Press, 1982), pp. 3–4.
6. For comprehensive treatments of the Dominican crisis, see John B. Martin, *Overtaken by Events* (New York: Doubleday, 1966); and Robert J. Barnet, *Intervention and Revolution: America's Confrontation with Insurgent Movements around the World* (New York: World Publishing, 1968), pp. 153–181.
7. Samuel F. Bemis, *Short History of American Foreign Policy and Diplomacy* (New York: Holt, Rinehart & Winston, 1959), pp. 673–690.
8. See article 5 of the NATO Treaty, and article 3 of the Rio Treaty.
9. *World Peace through World Law* (Cambridge, Mass.: Harvard University Press, 1958).
10. Marion J. Levy, Jr., *The Structure of Society* (Princeton, N.J.: Princeton University Press, 1952), p. 64.
11. Ibid., pp. 57 and 62, respectively.
12. For example, David Easton, *A Framework for Political Analysis* (Englewood Cliffs, N.J.: Prentice-Hall, 1965); Gabriel Almond and James Coleman (eds.), *The Politics of Developing Areas* (Princeton, N.J.: Princeton University Press, 1960), especially the Introduction. See also Michael Haas, "A Functional Approach to International Organization," in *International Politics and Foreign Policy*, edited by James N. Rosenau (New York: Free Press, 1969), pp. 131–141.
13. The most prominent representative of the realist school of thought is Hans J. Morgenthau. See his *Politics among Nations*, 5th ed. (New York: Alfred A. Knopf, 1973).
14. For a discussion of various balance-of-power systems, see Morton A. Kaplan, *System and Process in International Politics* (New York: John Wiley & Sons, 1964—Science Edition), pp. 22–53.
15. Richard C. Snyder and Edgar S. Furniss, Jr., *American Foreign Policy* (New York: Rinehart, 1954).
16. Joseph Frankel, *The Making of Foreign Policy* (New York: Oxford University Press, 1963).
17. Ibid,. p. 3.
18. James E. Dougherty and Robert L. Pfaltzgraff, Jr., *Contending Theories of International Relations* (Philadelphia: Lippincott, 1971), p. 312.
19. Ibid., pp. 316–317.

A

FORMULATION OF FOREIGN POLICY

CHAPTER 2

Tools for Analysis

SOURCES OF EXPLANATION

This chapter discusses the problem of causality between pertinent variables and the formulation of particular variables, presents a classification of these variables, and examines three models of the foreign policymaking process that constitute idealized versions of this process and have received prominent, and at times critical, attention in the scholarly literature.

The Problem of Causality

If one could identify with precision the specific factors determining the formulation of an individual foreign policy in a particular issue area, it would be possible to establish with confidence the causality between these factors and the resulting policy. Indeed, this might also furnish a sound basis for projection of future policy developments in this issue area, although we must recognize that each subsequent policy formulation may be subject to influence by new and different factors not yet identified by the analyst.

Unfortunately, the precise identification of particular policy-determining factors is usually extremely difficult or downright impossible. One reason is that the number of actors or variables that *might* influence policy formulation is very large, and decision makers rarely articulate the exact reasons and motivations that led them to make or accept a specific decision. Nevertheless, while the number of variables is large indeed, it is possible and useful to categorize them; moreover, the establishment of such categories will systematize the search for the appropriate explanation of why particular foreign policies may have been adopted. In this connection, it is important to stress that the analysis and identification of different variables in a particular category that are assumed to have influenced and perhaps led to a particular foreign policy decision *do not* generally suggest *causality* between the so-called independent variable or variables* and the foreign policy (dependent variable) that the analyst is seeking to explain.[1] The most that can be asserted in most cases is a positive correlation between the independent and dependent variables, and this only after an exhaustive empirical inquiry into the circumstances surrounding the decision-making process with respect to the policy or policies we want to explain.[2] If we try to look into the future, we may speak of tendencies of positive correlations between independent and dependent variables resting on past experience, and it is on this basis that we can make informed projections for the future. At times, intervening variables may have to be considered by the analyst, as such variables are apt to modify the influence and impact of independent variables. We will return to this subject with some examples later in this chapter.

Having generally rejected strict single or multiple causality between independent and dependent variables in explaining particular foreign policies, analysts must neverthelesss evaluate the potency of relevant variables. It is reasonable to assume that, in any instance of policymaking, some variables have exerted greater influence on policy formulation than others; the recognition of such differences not only is essential for explaining foreign policies, it strengthens the value of the explanation. For example, in the summer of 1982, a change of American policy toward Western Europe's decision to support the construction of a gas pipeline from the Soviet Union to selected West European countries occurred. The U.S. government had always opposed the building of this pipeline but had not succeeded in persuading its West European allies to accept this position. During the June 1982 economic summit in Versailles, the Reagan administration's action against pipeline construction seemed to consist mainly of the denial of export licenses for the American supply of high-technology items needed for the pipeline pumps. However, a week after the summit, the U.S. government expanded this ban to include European licenses for the manufacturing of these items. Who initiated this change of policy in the Reagan administration, and what were the motivations for this change, which was carried out in opposition to Secretary of State Alexander Haig's expressed policy in Versailles? This policy change was a

---

* *Independent variables* refer to those changes and differences in factors or behavior that are associated with changes and differences in the foreign policies developed, and these policies are the *dependent variables*. The dependent variable is presumed to be predictable from the independent variable. A third type of relationship is introduced by so-called *intervening variables*, which represent relevant factors that may modify the link between independent and dependent variables.

contributing factor to Haig's resignation from his post. Its consequences were not only the generation of enormous tensions between Washington and its European allies, but perhaps also lasting damage to the NATO alliance. In cases such as these, it is essential to evaluate carefully the potency of the variables that were likely to have influenced this policy decision.

Thus it is important to subject independent variables to comparative evaluation; indeed, we must if we are to make sound judgments of which of the independent variables shows the highest correlations with regard to the policies formulated. Another factor analysts must consider is the feedback for the array of possible independent variables flowing from the implementation of particular foreign policies. As pointed out in Chapter 1, the outcome of policy implementation may be at variance, sometimes considerable, with the intended purpose of a particular policy. If that should be the case, it is likely that such an outcome could favorably or adversely affect other pertinent independent variables. Alternatively, we could consider outcome feedback as a separate independent variable, so that it becomes part of the policy assessment.[3]

The Categorization of Independent Variables

This book classifies independent variables to explain American foreign policy into four categories: idiosyncratic, institutional, societal, and international clusters. The last category is subdivided into international and systemic clusters.[4]

Idiosyncratic Variables   Our first cluster consists of idiosyncratic variables, focusing on the psychological and mental characteristics, tendencies, and interests peculiar to the individual chief decision makers on the American foreign policy scene. Examples are educational and family backgrounds, personality features, values espoused, moral standards held, past experience, and the types of images held of the world.

Institutional Variables   The second cluster of variables is composed of influences exerted on policy formulation by governmental and nongovernmental institutions. They include the foreign policymaking structure in the White House, the National Security Council, the Departments of State and Defense, other pertinent executive departments and agencies, and Congress. It is in this context that we will examine the impact of roles played by decision makers on the foreign policymaking process. Nongovernmental institutions include political parties and interest groups that, in certain foreign policy issue areas, have been known to be very influential through the close contacts they have with various governmental institutions involved in foreign policy formulation.

Societal Variables   The cluster of societal variables covers a broad range of phenomena. Examples are public opinion as perhaps the most specific variable, American value orientations and historical experiences that have led to the formation of particular traditions, the American "character," educational levels, and perhaps the context and nature of U.S. industrialization.

International Variables   The final cluster of variables serving as sources of explanation for American foreign policy, and especially important to those supporting a "distribution of international power" approach to the study of foreign policy, stems from the international arena. This category of international variables can be subdivided into (1) *interactional* variables, that is, those arising from the interaction of the United States with individual foreign countries, and (2) *systemic* variables, that is those flowing from the international system in which the United States conducts its foreign affairs. The military capabilities of the Soviet Union in general as well as in comparison to the United States, and Soviet actions and intentions in the world represent crucial "interactional" variables for U.S. foreign policy formulation. However, capabilities and actions of NATO allies or of neutral countries such as Sweden and Yugoslavia also have important impacts on America policy making. Systemic variables, in contrast, refer to global and perhaps sometimes regional systemic constellations of a strategic, political, or economic nature. Examples are the nuclear "balance-of-terror" system prevailing between the United States and the Soviet Union; the triangular political and military balance-of-power system that is by many perceived to exist among the United States, the Soviet Union, and the People's Republic of China; the international trade system symbolized by GATT (the General Agreement on Tariffs and Trade); and the implications of a possibly emerging New International Economic Order that might modify or replace the current basically capitalist-market force economic world system. Other significant systemic international variables are related to the exhaustion of raw materials, the decline of food production in parts of the world, and global pollution problems. We have mentioned some of these issues in Chapter 1 and will return to them in our discussion of particular American foreign policies.[5]

POLICYMAKING MODELS

The *process* of American foreign policy formulation has received much attention in the literature.[6] However, few scholars have developed particular models for this process.[7] The best-known models constructed during the recent past are those elaborated by Graham T. Allison.[8] They are useful for our purpose of gaining a better understanding of the intricacies of American foreign policymaking by offering three perspectives of this process:

1.   The *rational policy model* based on the assumption that foreign policy is made through a rational intellectual process.
2.   The *organizational process model* based on the concept that foreign policy is the output stemming from the interplay among major governmental organizations participating in the formulation of foreign policy actions.

3. The *bureaucratic politics model* based on the notion that foreign policy-making is the result of overlapping bargaining activities among officials in various governmental ministries and agencies.

Rational Policy Model

According to the rational policy model, the policymaking process consists of purposive acts of a rational, unitary decision maker, namely the national government. This model therefore sees the national government as having *one* set of major goals, *one* set of perceived objectives and alternatives and a *uniform* estimate of the existing situation, as well as of the consequences that may follow from each alternative. Such a government makes choices on the basis of the maximization of a value, such as a desired goal or a highly regarded objective. For example, to ensure maximum security against Soviet attack, U.S. policy has consistently supported the strength of the Atlantic Alliance. As we have intimated in the preceding chapter, to make such a choice requires consideration by the decision makers of (1) the alternative potential goals in relation to their value standards and their highest preference (perhaps the preservation of a "Free World"), (2) the alternative courses of action open to reach these goals, and (3) the probable significant effects of each of the possible alternate courses of action.[9]

Although the goal selection process may seem clear-cut at first, we are aware of many pitfalls. Since the selection of goals depends very much on the value standards of the individual policymaker, these values may be coherent or contradictory. Rational decision making may also be impaired by incomplete thought or information. There is often a tendency to make decisions intuitively or impulsively with regard more to personal experience than to actual knowledge of the situation obtained by outside agencies. There may also be the habit of conforming with tradition or what is conceived of as tradition. To return to our example, the United States has supported the Atlantic Alliance so long that other alternatives, such as defending America exclusively from American soil, tend to face an intuitive adverse bias, although some valid arguments could be made for the "Fortress America" concept.

Organizational Process Model

The second perspective, the organizational process model, recognizes that the government of a state does not really operate in a unitary fashion because it consists of a conglomerate of "semi-feudal, loosely allied organizations, each with a substantial life of its own."[10] While government leaders have formal control over the various ministries and agencies, they can only understand and solve problems and arrive at solutions through these organizations. The organizations involved are the Departments of State and Defense and, in almost all cases, the Department of Treasury. However these may not be the only organizations participating in policymaking processes: the Departments of Commerce, Agriculture, Labor, and Energy may also share to varying degrees in seeking to produce foreign policy decisions. Finally, the intelligence community, especially the Central Intelligence Agency (CIA) and the Defense Intelligence Agency (DIA), provides a significant input into foreign policymaking.

With so many agencies participating in the foreign policy process, coordination becomes one of the major tasks of governmental leaders. Coordination, however, must face and cope with so-called standard operating procedures (SOP) in the various departments and agencies, and from this point of view alone, coordination becomes difficult because individual departments and agencies have differing SOPs. Each of the organizations often is more concerned with its own goals and objectives than with a generally agreed-on program of policy, and these goals and objectives at times may not be compatible with rational conceptions of national goals. These organizations are concerned not only with the continued existence of their own institutions but also with expansion of their activities. They are frequently influenced by outside pressures from citizens and special-interest groups and by bargaining among their own officials.

As a consequence of this interplay among organizational goals, values, and interests, the final output in terms of foreign policy may not be what the governmental leaders had in mind originally. Yet, the organizational constraints that exist in the different participating departments and agencies are likely to make it impossible to modify the final decision to any significant extent. These problems occur not only in the United States but in almost all countries of the world, regardless of whether they have a democratic or dictatorial government. The tug-of-war that occurred between the State Department and the Department of Defense regarding the United States' negotiating stance in the Strategic Arms Limitation Talks (especially SALT II) with the Soviet Union is an interesting example. The State Department was much more supportive of reaching an agreement on SALT than the Pentagon, which viewed it as a threat to American security. Particular weapons systems were claimed to be endangered if the Soviet Union were permitted to retain missiles (SS-18s) that were much larger than those in the U.S. arsenal. This dispute has not remained under the Reagan presidency. Many officials in the State Department continue to press for a realistic arms control agreement while, for the Defense Department, upgrading the American nuclear arsenal has the highest priority.

Bureaucratic Politics Model

The third perspective of foreign policymaking focuses on the internal politics of the bureaucracy of the government and the bargaining that usually takes place between officials participating in the policymaking process. The essence of this model lies in the fact that civil servants, as human beings, look at the promotion of their own personal interests, including the expansion of their position of power and prestige, as important guides and motivations for their actions and decisions, and this colors their images of the public interest.[11] Of course, civil servants will not openly admit to this situation, but it is a problem found in all governments of the world. It produces bureaucratic attitudes and behavior, which tend to reduce the influence of the wishes of governmental and political leaders. Max Weber, a German sociologist living in the early part of this century, stressed in his study of bureaucracy that large, long-established state bureaucracies are capable of considerable independence and insulation from the political leadership and are far from being passive tools of those who wield power in a state.[12]

Former Secretary of State Henry Kissinger, recognizing that even on the highest level it is impossible to implement an order easily, made the following comments:

> When I first started advising at high levels of government in the early days of the Kennedy Administration, I had the illusion that all I had to do was walk into the President's office, convince him I was right, and he would then naturally do what I had recommended. There were a number of things wrong with this view. . . . Even if by chance I persuaded him that his whole bureaucracy was wrong and I was right, he would then have the next problem of going about implementing what had been suggested. And that is not a negligible issue. There is only so much that even a President can do against the wishes of the bureaucracy, not because the bureaucracy would deliberately sabotage him, but because every difficult issue is a closed one. The easy decisions are made at subordinate levels. A closed issue is characterized by the fact that the pros and cons seem fairly evenly divided and/or because the execution really depends on certain nuances of application. Unless you can get the willing support of your subordinates, simply giving an order does not get very far.[13]

Positions of power of individual civil servants, their prestige, their reputation for effectiveness, and their skill in using bargaining advantages are important variables for the results of bureaucratic bargaining with respect to a particular foreign policy decision. Sometimes coalitions are formed among individuals and departments to assure a policy output that they view as beneficial, not only for the national interest but also for their own personal advancement. This does not mean that the interests of the nation are sacrificed for primarily personal gains. The officials want to enhance these interests, and most of them share common basic values and traditions with respect to the ways of life within their nation and to its national purposes. However, the specific outcome on a particular foreign policy decision may well be conceived as flowing, according to Allison, from

> intricate and subtle, simultaneous, overlapping games among [civil servants] located in positions, the hierarchical arrangement of which constitutes that gov-

ernment. These games proceed neither at random nor at leisure. Regular channels structure the game. Deadlines force issues to the attention of busy [civil servants]. The moves in the chess game are thus to be explained in terms of the bargaining among [civil servants] with separate and unequal power over particular pieces and with separable objectives in distinguishable subgames.[14]

Another insightful proposition of Allison flowing from his bureaucratic politics model is "Where you stand depends on where you sit."[15] It means that whatever position a bureaucratic participant in the policy formulation holds is likely to shape his or her perceptions, priorities, and issues. It also means that the demands made on policymaking participants are quite different, whether they are the president, departmental secretaries, assistant secretaries, or merely staff members. In other words, the particular roles in which these individuals find themselves within the institutional framework of the government influence their policy decisions.

Although many students of foreign policy have praised Allison's three models, there has also been criticism by a number of scholars that the models downplay the roles of the president, of close presidential advisors, and of Congress in the formulation of policy, that they do not sufficiently appreciate the impact of electoral politics, and that they underestimate, if not ignore, the influence of the international system on American foreign policymaking.[16]

While these criticisms have some merit, it is our contention that these three models do offer important insights into the foreign policymaking process. However, we should note that instead of selecting one model or perspective as giving us the closest approximation to reality, this process is likely to contain elements of all three models, with more weight given to the organizational and bureaucratic models. Moreover, in most foreign policy issue areas, the external situation does have a distinct bearing on the policymaking process, because frequently policies are made in response to what happens beyond the national boundaries. This means that the promotion of the public interest according to the foreign policy direction of the top political leadership in a state is heavily dependent on the perceptions of domestic and external conditions, belief systems, and personal aspirations of major participating bureaucrats, and that the impact of these factors is in turn circumscribed by the interests, objectives, and procedure of the organizations in which these officials are employed. The end product, then, is the result of much skillful bargaining among the major participants in a particular foreign policy decision. As Kissinger observes, these "decisions emerge from a compromise of conflicting pressures in which accidents of personality or persuasiveness play a crucial role."[17] Bargaining may dominate over substance, and the quality of the decision may suffer.

SUMMARY

This chapter has focused on the classification of variables (in most cases, independent) that may explain the formation of particular U.S. foreign policies, and on three different models of the policymaking process.

Four categories of explanatory variables were identified: *idiosyncratic*, dealing with personal traits of top-echelon decision makers; *institutional*, referring to governmental and nongovernmental institutions and organizations; *societal*, flowing from the characteristics of American society and public opinion; and *international*, which were subdivided into *interactional* and *systemic* variables. Interactional variables emanate from the relations and interactions between the United States and other countries as well as IGOs. Systemic variables spring from global and regional international systems and from the physical international environment.

The three models of foreign policymaking processes are the rational policy, organizational process, and bureaucratic politics models. In the *rational policy model*, the government is seen as a unitary actor that makes rational decisions in the making of foreign policy. The problems and limitations of setting foreign policy goals are examined.

In the *organizational model*, the government is considered to be a coalition of semifeudal, allied organizations and agencies, many of which participate and have a stake in the foreign policymaking process. Foreign policy decisions are influenced by the interests and goals of the participating organizations, and compromises must be struck at times to accommodate the interests of the participants.

In the *bureaucratic politics model*, the emphasis is on the participating officials in the policymaking processes and in the bargaining that takes place among the civil servants as the process unfolds. In the bargaining, the personal interests of the bureaucrats, including the expansion of their positions of power and prestige, play important parts and tend to color their images of the public interest. The specific outcome on a particular foreign policy decision may depend on the skill with which individual civil servants may use the intricacies of the bureaucratic system to channel and guide the decision-making process.

All three models offer important insights into the foreign policymaking processes and, indeed, the formulation and implementation of individual foreign policies may contain elements of all three models.

NOTES

1. See Joseph Frankel, *The Making of Foreign Policy* (New York: Oxford University Press, 1963), p. 102.
2. See also in this connection James Rosenau, *The Scientific Study of Foreign Policy* (New York: Free Press, 1971), pp. 35–38 and 107–108.
3. Rosenau provides more details on feedback. See ibid., pp. 44–46.
4. In his book, *The Scientific Study of Foreign Policy*, ibid., pp. 108–109, Rosenau seeks to explain the external behavior of societies in terms of five sets or clusters of variables: the individual, role, government, societal, and systemic variables. The categories used for the conceptual framework of this book, while in many respects similar to those used by Rosenau, manifest some significant differences in substance and terminology. The most important difference is the elimination of the "role" variable, which leaves us with four clusters of variables.

5. See also the case studies in Werner J. Feld and Robert S. Jordan, *International Organization* (New York: Praeger, 1983), Chapters 4 and 5.

6. See, for example, Richard C. Snyder and Edgar S. Furniss, Jr., *American Foreign Policy* (New York: Rinehart, 1954); Burton M. Sapin, *The Making of United States Foreign Policy* (New York: Praeger, 1966); and Roger Hilsman, *The Politics of Policy Making in Defense and Foreign Affairs* (New York: Harpter & Row, 1971).

7. Snyder and Furniss, *American Foreign Policy*, falls in this category.

8. Graham T. Allison, *Essence of Decision: Explaining the Cuban Missile Crisis* (Boston: Little, Brown, 1971).

9. For more details about this model, see ibid., pp. 29–35. See also pp. 14–28 for illustrations.

10. Ibid., p. 69.

11. For details see ibid., pp. 162–180.

12. Max Weber, *Essays in Sociology*, translated and edited by H.H. Gerth and C.W. Mills (New York: Oxford University Press, 1958), pp. 228–235.

13. Henry A. Kissinger, "Bureaucracy and Policymaking: The Effects of Insiders and Outsiders on the Policy Process," in *Readings in American Foreign Policy: A Bureaucratic Perspective*, edited by Morton H. Halperin and Arnold Kanter (Boston: Little, Brown, 1973), pp. 45–83.

14. Graham T. Allison, "Conceptual Models and the Cuban Missile Crisis," in Halperin and Kanter (eds.), *Readings*, pp. 45–83, on p. 71.

15. Allison, *Essence of Decision*, p. 176.

16. See Stephen B. Krasner, "Are Bureaucracies Important? or Allison Wonderland," *Foreign Policy*, no. 7 (1972), pp. 159–179; Robert Art, "Bureaucratic Politics and American Foreign Policy," *Policy Sciences* (December 1973); Linda P. Brady, "Bureaucratic Politics and Situational Constraints," paper delivered at the 1974 Annual Meeting of the APSA, Chicago, August 27–September 2, 1974; and Howard Bliss and M. Glen Johnson, *Beyond the Water's Edge: America's Foreign Policy* (Philadelphia: Lippincott, 1975), pp. 127–180.

17. Kissinger, "Bureaucracy and Policymaking," p. 33.

3

Idiosyncratic Elements of Policymaking Participants

By their very nature, idiosyncratic variables as sources of explanation differ from policymaker to policymaker. Family and educational background, individual value structures, past experiences, personality features, perceptual screens, images held, the priority of interests pursued, and the information available *and* used tend to have an impact on a foreign policymaker's judgment and behavior. Obviously, the higher in the rank order a policymaker is the greater is likely to be the effect of his or her behavior and decisions on the formulation of policy. However, with the large number of decisions on various levels that precede the determination of major foreign policy goals and specific actions, and with decisions on such actions often taken in rapid succession, it would be an error to ignore lower-level policymakers, although research on their idiosyncrasies is much more difficult than on those in the top echelons.

Various methods can be applied to inquire into the idiosyncrasies of policymakers. They include documentary and library research, content analysis of their public statements and writings, and questionnaires and individual interviews, either structured in terms of possible response or open-ended. Before one can embark on fruitful, appropriate research, however, it is helpful to clarify the relationship between attitude and perception, the concept of "image," the role played by information and intelligence, and the nature of relevant interests of foreign policymakers.

ATTITUDES AND PERCEPTIONS

Attitudes constitute important idiosyncratic elements of decision makers and therefore can aid in explaining particular foreign policies. A number of definitions exist for the term attitude, but, for our purposes, it is defined best as an *enduring* organization of motivational, emotional, perceptual, and cognitive processes with respect to some aspect of the individual's world.[1] Attitudes are likely to predispose the judgments of individual decision makers to support or reject particular foreign policy goals or actions. In turn, attitudes are conditioned by the value and belief systems of the decision makers, and these tend to give attitudes their relatively enduring quality.

Nonetheless, attitudes can be modified through new perceptions or changes in the affective components of particular attitudes of policymakers. Perceptions denote sensory experiences that are registered as meaningful and interpreted according to the concepts of the external world held by the perceiving individual. As Allport puts it in a down-to-earth manner, perception "is the way things look to us, or the way they sound, feel, taste, or smell."[2] The nature of perception thus is mainly cognitive, but it also has evaluative components.

The degree of attitudinal *change* depends on whether new perceptions can pass through the screen formed by existing attitudinal elements of the policymaking participant. Hence, the *potency* of perceptions and the *persistence* of attitude factors, often significantly influenced by cultural, social, and educational backgrounds, affect the thought processes of policymakers and thereby can make important differences in the formulation of American foreign policy. The controversy in the fall of 1950 and spring of 1951 between President Truman and General Douglas MacArthur concerning how best to conduct the Korean War provides an interesting example of the interplay between the completely different backgrounds of the two men and their respective perceptual screens that, in the long run, harmed U.S. interests.

The Truman-MacArthur Impasse on Policy Goals

President Truman was born in 1884 into a very modest family of a farmer and livestock dealer. He finished only high school; although he was anxious to enter West Point, he was rejected because of poor vision. Before World War I, he held various, mostly blue-collar jobs. After serving in that war and advancing to the rank of major, he returned to civilian life and joined a men's clothing store that failed in 1921. Turning to politics, he was elected county administrator. In his free time, he went to law school and earned a law degree. In 1926 he was elected judge, and in 1934 he was elected to the U.S. Senate. During his Senate tenure, Truman earned a reputation for honesty and efficiency.

In contrast to Truman, General MacArthur was born into an upper-middle-class family. His father was a high-ranking army officer who ended his career as a lieutenant-general. Douglas MacArthur graduated from West Point as first in his class and was made brigadier general at the age of 38. He had a brilliant military career during World War II, mostly in Asia, and he was the U.S. commander-in-chief in the Far East when North Korean forces invaded South Korea in June 1950. After the U.N. Security Council branded North Korea the aggressor during a session from which the Soviet representative on the council was absent, MacArthur was named the U.N. supreme commander of the largely American military effort against the North Koreans and later the forces of the People's Republic of China (PRC).

At stake in the controversy between Truman and MacArthur were the priorities to be assigned to policies on the pursuit of the war effort in Korea. MacArthur, reflecting his impressive military background and career, his long successful years in Asia, his confidence in himself, and his general perceptions of the world, wanted greater priority to be given to utilizing military resources in Asia. He insisted that Korea be unified through the capture of North Korea. He advocated crippling the PRC through air bombardment of its industries and its communications network, and instituting a naval blockade along its coast. Troops from nationalist China on Taiwan were to provide reinforcements for the American units engaged in these tasks. The result would be a decisive weakening of the PRC's capability to wage aggressive war. All this could be achieved without risking military intervention by the Soviet Union, because Moscow would not resort to war until its nuclear and industrial capabilities reached some kind of parity with those of the United States.

These policy recommendations are consistent with MacArthur's beliefs, attitudes, and perceptions whose major elements have been compiled by Joseph H. deRivera as follows:

1. Asia was basically more important than Europe because she would be the power of the future. Communism and not the Soviet Union was the main enemy.
2. The United States could easily gain control over China at the present time.
3. If it failed to do so, it would lose its chance, for China's strength would grow relative to the United States.
4. Communism was an evil form of government, whereas the Chinese Nationalists would preserve freedom for China.
5. If the United States did oppose communism in China, the Soviet Union would not intervene.
6. If the Soviet Union did intervene, the United States might as well fight a world war then as later.
7. It was fundamentally immoral to sacrifice the lives of citizens without the nation making an all-out effort to help them.
8. The United States should keep control over its foreign policy and not allow other countries to influence its actions.[3]

Truman rejected the MacArthur proposals. He considered them too risky, because he felt that the Soviet Union could not ignore a direct attack on the

PRC, its largest and most important ally at that time. Moreover, the expenditure of large military resources in Asia would make it impossible to build strong defenses in Europe against Soviet aggression. Indeed, American weakness in Europe might invite a Soviet attack. Dissipating its power in a war against what Truman considered a secondary enemy might make it impossible for the United States to contain its principal enemy, the Soviet Union.

The Joint Chiefs of Staff agreed with the assessment of the Truman administration. They felt that the MacArthur proposals would involve the United States in the wrong war, at the wrong place, and with the wrong enemy. These views were shared by Britain and France, whose own security would be jeopardized by the diversion of American military resources to Asia, which would undermine NATO's strength and perhaps unity.

Truman's policy preference reflected his particular attitudes and perceptions as shaped by his background and career experiences. The failures in his early life were responsible for his social compassion and a certain lack of self-assurance, verging sometimes on feelings of inferiority when he had to deal with high-powered individuals within and outside the United States. Although he did not exude charisma, his political and governmental career suggests that he understood how to use the authority that was conferred on him through his place in the governmental organization, regardless of whether he occupied the position of judge or president. The famous sign on Truman's desk, "The buck stops here," also indicates that he was fully aware of his awesome responsibilities, which included the need to bring about social change if that was required.

The contrast to MacArthur's view of the strategic ramifications flowing from the Korean War is quite apparent from the elements listed by deRivera for Truman's perceptions of this situation and its possible consequences:

1. Europe was basically more important than Asia because of her ties to America and because she currently had more power.
2. The United States would have to expend all of its strength to control China, and this would leave Europe vulnerable to the major enemy, the Soviet Union.
3. The Chinese could be used in the future to counterbalance Russian power.
4. Time was on the side of the United States—time to arm, to gain more allies, to give rise to discontent in the Soviet Union.
5. The source of trouble in Asia was the poverty of her people and the ravages of colonialism. Social change was needed, and communism would provide it; whereas the Nationalists had been either unwilling or unable to do so.
6. Asians in general would perceive aid to the Nationalists as an imposition—a form of colonialism, and since the Nationalist leader's only hope was to provoke a major war between the United States and China, one should minimize involvement with the Nationalists.
7. The United States did not currently have the strength to fight both China and Russia, nor did the people of the United States want to fight in an all-out war.

8. An all-out war was immoral.
9. It was necessary to have allies; to keep them, one had to take their views into consideration.[4]

With the wide disparity in attitudes, beliefs, and perceptions between Truman and the general in command of the American forces, efforts at conciliation were difficult, if not impossible. Although a personal meeting was arranged in October 1950 between the two parties at Wake Island in the Pacific to bridge the perceptual gap and provide an intimate opportunity for the president to explain this policy preference of a limited war in Korea, the effort did not succeed in spite of the apparently friendly nature of the meeting. Even after the American and South Korean forces, which had reached the Yalu River separating the PRC from North Korea, were forced to withdraw as a result of a bitter defeat inflicted by PRC troops, MacArthur persisted in wanting to pursue his policy proposals and enlarge the war. He requested permission to bomb Manchuria, to use Chinese Nationalist troops, and to employ American forces that were at that time slated to go to Europe. The administration turned down all of these requests and asked him to defend South Korea as best as possible. This prompted the general to blame the administration for his defeat, because it seemed that his psychological makeup could not tolerate "his" defeat.

Although the situation of U.S. and allied forces in Korea began to improve in early 1951, and Seoul, the capital of South Korea, was recaptured, the Truman administration had decided to initiate negotiations for a settlement of hostilities that would restore the status quo that had existed before the North Korean invasion. MacArthur attempted to sabotage these plans. In a reply to a letter by the Speaker of the House of Representatives about the future course of the war, the general declared: "There is no substitute for victory."[5] This raised the question of who was authorized to formulate American foreign policy, and it prompted Truman to dismiss General MacArthur on April 10, 1951. This ended this particular challenge to the president's foreign policy prerogatives, but the war continued for another 2 years.

Perceptions and Misperceptions

As the preceding case suggests, the perceptions of the participants in the foreign policymaking process are influenced by their educational, social, cultural, and career experiences. While their perceptions may reflect reality more or less accurately, individual interpretations of and judgments regarding these perceptions may result in quite different conclusions about what policies to choose.

In some cases, however, it is also possible that perceptions completely diverge from reality. For example, was British Prime Minister Neville Chamberlain's perception in the late 1930s that Britain could work with Hitler a clear misperception? In contrast, was Winston Churchill's very opposite perception of Hitler correct? Was the Reagan administration's perception of West Europe's willingness to acquiesce to American sanctions imposed on suppliers of materials for the Soviet gas pipeline not in fact a gross misperception? Policymakers' misperceptions can have a crucial impact on policy formulation and should be considered in the analysis of idiosyncratic variables.[6]

IMAGES

Closely related to our discussion of attitudes and perceptions is the notion of the "image" that foreign policymakers hold of the external environment of their country and of its strengths and weaknesses. These images tend to shape the input into the policymaking process. During the last few years, psychologists and political scientists have studied more and more the problem of the image, and it is now fairly well known that past experiences, current attitudes, value commitments and beliefs, as well as the development of the individual's personality, bear on the manner in which an official or a political leader perceives the outside world. Because these factors vary from individual to individual, different decision makers look at the external and internal environment differently, and foreign policy decisions are significantly influenced by the perceptional components of their internal image of the world and special situations they face.

Open versus Closed Images

Images are regarded as either open or closed. Individuals who have an open image accept new information and adjust their image to this information. Such information may come from a variety of sources, such as advisors, supervisors, colleagues, intelligence agencies, or the press. In contrast, individuals with a closed image do not adjust to any information. They reject new conditions for a variety of reasons and thereby may move away from the reality of their country's environment and of the world. Even if people recognize that the new information is clearly discrepant with the image held, they doubt the validity of the information or interpret it in such a way as to obviate a change in attitude and image.[7] When in 1955 and 1956 the People's Republic of China attempted to start a friendly dialogue with the United States, John Foster Dulles (then U.S. secretary of state) rejected these overtures, because his image of the PRC as an evil communist force was so strong that any merit that this information might have for U.S.-PRC relations was dismissed out of hand.

It would be an error to assume that an individual's images fall entirely into either category: open or closed. There are many gradations between these two extremes; moreover, there are circumstances, such as a very radical change of the international environment, that compel even an official with a very closed image to adjust to a new situation. One example is the change in British governmental leaders during the late 1930s when Hitler attacked Poland and subsequently invaded the Soviet Union in 1941. Before the attack on Poland, many British leaders including Chamberlain felt that they could do business with Hitler and that somehow Nazism would go away. Deeply disillusioned after the German attack, Chamberlain resigned from office in early 1940.

Another example is President Carter's abrupt change in his image of the Soviet leadership after the Soviet invasion of Afghanistan in December 1979. Before that event, Carter believed that the Soviet leaders were sincere in trying to create a better relationship with Washington, and he was prepared to make some concessions necessary for such a development. However, the Afghanistan invasion shattered this image, and Carter expressed his deep disappointment about the dishonesty of the Soviet leadership.

One of the problems in changing a decision maker's image is the clearness with which that individual receives new information. Communication scientists call this the *clarity* of the signal received by the decision maker, and the more the signal is impaired, the greater is the probability that the meaning of that signal will be obscured. Spurious signals or static that interferes with signal reception is called *noise*, and the clarity of the signal is often expressed in terms of a signal:noise ratio. The higher this ratio is, the stronger is the signal, and the more likely is a change in the image of the decision maker. For example, when in the October 1973 Middle East War Israel appeared to be on the edge of defeat, the United States sent a very strong signal to the Soviet Union through placing U.S. military forces on a worldwide alert in order to deter Soviet intervention in that war.

The Conservative Nature of Images

The conservative nature of images developed at a certain time can be illustrated by some of the foreign policies in which the Kennedy administration engaged. Although it appeared at first that the liberal nature of John F. Kennedy, as portrayed in many of his speeches, would lead to an innovative foreign policy compared to that of his predecessor, Republican President Dwight D. Eisenhower, the old image of "evil communism" continued to persist, and the cold war mentality initiated right after World War II continued to control not only the president, but also his special assistant for national security affairs, McGeorge Bundy. As David Halberstam observed in his best-selling book, *The Best and the Brightest*, the men around Kennedy reflected the post-Munich, post-McCarthy pragmatism of the age. He goes on to say:

> One had to stop totalitarianism, and since the only thing the totalitarians understood was force, one had to be willing to use force. They justified each

decision to use power by their own conviction that the Communists were worse which justified our dirty tricks, our toughness.[8]

The result was that Vietnam became a reflection and a consequence of the containment policy initiated by President Harry S. Truman in 1947. If the images of the decision makers around Kennedy had been more open and they had been more willing to accept some of the new information that became available during the early 1960s, perhaps a different policy would have been followed.

Public versus Private Image

We should stress that the notion of image must be understood in psychological terms. It refers to what the individual decision maker perceives the world to be. However, today we frequently talk about the image the decision maker has as it *appears* to the world. Sometimes decision makers want to make their images public in order to defend their policies. Once they have done so, it is very difficult for them to change the impression they have created in their constituencies or in other people of their country and abroad. Under such conditions, decision makers may perceive new information as a threat that may destroy the integrity of their own image and undermine the political support they have built for themselves and their policies. In other situations, foreign policy decision makers may have two images of a particular situation, one for their own use and one for public consumption.[9] This may well have been true of President Kennedy and his associates. Many people considered him as wishing to take fresh approaches to foreign policy to overcome the confrontational nature of the U.S.-Soviet relationship that existed under the preceding Eisenhower-Dulles administration. However, he remained a prisoner of the foreign policy images built up during the 1940s and 1950s. When, during the Republican presidential primaries in 1976, Ronald Reagan challenged President Ford's foreign policies toward the Soviet Union as not being tough enough, the latter attempted to change the image projected by dropping the word "detente" from his foreign policy description.

INFORMATION AND INTELLIGENCE

Possible changes in the attitudes and images of policymaking participants may be especially crucial if affected by perceptions of new information on conditions and activities outside the United States. However, to have simply masses of raw information would not be significant. Only accurate, relevant information is useful to participants in the policymaking process, and it can aid in providing a sound basis for the formulation of effective policies. What is needed, then, is careful, selective collection and collation of information, followed by systematic analysis, interpretation, and evaluation. The end product of this sequence of steps is known as *intelligence*; when it pertains to foreign countries and the international environment in general, it is called *foreign intelligence*. Obviously, this latter type of intelligence is usually of the greatest interest to foreign policymakers, although *domestic intelligence* may also have to be taken into account in the foreign policy formulation process. The sources of foreign intelligence information are mostly found abroad, but some information is also collected from within the country through counterintelligence activities and debriefing of travelers who have been in foreign countries.

Intelligence Collection

The information may be collected by secret agents, diplomats assigned to the country's embassies in various capitals of the world, research officials in the intelligence agency headquarters, or by mechanical means and electronic devices. Spy-in-the-sky satellites take pictures of weapons installations, and governments monitor the coded international cable traffic of other governments. We should note that the bulk of pertinent information is gathered by researchers who scan every bit of printed material emanating from foreign countries, especially newspapers, scientific articles, and other publications available to the public-at-large and not classified as secret or confidential. On the other hand, the least information comes usually from secret agents, although from time to time their input may be most crucial. In this connection, we must draw attention to an important asymmetry in the collection of information encountered by intelligence agencies in (closed) totalitarian and (open) democratic countries. In the latter, many more open sources are available. For example, one can read about U.S. defense matters in American periodicals such as *Aviation Week and Space Technology* or even the *New York Times*. In totalitarian societies such as the Soviet Union, all publications are carefully censored to prevent disclosure of items useful to foreign intelligence organizations. Hence totalitarian governments have a distinct advantage over democratic societies in the information collection game.

As a background or basis for decision making, a foreign policy official may need encyclopedic knowledge about a foreign country: knowledge of military, economic, or technological vulnerabilities, knowledge about what kind of action one or several foreign states may be able to take in the world arena, or immediate spot knowledge about a current event. The first type of knowledge can be gleaned from so-called *national intelligence surveys*, which deal individually with most countries of the world and cover a broad range of topics, including geography and national resources, transportation and telegraph communication capabilities, every aspect of economic intelligence, complete sociological data about the population, education, and morale of the people, scientific and technological intelligence, an evaluation of the political structure and processes, and, finally, military resources and capabilities. These surveys also contain National Intelligence Estimates (NIEs), which furnish very useful knowledge to foreign policy officials. Spot knowledge about a current event is provided to policymakers by summaries prepared within a matter of hours and rushed to the officials in need via the fastest electronic means possible or through personal briefings.

All this knowledge is important, because foreign policy goals are not attained in a vacuum but in interaction with other states. Those who would pursue them must take into consideration the foreign policy aspirations of other countries, their pressures to have these aspirations recognized, and their capabilities of implementing their own policies.

Acceptance of Intelligence Information

Although the production of foreign intelligence is a very extensive and expensive activity, the acceptance of the knowledge received from the intelligence agencies as a basis for decisions is often uncertain. If the intelligence received confirms the image held by an official participating in the foreign policymaking process, it is likely to be considered accurate and to be accepted; however, if it conflicts with the image, it may be rejected.

As you might suppose, officials having closed images are more likely to reject intelligence information than are those with open images. There are a number of specific reasons for these rejections. In some instances, doubt is cast on the quality of the intelligence produced. In others, long-standing favorable perceptions of foreign policymakers regarding the reliability of *their own* knowledge (partly based on their own experience), coupled with a low regard for the performance of intelligence producers, leads to the partial or complete rejection of intelligence.[10] Finally, intelligence estimates of different U.S. agencies may be conflicting, as happened with respect to estimates of Soviet military capabilities in the mid-1970s, prompting policymakers to rely on their own judgments and perceptions.

When top-ranking governmental leaders or military commanders choose to disregard the products of their intelligence services, the consequences sometimes may be unfortunate. The Office of U.S. Naval Intelligence provided intelligence in December 1944 that the Japanese divisions stationed in Manchuria were skeleton units with very low troop strength and that the emperor himself had decided to explore the prospects of surrender. Had this intelligence been coordinated with similar information available in various intelligence offices of the U.S. Army, it might not have been disregarded in favor of the much more somber estimate of the situation by General George C. Marshall, then chairman of the Joint Chiefs of Staff. If the intelligence developed from naval sources had been given greater credibility, and efforts been made to confirm it by other sources, it might have led to foreign policy decisions different from those actually taken by President Roosevelt, who requested, in accordance with his image of a persistently strong Japan, that the Soviet Union enter the war against Japan in return for American concessions.[11]

More recent examples of ignoring intelligence reports include (1) the 1979 attack on the U.S. embassy in Teheran, Iran, and the seizure of the hostages about which President Carter had been warned, and (2) the Israeli invasion of Lebanon in 1982, which Reagan perhaps could have dealt with more effectively if he had heeded intelligence advice that the invasion was inevitable.

INTERESTS

Every participant in the formulation of foreign policy is likely to have perceptions of personal, organizational, and national interests that are likely to influence his or her preferences of the available policy choices. These perceptions may also reinforce or weaken existing attitudes and images. We will examine the concept of national interest later in this chapter; first we will briefly outline the personal and organizational interests of policy decision participants.

One of the most natural aspirations of every government official is to seek promotion, enhanced power and influence, greater prestige, and, of course, increased pay. The bureaucratic politics model of the policymaking process reflects these desires and motivations, and it is fair to assume that these objectives are to varying degrees consciously or subconsciously considered by all participants in the policy formulation processes.[12] How the promotion of personal interests is actually manifested depends on the skill of the individual, the position held in the policymaking hierarchy, and the interpersonal relationship with one's colleagues.

Since many foreign policy decisions are made by and within a group whose membership varies only slightly over a period of time, a participant might consider it best for the long-range pursuit of personal interests to accept a "groupthink" mold. This means that he or she will want to adopt the role of the perfect team player and, indeed, become the perfect team player by suppressing personal doubts, showing docility to the leadership, refraining from antagonizing new members of the group, and assuming the role of what Irving Janis calls a "mindguard."[13] Through such an attitudinal orientation, the governmental top leadership is protected from thoughts that might damage the collective confidence in the soundness of the policies to which the leadership is already committed or to which it is about to commit itself. Such a behavior pattern in policymaking has been characterized as "groupthink" and was a major feature of the policy decision to proceed with the ill-fated Bay of Pigs invasion of Cuba in 1961.

Plans for this invasion had begun during the Eisenhower administration and were based on the belief in the U.S. intelligence community that a small force of exiles from Castro's Cuba could land in Cuba and overthrow Castro.

The beachhead chosen for this operation was the Bay of Pigs. Kennedy decided to support this plan after he came into office, expecting that the exiles, once they had landed, would be received by the population as liberators. However, the outcome of the operation, launched in April 1961, was a dismal failure.

The decision to undertake the operation was made by a group of about a dozen high-ranking individuals, and the decision-making process followed the pattern of "groupthink" outlined above.

The group was headed by President John F. Kennedy and included Attorney General Robert Kennedy, Special Assistant Arthur Schlesinger, Jr., Special Council Theodore C. Sorensen, Director of Intelligence and Research of the Department of State Roger Hilsman, and other top-level officials.[14] By tending to seek concurrence rather than information and critical appraisal, the group's leadership gave rise to shared illusions and complacent overconfidence. Warnings and uncertainties were ignored, and as a result the serious risks of the clandestine operation were underestimated.

Organizational interests can also be very potent motivations for policy-making participants. The greater the role that an executive department or agency is likely to play in the implementation of a foreign policy, the greater may be the prestige and influence wielded by its officials. Hence, in interagency decision making on various foreign policy issues, the involvement of individual organizations can become an important consideration for the decision makers. Sometimes, in fact, pressures may be exerted on officials to conform with organizational norms and ideologies. Moreover, executive departments with important clienteles may feel pressed to promote the interests of their clients in the foreign policy deliberations. A case in point may be policy objectives in international trade and investment. Representatives of the Departments of Commerce and Agriculture always have a prime interest in international trade policy and have to take the demands and wishes of their respective clienteles into account. The Treasury and Justice Departments have substantial interests in international investment objectives and in this connection have special concerns regarding the transfer of technology to other countries and the nationalization-expropriation of American subsidiaries abroad. Powerful American multinational corporations are anxious to have strong representation by officials of these departments in relevant foreign policy deliberations.

THE NATIONAL INTEREST

A Variety of Notions

Winston Churchill said in 1939, "I cannot forecast to you the action of Russia. It is a riddle wrapped in a mystery inside an enigma; but perhaps there is a key. That key is Russian national interest."[15]

Although at first glance the notion of national interest seems to provide an objective guide to foreign policymaking, the term is elusive and has been understood by political scientists and public servants in various ways. Hence the particular definition of the national interest by a policymaker becomes an idiosyncratic variable that may influence the final foreign policy product. One way to define national interest is to consider it as an ideal set of purposes a nation should seek to realize in the conduct of its foreign relations. This concept of national interest is called *normative*: national interest is defined in terms of what *ought* to be done. National interest is often viewed in this way when citizens and politicians deliberate on the general goals for their nations. It is an appropriate use of the term for speeches by politicians on the Fourth of July.

A second definition focuses on what policies a state, through its leadership, has pursued over a period of time. This kind of definition deals with a *historical description* of facts but does not necessarily offer prescriptions for the future.

Finally, some observers look at national interest as a kaleidoscopic process by which forces in a society seek to express certain political and economic aspirations in world politics, usually through the highest organs of the state. To understand fully the configuration of national interest under this notion requires becoming familiar with the values and beliefs held by the people, inquiring into their concrete interests, and assessing the ideologies they may espouse. Again, we see in this definition primarily a description of what exists at present in terms of the national interest and a *functional view* as to the motivations for the continuance of or change in the way that interest is defined at a particular point in time.[16]

If we can learn one lesson from the three concepts delineated, it is that perceptions of national interest are likely to differ not only among individual decision makers but also among individual citizens. Your own view of the national interest may vary appreciably from that of your neighbor. Moreover, the national interest may change over time as domestic and external circumstances change, and the attitudes and perceptions of decision makers will be altered accordingly. Such a change is illustrated by the Monroe Doctrine, a policy regarded as a cornerstone in protecting U.S. national interests in the Western Hemisphere during the nineteenth century. This policy not only sought to prevent outside interference in the Western Hemisphere but also suggested that U.S. interests were mainly limited to North and South America. Today such a restricted view of American relationships with international society would be considered by most Americans as incompatible with the world leadership role assumed by the United States. Therefore, contemporary policymakers define American interests differently and seek to formulate policies to protect and bolster U.S. global responsibilities.

In view of the differing interpretations that may be attributed by different decision makers to the national interest and the difficulty of giving operational meaning to this concept, a number of international relations specialists have cast doubt on the reliability of using national interest as an objective guide to making or understanding the foreign policy of a country.[17] Nevertheless, by using the term in the plural and equating it to the vital interests of a state, a number of national interests applicable to all countries can be identified.[18] They are the protection of the integrity of a state's territory, the achievement of maximum security, the preservation of national self-determination, and the attainment and maintenance of optimum economic well-being.

The very breadth of these universal national interests makes them useful only as broad guides for foreign policymaking. It is yet necessary to determine more specific goals. For this determination, it is necessary to undertake a careful analysis of a country's capabilities and vulnerabilities, especially in the military, technological, economic, financial, and political fields. Not even the United States, undoubtedly in overall terms the most powerful country on earth, can embark on a realistic foreign policy without carefully assessing the needed resources to carry through such a policy and weighing them against internal and external weaknesses.

Capabilities and Vulnerabilities

What are the major U.S. capabilities and vulnerabilities? On the basis of its gross national product (GNP), a chief indicator of economic success, the United States leads all other countries of the world. The U.S. GNP in 1982 exceeded $3 trillion, but it is interesting to note that only slightly more than half of the GNP comes from the production of goods; the other half is derived from the provision of services such as banking, insurance, retail establishments, and tourism. Many items that used to be manufactured in the United States—for example, TV sets or radios—are now produced abroad by subsidiaries of U.S. multinational corporations or are imported from foreign firms. This may have lowered the production capacity of the United States, and this trend could create vulnerabilities under certain circumstances.

The level of technology in the United States for the production of civilian and military goods remains very high. However, other countries, such as Japan, West Germany, and France, are catching up with us in some aspects of research and development (R&D) and may have surpassed us.

In overall financial muscle, the United States remains dominant in the world. Although during the 1970s the value of the dollar had seriously declined, it regained its strength during the early 1980s. However, the continued heavy financing of continually rising government deficits may place severe constraints on foreign policy choices.

American military capability, which obviously is a crucial factor not only for our policies toward the Soviet Union, but also for our relations with our allies in Europe and Asia, is not easy to assess. As for hardware, it depends on whether one counts land-based or sea-launched nuclear missiles, whether emphasis is placed on throw-weight of missiles or the number of warheads, and which planes are to be included in determining the balance between the United States and the Soviet Union. In some conventional weapons such as tanks and missile launchers, the Pentagon has admitted inferiority, a subject discussed in more detail in later chapters. However, in viewing American military strength, the human factor must also be considered. How well can volunteers who now constitute the main element of the U.S. armed forces be trained, and how well will they fight? Was the abortive mission to rescue the American hostages in Iran in April 1980 an example, and evidently not a good one, of the capabilities of the U.S. military establishment? What is the effect of the current racial mix with its large percentage of blacks on army effectiveness?

Finally, an assessment of U.S. capability cannot ignore sociopolitical factors. They include racial cleavages with their political implications, which might be regarded as vulnerabilities. Similarly, the low esteem in which Congress and the Executive have been held by large segments of the population would raise a caution flag (see Table 3.1). Public opinion surveys have indicated strong support for rising defense expenditures during the 1970s (see Figure 3.1), which may have peaked in 1980 and declined in 1982 (see Table 3.2). A clearly positive element in the sociopolitical sector is the fairly high level of patriotism of the American people, in which, for better or worse, a substantial dose of ethnocentrism is mixed.

The need for a careful assessment of U.S. capabilities and vulnerabilities was borne out by the fiasco of the Vietnam War. The reason for failure was, however, not the lack or the lagging quality of military hardware, but the lack of the necessary emotional resources to carry through the battle. In addition, the U.S. political leadership did not comprehend the nature of the struggle on the part of the North Vietnamese, and the American military command was unable to devise and implement the appropriate counterinsurgency tactics. We will return to the Vietnam War in Chapter 10.

The foregoing brief survey of American strengths and weaknesses serves as

Table 3.1   Confidence in Institutions[a]

Institutions	1973	1974	1975	1976	1977	1978	1980
Big business	37.0	36.7	25.8	26.9	33.5	29.0	34.2
Organized labor	19.6	21.3	13.6	14.2	18.2	14.7	18.8
Organized religion	43.9	51.8	32.7	37.5	49.3	41.1	44.3
Education	46.7	57.4	41.6	45.8	50.1	38.2	37.5
Executive branch	37.0	15.9	17.9	16.5	34.4	16.8	15.2
Congress	28.0	19.1	16.1	15.5	22.1	15.5	10.9
U.S. Supreme Court	37.5	37.1	37.2	39.8	41.2	33.9	28.9
Medicine	68.3	70.6	67.8	66.3	63.5	61.7	65.8
Scientific community	43.9	50.3	45.5	48.1	47.3	43.6	48.6
Press	29.2	30.2	32.0	34.8	31.0	26.9	27.6
Television	23.5	27.4	23.9	22.9	21.5	18.4	20.1
Military	37.8	44.2	42.6	44.0	42.0	35.6	32.4

[a]Given the size of the data base, fractional percentages rather than rounded percentages have been reported.

Source: *General Social Survey* (GSS) of National Opinion Research Center (NORC), 1973–1980.

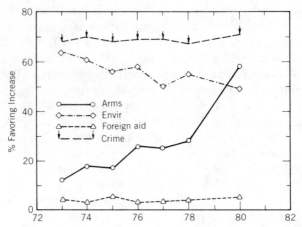

Figure 3.1 Selected U.S. spending priorities, 1973 to 1980.

Source: General Social Survey of National Opinion Research Center (NORC), 1973–1980.

Table 3.2   The Public's Sentiments on Defense Spending, 1960–1982[a]

Response	1960	1969	1971	February 1973	September 1973	CCFR 1974	1974	1976	CCFR 1977	1978	CCFR 1982
1. Too much	18%	52%	49%	42%	46%	44%	32%	36%	23%	16%	24%
2. About right	45	31	31	40	30	32	47	32	40	45	52
3. Too little	21	8	11	8	13	12	13	22	27	32	21

[a]*NOTE:* 1982, 1978, and 1974 Chicago Council on Foreign Relations (CCFR) results compared to Gallup Poll trend. Gallup did not collect data for the period 1960–1968. The CCFR questions were slightly different: (1) cut back, (2) keep same, and (3) expand.

Source: John E. Rielly (ed.), *American Public Opinion and U.S. Foreign Policy 1983* (Chicago: The Chicago Council on Foreign Relations, 1983), p. 28.

nothing more than a fragmentary illustration of how policymaking participants must make a careful analysis of U.S. capabilities and vulnerabilities in order to identify particular national interests that need to be pursued and for whose pursuit appropriate resources of every type are available. The identification and definition of these interests, in turn, is subject to influences emanating from considerations of the policymakers' personal interests and other idiosyncrasies including their personal traits and backgrounds.

For the determination of realistic foreign policy goals and actions, however, another step is necessary. The resources, such as well-trained and well-organized military forces, a powerful economy, adequate financial means, and extensive technological capabilities, not only must be measured in absolute terms, but also must be weighed in relation to the military, economic, and other capabilities of the states toward which a specific policy is being developed. Furthermore, in determining the proper policy goals and actions with respect to a particular area, it is necessary to evaluate the national interests of other states in the same area. The pursuit of these interests may compete with or perhaps reinforce the implementation of U.S. goals and therefore must be given close attention if the elaboration of *successful* American policies is to be assured.

Idiosyncratic Propensities in Foreign Policymaking

Can we discern any patterns between certain idiosyncrasies of policymakers and the formulation of policy goals and actions that may help not only in determining causality between independent idiosyncratic variables and policy content but also in predicting policy outputs? Margaret Hermann has advanced a number of pertinent propositions that can be applied to the American scene. Some of these propositions are very useful in gaining a better understanding of how particular characteristics or needs of individual presidents tend to produce differing foreign policy behavior.[19] Although somewhat paraphrased, they are outlined here:

• *The more nationalistic the president, the more conflictual his or her administration's foreign policy will be.* Strong nationalistic beliefs imply the goodness of the United States; thus certain other states tend to cause the world's problems, and these are seen as enemies. Confrontational behavior toward the latter is therefore natural. President Reagan is an example of this behavior.

• *The greater the president's need for achievement, the more cooperative behavior his or her administration will initiate.* Need for achievement is a motive and a generator of a particular view of the world. Presidents exhibiting this need offer cooperation in hopes that others will reciprocate and that, as a consequence, a trusting and mutually rewarding relationship can be established that can be expanded to different issue areas. President Carter's strategy in dealing with the Soviet Union is an example. He hoped to achieve an arms control agreement with Moscow and thus intensify detente. He abandoned this strategy when the Soviet Union invaded Afghanistan.

• *The more dogmatic the president, the less likely his or her administration is to change its position on a well-established policy.* Dogmatism suggests a rigid and inflexible set of ideas and thought patterns that emphasize one side of a problem. It stresses the importance of tradition, style, and rules. A dogmatic person is loath to change any policy or position once adopted. Again, President Reagan may be the best example. He is strongly committed to anticommunism and adamantly sticks to the basics of his defense and arms control policies, although he allows modifications—primarily for tactical, negotiating purposes. This was done with respect to the MX missile when Congress balked on providing the construction funds, and in the negotiations on the deployment of medium-range missiles in Europe to restore NATO's balance with the Soviet SS-20 missiles that were already in place.

• *The more Machiavellian the president, the more face-to-face foreign policy interactions his administration will have.* Machiavellianism refers to the manipulation of people or, in the context of foreign relations, of other governments. However, these manipulations will also have a domestic payoff. Direct communication with the other party is essential for the success of the manipulator, and therefore, in the foreign arena face-to-face contacts with other governmental leaders, either through regular bilateral meetings or though "summit" conferences, are stressed. President Nixon is the best example for this trait and style of foreign policy operations. Through this strategy he achieved the initial normalization of relations with the People's Republic of China and was able to conclude a strategic (nuclear) arms limitation agreement with the Soviet Union (SALT I).

In this discussion of idiosyncratic propensities regarding foreign policymaking, we must keep in mind that while the president may have the ultimate word in the decision-making, other, mostly high-level officials are also involved, and they have their own idiosyncrasies that may or may not have a bearing on the policymaking process. However, there will also be a tendency by the closest foreign policy advisors to adopt and support the president's traits and style, and therefore, at least to the outside, the administration will in most cases exhibit uniform foreign policymaking behavior. In some instances, however, it may be a very strong secretary of state whose particular idiosyncrasies set the behavioral tone for the administration; the best examples are John Foster Dulles for the Eisenhower administration during the 1950s and Henry Kissinger for the Nixon and Ford administrations in the 1970s.

SUMMARY

This chapter contains a discussion of *idiosyncratic variables* that may have a bearing on the formulation and content of American foreign policy. The *attitudes* of policymakers are significant variables, because they are likely to predispose the participants in the foreign policymaking process to support or reject particular foreign policy goals or actions. Attitudes have an enduring quality and are conditioned by the decision maker's value and belief systems, which, in turn, are influenced by social, educational, cultural, and career experience factors.

Attitudinal changes emanate from new perceptions that denote sensory experiences of the external world. Perceptions may also have evaluative components.

The notion of image has been examined in detail. *Images* refer to policymakers' view of the external and internal environment of their country and tend to shape their input into the policymaking process. Current attitudes, past experiences, value commitments and beliefs, as well as the development of a decision maker's personality bear on the manner in which he or she views the outside world. Images can be either *open* or *closed* depending on how extensively new information is accepted for the adjustment of the existing image. Changes of images also depend on the *clarity* with which new information is received. Usually, images have an enduring *conservative* quality; once developed, policymakers find it difficult to change them. This is all the more true when the image held by a high-ranking policymaker has become *public knowledge*.

Attitudinal and image changes may be especially crucial when new information is discovered on activities and conditions outside the United States. Such information may be converted into *foreign intelligence* after it has been analyzed, interpreted, and evaluated. The information processed into intelligence in most cases comes from *open sources*; *secret operations* contribute only a relatively small, although at times crucial, amount to the overall intelligence production process. A variety of means exist for the *dissemination* of intelligence. Their choice depends on the need of the recipient or "consumer" of the intelligence. Policymakers do not always accept and use the knowledge conveyed by the intelligence agencies. They either may have doubts about the accuracy of the intelligence provided or seek to rely on knowledge gained through their own experiences.

Personal and organizational interests of decision makers are also idiosyncratic factors influencing the policymaking process and the content of foreign policy. In the pursuit of personal interests (promotion, prestige, power), a participant in policymaking may accept a "*groupthink*" mold when policy is made within a small group of top-level governmental leaders. This implies assuming the role of a perfect team player, suppressing personal doubts about issues debated within the group, and displaying a high level of docility to the wishes of the leadership.

Although it is often believed that the notion of the *national interest* provides an objective guide for foreign policy formulation, this notion is subject to differing conceptualizations and to varying definitions by individual policymakers. Hence it becomes an idiosyncratic variable for the formulation of policy. According to the three main conceptualizations, national interest can be understood to be *normative* (a prescription of what *ought* to be done), *historical* (describing what the national interest had been), and *functional* (a process by which different forces in a society seek to express their aspirations in world politics at different points in time). In view of the unreliability of the notion of national interest as an objective guide because of the differing interpretations that can be attributed to this term by individual policymakers, other factors that lend themselves to a degree of empirical measurement must be and are used to determine foreign policy goals and actions. These factors are a country's *capabilities* and *vulnerabilities*, especially in the military, technological, economic, financial, and political fields. A comparative analysis of U.S. capabilities and vulnerabilities with those of a state or states toward which prospective American policies are directed is likely to provide a sound basis for policy content.

Finally, the chapter seeks to link particular idiosyncratic propensities of high-level policymakers with *patterns of foreign policy behavior*. The propositions discussed cover consequences for policy behavior by presidents whose personal characteristics display strong *nationalism*, a high level of *dogmatism*, a strong *need for achievement*, or a penchant for *Machiavellianism*.

NOTES

1. D. Krech and R.S. Crutchfield, *Theory and Practice of Social Psychology* (New York: McGraw-Hill, 1948), p. 152.
2. G. Allport, *Theories of Perceptions and the Concept of Structure* (New York: John Wiley & Sons, 1955), p. 17.
3. For details, see Joseph deRivera, *The Psychological Dimensions of American Foreign Policy* (New York: Charles E. Merriam, 1968), pp. 245–297.
4. Ibid., pp. 254–255.
5. Ibid., p. 294; pp. 247–297 give a full analysis of the dispute.
6. For a full treatment of this issue see Robert Jervis, *Perception and Misperception in International Politics* (Princeton, N.J.: Princeton University Press, 1976).
7. Ibid., 291–297.
8. David Halberstam, *The Best and the Brightest* (New York: Random House, 1972), p.22.
9. In this connection see also K.J. Holsti, "National Role Conception in the Study of Foreign Policy," *International Studies Quarterly* 14 (1970), pp. 233–309.
10. See, for example, Patrick J. McGarvey, "DIA: Intelligence to Please," *The Washington Monthly* 2 (July 1970), pp. 68–75.
11. Ladislas Farago, *War of Wits: The Anatomy of Espionage and Intelligence* (New York: Funk & Wagnalls, 1954), pp. 25–29; Ellis M. Zacharias, *Secret Missions* (New York: G.M. Putnam & Sons, 1946), p. 335; and ibid., *Behind Closed Doors* (New York: G.M. Putnam & Sons, 1950), p. 57.
12. See Anthony Downs, *Inside Bureaucracy* (Boston: Little, Brown, 1967), pp. 81–89. For a discussion of how the positions held influence perceptions and attitudes, see Andrew K. Semmel, "Some Correlations of Attitudes to Multilateral Diplomacy in the U.S. Department of State," *International Studies Quarterly* 20 (June 1976), pp. 301–324.
13. Irving L. Janis, *Victims of Groupthink*, 2nd ed. (New York: Houghton Mifflin, 1982), pp. 40–41.
14. For a full account of the group's deliberations, see ibid., pp. 14–47.
15. Statement in London, October 1, 1939.
16. For a more comprehensive discussion of the notion of national interest, see James Rosenau, *The Scientific Study of Foreign Policy* (New York: Free Press, 1971), pp. 239–249; and Hans J. Morgenthau, *In Defense of the National Interest: A Critical Examination of American Foreign Policy* (New York: Alfred A. Knopf, 1951).
17. See Morton A. Kaplan, *System and Process in International Politics* (New York: John Wiley & Sons, 1964—Science Edition), pp. 151–165; and Stanley Hoffmann, *Contemporary Theory in International Relations* (Englewood Cliffs, N.J.: Prentice-Hall, 1960), p. 33.
18. Frederick H. Hartmann, *The Relations of Nations*, 4th ed. (New York: Macmillan, 1973), pp. 6–12.

19. Margaret G. Hermann, "Effects of Personal Characteristics of Political Leaders on Foreign Policy," in *Why Nations Act*, edited by Maurice A. East, Stephen A. Salmore, and Charles F. Hermann (Beverly Hills, Calif.: Sage Publications, 1978), pp. 49–68, on pp. 65–67. See also Hermann's "Leadership Personality and Foreign Policy Behavior," in *Comparing Foreign Policies*, edited by James N. Rosenau (New York: John Wiley & Sons, 1974), pp. 201–234.

CHAPTER 4

Institutional Variables: The Executive Branch

Having discussed in Chapter 3 the idiosyncratic variables, we now move to a discussion of the institutional variables. In this chapter we will focus on the executive branch, and in Chapter 5 will examine the role of Congress and interest groups in the formulation of foreign policy.

The Constitution does not clearly circumscribe the role of the president in the formulation of foreign policy. Article II grants to the president the power to make treaties and to appoint ambassadors and other public ministers and consuls, but only with the advice and consent of the Senate. The president is also authorized to receive ambassadors and other ministers. Additional and, in fact, broader powers stem from presidential functions of chief executive officer and commander-in-chief of the armed forces. In a famous Supreme Court decision [*United States* vs. *Curtis-Wright Export Corporation*, 299 U.S. 304 (1936)], Justice Sutherland issued an *obiter dictum* assigning to the president the foremost position in foreign policy activities:

> In this vast external realm, with its important, delicate, and manifold problems, the President alone has the power to speak or listen as a representative of the Nation.

However, the Constitution is far less enthusiastic than Justice Sutherland in conveying foreign policy powers to the president. Congress has specific grants of authority in the foreign policy field that impose important limitations on the president. It is up to Congress to raise and maintain the armed forces. However, Congress' competence to declare war is obviously less important in the second half of the twentieth century than it was previously, because even extensive hostilities such as the U.S. involvements in Korea and Vietnam have not been regarded as "wars" in the sense of the Constitution.

Other specific constitutional grants of power to Congress deal with the regulation of international commerce, the punishment of piracies and felonies committed on the high seas, and offenses committed against the laws of nations. Finally, the president's foreign policy powers can be restricted by Congress' authority to raise revenues for the payment of debt and for the appropriation of funds for the common defense and welfare, and by its general legislative authorizations.

The Constitution has been characterized as an open invitation for struggle between the executive and the legislative branches of government for the privilege of directing American foreign policy—and certainly American history in the foreign policy field has borne this out, especially since Vietnam and Watergate. Before we examine this struggle with its manifold implications for the explanation of U.S. foreign policies, however, we must first describe and assess the institutional features of the executive branch bearing on the formulation of policy.

THE WHITE HOUSE

While the Constitution is ambiguous about the role of the president in foreign policy formulation, there is no question that the president is ultimately responsible for all major foreign policy decisions. As the well-known sign on President Truman's desk proclaimed: "The buck stops here."

Indeed, some of the major foreign policy events of the past have borne the clear imprint of the president in office and of his personality. For example, President McKinley bore the responsibility for the acquisition of the Philippines at the end of the nineteenth century and for the war with Spain.[2] President Franklin Roosevelt, in 1940, was instrumental in the exchange of fifty American destroyers for the American use of eight British bases stretching from Newfoundland to British Guiana. President Truman made the fateful decision to commit American forces against the North Koreans invading South Korea in the summer of 1950. President Kennedy assumed full responsibility for the 1961 debacle of the attempted invasion of the Bay of Pigs by Cuban exiles under the direction of CIA operatives. He also made the final choice in October 1962 to face down the Soviet Union when it attempted to introduce offensive missiles into Cuba that could easily threaten large parts of the U.S. mainland. President Nixon was instrumental in beginning the diplomatic recognition process of the People's Republic of China in the early 1970s, and he personally was responsible for the gradual disengagement of U.S. forces from Vietnam. The Camp David accords between Israel and Egypt in 1978 clearly show the mark of President Carter; in addition, the possible utilization of U.S. Marines in the 1982 evacuation of PLO forces from Lebanon may reflect the very close, personal involvement of President Reagan in the solution of the Israeli-PLO-Syrian conflict.

Although ultimate responsibility in all the above and many other foreign policy issues was clearly in the hands of the president as a *personal* participant in the decision-making process, personal staff members in the White House and Executive Office assisted him through a continuous flow of information and intelligence, the preparation of position papers, and, most of all, personal consultations and advice. This advice included, and continues to include, the constitutional limits of the president's powers in the foreign policy field. Although as commander-in-chief the president can employ the armed forces, the question arises as to the precise conditions under which this can be done. The War Powers Act of 1973, to be examined in detail later, is an obvious limitation. Furthermore, as chief executive officer, how far can the president go in concluding so-called executive agreements, and under what conditions would such an agreement—for example, the destroyers-for-bases swap mentioned earlier—impinge on the Senate's right to consent to an international "treaty" negotiated by the president? Again, this will be examined more thoroughly later. Whatever the final judgment in these questions, the president needs to have available advisors on these issues, and they can play influential roles in the development of American foreign policy.

Presidential Advisors

Since 1939, when the White House office was formally established by executive order, some of the officials assigned to this organization have specialized in furnishing information and offering counsel to the presidents on foreign policy issues. Other officials have been primarily concerned with domestic matters and have provided liaison with Congress.

Members of the White House office staff are not subject to Senate confirmation of their appointments. This makes good sense, because the relationship between presidents and their advisors rests on a very personal basis. Unless presidents can feel thoroughly comfortable with their advisors, the quality of policy development may suffer. Unfortunately, the presidential choice of a foreign affairs advisor is not always based on highest intelligence and experience in foreign policy. Other pertinent factors include expected loyalty, long-standing friendship, and perhaps political expedience. However, such attributes may well combine with superior foreign policy knowledge and savvy.

Before 1939, presidents also had their personal advisors, although their positions rested on a more informal basis. For example, Colonel E. M. House was President Woodrow Wilson's intimate advisor. Before World War I, he attempted unsuccessfully to bring Great Britain and Germany together. He also helped Wilson with the formulation of the famous "Fourteen Points," but Wilson rejected his wise counsel to leave to the Senate full responsibility for the Treaty of Versailles. Had his advice been heeded, the treaty might have been accepted and, with it, the League of Nations.[3]

Even after the formal establishment of the White House office, presidents sought the advice of individuals not formally assigned to that office. For example, President Franklin Roosevelt highly valued the foreign policy advice of Harry L. Hopkins, a New York social service worker who had risen rapidly to high rank in the administration and had served as secretary of commerce. In the presidency of John F. Kennedy, his brother Robert, holding the post of attorney general, played a crucial role as special foreign policy advisor during the Bay of Pigs episode and the Cuban missile crisis. In the administrations of Presidents Johnson and Carter, their wives (Lady Bird and Rosalyn, respectively) had substantial political influence on specific issues; how much Johnson and Carter actually listened to their wives with respect to foreign policy is difficult to ascertain, however.

The exact organization of the White House office depends on the personal preferences of the current officeholder. Under President Reagan, the top jobs are held by James Baker, the chief of staff; Michael Deaver, deputy chief of staff; and Edwin Meese, "counselor." To be added, especially for foreign policy matters, is William Clark, the national security affairs advisor, whose functions we will examine in the next section. It is noteworthy, but not surprising, that the number of employees on the White House staff increased from 45 in 1939 to over 600 in 1975, but in 1982 the number had declined to 361.[4] In addition, personnel may be temporarily assigned to the presidential staff from various departments, and, or course, the cabinet members may also be asked by the president for their advice on specific foreign policy matters.

National Security Council

The importance of the national security affairs advisor for the president's involvement in the formulation of foreign policy is highlighted by the fact that this advisor plays a very significant role in the operations of the National Security Council (NSC). This is not a statutory role but one that has developed since President Kennedy's administration when McGeorge Bundy was the national security affairs advisor.

In statutory terms, the National Security Council consists of the president as chairman, the vice-president, and the secretaries of state and defense. Other high-ranking officials frequently invited to sit in on NSC sessions include the secretary of the treasury, the chair of the Joint Chiefs of Staff, and the director of the Central Intelligence Agency. Other invited participants may be the heads of the Department of Energy and the Office of Management and Budget, the attorney general, the director of the FBI, and sometimes during earlier periods the U.S. ambassador to the United Nations.

The statute creating the NSC was passed in 1947. Its specified task is

> to advise the President with respect to the integration of domestic, foreign, and military policies relating to the national security so as to enable the military services and other departments and agencies of the government to cooperate more effectively in matters involving national security.[5]

Although it seems obvious that the coordination of foreign, military, and domestic policies for the assurance of national security should have the highest priority, the utilization of the NSC has not been uniform. Under President Eisenhower, the NSC followed a clearly defined schedule and met every week. Presidents Kennedy and Johnson relaxed the NSC schedule, and meetings took place less frequently. President Nixon, in his first term, returned to the weekly schedule; however, beginning in 1971, NSC meetings sometimes occurred only once a month or even less often. President Ford more or less followed the pattern Nixon had established toward the end of his tenure, whereas President Carter restored the NSC to greater prominence. Under President Reagan, it appears that the NSC, which meets more sporadically, is given less significance, and other means of policy coordination are emphasized. Three senior interdepartmental groups (SIGs) have been established; they are chaired by high officials of the departments of state and defense and the CIA, and their function is to deal with aspects of national security flowing from the formulation and implementation of foreign policies, defense policies, and intelligence policies.[6]

Over the years, not only the personal preferences of presidents but also the professional experience, style, and bureaucratic skill of the national security affairs advisors as well as of the secretaries of state and defense have shaped the organizational framework of the NSC. With strong secretaries of state, such as Dean Acheson under President Truman and John Foster Dulles under President Eisenhower, the NSC structure consisted of a hierarchy of interdepartmental committees to which Eisenhower added a Planning Committee and an Operations Coordinating Board (OCB). After the NSC had made a formal decision, the OCB took over with monthly, quarterly, and annual reviews to ensure that each department and agency carried out the approved policy. This board was eliminated after Eisenhower left office.

Under the Kennedy administration, McGeorge Bundy, the national security affairs advisor, changed the NSC structure by abolishing the OCB, which eliminated over forty-five interdepartmental committees. As already mentioned, the NSC met less often under Kennedy, and the emphasis—as promoted by Bundy—shifted to less formal meetings in which many of the same people were present that used to participate in the NSC sessions. During the Kennedy years, Secretary of Defense Robert McNamara, an imaginative and forceful leader, became a closer advisor in foreign policy matters than Secretary of State Dean Rusk, although initially Rusk wanted the Department of State to play the top role in foreign and national security affairs. At the same time, Bundy also remained a trusted and influential advisor.

Bundy continued in this position under President Johnson until 1966 when Walt Whitman Rostow took over as national security affairs advisor and retained and exercised a similar influence on foreign policymaking as did his predecessor. In a similar fashion, McNamara also remained a close advisor of President Johnson.[7] However, the structure of the NSC gained again in organizational mechanisms through the creation of interdepartmental committees chaired by top officials of the State Department. Interdeparmental regional groups (IRGs) were supposed to coordinate regional policies in such areas as Africa or Asia, and were to report to a senior interdepartmental group (SIG) chaired by the undersecretary of state.

Henry Kissinger, as special assistant for national security affairs under President Nixon, modified and strengthened the NSC structure further, as can be seen from Figure 4.1. But strengthening the structure must not be equated with increasing its actual power in the foreign policymaking process. Indeed, as already noted, the NSC meetings, after a good start, met less and less frequently in the Nixon and Ford administrations, and what meetings were held assumed a *pro forma* nature, whereas major decisions were taken by Nixon and Kissinger in personal consultations. This pattern of consultation in foreign policy formulation was further intensified and "legitimized" when Kissinger became secretary of state in 1973.

Regardless of the actual power exerted by the NSC on foreign policy formulation and implementation, Figure 4.1 shows the very complex nature of the NSC framework at that time and *the strong personal influence of Henry Kissinger*. He chaired the Senior Review Group (SRG), the Defense Program Review Committee (DPRC), the Forty Committee, and the Washington Special Actions Group (WSAG); he was a member of the undersecretaries group (USG); he also had representatives on each interdepartmental group (IG), the Verification Panel, and the Vietnam Special Studies Group. The IGs numbered six: five covered the major regions of the world, and one represented politicomilitary affairs. The USG had as its major task the coordination of implementing the presidential decisions. The DPRC was to coordinate defense spending with foreign policy objectives, while the Verification Panel had as its primary function the monitoring of negotiations on the Strategic Arms Limitation Talks (SALT). The Forty Committee supervised covert intelligence activities conducted by agencies of the U.S. government, and WSAG was in charge of the White House operation center in the event of sudden international emergencies.

Under the Carter administration and Security Advisor Zbigniew Brzezinski,

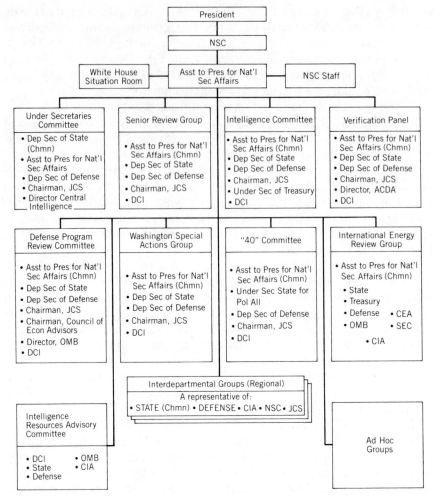

Figure 4.1 The National Security Council, 1969–1974.

Source: Adopted from Committee on Foreign Relations, United States Senate, *The National Security Adviser: Role and Accountability* (April 17, 1980), p. 97.

the organization pendulum of the NSC swung again in the opposite direction, and the structure became less complex. The WSAG was discontinued, and, although the SRG, IGs, and USG were retained, most authority was given to a cabinet-level Policy Review Committee, which sought to define foreign policy problems and coordinate research on long-range foreign policy issues. A Special Coordinating Committee handled immediate crisis problems. Brzezinski reduced the policymaking power of the NSC and strengthened its role of providing information and advice from the executive departments and agencies concerned with national security to President Carter. For this reason,

Brzezinski spent at least an hour each day with the president, briefing him on the latest intelligence developments and discussing with him foreign and national security policy problems and possible solutions.[8] The advice thus given to the president was not always what seemed best to Secretary of State Cyrus Vance, who had a less bellicose and assertive nature than Brzezinski. Indeed, during the Iranian hostage crisis, when Carter seemed to have accepted the latter's counsel to mount a complicated and daring military rescue mission for the hostages, Vance turned in his resignation.

Under President Reagan, the NSC system may have lost additional strength as an effective influence in the foreign policymaking processes. This is suggested by former Secretary of State Haig's insistence that he would be the "vicar" of foreign policy, and it is confirmed by the establishment of the three senior interdepartmental groups (SIGs), mentioned earlier, which replaced Carter's Policy Review Committee. Still further changes may well be in the offing. Reagan's first special assistant for national security affairs, Richard V. Allen, did not have direct access to the president and had to go through Counselor Edwin Meese. However, the current advisor, William Clark, has unrestricted access to the president and is becoming a growing power in foreign policy formulation in spite of his limited knowledge of international affairs. (He was formerly a judge in California.) The position of the current secretary of state, George Shultz, is still evolving at this writing, and his attitude toward the NSC as well as the nature of his relationship with the president will be important factors for the formal and informal processes and presidential management style in the formulation of American foreign policy.[9]

THE DEPARTMENT OF STATE

Scope and Functions

The president's time cannot be occupied with every aspect of foreign policy formulation; indeed, many decisions are made at lower levels. For the majority of these decisions, the staff work and preliminary decision making takes place in the Department of State, which has the prime interest in and functional responsibility for the relations of the United States with foreign countries and intergovernmental organizations (IGOs).

The chief officer of the Department of State is the secretary of state, who by law and delegation of presidential powers is, at least in formal terms, the president's principal advisor in formulating foreign policy and principal agent in policy implementation. This person is also the first-ranking member of the cabinet and fourth in line (following the vice-president, Speaker of the House, and president pro tempore of the Senate) in the event of presidential incapacity. However, as we have seen, the secretary's effective influence in foreign policymaking varies depending on experience and personality as well as the president's predilection for personal advisors, including the special assistant for national security affairs, which has sometimes led to informal consultation and decision making such as President Johnson's "Tuesday lunch group."[10]

As we already mentioned, Dean Acheson and John Foster Dulles were strong secretaries of state whose counsel on foreign policy was generally accepted by their presidents. Dean Rusk, secretary of state in the Kennedy and Johnson administrations, was considerably weaker and was overshadowed in the presidential foreign policy deliberations by the national security affairs advisors and Secretary of Defense McNamara. Henry Kissinger dominated the foreign policy process in both the Nixon and Ford administrations; Cyrus Vance, whose influence as secretary of state during most of the Carter presidency was initially strong, lost out toward the end to the rising power of Brzezinski. Alexander Haig, who had considered himself the "vicar" of American foreign policy, apparently with President Reagan's approval, later ran afoul of the group of close top advisors of the president and lost Reagan's backing. Although Haig was able to have the White House relieve National Security Advisor Richard Allen of his job, he seemed eventually to have lost the "turf" battle about whose views on foreign policy should prevail, with both the White House advisor group and perhaps Secretary of Defense Caspar Weinberger emerging as the victors in June 1982. The present secretary of state, George Shultz, is likely to have a better chance of exerting effective influence on the final shape of policy, because he is a long-standing friend of President Reagan and is considered to be more of a "team player" than Haig was, an attribute that seems to be highly appreciated in the Reagan White House.[11]

Haig had a penchant for dramatic statements and sensational actions, as characterized during his early tenure by his threats against Cuba to interdict communist arms deliveries to El Salvador and later, in 1982, by his 6000-mile shuttle diplomacy between London, Washington, and Buenos Aires to prevent a war over the Falkland Islands between Great Britain and Argentina. Shultz, by contrast, preferred a quieter, more restrained style in foreign policy. Yet he showed considerable energy and success in the 1983 negotiations between Lebanon and Israel on the withdrawal of Israeli troops from Lebanese soil, although the implementation of the agreement reached may be in jeopardy unless Syria accepts the content of this accord and also withdraws its forces.

The functions of the secretary of state and the State Department are many and extremely varied. They range from concern about U.S. security to economic well-being. This includes relations with our allies in various parts of the world, often formalized in IGOs such as the North Atlantic Treaty Organization (NATO) or the Organization of American States (OAS), as well as relations with potential enemies. The crucial and sensitive interaction process with the Soviet Union and the search for the prevention of nuclear hostilities are examples of this later purview. Close attention must be paid to the problems of international trade and international investment, including such issues as the transnational transfer of technology and new developments regarding the law of the sea. Finally, there are the problems of the developing countries with their low per capita incomes, high rates of disease, mostly traditional and primitive agricultural economies, and their search for industrialization and a new economic order to improve their standards of living. The extensive scope of the secretary's activities as head of the Department of State can be seen by reading various interviews given by Haig in 1981.[12] A summarization of the most crucial problems can be found in a statement given by Secretary Haig of the House Foreign Affairs Committee on March 2, 1982, of which excerpts are reproduced below:

> Over the past year, the President has frequently expressed the desire for a constructive and mutually beneficial relationship with the Soviet Union. At the same time, we have made clear that such a relationship must be based on Soviet restraint, especially in the use of force or the threat of violence. The role of Soviet threats in the Polish crisis, coming while Soviet troops occupy Afghanistan and Moscow's arms flood Cuba, undermines the very basis for productive East-West relations. . . .
>
> Mr. Gromyko [the Soviet Foreign Minister] and I also had a detailed discussion of arms control, providing me the opportunity to explain President Reagan's initiative of last November for zero levels of intermediate-range missiles. I noted that the United States is actively preparing for START [Strategic Arms Reduction Talks] negotiations, which we will initiate when conditions permit. . . .
>
> It is crucial that we understand the historic events taking place in Poland, what they mean for East-West relations, and what we can do to influence the situation. . . .
>
> Now let me turn to another area of great concern to us, the Caribbean Basin, where we face two distinct but related challenges: first, the economic and social upheavals that mark the development process; second, the threat to democracy and individual rights from the forces of totalitarianism in Cuba and elsewhere, supported by the Soviet Union.
>
> Last week the President spoke at length on our new Caribbean Basin initiative. This program is a first step toward meeting these challenges. As the President explained, the United States will work with Mexico, Canada, and Venezuela to assist countries facing severe economic problems. The American part of the package includes trading opportunities, investment incentives, and increased financial assistance. . . .
>
> In recent years, Cuba has embarked on a systematic campaign to destabilize legitimate governments in Jamaica, Colombia, Honduras, El Salvador, and elsewhere. At the same time, Cuba has systematically expanded its ability to project its military power beyond its own shores. . . .
>
> The threat to democracy from opponents of peaceful change is particularly acute in El Salvador. . . . In the face of such threats to the democratic process, the United States has firmly stated its commitment to free elections.[13]

To manage all these tasks, the Department of State is organized along both geographical and functional lines, as can be seen from Figure 4.2. The geographical breakdown is reflected by the Bureaus of European Affairs, African Affairs, East Asian and Pacific Affairs, Inter-American Affairs, and Near East and South Asian Affairs. The Bureau of International Organization Affairs can be regarded only partially as a geographical subdivision and resembles more a functional unit. Other functional bureaus deal with economic and business affairs, human rights and humanitarian issues, politicomilitary affairs, international narcotics matters, terrorism, refugee programs, and intelligence and research. Some bureaus have primarily administrative functions—the comptroller, inspector general, the legal advisor, congressional relations, protocol, and consular affairs.

The various bureaus in the State Department are headed by assistant secretaries of state and major subdivisions by deputy assistant secretaries. In the geographical bureaus, the relations with individual foreign countries are handled by country directors managing a collective "country desk," which, depending on the importance of the country involved, is serviced by an appropriate number of officials. The country director is not only in daily communication with the American embassy in the foreign country but also has frequent contacts with the embassy of that country in Washington and with his or her counterparts in other executive departments that have a particular interest in the country whose affairs that director handles. The country director plays an important role in the execution of foreign policy actions toward individual countries, because he or she is usually authorized to send telegrams to American embassies over the signature of the secretary of state. Most of these telegrams deal with routine problems; when controversial issues are involved, however, the desk officer may have to seek concurrences from other officials who are responsible for the relations with countries that might be affected. For example, U.S. actions toward West Germany must take into consideration reactions by neighboring France and the Netherlands.[14]

Between the secretary and the assistant secretaries is the deputy secretary, not only the alter ego but also the chief deputy and advisor of the secretary, who runs the day-to-day operations of the department. The main assistants to the deputy secretary are the undersecretaries for political affairs, economic affairs, security assistance, and management. Depending on the complexity of the situation for which policies must be formulated, the levels of policy formulation range from the country director to the secretary of state and, on major issues,to the presidential level. Input is also likely to come from U.S. diplomatic missions abroad.

Minor decisions can be made by the country directors, but their influence is also felt in policy decisions made on higher levels because of the information and recommendations they provide for the higher echelons. More significant decisions on foreign policy formulation may come from the assistant secretaries, but they too are likely to furnish only salient inputs in terms of information and

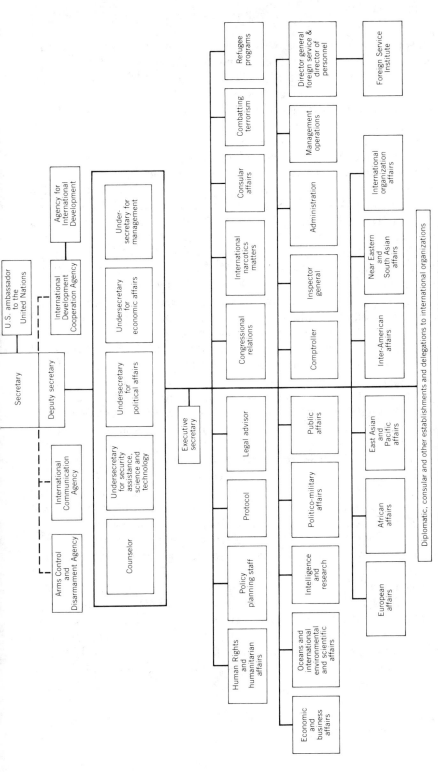

Figure 4.2 U.S. Department of State organizational chart.

Source: United States Government Manual 1981–82.

Diplomatic, consular and other establishments and delegations to international organizations

policy positions to the top echelons of the State Department where the truly significant decisions are made. For the most crucial and basic decisions, the secretary has to go to the White House level, where ideally his policy recommendations will find a favorable response.[15]

Position papers by proponents of particular policies, clearances, and concurrences by involved officials, and opposition by other officials characterize as well as complicate the policymaking processes on most levels. As the files become heavier and proceed laterally on their way up, they reflect the interests and attitudes of the policymaking participants. Important support agencies for the State Department, although organizationally independent, are the United States Information Agency (USIA), the Arms Control and Disarmament Agencies (ACDA), the Agency for International Development (AID), and the International Development Cooperation Agency (IDCA). The last two are concerned with the United States' relations with Third World countries: IDCA seeks to coordinate all governmental efforts toward Third World development goals, while AID is responsible for administering the overseas assistance programs. The ACDA has two tasks: (1) research on arms control and disarmament possibilities, and (2) participation in bilateral and multilateral negotiations that deal with the possible realization of these objectives.

The USIA, for a number of years known as the ICA (International Communications Agency), carries out information functions on a worldwide scale through public information officers assigned to U.S. diplomatic missions, the operation of libraries in foreign countries, and the Voice of America and other international broadcast facilities. We will have more to say about these activities in Chapter 8. In addition, the USIA handles programs of lectures in foreign countries, mostly by American scholars, and sponsors public opinion research on subjects relevant to foreign policy formulation.

The staff of the Department of State consisted in 1981 of about 23,500 employees,[*] of which approximately 3500 are foreign service officers (FSOs). Their functions and problems will be examined in Chapter 8, when we will discuss the instruments for policy implementation. Suffice it to say here that the foreign service as a relatively small, distinctive bureaucracy has developed a certain elite status that is often resented by non-foreign service officials. At the same time, many FSOs have tended to follow precedent and tradition, and to shun rocking the boat. Risk-taking and aggressive, innovative behavior have mostly been avoided because, in a very competitive climate, such traits might unfavorably affect the efficiency ratings given them periodically by their superiors. Nevertheless, most FSOs are intelligent and capable and have made important contributions to policy formulation and implementation. To appreciate the workload of the FSOs and the department itself, it should be noted

---

[*]It is interesting to note that in 1970 the number of State Department employees was 39,753, but has declined ever since that year.

that some 10,000 messages, reports, and instructions are sent and received every day, of which 2000 are telegrams requiring action or attention of some kind.

THE DEPARTMENT OF DEFENSE

If only the State Department and the White House foreign policy organizations were involved in the formulation of policy, the number of variables to be analyzed would be greatly reduced and explanations for particular policies might be simpler. However, with other executive departments and agencies also participating in the policymaking process, each with its own set of organizational objectives and interests, the number of institutional variables to be examined proliferates. One of the most interested and influential of these organizations is the Department of Defense (DOD).

The interest of the DOD in foreign policy formulation stems from several sources. The military establishment provides important resources and capabilities for the potential implementation of policies and therefore needs to be intimately involved in the formulation of all policies whose execution might depend on these capabilities. Military officers provide training to the armed forces of foreign states and supervise the maintenance of arms and equipment supplied to different countries under various U.S. programs. Finally, the military establishment develops strategies and tactics for the armed services that need to be related to foreign policy needs. The development of the Rapid Deployment Force (RDF) in the early 1980s is a case in point. The RDF is composed of elements of all major military services; the Carter administration initiated its creation toward the end of the 1970s. Its main purpose was rapid military intervention in the Persian Gulf region and other parts of the Middle East in the event of Soviet aggression anywhere in that area.

The foreign policy concerns of the Defense Department are revealed in its 1982 statement regarding the United States' basic national interests for the coming years:

> • *To maintain the security of our nation, as well as that of our allies and friends around the world.* We seek to deter any aggression that could threaten that security, and, should deterrence fail, to repel or defeat any military attack.
> • *To manage East-West relations, in conjunction with our allies, so as to preserve our interests and the peace.* It is incumbent on the United States, as the leader of the Atlantic Alliance and the center of other collective security frameworks, to cultivate the cooperative aspects of East-West relations, while simultaneously leading renewed efforts on the competitive aspects, channeling them into less dangerous routes wherever possible.
> • *To respond to the twin challenges of global economics and energy.* Interdependence has long been a truism, but the extent of our resource dependence, the vulnerability of our supply lines, and the need to do more than merely

acknowledge these realities, are now issues of considerable significance to us and to our allies and friends.

• *To resolve peacefully disputes in troubled regions of the world.* Such regional conflicts may involve allies or friends of the United States, may threaten U.S. interests (such as access to oil or other natural resources, or to lines of communication), and almost always carry the risk of escalation to a wider conflict.

• *To build positive bilateral relations with every nation with whom there is a basis of shared concerns.* There are over 150 nations in the world today—no one of them is our equal in total wealth or power, but each is sovereign, and most if not all of them touch our interests directly or indirectly.

• *To make a renewed assertion of fundamental American values—human rights.* This nation was predicated on certain principles—freedom and the right of peoples to choose their own form of government. In our human rights policy we uphold these and other basic principles, including the right to at least some minimum living standard.

• *To direct our attention to critical global problems, which, whether or not they now afflict us directly, will, if they remain unsolved, surely affect our lives in the future.* Among these are overpopulation, world hunger, the depletion of natural resources, the worldwide flood of refugees, the international narcotics traffic, nuclear proliferation, and terrorism.[16]

In terms of personnel and financial muscle, the DOD outstrips the State Department by a wide margin (see Figure 4.3 for an organizational chart of the Department of Defense; compare with Figure 4.2). In 1983, the budget for defense was approximately $214.8 billion, while the State Department received about $2.5 billion. The DOD budget is expected to rise by 11 to 15 percent annually until 1986.[17] Of course, the mission of the Pentagon far exceeds concerns with foreign policy; its prime task is to ensure the security of the nation.

International Security Affairs (ISA)

In spite of its broad mission, the Department of Defense has a legitimate interest in foreign policy formulation; for this reason, in 1961 an Office of International Security Affairs (ISA), headed by an assistant secretary of defense, was established.

Located in the office of the secretary of defense, ISA is one of three offices concerned with international security affairs and policy (planning and review) under the direction of the undersecretary for policy, who also supervises the Defense Security Assistance Agency (see Figure 4.3). This organizational structure suggests the great importance the Defense Department attributes to its involvement in foreign policy formulation.

Sometimes referred to as "the little State Department of the DOD," ISA is organized along both geographical and functional lines, similar to the Department of State. Its basic functions are as follows:

1. To determine DOD policy positions in the area of foreign affairs, especially foreign military assistance, arms control, and disarmament.
2. To provide a contact point within the Pentagon for interaction with State Department officials.
3. To offer the secretary of defense expert foreign policy advice to complement the views of the Joint Chiefs of Staff channeled to him.

At the present time, the assistant secretary for international security affairs is Richard N. Perle. He occupies an influential position in the upper levels of the Pentagon bureaucracy, and even the secretary of defense, Caspar Weinberger, often accepts his views on U.S.-Soviet relations and arms control. Perle's attitudes lean strongly to the right, and he maintains close contacts with conservative groups in Washington and elsewhere. He used to be a staff member and long-time advisor to Senator Henry Jackson before moving to the Pentagon and now has close relations with William P. Clark, the president's special assistant for national security affairs.[18]

Defense Security Assistance Agency

Until 1971, ISA was in charge of the military assistance program (MAP), which now is handled by the Defense Security Assistance Agency. This agency also is responsible for the DOD's review of military assistance programs and foreign military sales, a task in which it cooperates with the State Department's Bureau of Politico-Military Affairs. To carry out its functions, the agency works closely with military assistance advisory groups (MAAGs) assigned to selected foreign countries. We will return to the subject of foreign military assistance and sales later in the book.

The Influence of the Pentagon

In the overall formulation of foreign policy, it is not so much the ISA but the personality and attitudes of the secretary of defense and his relationship with the Joint Chiefs of Staff (JCS) that affect the policymaking process. During the Truman and Eisenhower years, the JCS played an important role in influencing the shaping of foreign and national security policies. General George C. Marshall, former chief of staff of the army, was secretary of defense in 1950–1951.* However, he was generally not perceived as a man who would

---

*Marshall will probably be better remembered for the program for economic recovery of Europe after World War II, the Marshall Plan, which was formulated during his tenure as secretary of state in 1947–1949.

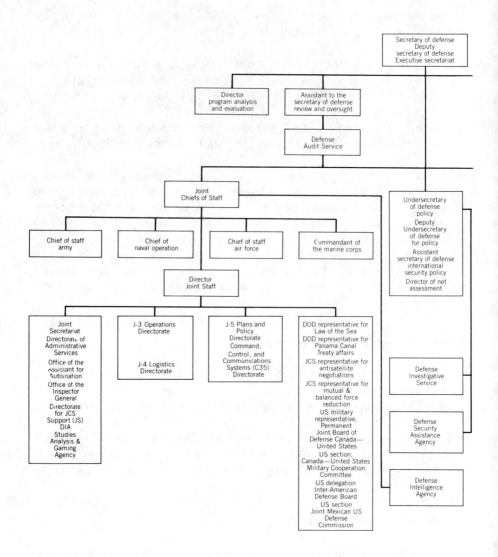

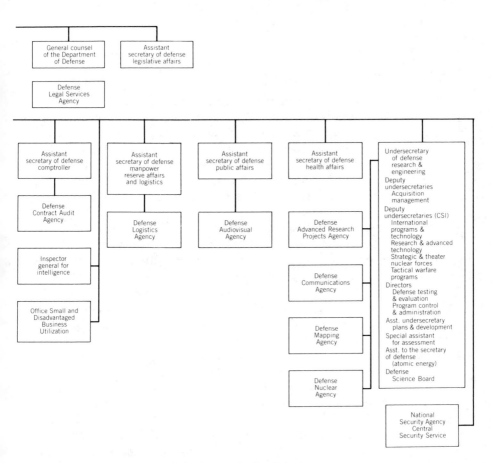

Figure 4.3 U.S. Department of Defense organizational chart.
Source: Department of Defense.

allow his loyalty to the military establishment to dominate his judgment.[19] During the Kennedy and Johnson administrations, the influence of the JCS declined. Secretary of Defense McNamara's sophisticated management style and his insistence on cost effectiveness strengthened the hand of the civilian leadership over the military establishment in foreign policy development. Indeed, as the Vietnam conflict proceeded, McNamara assumed an increasingly dovelike attitude.[20]

The trend toward the greater voice of the civilian leadership in the Pentagon was temporarily halted during the Nixon years, especially with Melvin Laird's tenure as secretary of defense. A basically conservative former Republican congressman, Laird was a strong, knowledgeable and capable secretary who had close relations with the Joint Chiefs of Staff. Under President Carter and his defense secretary, Harold Brown, the power over policy by the JCS waned again; Brown's recommendations to the White House were often unsuccessfully opposed by the military, the cancellation of the B-1 bomber by Carter being a prime example.

The Reagan administration has again given the JCS a greater role in the policy field and has involved them in budget planning, an important factor in molding basic policy lines. The generally hawklike attitudes of President Reagan and Secretary of Defense Weinberger are likely to be much more congenial to the military minds in the Pentagon than the attitude of their predecessors. Moreover, the tremendous increase in budgetary allocations to the military establishment during the first half of the 1980s cannot but find favor with the chiefs of the armed forces.

Several factors give the Pentagon particular clout in influencing foreign policy formulation. First, during the late 1970s and early 1980s, perceptions of many American elites and the public at large about the threat of Soviet attack on the United States have intensified. The protracted cold war had stimulated beliefs that a large military establishment was needed in "peacetime" and that, as a consequence of the possibility of the employment of nuclear weapons, no time would be available for mass mobilization. Whether justified or not, the impression has been gained that U.S. military strength has become inferior to that of the Soviet Union. Combined with the generally prevailing strong anticommunist sentiment, the grass roots support exists for policies designed to regain the military superiority over the Soviet Union that the United States once possessed, or at least to achieve "advantageous equivalence." At the same time, cooperation with the Soviet Union has had little support, especially since the Soviet invasion of Afghanistan in 1979.

Another element strengthening the Pentagon's clout in foreign policy development is the flow of funds from arms procurement and military installations into the economies of the states. The power to spend the enormous sums of money for upgrading the military posture of the United States means that large and small defense contractors have vested interests in the thrust of American foreign policy advantageous to their revenues, and labor unions have similar interests with respect to their members. It is noteworthy that the construction of the B-1 bomber by Rockwell International involves subcontractors in forty-eight states and eventually may create 200,000 jobs. Similar job-creating trends may occur with the production of other weapons systems.

Military installations in various states also bring about vested interests, and both arms producers and communities with installations as well as members of Congress wishing to serve their constituencies become powerful and insistent lobbyists in Congress for foreign policies promoting their particular goals. Corporations and interest groups with defense production interests may also use membership in State Department advisory committees for that purpose.

The Defense Department task of deterring Soviet nuclear aggression against the United States by itself carries a measure of influence on foreign policy formulation. It intensifies existing American distrust of the Soviet Union and tends to skew attitudes of most participants in foreign policymaking toward assurance of the least risk in U.S. relations with the Soviet Union.

Finally, several hundred army, air force, and naval attachés are assigned to diplomatic missions and military assistance advisory groups (MAAGs) in different countries. They make their reports to their own services and interact on a daily basis with U.S. foreign service officers in the capitals where they are assigned.

It is difficult to define what a particular "military mind" is, if in fact it exists at all. But it is fair to assume that military officers look at the international arena in terms of competition as well as natural and potential conflict to be resolved through either the threat or actual use of arms. As Nash states, according to typical military thinking:

> The one way to make the world less threatening was to use force to compel other nations to comply with some standard of behavior. In this characteristically military point of view, force represented the appropriate means to correct an unacceptable (therefore "wrong") international situation.[21]

Closely related to this perspective of military views is the tendency to look at international situations and problems in terms of "worst case" scenarios for which the only solution is the application of highly effective armed forces. There is a tendency to play it safe—to seek a margin of safety through more weapons and personnel. The creation of such forces then becomes the goal of highest priority, and such conviction colors the input into foreign policymaking not only by military attachés whose influence generally is limited to local contacts with ambassadors and other foreign service officers at a particular mission but also by high-ranking officers at the Pentagon, NSC, and White House levels.

What we see, then, is that the Defense Department impact on foreign policy formulation goes much further than the formal contacts through ISA. Looking at the total effect achievable through a variety of formal and informal channels as well as through the enormous economic impact of the Defense Department activities throughout the United States, it is evident that many variables must be considered to appreciate and assess the role of the DOD on the formulation of American foreign policy.

OTHER INTERESTED EXECUTIVE DEPARTMENTS

Other departments involved in the formulation of foreign policy include Commerce, Agriculture, Labor, the Treasury, and Energy. Officials of these departments also serve as attachés in the larger U.S. diplomatic missions around the world.

The Department of Commerce

Foreign economic policy formulation is of particular interest to the Commerce Department and its clientele. This prime concern is international trade and the implementation of the multilateral trade agreements that have been negotiated from time to time since the 1930s by the United States with foreign countries and that have led to successive reductions in tariffs. The negotiations themselves, however, are carried out by the Office of the United States Trade Representative, which is part of the Executive Office of the President. Negotiations since 1947 have been held under the auspices of the General Agreement on Tariffs and Trade (GATT) and have always been drawn-out, highly complex affairs. We will examine various aspects of foreign economic policy in Chapter 8.

The special responsibilities of the Commerce Department dealing with international trade include the administration of export control, the implementation of trade agreements including supervision of antidumping rules, the distribution of adjustment assistance to business firms and communities that have sustained injury as the result of lower-priced imports, and foreign commercial representation. The latter function has assumed increasing importance in view of the need to enhance American exports in order to redress recurring deficits in the international trade balance.

The range of interests with which the Commerce Department is concerned is broad and its impact on the foreign policymaking process important and legitimate. As a typical clientele department, it often seeks the advice of business corporations and economic interest groups, whose views frequently become part of the policy proposals promoted by the department.

The Department of Agriculture

The Department of Agriculture also has a major interest in foreign economic policy and especially export policies. United States exports of grains represent nearly 66 percent of the world's total export shipments of such commodities, and agricultural commodities in general represent about 20 percent of total U.S. exports.

The Agriculture Department also administers Public Law 480, which provides free shipments of U.S. government-owned farm commodities for humanitarian reasons and for the enhancement of Third World development goals. Farm products worth $1.3 billion were shipped in 1982 to the poorest countries of the world, to countries of high importance to the United States, and for refugee needs.[22]

The Foreign Agricultural Service (FAS) promotes sales of agricultural commodities overseas and provides technical aid to developing countries to make their agricultural production more efficient. Another typical clientele department, Agriculture works closely with farm organizations and large agri-businesses representing their interests in the formulation of policy. Secretary of Agriculture John R. Block strongly urged in 1982 that the maximum amount of grain should be sold to the Soviet Union, although the Department of State considered such sales inconsistent with U.S. policies of selective sanctions against the Soviet Union for its part in the imposition of martial law in Poland.

The Department of Labor

The third clientele department with varied interests in foreign policy formulation is Labor. As noted earlier, adjustment assistance payments are often made to communities suffering unemployment from low-priced imports. This is one indication of the significant interest the Department of Labor has in international trade negotiations.

The United States is a member of the International Labor Organization (ILO), an agency associated with the United Nations and concerned with the training of workers and their protection against poor working conditions. This is an important field for the department and its clientele, the large labor union federations such as the AFL-CIO and the Teamsters. For political reasons, the United States relinquished its membership in the ILO for 2 years in the late 1970s, mostly in response to demands by the AFL-CIO that complained about the increasing politicization of the ILO by the Soviet Union. When this process was stopped, the United States rejoined.

Other concerns of the Department of Labor include technical assistance to Third World countries carried out by AID. For example, help is provided for particular job training and for accident prevention in the workplace.

The Department of the Treasury

The complexities of international monetary relations have always required a high degree of technical expertise, which was much more readily found in the Department of the Treasury than in the State Department. This may have been one reason that the secretary of the treasury assumed, historically, such an influential role in the cabinet, dating back to the time of Alexander Hamilton and continuing today.

The secretary of the treasury holds a key position in a number of international financial organizations. As one of the governors of the International Bank of Reconstruction and Development (the World Bank), the International Monetary Fund, and the Inter-American Development Bank, this officer has the opportunity to play important roles in these institutions, not only safeguarding the U.S. interests but keeping in mind also the broader interests of the world community. In addition, the treasury secretary maintains frequent contacts with finance ministries of the major Western countries and important Third World nations.

An important function in terms of foreign policy formulation is the secretary's task of coordinating foreign economic and financial policies. This is carried out through close relationships with the other members of the president's cabinet and chief White House advisors. Close liaison is also necessary with appropriate committees of Congress.[23] Because of the influential position of the Department of the Treasury, when American ambassadors assigned to major capitals around the world are on official visits to Washington, they usually spend several hours with Treasury officials in consultation on matters of common concern. The need for cooperation and coordination is also reflected in the formulation and implementation of most phases of foreign economic policy. Private foreign investments, the conduct of multinational corporations, exchange rate realignments, and balance of payments are some of the issues for which common positions between the Treasury and State Departments have to be devised. Again, advisory committees on international investment and related subjects composed of business representatives and members of the public have an input in the decision-making process.

The Department of Energy

The role of the Department of Energy in the formulation of foreign policy is much narrower than that of the Treasury. It is involved in policies and measures assuring the supply of crude oil to the United States and its allies in Western Europe, Japan, and the Australia-New Zealand region. The Paris-based International Energy Agency's emergency program in the event of renewed oil embargoes is closely monitored by the Department of Energy.[24]

The department, which has an Office of International Affairs, is also in charge of conducting nuclear weapons research, development, production, and surveillance programs—all activities bearing on the formulation of foreign policy. The Energy Department also monitors foreign nuclear blasts and verifies compliance with nuclear test-ban treaties and with the Non-Proliferation Treaty (NPT), especially with respect to countries that may be developing a nuclear weapons capability (e.g., Israel and Brazil). Thus the Energy Department's influence on policymaking can be crucial.

THE INTELLIGENCE COMMUNITY

The so-called intelligence community is made up of several intelligence-producing agencies coordinated by the Central Intelligence Agency (CIA). Other agencies include the Defense Intelligence Agency (DIA); the National Security Agency (NSA), concerned primarily with monitoring international electronic communications and cryptographic work (the development of U.S. codes and breaking of secret codes of foreign governments); the Bureau of Intelligence and Research of the Department of State, dealing mainly with political and economic intelligence; the Department of Energy, focusing on developments in the nuclear field; and the FBI, whose function in the field of foreign affairs is primarily to engage in counterintelligence activities. Other executive departments, such as Commerce, also have sections concerned with the production of specialized intelligence. Nongovernmental research organizations have also been drawn into the intelligence-producing efforts. Some examples are the air force-supported Rand Corporation and the Lincoln Laboratories of the Massachusetts Institute of Technology (MIT). Figure 4.4 shows the organization of major intelligence producers.

The CIA

The Central Intelligence Agency (CIA) is the leading producer of foreign intelligence; in addition, it has the mission of coordinating the activities of the agencies making up the intelligence community.

The bulk of intelligence produced by the CIA comes from overt sources, but some very crucial intelligence pieces such as warnings of impending events (some of which have gone unheeded) may be derived from covert sources, at times long-term agents who are high officials of another country. The dissemination of all relevant intelligence is a very important process: it must go in appropriate form to those individuals and agencies who need it for different purposes, prominently of course for the making of foreign policy.

The CIA is believed to have 18,000 employees plus a budget of more than $1 billion.[25] It is organized into four directorates:

The Directorate of Intelligence—concerned with the analysis and evaluation of information derived from open sources.

The Directorate of Operations—concerned primarily with covert intelligence programs and activities.

The Directorate of Science and Technology—whose task is to collect and analyze foreign information pertaining to science, technology, and weapons.

The Directorate of Management and Services—handling administrative and personnel services.[26]

Covert operations of the CIA, by their very nature, have always aroused the greatest curiosity and controversy. The record of these operations, which are attempts to influence events in foreign countries directly through secret activities against foreign governments, installations, or individuals (assassinations, for example), has been spotty. The 1961 Bay of Pigs operation, mentioned earlier, was a fiasco; however, the overthrow of Premier Mohammed Mossadegh in Iran in 1953 and the ouster of President Jacobo Arbenz in Guatemala were successful.[27] The overthrow of the Allende regime in Chile in 1973 can be attributed at least in part to CIA covert operations. More recent examples are attempts in 1982 and 1983 to run guns (at a minimum) to rebels fighting the Soviets in Afghanistan and to the various groups in Central America fighting the Sandanista regime in Nicaragua.

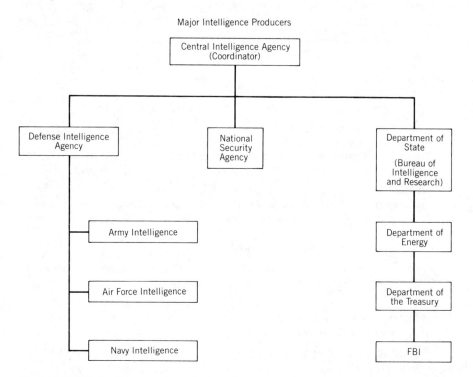

Figure 4.4 U.S. intelligence community. Total budget: About $10 billion (*U.S. News and World Report*, June 1, 1981).

The DIA

The Defense Intelligence Agency (DIA) ties together and seeks to strengthen the intelligence-producing efforts of the army, navy, and air force. However, its budget and work force are much smaller than those of the three military services. This may be one reason the DIA often has difficulty in properly executing of its missions. Another reason may be the following, as stated by Nash:

> The integrating task of DIA, the responsibility of the Assistant Secretary of Defense for Intelligence, was never performed with complete effectiveness due to the specialized services and the strong sense of service identity which affected the outlook of army, navy, and air force officers. Each officer tended to see his career advantages in terms of his particular service, he knew that after one or two tours of duty in DIA he would return to regular line service, and, as a consequence, the policy positions he supported and the intelligence conclusions he developed were conditioned by the stated or implied preferences of superior officers in his branch of the service. Military tribalism ran strong in DIA.[28]

Similar problems have surfaced in the intelligence services of the army, navy, and air force, including the latter's National Reconnaissance Office (NRO), whose overall task is the production of combat and strategic intelligence. Nor has the State Department's Bureau of Intelligence and Research been immune to these problems. It seems that assignment to intelligence functions in both the armed services and in the State Department is not considered useful for career purposes, and, in fact, it may be seen as a dead end. In contrast, operational posts such as company, batallion, and regimental command or equivalent positions in the navy, air force, and the foreign service are perceived as a source of good opportunities to reach top ranks. Therefore, capable military and foreign service officers attempt to avoid intelligence assignments, an attitude that may adversely affect the quality of intelligence production.

SUMMARY

The discussion of inputs into the formulation of American foreign policy suggests that a large number of executive branch departments have particular interests and concerns to be embodied in different policies. The State Department is responsive to these interests and concerns, and *interagency coordination* must be a priority task. The NSC performs this task for policies involving national security matters. On controversial issues, such as whether the United States should negotiate a long-term contract on the sale of grains to the Soviet Union in contravention to its policy on sanctions against the Soviet role in the Polish government's imposition of martial law, the Secretary of Agriculture is likely to seek a decision on the White House level.

In terms of variables to explain the content of particular foreign policies, it is necessary to make careful judgments as to which variables might have the greatest explanatory power. Our discussion suggests that in most policies dealing with *security matters*, the Defense Department has the major influence, including those dealing with U.S.-Soviet relations. However, as the policies bear on *economic matters*, the Departments of Commerce and Agriculture will also have important interests and concerns whose pursuit will, in all likelihood, be backed by powerful lobbies. Finally, for most foreign economic policies, the most relevant variables may be found outside the State Department; the organizational and substantive interests of the Department of the Treasury, Commerce, and Agriculture will play a major role. It is difficult to determine the impact of *covert intelligence operations*, but the CIA involvements in Central America and other places suggest that indirectly ultimate policy-making may well be influenced.

NOTES

1. Edward S. Corwin, *The President: Office and Powers*, 4th ed. (New York: New York University Press, 1957), p. 171.
2. See Samuel F. Bemis, *Short History of American Foreign Policy and Diplomacy* (New York: Holt, Rinehart & Winston, 1959), pp. 293–294.
3. Ibid., pp. 378–379, 412, 415, 439–440.
4. U.S. Department of Commerce, *Statistical Abstract of the United States*, 1982, p. 266, Table 454.
5. National Security Act of 1947, Title I, Section 101(a).
6. For details see Roger Hilsman, *The Politics of Policy Making in Defense and Foreign Affairs* (New York: Harper & Row, 1971), pp. 155–156.
7. Ibid., p. 161.
8. See Henry T. Nash, *American Foreign Policy: Changing Perspectives on National Security*, rev. ed. (Homewood, Ill.: The Dorsey Press, 1978), p. 195.
9. For an interesting analysis and models of presidential management styles in foreign policy-making since Franklin D. Roosevelt, see Alexander L. George, *Presidential Decision Making in Foreign Policy: The Effective Use of Information and Advice* (Boulder, Colo.: Westview Press, 1980), pp. 145–168.
10. Irving L. Janis, *Victims of Groupthink* (Boston: Houghton Mifflin, 1972), p. 130. The "Tuesday Lunch Group" included the secretaries of state and defense, the chairman of the Joint Chiefs of Staff, the director of the CIA, and several White House assistants. Deliberations of the group revolved around military aspects of the Vietnam War and the choice of strategies and tactics in this war.
11. *Times Picayune* (New Orleans), July 11, 1982, p. 35.
12. See U.S. Department of State, *Bulletin* 8, 2050 (September 1981), pp. 10–32.
13. U.S., Department of State, Bureau of Public Affairs, *Update of Current Policy*, No. 373, March 21, 1982.
14. For a detailed description of country directors' activities see Burton M. Sapin, *The Making of United States Foreign Policy* (New York: Praeger, 1966), pp. 383–392.
15. John H. Esterline and Robert B. Black, *Inside Foreign Policy: The Department of State Political System and Its Subsystems* (Palo Alto, Calif.: Mayfield Publishing, 1975), pp. 44–64.

16. U.S., Department of Defense, *Annual Report*, FY 1982, pp. 13–14.
17. *OMB, The U.S. Budget in Brief FY 1984*, pp. 68–69.
18. Alexander Dallin and Gail W. Lapidus, "Reagan and the Russians: United States Policy toward the Soviet Union and Eastern Europe," in *Eagle Defiant*, edited by Kenneth A. Dye, Robert J. Lieber, and Donald Rothschild (Boston: Little, Brown, 1983), pp. 191–236, on pp. 203 and 209.
19. See Janis, *Victims of Groupthink*, p. 54.
20. Ibid., pp. 123–124.
21. Nash, *American Foreign Policy*, p. 65.
22. *The United States Budget in Brief*, FY 1982, p. 38.
23. Marian D. Irish and Elke Frank, *U.S. Foreign Policy* (New York: Harcourt Brace Jovanovich, 1975), pp. 279–280.
24. For additional details, see U.S. Department of Energy, *Secretary's Annual Report to Congress*, 1980, pp. 9–1 to 9–7.
25. Nash, *American Foreign Policy*, p. 212.
26. Ibid., pp. 212–215.
27. For a more detailed treatment of CIA covert operations, see Victor Marchetti and John D. Marks, *The CIA and the Cult of Intelligence* (New York: Dell Publishing Co., 1974).
28. Nash, *American Foreign Policy*, p. 209.

5

Institutional Variables: Congress and the Influence of Interest Groups in the Formulation of Policy

As pointed out in the preceding chapter, the Constitution with respect to foreign policy formulation had been characterized as an open invitation for struggle between the executive and legislative branches of the U.S. government. In this chapter we will examine the evolution of the congressional role in policy formulation and discuss the influence on this process exerted by nongovernmental institutions, in particular economic and other interest groups. This chapter then continues our inquiry into the institutional sources of explanation of American foreign policy. The first issue to be examined will be the assertiveness of Congress to become involved in the making of foreign policy.

CONGRESSIONAL ASSERTIVENESS

International Agreements

The swing of the power pendulum between the president and Congress in foreign policy has become most visible in the years following World War II. However, the issue had been raised before that time, especially when the increasing use of "executive agreements" by presidents, beginning with George Washington, appeared to undermine if not circumvent the authority of the Senate's participation in U.S. treatymaking.

Executive agreements are binding international obligations based on powers vested in the presidential office. Such agreements enter into force when signed although on a few occasions this may be delayed until Congress gives its specific approval.*,[1] Since congressional bills require only a simple majority rather than the two-thirds vote needed for treaty ratification in the Senate, it has been asserted that even if executive agreements are to depend on congressional approval for their validity, the procedure is a more streamlined method of dealing with foreign countries than the route through the Senate. Indeed, in some cases executive agreements are negotiated on the basis of prior congressional authorization.

The subjects of executive agreements vary widely from routine regulations of international aviation to "high politics" areas such as the Yalta and Potsdam agreements dealing with the end of World War II and the postwar period. George Washington negotiated an executive agreement in 1792 providing for reciprocal mail delivery, and Franklin D. Roosevelt initiated the reciprocal trade program during the 1930s through executive agreements that have led to continuing reductions of tariffs in international trade and a tremendous increase in international trade. In 1973 the war in Vietnam was ended by an executive agreement between the United States and North Vietnamese governments. During the 1970s and early 1980s a number of executive agreements were concluded by the United States with Spain for U.S. bases in that country in return for American economic trade-offs.

The number of executive agreements exceeds by far the number of formal international treaties subject to Senate ratification. Since World War II, less than 1 percent of all international accords between the United States and other countries were formal treaties, while the number of executive agreements exceeds several thousand. It is therefore not surprising that periodic efforts have been mounted in Congress to limit the ability of the president to conclude executive agreements. One of the most significant efforts was the introduction of a constitutional amendment in the early 1950s by Senator John Bricker of Ohio that would make an international treaty effective as internal law in the United States only through legislation "valid in the absence of treaty." Congress was also to be given the power to "regulate all executive and other agreements with any foreign power or international organization."[2] The proposed amendment was defeated in the Senate by one vote.

Another limited effort to at least have full knowledge about the content of executive agreements concluded by the president has been the enactment of a statute, the Case Act, in 1972. The Case (or Executive Agreements) Act required the Executive to submit to Congress all international agreements within 60 days of their execution. The passage of this law was the consequence of hearings held by a subcommittee of the Senate Foreign Relations Committee, chaired by Senator Stuart Symington of Missouri, which made a detailed

---

*An example is the United States-Canada Fur Seal Agreement of 1942, which was approved by Congress in 1944.

study during 1969 and 1970 of existing U.S. security agreements and their impact on American foreign policy. The subcommittee found a large number of secret agreements, de facto understandings, covert activities, and paramilitary operations that had been authorized by the executive branch without congressional knowledge. By the end of 1980, 3013 agreements had been provided to Congress, of which 122 were transmitted under injunctions of secrecy as authorized by the Case Act.[3]

The Conduct of Hostilities

The apex of post-World War II congressional support for administration initiatives in hostile situations was the Gulf of Tonkin Resolution in 1964 during the Vietnam War. By a unanimous vote in the House and with all but two votes in the Senate, Congress gave President Lyndon Johnson virtually a free hand to conduct this war. A year later, however, following the U.S. intervention in the Dominican Republic, Congress began an active investigation of foreign policy actions formulated and implemented by the executive branch. In 1971 the Gulf of Tonkin Resolution was repealed, and in 1973 Congress mandated American disengagement from Vietnam.

Probably the most significant congressional action affecting the conduct of future hostilities was the 1973 passage of the War Powers Act, overriding a veto cast by President Richard Nixon. According to this act (Section 2c), the president may initiate military activity involving hostilities or imminent hostilities only pursuant to a declaration of war, specific statutory authorization, or a national emergency created by an attack on the United States, its territories or possessions, or its armed services. Within 48 hours of initiating military activity, the president must report the action to Congress; if possible, Congress is to be consulted before taking such action. If Congress does not authorize this activity by legislation or a declaration of war within 60 days, the president must terminate this activity (Section 5b). If the president certifies that more time is needed for the deployed armed forces' safe withdrawal, Congress may authorize 30 more days for this task. This provision, which allows termination without passage of a bill, circumvents the possibility of a presidential veto. At the same time, it gives the president usually 90 days to maneuver the armed forces to achieve the objective.

Congress may terminate military activity initiated by the president before the 60-day period by concurrent resolution ordering the immediate withdrawal of the armed forces by the president. Since a concurrent resolution is not subject to the president's signature, no veto is possible.

The question has been raised whether the War Powers Act is an unconstitutional infringement of the president's authority as chief executive and commander-in-chief. During the last 25 to 30 years, presidents have also claimed special authority on the basis of "inherent" power.[4] The constitutionality of the

War Powers Act may be tested in the courts, but the outcome is quite uncertain because the issue may be more political than legal, and the courts may therefore shy away from a substantive decision. So far it seems that the act has not impeded the conduct of foreign policy; indeed it may have the salutary effect of placing the administration on guard and making it more cautious before undertaking military action. Nevertheless, such action was taken when it appeared necessary, although not always successfully. Examples are the successful rescue of the Mayaguez, an American ship attacked in 1975 by Cambodian military forces beaten back by U.S. Marines, and the aborted attempt to free the American hostages in Iran in 1980, and the landings of marines in Lebanon in 1982.

Political and Economic Matters

The attitudes of members of the House toward foreign policy formulation often depend on the domestic constituencies that they serve or would like to please. Many Jewish voters linked the issue of human rights to Soviet emigration policies and objected to granting the Soviet Union most-favored-nation (MFN) status in international trade with the United States.* When in 1974 the administration was anxious to expand trade relations with the Soviet Union, Congress, in response to domestic pressure, passed an amendment to the Trade Expansion Act, sponsored by Senator Henry M. Jackson of the state of Washington and Charles A. Vanik of Ohio, to deny most-favored-nation status to Moscow unless it permitted a greatly increased emigration of Jews. Congress thereby impeded President Ford's and Secretary of State Henry Kissinger's goals of increased world trade and better relations with the Soviet Union.[5]

Another example of congressional assertiveness in the field of American foreign policy, although not related to the human rights issue, was the action to cut off military aid to Turkey in 1974 over strong protests of Kissinger. The reason for Congress to take this action was heavy pressure by American voters of Greek origin who wanted to punish Turkey for the military invasion of Cyprus. It was also asserted that Turkey, by using United States-supplied weapons for "offensive" purposes, had violated U.S. law that specified only "defensive" employment of these weapons. The powerful Greek lobby in Congress maintained the embargo until 1977 when President Carter was able to change Congress' mind regarding this matter.[6]

Congressional assertiveness has also been motivated by apprehension about an overzealous intelligence community, especially as far as covert opera-

---

*Countries that have been granted MFN status are eligible to receive the lowest possible tariffs for imported goods from their trading partners. International trade as a tool of U.S. foreign policy will be discussed in detail in Chapter 8.

tions were concerned. One of the issues arousing suspicion in Congress was alleged CIA involvement in the 1970 opposition to and later the overthrow of President Salvador Allende of Chile in 1973. The International Telephone and Telegraph Co. (ITT) was said to have tried to persuade the CIA in 1970 to intervene clandestinely against the possibility that Allende, a socialist, would be elected as president by funneling funds to certain parties, newspapers, and groups opposing Allende. Congressional hearings were held in 1973 and 1974 to delve into ITT and CIA activities in Chile; the longer-range objective of the hearings was to establish effective oversight procedures by Congress for secret intelligence operations.[7]

Whereas the events in Chile occurred before Congress began its investigations, in 1975 congressional action in fact prevented the United States from covertly aiding political factions in the Angolan civil war. Angola, an African country that in 1975 was about to receive its independence from Portugal, found itself in a divisive political struggle as to which political group or groups was to assume governmental power. United States covert involvement in Angola began very modestly through cash subsidies paid to one of the non-Marxist parties. However, in order to compete with the Soviet Union, and later Cuba, which supported the Marxist faction, as well as with South Africa, the U.S. budget for the Angolan operations escalated materially into the millions of dollars. When the Defense Department appropriations bill, with its hidden funds for the CIA, made its way through Congress, Senators John Tunney of California and Dick Clark of Iowa prevailed on their colleagues with respect to an amendment prohibiting use of any funds for any activities involving Angola directly or indirectly.[8] The House concurred a few weeks later in January 1976.

The results of the various congressional committees investigating mostly covert intelligence activities were finally the establishment of two permanent oversight committees. The Senate created in 1976 the Select Committee on Intelligence, and the House established in 1977 the Permanent Select Committee on Intelligence. The authority given the two committees varies: the jurisdiction of the House committee is broader than that of the Senate. The real power of both committees stemmed from their legislative jurisdiction over authorizations for appropriations for the intelligence agencies and for provisions specifically prohibiting appropriations that had not been authorized. The committees thus were given not only the details about the secret intelligence budgets and activities, but they could also disapprove it, either wholly or in part, if they considered this advisable.[9] However, later legislation in 1980 reduced the scope of the committees' oversight functions. While requiring the executive branch to keep the committees fully informed of current intelligence activities, they cannot anymore disapprove such operations.[10] Nevertheless, the committees captured the spotlight in 1983 during the controversy about the utilization of CIA funds for various purposes in Central America.

Crabb and Holt put the functions of the congressional intelligence committees in the proper perspective when they observe:

The basis of congressional concern about the intelligence community has nearly always been political—that is, concern on Capitol Hill about the consequences of failures. This concern has been mainly directed to covert action, less so to intelligence collection and analysis. With the two Intelligence committees now voting on line item authorizations for covert actions, Congress, or at least the members of the committees, will share the burden of future intelligence failures. In the past, Congress has generally been reluctant to assume this kind of responsibility, and it may be questioned whether legislative attitudes have changed fundamentally.

Effective legislative oversight, however, involves a great deal more than simply keeping intelligence operations and related policy decisions from going awry. Legislative oversight is also concerned with making things go right, or making them go better. In the attention the Intelligence committees have given to the quality of the intelligence product and analysis in recent years, they have demonstrated their awareness of broader concerns.[11]

Miscellaneous Instances of Assertiveness

The cases of congressional assertiveness in foreign policy formulation described briefly in the preceding pages exemplify some of the causes of congressional presidential conflict in this policy area, but they are far from exhaustive. Other examples include the Cooper-Church Amendment to the foreign military sales bill in 1970 prohibiting the expenditure of funds in support of military operations, which prevented the administration from reintroducing U.S. ground and air forces into Cambodia when the military situation later deteriorated. Similar restrictions were approved in 1973 and 1974 regarding the financing of U.S. military involvement in hostilities in North and South Vietnam as well as in Laos and Cambodia unless specifically authorized by Congress.[12] In the Atlantic area, beginning in 1966, the Senate Majority Leader Mike Mansfield attempted to induce Congress to vote for a reduction of American troops in Western Europe. First, he introduced a resolution expressing the sense of the Senate to that effect, but in spite of the prominence of the sponsor, no action was taken. Later, in 1971, Mansfield sought to invoke the power of the purse to compel a 50 percent reduction in the American troop strength in Western Europe, but this strategy also failed.

Other instances of congressional assertiveness surfaced during the negotiations on the Panama Canal's gradual transfer to the control of the Republic of Panama and the drawn-out ratification process of the pertinent treaties. Congress made some modifications in these treaties. However, President Carter ultimately was successful in their ratification. Similar problems arose in the ratification process of the SALT II treaty, but in this case the president failed to achieve his goal, with the Soviet invasion of Afghanistan bearing a major responsibility for this outcome.[13] In both cases, purely domestic politics provided significant motivations for congressional claims and suspicions. Whether justified or not, these claims and suspicions must and did reflect serious national security concerns.

Finally, congressional anxiety about human rights led to changes in the Foreign Assistance Act in 1974 and 1976. Except in extraordinary circumstances, the president must reduce or terminate security assistance to any government that grossly violates internationally recognized human rights. Tightening the standards and procedures further in 1976, Congress mandated as U.S. foreign policy the promotion of increased observance of such rights by all countries and prohibited security assistance except in specified circumstances.[14] In 1979 Congress directed that significant improvements in human rights records should be taken into account when allocating security assistance.[15] The allocation of development assistance and food shipments were also linked to human rights performance of recipient countries.[16] Again, these actions do not exhaust efforts by Congress to inject itself into foreign policy affairs on the basis of human rights concerns, but they illustrate a broad trend during the 1970s.

More recently, the House Foreign Relations Committee objected to sanctions imposed by President Reagan on American and European manufacturers intent on participating in the construction of a natural gas pipeline from the Soviet Union to Western Europe. These sanctions prohibited the manufacturers from using U.S. patents in the production of necessary parts for the pipeline. Constituency pressures, more likely than apprehension about deteriorating relations with the United States' European allies who considered the sanctions a violation of international law, stimulated proposed legislation in the House against the president's policy. The proposal was passed in the committee by a vote of 22 to 12, including seven Republicans,[17] but the whole House rejected it with a majority of only three votes.

Policy Implications

If the foreign policies formulated by the executive branch were always fully coherent and represented careful, rational choices, then repeated assertiveness of Congress in the field of foreign policy and the ensuing executive-congressional conflicts would seriously harm the interests of the United States and the American people. However, deep cleavages often tend to exist in the policy-making processes of the executive branch because of conflicting images and views among top-echelon decision makers and because of diverging organizational interests as well as bureaucratic infighting. Hence, if and when Congress injects itself into foreign policy formulation and even implementation (e.g., intelligence operations or foreign aid), the outcome does not always have to be damaging to American interests. Nevertheless, the executive branch generally has the constitutional initiative in foreign policy formulation and has the benefit of the very extensive and comprehensive information-collecting apparatus at its disposal, both important advantages in any conflict with Congress on foreign policy. However, Congress does have effective means to make its will in foreign affairs felt—control over appropriations, treaties, and appointments, as well as general legislation.

What are the broad reasons for congressional involvement in foreign policy formulation? If we understand these reasons, it will help in discovering more specific sources of explanation for individual policies.

As already noted, responsiveness to their constituencies and electoral considerations are important motivations for members of Congress to adopt particular positions on foreign policy, at times at variance with administration policy. Advertising such positions, especially if the member has a seat on the prestigious Senate Foreign Relations Committee or on the House Foreign Relations Committee, produces welcome publicity, and if Congress should approve his or her position, the legislator can claim credit for having effectively influenced congressional or U.S. policy in favor of important groups such as the Jewish or Greek lobby or a particular economic interest group.

Another reason, albeit more indirect, is the proliferation of the committee system in Congress. Whereas in 1920 Congress had 47 committees and subcommittees, the number today approaches 400. The position of committee chairperson is highly desirable, because it enhances one's prestige and power and it greatly improves the prospects for reelection. Chairpersons want their committees to participate in as much legislation and policymaking as possible. Although Congress plays a greater role in the formulation of domestic than foreign policy, relevant subcommittees do get a share of the policymaking process in the latter area, and this offers chairpersons and members of these committees opportunities to make their input into policymaking and the legislative process if they pertain to foreign affairs.[18]

There is no question that action by individual members of Congress to promote particular foreign policies or approving policy goals of the administration can have disruptive effects. It also may hinder the president's ability to negotiate with foreign powers, because the representatives of the latter never really know whether what the executive branch has promised or, in the case of treaties, has signed, will be accepted by Congress. The establishment of the League of Nations in 1919, rejected by the Senate in the ratification procedures, and the SALT II treaty's fate in the late 1970s are prime examples for this dilemma. Moreover, I.M. Destler observes:

> Congressional foreign policy leverage depends ultimately on handles that are blunt instruments—cutting off funds, rejecting or amending painfully negotiated

treaties. The costs to foreign policy of actually employing these instruments are often severe, and this is recognized on both ends of Pennsylvania Avenue.[19]

The remedy for this situation appears to be consultation among executive and legislative leaders as policies are taking shape. This would make it possible to incorporate congressional views into executive policy proposals and provide opportunities to the executive branch for trade-offs. However, this prescription may not always work in practice. Policy may have to be developed very rapidly, especially in military and strategic situations. Secrecy may be essential, and that would be sacrificed in prolonged consultations with congressional leaders. Necessary flexibility by the administration in dealing with third countries may have to be given up. Finally, as Destler points out:

> The day-to-day costs of consultation may be greater to politicians than they appear at first glance. One cost is in time and attention—overtaxed resources that legislators must allocate with care. . . . Consequently, legislators are reluctant to give detailed attention to a particular issue until they have to. Not surprisingly, those who consulted with senators on Panama in early 1977 found it difficult to get them to focus on the specifics that became so crucial in early 1978. The same was true on SALT a year later.[20]

In the last analysis, executive-congressional conflict in foreign policy will be with us in the years to come simply because it is part of our constitutional system. What is needed is leadership of the highest order on the part of both branches of government aiming at the most effective management of this conflict. In this connection, we must not forget that Congress makes an essential contribution to foreign policymaking by furnishing a base of legitimacy, an essential element in a democracy. For example, by prescribing limits to the president's use of the armed forces, Congress creates "powerful restraints upon diplomatic adventurism" and "upon a tendency by the United States to become overextended abroad."[21] Congressional assertiveness may also help the United States to find the proper balance between what Americans would *like* to accomplish through their foreign policies and what they are *able* to accomplish on the basis of available resources and capabilities.

THE INFLUENCE OF INTEREST GROUPS

In the preceding pages we have referred several times to constituency pressures on House members and senators inducing them to take particular positions on foreign policy issues. Many of these pressures come from well-organized nongovernmental groups that pursue not only economic but also a variety of other interests. The pressures of these groups can become significant variables explaining the formulation or changes of policies by both the executive branch and Congress, although views about the magnitude of the influence these groups possess may at times be exaggerated. As we will see, the extent of this influence depends on the power and finances of the groups involved as well as on the foreign policy issue area.

In his seminal work, *The American People and Foreign Policy*, Gabriel Almond has identified four categories of influential domestic groups who seek to have their goals and values reflected in the formulation of foreign policy.[22] They are:

1. The *administrative* or *bureaucratic elites*, which include the professional corps of the executive establishment who enjoy special powers by virtue of their interest in and familiarity and immediate contact with particular policy problems.
2. The *interest elites*, which include the representatives of the vast number of private policy-oriented associations, ranging from huge nationwide aggregations to local formations and organized around aims and objectives that in their variety reflect the economic, ethnic, religious, and ideological complexity of the American population.
3. The *political elites*, which include the publicly elected, high-appointive, as well as party leaders.
4. Finally, there are the *communications elites*, the most obvious representatives of which are the owners, controllers, and active participants of the mass media—radio, television, press, and movies.

We have already discussed the participation of civil servants in the foreign policy formulation process in previous chapters, and we have examined the motivations and roles of senators and House members in making policy in the preceding pages of this chapter. Our focus now is therefore on what Almond calls the interest and communications elites.

Interest Group Activities

Interest groups whose leading echelons may want to have a hand in shaping foreign policy are found in all segments of the society, but without doubt, the most important groups are in the economic field. Business associations (and some individual large corporations), farmers' organizations, and labor union federations often have a major stake in a specific kind of policy and possess the staff and financial resources to engage in extensive lobbying. Most of the lobbying activities are concentrated in Congress, but representatives of major economic interest groups and large corporations are also appointed to advisory committees in the State Department, and thereby can exert and have exerted considerable influence on policy formulation and implementation. An example is the Advisory Committee on International Investment, Technology, and Development to the Office of Investment Affairs of the Department of State and various working groups of this committee, which has been instrumental in shaping U.S. policy on the U.N. negotiations regarding the Code of Conduct for Transnational Corporations (TNCs), the International Code of Conduct for the Transfer of Technology being negotiated under the auspices of the U.N. Conference on Trade and Development (UNCTAD), and other international investment issues. Other advisory committees in the State Department deal with law of the sea problems, and the lobbying in both the executive branch and Congress by large corporations concerned with the exploitation of the minerals found in the deep sea bed was responsible for the U.S. government's decision to reject the draft treaty on the law of the sea that had been negotiated during the long, drawn-out U.N. Conference on the Law of the Sea (UNCLOS III).[23]

Another instance of effective lobbying for the particular interests of an American industry occurred after the negotiations to reduce tariffs on international trade during the Kennedy Round had been concluded in 1967.

> The American chemical industry opposed the elimination of certain nontariff barriers against foreign imports of tar products (the so-called American Selling Price Clause) which were contained in the international agreements ending the multilateral Kennedy Round negotiations on the reduction of trade barriers between the United States and her major trading partners in the world. Although the agreement bore the signature of the duly authorized American negotiator, Congress gave in to pressure by the chemical industry and refused to approve legislation for the elimination of this clause, which adversely affected the American administration's credibility for future trade negotiations.[24]

Finally, successful economic interest group lobbying activities were reflected in the lifting of U.S. sanctions on grain sales to the Soviet Union in 1981. Political pressure from the AFL-CIO induced temporary withdrawal of the United States from the International Labor Organization (ILO) during the late 1970s.

Despite the success stories alluded to in the above examples, we must guard against overestimating the influence of economic interest groups in shaping foreign policy. In the formulation of national security policy and the strictly political aspects of foreign policy, their influence is often likely to be minimal. Moreover, even in the field of economic foreign policy where, according to one of the myths about American politics, economic interest groups are assumed to be especially successful, this claim may at times be exaggerated. There can be little doubt that members of Congress are apt to take economic group pressures more seriously when it comes to the definition of economic foreign policy than national security policy, but on many occasions conflicting interests may mitigate the pressures and encourage a measure of responsibility that looks beyond the economic interests immediately affected and takes into account long-range national goals.[25] As Bauer, Pool, and Dexter point out:

> There . . . is no straight-line process in which businessmen receive messages about foreign economic affairs, respond by messages to their trade associations, which in turn respond by messages to Congressmen, who to some measure respond by action. The low saliency of foreign trade matters and the competition of other matters for time means that at every level there is only a limited amount of actual communication and a great deal of speculative imagination of what each relevant group must be thinking and feeling.[26]

As we have seen in our discussion of congressional assertiveness in foreign policy formulation, groups other than those representing economic interests are at times also eager to influence the policymaking process. The Jewish and Greek lobbies are the outstanding examples, but other groups, often ideologically or ethnically motivated, have also manifested foreign policy interests. They include the National Council of Churches, League of Women Voters (LWV), Women's Strike for Peace, United Nations Association, Federation of American Scientists, Council for a Liveable World, the American Legion, Veterans of Foreign Wars (VFW), and the Committee on the Present Danger. Some of these groups, especially the last three listed, strongly supported and lobbied for President Reagan's sharp increase of the defense budget in 1981.* Most of the others enumerated had strong reservations and were afraid of a nuclear holocaust, and voiced concerns about a sharp confrontation with the Soviet Union.

Apart from the support given President Reagan in his increases of the defense budget, the American Legion and the VFW as well as other veterans' groups have been active in the foreign policy field since World War II. Some church organizations, such as the National Council of Churches in the United States, opposed the Vietnam War. Ethnic groups have also attempted to involve themselves in foreign policy. As already noted, Jewish organizations have played an important role in influencing American policy toward Israel, and Polish and Hungarian groups have often wanted the United States to pursue a strongly anticommunist policy toward the Communist People's Democracies of Eastern Europe.**

Scientists have also formed groups to influence foreign policy. They have

---

*Other supporters were the American Security Council, the American Conservative Union, the Conservative Caucus, and the Coalition for Peace through Strength.

**They are the German Democratic Republic (often referred to as DDR, the Deutsche Demokratische Republik), Poland, Czechoslovakia, Hungary, Romania, and Bulgaria.

claimed that scientific achievement gives them special insights into world politics to make decisions on arms and arms control. The Association of Atomic Scientists has been particularly active and has opposed as much as possible any use of nuclear weapons. Their publication, *The Bulletin of Atomic Scientists*, has obtained a readership going far beyond the circle of specialists it was originally designed to serve.

Finally, especially the LWV undertakes periodic reviews of particular foreign policy issues and takes definite positions on these issues. For example, during 1976—1977, the American stand on the United Nations was discussed and reevaluated by all units in the United States, and, considering the extensive membership, LWV positions adopted nationally have a measure of influence on American policymakers.

So far, we have discussed American interest groups intent on influencing U.S. foreign policy. However, private groups from foreign countries may also be affected by U.S. foreign policy decisions and therefore have an interest in influencing the policymaking process. Indeed, several hundred agents are registered with the attorney general under the Foreign Agents Registration Act of 1918, and some of them represent private groups located abroad.

It is important to note that many of the noneconomic interest groups are concerned only with a single issue, as exemplified by the interest of the Greek lobby in the Turkish invasion of Cyprus. In many cases, the pursuit of their interest or interests is fed strongly by a high level of emotional fervor and intense commitment to a particular ideology. This makes for a very aggressive lobby, and—when circumstances are right, such as in the agony of the Vietnam War—the lobbying efforts can be quite effective. In contrast to single-issue organizations, multipurpose groups such as the typical business or agricultural federation find it hard to engage in overly hard-hitting tactics. They are hampered by saying or doing things that might offend some of their members, and therefore their style is often much more low-key.[27]

The effectiveness of interest group activities depends not only on the issue itself but also on the importance of the issue. As Lester Milbraith observes, it seems that the *less* important the issue, the greater is the likelihood of successful interest group influence. In contrast, as crisis levels increase, groups may desire to increase their influence efforts if their interests are at stake; however, as decision time shortens because of the crisis, there is less likelihood that group interests are taken into account by policymakers.[28]

Lack of success of economic interest groups in influencing security policy does not mean that efforts to modify such policies are not made. An example is the attempt of two large American oil companies (Standard Oil Company of California and Mobil) to force the United States to toughen its stand toward Israel, to gain assurances of the continued flow of petroleum to America from the oil-producing states of the Persian Gulf, and, implicitly, to elicit a benevolent attitude toward the American petroleum industry.[29]

The Military-Industrial Complex

The notion of a "military-industrial complex" tilting American foreign policy toward war and preventing peace has spawned a continuing debate in the popular and scholarly literature going back to the time when Franklin D. Roosevelt campaigned in 1932 for the presidency of the United States. He attacked the "merchants of destruction" and promised to take the profits out of the war. In his farewell address, President Eisenhower warned against the influence that could be exerted by the conjunction of an immense military establishment and a large arms industry.[30]

The military-industrial complex is generally understood to consist of business firms directly and indirectly engaged in the production of arms and military equipment for which they receive purchasing contracts from the U.S. government. It is reasonable to assume that the leaders of industries producing weapons systems and war materiel have a vested interest in seeing that their country pursues policies requiring large financial outlays for armaments, either for the conduct of hostilities or to be prepared for them. There can be little question that, when large manufacturing concerns such as Rockwell Industries, Lockheed, or Colt Industries are dependent on the national government for a substantial part of their business, they are likely to prefer national situations and policies that keep orders coming into their plants. In the United States, defense spending generates employment for 7 to 8 million persons directly, close to 10 percent of the total work force. There is also little doubt that the 2000 high-ranking retired officers hired by large American corporations with military hardware for sale[31] can be utilized not only for the procurement of orders but also indirectly for influencing national policies through close personal ties and social contacts with their former brother officers still on active duty. Finally, members of Congress eager to attract manufacturing plants into the districts they represent may well support the aims of the military-industrial complex.

However, whether the complex, if in fact it exists as such, has been a major influence in formulating American security policy or may ultimately be able to prevent peace is questionable. While obviously, with so many civilian jobs at stake, tremendous pressures can be exerted directly and indirectly on national policymakers in the executive branch and Congress to continue and perhaps increase the budget of the Pentagon for the acquisition of military hardware, there is no evidence that decisions to enter the Korean War or concerning Vietnam were initiated by the military-industrial complex per se. Some of the top executives of affected corporations may have been pleased initially with these events, and the military leadership is likely to have supported these decisions, but their influence was very minor as far as the grand design was concerned.[32]

In this connection, it may also be significant in terms of the profit expectations of many defense contractors that companies heavily dependent on Pentagon contracts have in recent years attempted to diversify their product line into nonmilitary goods. Indeed, during the 1970s, increases in defense spending lagged behind inflation, and as profits on defense contracts have dwindled, the investment community has become disenchanted with those companies relying too much on government work. This may of course change, at least temporarily, during periods of intensive rearmament, as is the case during the Reagan administration. However, over the long haul, the influence on foreign policy formulation exerted by defense contractors and their allies is likely to be quite limited.

A case in point is the rejection of the B-1 bomber by President Carter in 1977. In 1970, Rockwell International had been awarded a contract to develop a prototype of the bomber, an important first step in favor of adding the B-1 to the U.S. arsenal. Totally committed to the plane were the U.S. Air Force, the UAW (United International Union of Automobile, Aerospace, and Agricultural Implements Workers of America), the AFL-CIO, high-ranking members of the House and Senate Armed Services and Appropriations Committees, and numerous potential subcontractors. Supporters for the B-1 were well established and well funded to lobby for the plane on a common ground of strategic and economic considerations. The opposition was a coalition of religious, environmental, consumer, peace, and labor groups operating on a "shoestring" budget.[33]

Although the pro-B-1 lobby had all the facilities for effectively influencing the decision-making process, it did not prevail; furthermore, some B-1 supporters complained that the lobby did not fully exploit its many advantages. Even attempts to overturn the president's decision in Congress failed. Obviously Carter's own inclinations played an important role, but as president and the leader of the Democratic party, he had to consider the large contingent of labor and business representatives who supported the B-1. Under President Reagan, whose idiosyncrasies and image of the world were, of course, quite different from those of Carter, the outcome of the lobbying battle was the opposite—and the plane was put into production. However, the pro-B-1 decision was not a pushover, and anti-B-1 forces fought a valiant battle inside and outside of Congress.

The Interests of the Mass Media

Few organizations have a greater *potential* to influence public policy than the mass media, but which specific policy goals individual news organizations pursue and how intensively these goals are pursued often remains unclear. Moreover, it is difficult to determine how much the public *accepts* of what it reads, sees, and hears. Nevertheless, the correspondents and editorialists of the media are in a position to determine *what* the public will read and hear, and consequently they can influence what it may remember. They have the power to emphasize certain news items or to play them down; they can conceal or expose, support or attack particular courses of action in a country's foreign policy. Despite governmental warnings of media excesses in reporting, they can embarrass individual officials and others in prominent places by making them look ridiculous, by publishing alleged wrongdoing, and by revising and distorting inconvenient incidents from the past. In all these ways, the press, radio, and television tend to influence foreign policy decisions by acting as mediators between the interested sectors of broad public opinion and the various elites that participate in the decision-making process of foreign policy formulation and execution. At the same time, the press, radio, and television present and interpret elite views and actions to their readers and listeners; conversely, they are in a position to exert influence over members of the elites in the name of the public they claim to represent.[34]

While the American press has become an integral factor in foreign policy-making, it does not function as a pressure group per se. Rather, it seeks to link widely scattered parts and splice them with political and intellectual criticism. Major wire services are mostly only factual conveyors of foreign policy news.

In many respects, the press functions are similar to those of intelligence organizations—the collection, evaluation, and dissemination of information. Roger Hilsman describes this function well in his book, *The Politics of Policy Making in Defense and Foreign Affairs*:

> An American correspondent in a foreign capital must, of course, rely on public announcements by the local government for much of his information and on briefings by the staff of the American embassy for a lot more. As a result much of what he reports is not new to Washington officials. But foreign correspondents are able to gather information on their own, and what they do gather is useful. So also is their independent judgment and interpretation of events. Wise Washington officials will always welcome the opportunity to hear an independent opinion to compare with the opinion forwarded by the embassy, even though they may not agree with it. Throughout the Vietnam struggle, for example, the views of the reporters who were critical of the Saigon regime and the American effort in Vietnam were valued by at least some of the officials in Washington as an antidote to the sometimes excessive optimism coming through official channels. In these circumstances the press constitutes a *competing* source of judgment and interpretation.[35]

Individual newspapers have the unusual power to place issues they want to emphasize on the front page and report on these issues more heavily than on others. By doing so, they focus attention on a particular issue and may bring enormous pressure to bear on government officials to take action. At the same time, this power to focus attention on an issue gives newspapers the power to kill a planned move by the government by merely publicizing it. An example is the Bay of Pigs fiasco. The *New York Times*, aware of the planned invasion of the Cuban Special Forces group under the sponsorship of the CIA, intended to reveal the plan and thus to put a stop to it. President Kennedy telephoned the publisher of the *New York Times* and asked him not to print the story. In this instance, the *New York Times* acquiesced. As a practical matter, the news media are normally very careful before publishing information of this kind. Had the *Times* gone ahead with its plans to publish, it might have gotten credit not for preventing a disaster, but for wrecking a victory.

In addition to television and daily newspapers, news magazines such as *Time, Newsweek*, and *U.S. News and World Report* also display particular attitudes on foreign policy and may promote specific policy goals that correspond to their editorial views and perhaps ideologies. More specialized magazines such as *Business Week* or *Aviation Week* may also pursue interests that they would like to be reflected in policy formulation.

One of the most important reasons for the power of the press and television in influencing foreign policy is that they are a principal source of the interpretation of events to the public at large. This interpretation is not always clearly labeled as such, as in the writings of the syndicated columnists such as James Reston and Joseph Kraft. Interpretation in a particular sense may also take place when news is ostensibly presented in a straightforward manner on television. The news is "interpreted" not only in editorials, or in the "instant analysis" after a particular speech, but also when Dan Rather of CBS or Tom Brockow of NBC determines the sequence of news items to be presented in his nightly news programs.

For the Department of State, support of official policy by the news media has become an important aspect of foreign policymaking. Because disclosures about impending policy actions can be very embarrassing, high officials often seek to establish very good and personal relations with important news writers and TV news commentators.

SUMMARY

In the struggle between the president and Congress over control of the foreign and security policymaking process, it is evident that the *congressional influence* has grown materially during the 1970s. However, it is not certain whether this trend will continue in the 1980s. The reduction in the power of the Intelligence Oversight Committee may hint at a reversal of this trend, but the increasing opposition in Congress to the steeply rising defense budget and the growing concern about the need for effective arms control sends different signals.

The *institutional variables* emanating from Congress, as reflected by the pursuit of various political interests on the part of members of Congress, need to be screened carefully to determine their influence on particular foreign policies. *Content analysis* of statements by members of Congress in the *Congressional Record* and elsewhere may be useful in assessing the degree of potency of these variables. The impact of *interest group lobbying activities* and of *media influences* can also be subjected to empirical research, but the identification of independent variables with causal effect on or high correlation with particular policies may be more difficult, since interest group channels of influence must pass through either favorable congressional or favorable executive branch conduits. These channels are at times well concealed, and therefore the assessment of variable potency can be very complex.

NOTES

1. Gerhard von Glahn, *Law among Nations* (New York: Macmillan, 1965), p. 416.
2. For details see Stephen A. Garrett, "Foreign Policy and the American Constitution: The Bricker Amendment in Contemporary Perspective," *International Studies Quarterly* 16, 2 (June 1972), pp. 187−219.
3. Charles W. Kegley and Eugene R. Wittkopf, *American Foreign Policy*, 2nd ed. (New York: St. Martin's Press, 1982), p. 417; and Marian D. Irish and Elke Frank, *U.S. Foreign Policy* (New York: Harcourt Brace Jovanovich, 1975), pp. 170−171.
4. For detailed arguments, see Enid Sterling-Conner, "The War Powers Resolution: Does It Make a Difference?" in *The Growing Powers of Congress*, edited by David M. Abshire and Ralph D. Nurnberger (Beverly Hills, Calif.: Sage Publications, 1981), pp. 284−317.
5. For details see Dan Caldwell, "The Jackson-Vanik Amendments," in *Congress, the Presidency and American Foreign Policy*, edited by John Spanier and Joseph Nogee, Jr. (New York: Pergamon Press, 1981), pp. 1−21.
6. For a detailed account, see Keith R. Legg, "Congress as Trojan Horse? The Turkish Embargo Problem, 1974−1978," in Spanier and Nogee (eds.), ibid., pp. 107−131.
7. For more details see Cecil V. Crabb, Jr., and Pat M. Holt, *Invitation to Struggle: Congress, the President and Foreign Policy* (Washington, D.C.: Congressional Quarterly Press, 1980), pp. 145−146.
8. Ibid., p. 148.
9. Ibid., p. 155.
10. Kegley and Wittkopf, *American Foreign Policy*, p. 430.
11. Crabb and Holt, *Invitation to Struggle*, pp. 157−158.
12. For 1973, Public Law 93-126, Sec. 13, October 18, 1973.
13. For details see William L. Furlong, "Negotiations and Ratification of the Panama Canal Treaties," and Stephen J. Flanagan, "The Domestic Politics of SALT II: Implications for the Foreign Policy Process," in Spanier and Nogee (eds.), *Congress, the Presidency and American Foreign Policy*, pp. 77−106 and 44−76, respectively.
14. The Foreign Assistance Act of 1974, approved December 14, 1974, and the International Security Assistance and Arms Export Control Act of 1976.
15. The International Security Assistance Act of 1979, approved August 14, 1979.
16. The International Development and Food Assistance Act of 1975, approved December 20, 1975.
17. *New York Times*, August 11, 1982.
18. For further details see B. Hughes, *Domestic Context of American Foreign Policy* (San Francisco: W.H. Freeman, 1978).
19. I.M.Destler, "Executive-Congressional Conflict in Foreign Policy," in *Congress Reconsidered*, 2nd ed., edited by Lawrence C. Dodd and Bruce I. Oppenheimer (Washington, D.C.: Congressional Quarterly Press, 1981), pp. 296−316; p. 310.
20. Ibid., p. 311.
21. Crabb and Holt, *Invitation to Struggle*, p. 218.

22. Gabriel Almond, *The American People and Foreign Policy* (New York: Praeger, 1962), pp. 139–140. The listing of the elites is in a somewhat different order from that in Almond's book.
23. For details see Werner J. Feld and Robert S. Jordan, *International Organizations* (New York: Praeger, 1983), Chapter 7.
24. Werner J. Feld, *The European Common Market and the World* (Englewood Cliffs, N.J.: Prentice-Hall, 1967), pp. 100–107, containing also accounts of other effective lobbying activities.
25. Raymond A. Bauer, Ithiel de Sola Pool, and Lewis Dexter, *American Business and Public Policy*, 2nd ed. (Chicago: Aldine-Atherton, 1972), pp. 475–482.
26. Ibid., p. 479.
27. Ibid., p. 477.
28. Lester W. Milbraith, "Interest Groups and Foreign Policy," in *Domestic Sources of Foreign Policy*, edited by James N. Rosenau (New York: Free Press, 1967), pp. 231–251, on pp. 249–250.
29. *Wall Street Journal*, August 15, 1973, pp. 1 and 19.
30. For a concise discussion and theoretical analysis of this issue see Marc Pilisuk and Tom Hayden, "Is There a Military-Industrial Complex Which Prevents Peace?" in *The Triple Revolution Emerging*, edited by Robert Perrucci and Marc Pilisuk (Boston: Little, Brown, 1971), pp. 73–94. See also C. Wright Mills, *The Power Elite* (New York: Oxford University Press, 1956); and Steven Rosen (ed.), *Testing the Theory of the Military-Industrial Complex* (Lexington, Mass.: D.C. Heath, 1973).
31. Patrick M. Morgan, "Politics, Policy, and the Military-Industrial Complex," in *The Military-Industrial Complex and U.S. Foreign Policy*, edited by Omar L. Carey (Pullman, Wash.: Washington State University Press, 1969), pp. 55–66.
32. Ibid.
33. See Norman J. Ornstein and Shirley Elder, *Interest Groups, Lobbying, and Policy Making* (Washington, D.C.: Congressional Quarterly Press, 1978), pp. 187–220, for a complete discussion of this case.
34. For a more comprehensive discussion see Bernard C. Cohen, "Mass Communications and Foreign Policy," in Rosenau (ed.), *Domestic Sources of Foreign Policy*, pp. 195–212.
35. Roger Hilsman, *The Politics of Policy Making in Defense and Foreign Affairs* (New York: Harper & Row, 1971), p. 110.

CHAPTER 6

Societal Factors and American Foreign Policy

Foreign policy formulation does not take place in a societal vacuum. Rather, the nature of the society within which national decision makers seek to determine broad goals and produce specific courses of action tends to make its imprint on the policies formulated.

What are the particular features of a society that have relevance for policy formulation? *Common historical experiences* leave a definite mark on a society and are apt to create traditions that bear on the pursuit of national objectives and on their morale. If the historical experiences have been favorable, they are likely to bolster the resolve of a people to persevere in the face of serious obstacles. If the reverse is true, grave demoralization may set in. Thus, the dead hand of the past continues to influence the present and may become a factor of either strength or weakness. Foreign policymakers must keep in mind historical experiences and tradition, because they may affect a country's overall capabilities to implement a particular foreign policy.

Another important societal feature having broad bearing on policy formulation refers to the *values and belief systems* that the people of a country hold. These systems contribute to the nature of the images that the people of a country hold of themselves and other peoples of the world, and thus may affect their social behavior as well as their national character. These factors can produce definite implications for the formulation of foreign policy, especially as far as the assessment of the implementation potential is concerned.

A third societal feature that might affect the implementation potential of foreign policies pertains to cleavages in a society caused by *racial, ethnic, or religious divisions*. Such cleavages are likely to have negative influences on the capabilities of a country and may constitute a serious vulnerability that foreign policymakers must take into consideration.

Ideological cohesion, a fourth societal feature having a bearing on the capabilities of a country, can affect foreign policymaking. Ideologies, when combined with the value and belief systems of a people, can become powerful elements strengthening the capabilities of a country; when associated with serious cleavages in a society, they are likely sources of major vulnerabilities. In either case, foreign policymakers must take these factors into account as they ponder the formulation of policies and policy goals.

Finally, the *public opinion* of the people of a country can have a major bearing on foreign policymaking. However, under which circumstances the influence of public opinion on policy formulation becomes significant is a controversial question not only in the United States but elsewhere as well.

In the pages to follow, we will examine the relevance and impact of the various societal features identified on U.S. foreign policy formulation. We will start with a discussion of relevant American traditions, value and belief systems, and other societal features that may affect the context of policymaking, and then inquire into the potency of public opinion as a factor in policymaking and the relationship between public opinion, foreign policy, and domestic politics.

AMERICAN HISTORICAL EXPERIENCE
AND VALUE SYSTEM

History and Geography

The historical experiences of the American people, beginning with statehood in the late eighteenth century and continuing to the middle of the twentieth century, combined with a favorable geography, have instilled in U.S. citizens a basic feeling of pride and confidence. After the original thirteen states along the Atlantic had been established in 1790, Jefferson's Louisiana Purchase (from France) of vast tracts of land added greatly to U.S. expansion. By 1853, the territory known later as the continental United States had been put together. Alaska, with its vast natural resources, was purchased from Russia in 1867, and Hawaii was added in 1898. Puerto Rico, Guam, American Samoa, and the Virgin Islands came under various types of U.S. control between 1899 and 1917.

This large area of the world's surface had the important advantages of being, to a large extent, in the temperate zone; it was endowed with extensive natural resources, and nearly all of it was habitable. The foundation was thus laid for the creation of an economic empire, and the energy of Americans and immigrants, driven westward by the search for land and riches, made the

United States by the middle of the twentieth century a country of premier economic and military status in the world.

For most Americans, this evidence of supreme achievement was a clear indication that the U.S. economic and political system offered the appropriate prescription for material success that should be emulated by less fortunate countries. However, many Americans overlooked that certain fundamental factors aided the United States in its accomplishments such as enormous space for expansion in an underpopulated nation, weak neighbors both north and south, vast oceans east and west providing protection for the American people from hostile action, and, as already noted, important natural resources.[1]

Major U.S. foreign policies during the nineteenth century were instrumental in supporting American economic expansion. They were:

- Isolation (nonintervention, noninvolvement, and no entangling alliances)
- The Monroe Doctrine (request for Europe to stay out of the Americas)
- Pan-Americanism (cooperation with republics of the Western Hemisphere)
- The "Open Door" policy (fair competition for American business firms to compete with companies of other countries, especially in China)
- Freedom of the seas
- The peaceful settlement of disputes (arbitration).[2]

The historical experiences and the supporting nineteenth-century foreign policies reflected indeed an American success story reaching beyond the confines of the continental United States. As the result of the Spanish-American War, the Philippines came under U.S. control, and in both World War I and World War II the United States emerged as one of the victors. However, World War II and the immediate aftermath constituted the apex of U.S. military power and success. The Korean War ended in a draw, and Vietnam spelled a defeat of American military forces.

It is not quite clear how the Vietnamese debacle affected the long-range attitudes of Americans. Without doubt, it left emotional scars and negative attitudes about U.S. policies and institutions, especially among those who bore the brunt of fighting and suffering in Vietnam. However, longitudinal surveys of American attitudes toward various aspects of American politics and institutions suggest that, while the perceptions and attitudes of the age groups mostly involved in the Vietnamese fighting differed materially from those older and younger during the early and middle 1970s, a gradual convergence can be observed in the late 1970s. Table 6.1 and Figure 6.1 show generational attitudes with respect to spending priorities on arms, space, foreign aid, and welfare. All of the statistics presented indicate a modicum of convergence among the three age groups. As far as support for arms is concerned, according to Table 6.1, the pre-Vietnam group shows the highest percentage, but the Vietnam generation is not far below the average (21 percent). Regarding increases in

Table 6.1   Responses Regarding Spending Priorities on Selected Issues by Age Groups[a]

	1973	1974	1975	1976	1977	1978
Military						
Presuccessor generation	13.07	20.72	20.64	29.44	29.92	35.10
Vietnam generation	8.51	12.66	11.96	19.13	19.84	21.57
Post-Vietnam generation	16.67	12.90	15.19	19.39	20.00	20.81
Space Exploration						
Presuccessor generation	6.82	8.16	7.49	8.33	9.90	10.26
Vietnam generation	10.38	7.52	9.18	12.56	13.02	16.59
Post-Vietnam generation	0.00	3.33	3.70	7.00	9.92	10.76
Welfare						
Presuccessor generation	19.82	21.71	22.19	11.71	12.37	9.69
Vietnam generation	23.12	25.86	30.87	16.08	12.31	15.58
Post-Vietnam generation	16.67	30.00	24.68	26.32	19.51	27.85

[a]Given the size of the data base, fractional percentages rather than rounded percentages have been reported.

Source: Werner J. Feld and John K. Wildgen, *The Attitudes and Values of the Successor Generation in the United States.* (Washington, D.C. The Atlantic Council of the United States, 1980), p. 13.

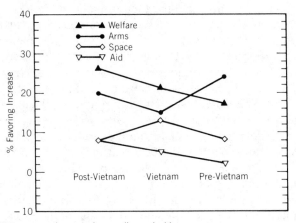

Figure 6.1   The generations and spending priorities.

Source: *General Social Survey* of National Opinion Research Center (NORC), 1972–1980.

spending on welfare, the Vietnam generation is right in the middle, but again the differences are not significant; here one should remember that the percentage of those supporting a rise in welfare expenditures has been declining steadily. Finally, the differences between the three generations on spending for foreign aid and space exploration are also insignificant.

Therefore, it is reasonable to assume that the trauma of Vietnam has somewhat eased. However, this does not mean that the Vietnamese experience has been forgotten. It only suggests that the differences in attitudes of various generations have begun to disappear. Indeed, Vietnam is likely to have a lasting effect on the attitudes of all Americans toward the distribution of military and economic power throughout the world and may well have diminished the confidence in the American prescription of promoting economic welfare and for the achievement of national military and political power.

Values and Belief Systems

The possible cognitive and perhaps affective change in the attitudes of Americans described in the preceding paragraphs is apt to be counteracted by the earlier socialization processes having taken place and continuing to take place in the American elementary and sometimes secondary school systems. Many pupils recite the Pledge of Allegiance to the Flag each morning and are taught to sing "America the Beautiful" and "My Country, 'Tis of Thee," activities that tend to strengthen loyalty to the nation and sentiments of patriotism. Elementary schools in other countries also extoll the virtues of their respective countries to their pupils and are socializing agents for the adoption of values considered supportive of their political system.

However, in other democracies the emphasis on such values appears to be less pronounced than in the United States. On the other hand, in totalitarian systems such efforts are much more sophisticated and aim not only at imparting strong loyalty to the nation but also the indoctrination of supporting ideologies. The establishment of youth groups for this purpose, such as the Komsomols in the Soviet Union, is widespread in totalitarian countries.

In the United States, the teaching of democratic values in the elementary and perhaps secondary schools has been controversial. It has often been argued, especially during the 1960s, that all teaching should be "value-free." However, whether there is such a thing as teaching any social subject devoid of all values is doubtful. During recent years, the need for imparting democratic values into schoolchildren is again more and more recognized. The supporting argument is that children must understand the working practices of democracy in order to become informed citizens who can be full participants in democratic systems. Hence, such values as periodic elections to public office, governance by majority vote, and observance of the rule of law by all participants in the political and governmental processes are considered to be essential for schoolchildren to understand. Complementary values pupils are to appreciate are integrity, fair play, and justice. The adoption of these values also requires familiarity with the philosophy contained in the Declaration of Independence, the principles of the U.S. Constitution, consent of the governed as an operational concept, and the notion of "limited government."[3]

Closely related to the commitment to democracy that the teaching of democratic values is to achieve in the minds of American pupils is the American economic credo of private enterprise and a free-market economic system. While the U.S. Constitution prohibits the taking of private property except for public use, with due process of law, and with just compensation, it does not ordain either free enterprise or a free-market economy. Nevertheless, the "American way of life" is frequently equated with such an economy and with the widely held assumption that such an economic system is capable of producing for the people of the United States a very high standard of living. Of course, giant corporations have at times been successful in manipulating the free-market system through their power of "administering prices" regardless of the working of the demand-supply mechanism, and the U.S. government has intervened in the interplay of market forces through subsidies and various regulations. But these interventions in the free-market system have not been fully comprehended by the public at large and therefore have not perceptibly undermined the general support for the free-enterprise and free-market system.

Although racial, ethnic, and religious divisions exist in all parts of the United States, more obviously in the South and Southwest because of the large number of blacks and Hispanic influence, the fabric of American society has not suffered seriously. During the last two decades, relations between blacks and whites have greatly improved, although tensions continue to exist in many places. Similarly, the large influx of Mexican and other Central Americans, while often deplored as harming the economic prospects of native American workers, has been accepted although not with enthusiasm. Religious cleavages in the United States do not present any *serious* problems in spite of the diversity of groups that include Jews, Muslims, Fundamentalist Christians, Krishnas, and "Moonies." Indeed, among many denominations of the Christian faith an ecumenical spirit prevails.

As a consequence, U.S. capabilities relevant for foreign policy formulation and implementation are *generally* not adversely affected by these divisions. However, in specific instances, religious, ethnic, and racial groups may seek to influence policy formulation in accordance with what they perceive as their interests; they sometimes also view these interests as converging with American interests, or they believe they should do so. Examples have already been mentioned: the interests of the Greek lobby in policy toward Turkey in connection with the Cyprus dispute, and the goals of the Jewish groups regarding U.S. policy in the Middle East. The World Council of Churches, with which the National Council of Churches is affiliated, has shown recurring inclinations to support revolutionary groups in different parts of the globe. The affinity of American blacks with the countries and peoples of Africa has also led to differences of perceptions and attitudes between U.S. black leaders and the various American administrations regarding policies toward Africa and the Middle East. More will be said about this issue in later chapters.

Implications for Policy Formulation

Although the historical experiences and the value and belief systems of a people affect foreign policy formulation and provide important sources of explanation, it is usually difficult to establish specific correlations between societal variables as described above and particular American foreign policies. However, a number of general conclusions can be drawn and propositions put forth as to how policymakers respond to societal factors or reflect them in their decisions.

1. The successful expansion of American economic, political, and military power during the eighteenth and the first half of the nineteenth centuries has not only instilled pride in many Americans but also convinced them that, because of their successes, most tasks they set for themselves in the world are "do-able." This self-confidence, although undermined somewhat by the Vietnam experience, often leads to a distinction made between a superior United States and the inferiority (in varying degrees) of most other countries. This produces tendencies toward "looking down" on other countries and results in "we-they" dichotomies. If the other countries were only to follow the American prescription for success, things would be well everywhere. Foreign policy officials, although much more sophisticated than the public at large, nevertheless cannot help but reflect these common experiences in their attitudes when engaged in various phases of policymaking.

2. The value and belief systems with which Americans are socialized in school (and to a lesser degree at home) reinforces sentiments of pride in the American way of life engendered by the historical experience. It leads to the belief that a democratic system of government is the solution for the problems of all countries and assures both fairness to all citizens and harmonious relations among countries. Hence, U.S. calls for more democracies in the world have the additional purpose of remedying human rights problems. Emphasis on the rule of law in the American system and on the notion of justice in general has given many Americans the view that foreign policy problems and international issues can be settled best by resort to treaties, arbitration, and courts. The great hopes placed in the Kellogg-Briand Pact of 1928, which was to outlaw war but failed to do so, and the great American expectations for the peace-keeping mechanism of the United Nations, although disappointed, indicate the faith of Americans in the effectiveness of international law. Again, American officials participating in foreign policy formulation are likely to have a more balanced and less affective view of the international arena, but the validity and advantages of democracy and the commitment to legal solutions of international problems tend to permeate much of the rhetoric and undoubtedly some of the thinking in high U.S. policymaking echelons.

3. General support for democracy and pervasive belief in free enterprise and the free-market system are powerful sources of strong opposition to

totalitarian regimes, especially of the communist variety, and to socialist economic systems. Hence strong anticommunist sentiments of the American people have had a very potent and persisting influence on the formulation of American foreign policy. These sentiments have also been most persuasive to policymakers in the executive branch and Congress to expand U.S. armaments whenever America's chief foe, the Soviet Union and its Warsaw Pact allies, *appeared* to attain a position of superiority vis-à-vis the United States.

4.   American value preferences and beliefs have had a bearing not only on foreign policy formulation but also on its implementation. Because of a wide-spread belief that most problems once identified are solvable, the approach to policy formulation and implementation often tends to be ad hoc and prag-matic. In addition, since pragmatism is based on the conviction that the context of events produces a solution, there is a tendency to await develop-ments. The belief is prevalent that every problem will be solvable if attacked with sufficient energy. It is therefore inconceivable that delay might result in irretrievable disaster; at worst it is thought to require a redoubled effort later on.

This tendency is reinforced by the special qualities of the professions—law and business—that furnish the core of the leadership groups in America. Lawyers, at least in the Anglo-Saxon tradition, prefer to deal with actual rather then hypothetical cases; they have little confidence in the possibility of stating a future issue abstractly. In the business world executives are rewarded for their ability to manipulate the known, in itself a conciliatory procedure. The special skill of the executive is thought to consist in coordinating well-defined func-tions rather than in challenging them. The procedure is relatively effective in the business world, where the executive can often substitute decisiveness, long experience, and a wide range of personal acquaintances for reflectiveness. In international affairs, however—especially in a revolutionary situation—the strong will, which is one of the business executive's notable traits, may produce essentially arbitrary choices.

All this gives American policy its particular cast. Problems are dealt with as they arise. Agreement on what constitutes a problem generally depends on an emerging crisis that settles the previously inconclusive disputes about priorities. When a problem is recognized, it is dealt with by a mobilization of all resources to overcome the immediate symptoms. This often involves the risk of slighting longer-term issues that may not yet have assumed crisis proportions. Administrative decisions often reflect compromise under the maxim that "if two parties disagree the truth is usually somewhere in between." Unfortunately, the pedantic application of such truisms causes the various contenders to exaggerate their positions for bargaining purposes or to con-struct fictitious extremes to make their position appear moderate. The sub-stantive quality of the decision suffers as a result.

Miscellaneous Cultural Tendencies

American society displays certain cultural traits that often are considered as factors influencing the character of American foreign policy. One such factor is an inclination toward moralizing, although such an inclination does not imply that American policy has always a truly "moral" character.

Americans have often believed that their role in world politics was determined by something called "manifest destiny." American expansion within and beyond the continent was justified by this belief in manifest destiny; such rationalization, however, is rarely heard today.

Another rationale for American policy has been the maxim of "no compromise with principle." This principle was applied successfully during World Wars I and II and may well have contributed to the total defeat of Germany and its allies in these wars. Today, this theme is invoked from time to time in our relations with the Soviet Union and the Warsaw Pact countries. However, pragmatism and realism seem to be the mostly used axioms for U.S. foreign policy, and, in as complex a world as the one in which we live, this makes good sense.

Finally, isolationism has been a theme of U.S. foreign policy that during the nineteenth century was often attractive to policymakers and that has had recurring appeal to many Americans to this day. However, for a superpower such as the United States, isolationism cannot be an appropriate motivation for foreign policy. Therefore, while withdrawal into a fortress America may seem to promise pastoral peace and happiness, it is an option that in realistic terms simply does not exist for the United States.

PUBLIC OPINION

What Kind of Impact?

While the societal factors examined so far have a broad impact on the content of American foreign policy, they affect, as already noted, the general nature and style of policy more than the specifics of particular policies. Yet, as Vocke points out, societal sources should not be considered as marginal sources of policy. They are pervasive in their impact, but they best explain long-term trends in policy.[4] Public opinion, also a societal variable, can be a critical factor on specific issues, however; furthermore, under certain circumstances, such as Vietnam, its impact can be traced clearly on a number of foreign policies formulated, especially during the Nixon and Ford administrations.

There has been considerable argument about the importance of public opinion in foreign policymaking. Gabriel Almond has divided the public into a mass or general public and the so-called attentive public as far as foreign policy is concerned.[5] Almond and many other observers hold that the mass and general public, consisting of 75 to 90 percent of the adult population, is uninformed about specific foreign policy issues or foreign affairs in general. It is without initiative, pays little attention to what goes on, and has no structured opinion. Whatever response it has is mainly emotional and highly fluctuating. It often moves rapidly from pessimism to optimism and vice versa regarding a particular foreign policy issue. Vietnam is an excellent case in point.

The attentive public is small, about 10 percent of the adult population, but it may be increasing because of the growing attention paid by the news media to foreign policy programs. Members of the attentive public are interested business managers, educators on all levels, professional men and women, and increasingly, women's organizations such as the League of Women Voters. These individuals are often members of foreign policy associations and read a number of publications, such as *Time* and *Newsweek*, thereby becoming better informed on foreign policy matters. They are interested in participating in opinion making and are doing so by expressing their views in a variety of public forums, including letters to the editor. In general, these people have higher incomes and are better educated, and their opinions are often more differentiated than those held by the mass public. They constitute the primary and often critical audience for foreign policy discussions among the elites.

There has been much argument of how useful it is to mobilize public opinion in support of a particular stand on foreign policy issues. Even though in a democracy public opinion appears to have a central role, and even though the people can express their displeasure with policies in political elections, experience has shown that in the field of general foreign policy the voice of the public at large usually plays a distinctly minor role. Again, there are exceptions: issues of war making and protracted war as well as certain aspects of foreign economic policy such as protectionism to save American jobs may well fall into this category. The changes of American policy in Vietnam offer a striking example of an exception. Moreover, as pointed out in Chapter 5, foreign policymakers value the support of public opinion for their decisions.

The question must be asked whether, in spite of the general public's low level of information regarding international affairs and their frequent disinterest in foreign policy, public opinion nevertheless has a latent influence on foreign policymakers. William R. Caspary contends that American public opinion is characterized by a strong and stable "permissive mood" toward international involvement.[6] This may be an overly positive view of the effect of public opinion; it may be more appropriate to say that public opinion sets broad limits for foreign policymakers. These limits are altered, however, if a strong emotional issue comes to the fore and captivates American public opinion. The U.S. involvement in Vietnam agains provides a good example. During most of the 1960s, this involvement was accepted and even supported in many quarters, although voices of protest were heard increasingly and with greater pungency. Toward the end of the Johnson presidency and the advent of the Nixon administration, however, public opinion became captivated by a rapidly growing, very emotional opposition to the war; the new majority of the public, whose opinion was specifically aimed at ending the Vietnam War, not only could not be ignored by the foreign policymakers but had to be accommodated for domestic political reasons. Table 6.2 provides relevant survey data.

The Manipulation of Public Opinion

If public opinion could be manipulated by interested groups or even individuals in such a way as to provide definitive support for a particular cause, its impact on foreign poliycmaking may be enhanced. Such efforts have been made again and again. Examples are (1) the previously mentioned efforts of the Jewish and Greek lobbies to shape policy in accordance with their interests, efforts that included full-page advertisements in large-circulation newspapers such as the *New York Times*, (2) the more recent attempts by organizations sympathizing with the Palestinians to influence elite opinions by the circulation of brochures and newsletters, and (3) the endeavors of some labor union federations, especially the UAW and the steel workers (USW), to change American commitments to the liberalization of international trade by the imposition of restrictions on automobile and steel imports.

Public opinion concerns with foreign policy have also been manipulated for domestic political purposes by governmental leaders. In such an event, we can no longer speak of the influence of public opinion on foreign policymaking. Indeed, public opinion manipulated by the government becomes a tool to assure support for government-directed policy formulation.

Table 6.2   American Public Support for the Vietnam War[a]

		Percentage of "No" Responses				
August 1965	*September 1966*	*October 1967*	*October 1968*	*May 1970*	*May 1971*	*January 1973*
61	48	44	37	36	28	29

[a] As measured by "No" responses to the following question: "In view of developments since we entered the fighting in Vietnam, do you think the United States made a mistake sending troops to Vietnam?"

Sources: Adapted from William L. Lunch, "American Public Opinion and the War in Vietnam," *Western Political Quarterly* 32, 1 (March 1979), pp. 21–44, on p. 25, Table 1; and George H. Gallup, *The Gallup Poll: Public Opinion 1972–77*, Vol. 1 (Wilmington, Del.: Scholarly Resources, 1978), p. 87.

Public Opinion, Foreign Policy, and Domestic Politics

The tendency of any president and associates to maintain and improve their political positions has definite consequences for the formulation of foreign policy goals. Their aim must be "achievement" in the foreign policy field and avoidance of failures and reverses. It may produce an attitude that what is good for the president politically may also be good for the country.

The area of national security in the broadest sense has best served the ambitions of most political leaders. Although emphasis on national security has generated long debates with domestic political opponents over what the "true" national interest of a country is or should be, the alleged needed counteraction to threats to a country's security has often resulted in bigger budgets and thereby the ability to fulfill more political promises. Able to claim superior knowledge of existing conditions, governmental leaders can criticize opponents with relative ease and contend in the face of dissent that disagreement with the proposed policy will endanger the chances of the state to assure its security. A number of President Reagan's comments about the burgeoning nuclear freeze movement in 1982 and 1983 have struck this theme. For example, on March 31, 1983, he said in a speech to the Los Angeles World Affairs Council:

> The Freeze concept is dangerous for many reasons. It would preserve today's high, unequal and unstable levels of nuclear forces and, by so doing, reduce Soviet incentives to negotiate for real reductions.
>
> It would pull the rug out from under our negotiators in Geneva, as they have testified. . . .
>
> The freeze proposal would also make a lot more sense if a similar movement against nuclear weapons were putting similar pressures on Soviet leaders in Moscow. . . .
>
> Finally, the freeze would reward the Soviets for their 15-year buildup while locking us into our existing equipment, which in many cases is obsolete and badly in need of modernization. Three quarters of Soviet strategic warheads are on delivery systems 5 years old or less. Three quarters of the American strategic warheads are on delivery systems 15 years old or older. The time comes when everything wears out. The trouble is it comes a lot sooner for us than for them. And, under a freeze, we couldn't do anything about it.[7]

Perceptions of national security, detente, and peace were closely intertwined when President Nixon made his trips to China and the Soviet Union in the winter and spring of 1972 to open a new era of relations with the two Communist giants. These visits, covered most extensively by television, made him a hero and contributed mightily to his impressive victory in the presidential election in November of that year. President Nixon's initiation of the new relationship with the Soviet Union and China was not without some political risks, because conservative Republicans were likely to look with disfavor on these new policies; however, the gamble paid off handsomely, although the long-range effect on U.S.-Soviet relations is not clear as yet.

During the 1976 presidential election campaign, President Gerald R. Ford presented his experience in foreign policy as a strong reason the American people should choose him rather than Carter. Before the 1980 election campaign, Carter was anxious to be seen at the economic summit meeting in Venice, Italy. There he could mix with the other leaders of the most powerful democracies in the world and perhaps hopefully expunge some of the negative impressions that were caused by the low esteem that West German Chancellor Helmut Schmidt was said to have for Jimmy Carter, and by other improvident behavior in the international arena. One such incident involved kissing Leonid Brezhnev's cheek during the SALT II signing ceremonies in Vienna a year earlier.

President Reagan's TV-fanfare trip to the economic summit in Versailles in 1982 also falls into the category of influencing American public opinion through displays of foreign policy expertise by an American president. Before the summit, Reagan was shown on TV while riding horseback with the Queen of England and addressing British parliamentarians at Westminster Abbey. After the summit, he was seen addressing the German Bundestag and visiting the Berlin Wall, a ritual that all American presidents feel obliged to perform to symbolize our close relationship with the Federal Republic of Germany despite recurring deep differences of views.

Other U.S. presidents have of course also intemingled foreign policy with domestic politics; Halperin and Kanter cite several main concerns guiding these efforts[8]:

1. The most important concern is getting and keeping office. For this reason presidents easily adopt the belief that their reelection is in the national interest and that their ability to be reelected should not be adversely affected by a controversial foreign policy decision. An example is President Dwight D. Eisenhower's decision not to support the British-French-Israeli efforts in the Suez crisis of 1956 to oust Egyptian President Nasser to ensure the international nature of the Suez Canal. Alternatively, a president may also see a particular foreign policy decision as an effective appeal to a particular group of potential supporters, such as voters of Polish extraction during the Poland crisis from 1981 to 1983 or a group of manufacturers and labor unions whose economic well-being may depend on a particular trade policy.

2. Presidents must avoid the appearance of failure and therefore are reluctant to undertake policies that have a high risk potential. Each failure tarnishes their reputation for success and creates perceptions in the public mind of reduced probability of success in the future. The fiasco of the Bay of Pigs venture aimed at toppling Fidel Castro could have had this effect on President Kennedy's reputation. However, his reputation was restored 18 months later

(in 1962) by his efficient handling of the Cuban missile crisis, which led to the withdrawal of Soviet missiles installed earlier on that island.

3.   Presidents should avoid rows with Congress, the press, or the public. Even if the president is initially successful in these rows, he may have paid too high a price in terms of generated antagonism, bitterness, and resentment. This was President Kennedy's assessment of his fight with Congress over the B-70 manned bomber.

4.   The president must seek to develop a consensus of support for a particular policy. In seeking this support, he must create the feeling that consistency is maintained. An example is a decision by President Truman to defend Taiwan in 1950, as otherwise he may not have been able to obtain popular support for his defense of Korea. Reagan's desire to aid Taiwan in 1982 fits here as well.

5.   Presidents must be aware at all times that domestic interests and foreign policy interact in the clash over the use of scarce resources. Domestic needs may be so overwhelming as to necessitate economizing in the defense field, with the result that aerospace procurement may be reduced or military bases may have to be closed. However, if public opinion is in favor of strengthening defense as was the case in the late 1970s and very early 1980s, a president can increase defense expenditures with impunity until such time when elites and the public strongly articulate domestic priorities of an economic, nondefense nature such as the need to counter pervasive unemployment and astronomical budget deficits. This is a dilemma that faced President Reagan in the spring of 1983. Although the presidentially approved 1984 budget resolution could not be passed in the Senate in spite of the latter's Republican majority because the senators sensed the declining support of the public for defense expenditures, Reagan remained adamantly opposed to lowering the increase of defense expenditures to the percentage the Senate wanted (slightly above 6 percent). Ultimately, however, Congress passed a compromise 1984 budget resolution on the last day of the 1983 fiscal year which was signed by the President.

SUMMARY

The explanatory variables for American foreign policies examined in this chapter emanate from different features of the American society. Some of these variables, at times difficult to identify, have only a very broad influence on the nature and style of policymaking, whereas one variable, public opinion, can be more specific in its causal relationship.

Four American societal features with a broad and diffuse impact on policy formulation are:

• Common historical experiences
• Values and belief systems

- The degree of ideological cohesion
- The degree of racial, ethnic, and religious cleavages

The *historical experience* of the American people have been very positive and have spawned policies during the nineteenth century that were instrumental in supporting American economic expansion. By the middle of the twentieth century, the United States had achieved top-level economic and military status. However, the trauma of Vietnam may well have undermined the confidence of Americans in their time-proven prescription for promoting economic welfare and gaining military successes.

The *values and beliefs* of Americans reflect admiration of and loyalty for their country. Democracy is ranked very highly including periodic elections to public office, majority vote decisions, and the rule of law. Closely related is their credo for free enterprise and the free-market system. This strong preference, coupled with the pervasive commitment to democracy, has produced a high degree of ideological cohesion.

Although *racial, ethnic, and religious differences* exist within American society, they have not seriously damaged its fabric. Hence the formulation of foreign policies, while on occasion under heavy pressure from different minority groups, has been able in most but not all cases to achieve reasonable, satisfactory results although not every group was pleased.

American societal features give its policy a particular cast:

- Problems are dealt with as they arise.
- Most tasks for American foreign policy are "do-able."
- There is a tendency to "look down" on other countries.
- Democracy and free enterprise are the solution for the problem of all countries.
- Americans have great faith in international law.
- A strong anticommunist mood is widespread.
- There should be no compromise with principle.

Public opinion, another societal variable, can be a critical factor on specific foreign policy issues. Vietnam is a prime example where public opinion led ultimately to the government terminating the war.

The public can be divided into the mass or general part (75−90 percent of the population) and the attentive part, which pays attention to foreign policy problems. Public opinion as a whole tends to set limits for foreign policymakers within which they have a high degree of discretion for the policies they may want to formulate. But these limits may be narrowed if highly emotional issues come to the fore and capture the public's opinion.

There are often interesting interplays between domestic politics, foreign policy, and public opinion through which presidents seek to improve their standing with the American people. Presidents like to show off their foreign policy expertise through the news media, and the chapter closes with a discussion of cases from Eisenhower to Reagan and the lessons learned from these cases.

NOTES

1. Thomas A. Bailey, *A Diplomatic History of the American People*, 6th ed. (New York: Appleton-Century-Crofts, 1958), p. 4.
2. Ibid., p. 2.
3. For a comprehensive discussion of the issue of teaching "democratic values" see Jeane Kirkpatrick, "The Teaching of Democratic Values," *The American Educator* (Spring 1977), pp. 35–37.
4. William C. Vocke, *American Foreign Policy: An Analytical Approach* (New York: Free Press, 1976), p. 186.
5. Gabriel Almond, *The American People and Foreign People* (New York: Praeger, 1962), p. 138.
6. William C. Caspary, "The 'Mood Theory': A Study of Public Opinion and Foreign Policy," *American Political Science Review* 64 (1970), pp. 536–546.
7. *U.S. News and World Report*, April 25, 1983, p. 19.
8. Morton H. Halperin and Arnold Kanter (eds.), *Readings in American Foreign Policy: A Bureaucratic Perspective* (Boston: Little, Brown, 1973), pp. 13–14.

CHAPTER 7

The International Situation and Foreign Policy Formulation

In Chapter 1 we briefly discussed the "distribution of international power" approach to the study of American foreign policy. The basic argument for this approach is that the United States as part of the international system can develop realistic policies only by taking into careful consideration the capabilities and vulnerabilities of other countries in this system when formulating its foreign policy.

The constellation of military, economic, and political power in the international arena as well as the capabilities and vulnerabilities of individual foreign countries are indeed important variables that help to explain the formulation of American foreign policies. However, this cluster of independent variables does not tell the whole story. As we have seen, idiosyncratic, institutional, and societal variables exert their influence on policy formulation and therefore cannot be ignored. In many cases the international variables may be particularly issue-specific, especially when policy is formulated in response to an international event such as the 1982 Israeli invasion of Lebanon, and thereby these variables become very significant sources of explanation for U.S. policies.

For analytical purposes, it is useful to make a distinction between international variables flowing from specific bilateral (also referred to as dyadic) and multilateral relations between the United States and other countries or IGOs, and those growing out of the international system itself. The latter may be the politicomilitary or the economic international system and their subsystems and, for our purposes, also include the global physical environment. These variables are called systemic, while the first category of variables are labeled interactional.[1] The examination of international variables will first focus on the interactional type. This cluster of variables will be discussed under two headings: (1) the nature of the relationship, that is, friendship (alliance) or hostility between the United States and other international actors, and (2) the comparative capabilities of the United States and other countries, especially as far as geographical, demographic, economic, technological, and military dimensions as well as governmental effectiveness are concerned. Since IGOs are composed of sovereign states and depend for their capabilities on the strengths and/or weaknesses of their members and the interrelationship among the latter, variables flowing from interactions between the United States and IGOs will only be examined later within the context of actual policy content.

The systemic variables also will be considered under two headings: (1) persistence and change in the international politicomilitary and economic systems, and (2) changes in the global physical environment, particularly the exhaustion of natural resources. We should note that systemic variables can be of either the independent or the intervening type. For example, the U.S. relationship and interactions with Iran during the 1970s produced a number of issue-specific variables influencing American foreign policy formulation toward that and other countries. The exhaustion of crude oil resources on a global level reinforced and accentuated some of the interactional independent variables (recall the hostage crisis of 1979–1981), and therefore the systemic variables should often be characterized as "intervening" rather than "independent," with the dependent variable of course being U.S. foreign policy or policies.

Figure 7.1 is a diagrammatic breakdown of the international variables discussed in this chapter. It may be helpful to refer to this diagram as the discussion proceeds.

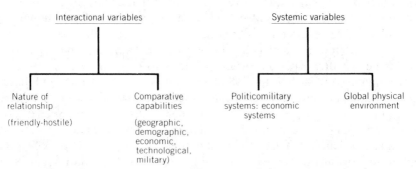

Figure 7.1 Breakdown of international variables involved in foreign policy.

THE INTERACTIONAL VARIABLES AS SOURCES
OF POLICY EXPLANATION

The Nature of the Relationship

The relationship and interactions between the United States and other individual states are strongly influenced by perceptions of enmity or friendliness. These perceptions are compounded and often strengthened by ideological conflicts. Policy development in response to interactions between the United States and countries espousing ideologies opposed by American decision makers are likely to be colored by this opposition. An example is the U.S. negotiating stance in joint American and Soviet attempts to reduce the number of warheads and missiles, both intercontinental and within Europe. The controlling perception for the American negotiators, as suggested by the director of the U.S. Arms Control and Disarmament Agency, is the Soviet aim of bringing "all Europe, Asia, Africa, and the Middle East under its control, leaving the United States no choice but to acquiesce in Soviet hegemony."[2] Such a goal is seen frequently as an integral part of Marxist-Leninist doctrine, which American policymakers have always rejected in its entirety.

When ideological rivalry is intense, decision makers are likely to attach considerable import to governmental changes abroad, and the desirability of such changes may generate interventionary behavior.[3] American interventions in Guatemala in 1954 leading to the overthrow of left-leaning President Jacobo Arbenz, and in Chile in 1973 aiding indirectly in toppling the Marxist-oriented government of Salvador Allende, are cases in point. However, ideological divergencies may not always be decisive for American policy formulation. Witness the U.S. relationship with the People's Republic of China, where President Nixon and Henry Kissinger considered strategic concerns regarding the Soviet Union more salient than ideological differences.

In contrast, ideological compatibility aids in the formulation of favorable policies toward those countries the United States considers as friendly. This proposition was illustrated during the Falkland hostilities between Great Britain and Argentina in the spring of 1982. Initially, the United States tried to act as an "honest broker" and to conciliate between the two warring countries. Alexander Haig, then secretary of state, shuttled among the cities of London, Washington, and Buenos Aires attempting to head off hostilities by seeking to persuade the Argentine government to withdraw its troops that had occupied the Islands and to subject to arbitration its claim of sovereignty over the Falkland Islands. When Haig's efforts collapsed, American policy tilted toward Great Britain. This was a difficult decision for American policymakers, since both Britain and Argentina were allies. However, once the United States decided to enter the fracas, the old cliché, "blood is thicker than water," seemed to come to the fore. Britain was not only a close ally in two world wars and a member of NATO, its goals and ambitions were much more compatible with those of the United States than were those of Argentina, which was controlled by a military junta and has been accused of harboring Nazi war criminals. The fact that more U.S. policymakers are of Anglo-Saxon than Spanish origin may have also played a part in the final choice to support Great Britain in this dispute.

The "friend or foe" factor in a relationship between the United States and other countries in some cases is likely to have a secondary potency as an independent variable for the explanation of American foreign policy. For instance, the United States imposed sanctions in 1982 on British, French, and Italian firms shipping products embodying U.S. patents to the Soviet Union for the construction of the gas pipeline, in spite of the Atlantic Alliance relationship with these countries. Here, other policy considerations, such as punishing the Soviet Union for its alleged instigation of Polish martial law measures, had a greater potency than the Atlantic Alliance factor. In general, primary weight in the formulation of foreign policy is given to international variables stemming from the impact of comparative capabilities and specific interactions with particular third countries. Nevertheless, the "friend or foe" factor and ideological rivalries are significant, albeit sometimes secondary, sources of foreign policy explanation and therefore must be considered by policy analysts.

Comparative Capabilities

No formulation of American foreign policy toward particular countries, if it is to be implemented successfully, can ignore the capabilities of those countries, especially in the economic, technological, and military spheres. The magnitude of these capabilities (or their absence) constitutes a measure for the actual and potential power that individual countries possess in the international arena. In other words, the capabilities reflect the elements of power of states and thus are important guides for American policymakers when, for example, countries are considered for alliance status. In such a case, attention must be paid by the formulators of American foreign policy to the elements of power over which a prospective ally can dispose and which contribute to the strength of the alliance. This was an important consideration when the United States promoted the admission of Spain to NATO; indeed, Spain had a geographically advantageous location and economic capabilities that appeared to be useful to the strategic calculations of NATO and of the United States. Capability evaluation by policymakers is equally if not more crucial when policy is formulated toward potential enemies.

The basic elements of power determining a state's capabilities are geography, including natural resources, the nature of its population, economic development, science and technology, military organization, and the quality of governmental administration. We will briefly discuss aspects of these elements.

Geography   In any discussion of capabilities (and possible vulnerabilities) of states, the size and shape of the territories and the locations of these states relative to other countries are significant. Large size is a clear advantage. It was the ability of Russia to give up space for time to organize its military defense that proved to be decisive in 1812 and 1941. Moreover, the difficulty of occupying captured territory is directly proportional to its size. Today, when invasion forces are often airborne, space is a much less significant factor in countering attacks; its value may lie instead in making possible the dispersion of vital industries to avoid complete nuclear destruction. Although the United States has sufficient space, the Soviet Union has achieved a much higher degree of dispersal of industrial capacity. The vast expanses of the People's Republic of China's territory offer many opportunities for dispersal.

It is noteworthy that, while small countries have never achieved great power status, middle-sized countries such as Great Britain and France were able to attain the status in the nineteenth and early twentieth centuries as the result of early industrial development, a strong military establishment, and colonial conquest. In a sense, these conquests added to their size, suggesting again the importance of the geographical factor. However, size remains only one of many elements determining the total power of a country. Many of the states possessing vast territories are not popularly identified as powerful.

Relative Location   The relative location of countries has been the basis for many theories of geopolitics. One of these, propounded in 1904 by Sir Halford Mackinder in London, has as its central concept that the pivotal area for international power is Euro-Asia, a region stretching from the Volga River in Russia to the Yangtse River in China, and from the Himalayas to the Arctic Ocean. This, according to Mackinder, was the "heartland" of the world, which was surrounded by an inner crescent (running from Germany, Turkey, and India to China) and an outer crescent (made up of Britain, South Africa, Antarctica, Japan, the United States, and Canada). Europe, Asia, and Africa were regarded as the "world-island," and the principal conclusion was: "Who rules East Europe commands the Heartland; who rules the Heartland commands the World-Island; who rules the World-Island commands the world."[4] Figure 7.2 provides a graphic illustration of Mackinder's geopolitical concept.

If the Mackinder propositions were considered today to be valid, the Soviet Union would present a particular challenge to American foreign policy-makers merely on the basis of geopolitics. However, the "science" of geopolitics has become discredited, because it sought to make an element of geography into an absolute law by which the power of states could be determined. While the relative location of states does influence their power status, it is only one factor among many. For example, Austria's location close to the Soviet Union has caused it to defer to its big neighbor on strategic and economic matters. However, the vulnerability of relative location can be overcome by countervailing forces: Gibraltar's proximity to Spain has not led to Spanish control because of British power and political skill.

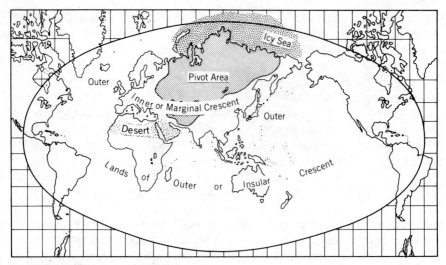

Figure 7.2   Mackinder's geopolitical world.

Source: Hans W. Weigert et al., *Principles of Political Geography* (New York: Appleton-Century-Crofts, 1957), p. 210, Figure 8.1.

Natural Resources   An aspect of great importance in determining the capabilities of a country is the availability of natural resources within its borders. These resources consist of minerals (fuels and metals) and of the products of the soil. Without these resources, modern economics cannot operate, the construction of a viable military force is impossible, and large populations cannot be fed. When vital resources are not available within a country, they must be imported. For many developing countries, the export of natural resources and agricultural products is essential for their economic survival and political stability.

It is important to understand that both the needs for natural resources and their availability change for particular countries over time. Altered economic conditions and technological advances bring about different needs in different countries, accelerating or slowing down the consumption of existing resources and requiring greater imports or the discovery of substitutes. At the same time, the resource availability expands when nations find new reserves of minerals or discover new methods for expanding or speeding up crop growth.

The two largest powers in the world, the United States and the Soviet Union, have been self-sufficient not only in coal and iron ore but also in many other minerals. During the past decade or two, however, the United States has been compelled to import iron ore from Venezuela, Canada, and other places, because it was exhausting domestic sources of high-grade ores. The United States must import many other materials needed to keep the American industrial machinery running as well, as indicated in Tables 7.1 and 7.2. Some of these materials, such as chromite and industrial diamonds, come from potential enemies, such as the Soviet Union.

Table 7.1   Major Vital Minerals Imported into the United States, 1980 and 2000

	Percentage Imported	
Mineral	*1980*	*2000*
Columbium	100	100
Manganese	97	100
Aluminum and bauxite	94	80
Cobalt	93	76
Chromium	91	80
Platinum	87	83
Tin	84	79
Flourspar	84	96
Nickel	73	46
Zinc	58	55
Tungsten	54	74
Mercury	49	38
Iron	22	22
Vanadium	15	71
Copper	14	10

Source: U.S., Department of Interior, Bureau of Mines, *Mineral Commodity Summaries, 1981.*
Estimates for the year 2000 from U.S., Bureau of Mines, *Mineral Trends and Forecasts, 1979.*

The increasing need for petroleum products has become the Achilles' heel of industrial advanced countries. The United States, which for many years was almost entirely self-sufficient in its petroleum needs, must import substantial amounts from other countries. Although new reserves have been found in the United States and along its shores and are beginning to be exploited in the North Sea near Great Britain, Norway, and the Netherlands, the United States and other highly industrialized nations of the Free World will probably remain dependent for adequate oil supplies on the Arab world. See Table 7.3 for U.S. import data in 1981 and 1982. While the very large oil reserves of many Arab states are by themselves a factor of considerable strength, this dependence reinforces their power considerably, and any threat by the Arab states to withhold oil from certain countries or to reduce the permissible output of the wells owned by the international oil companies is not taken lightly. It is therefore not surprising that this threat has been used again and again by the Arab countries in the Israeli-Arab conflict to put pressure on the governments of the industrially advanced countries to make their policies more favorable to the Arab cause. Although the oil glut of 1982 and 1983 has caused dissension among the members of the Organization of Petroleum-Exporting Countries (OPEC) and lowered oil prices, the situation may be reversed when oil consumption again rises because of an improved world economy. This points up the persistent need for adequate energy resources and makes the continued construction of the gas pipeline between the Soviet Union and Western Europe, to which West Germany and other West European countries remain committed in spite of the American sanctions, a very understandable enterprise.

Table 7.2   Critical Materials Used for Jet Engines

Mineral	Pounds Used in Jet Engines	Imports as Percent of Consumption	Where Material Is Produced (%)
Tungsten	80–100	24	United States (30) South Korea (19) Canada (12) Australia (8) Bolivia (8) Portugal (7)
Columbium	10–12	100	Brazil (54) Canada (21) Mozambique (18)
Nickel	1300–1600	75	Canada (71) New Caledonia (20)
Chromium	2500–2800	100	South Africa (31) Turkey (19) S. Rhodesia (19) Philippines (18)
Molybdenum	90–100	0	United States (79) Canada (10)
Cobalt	30–40	100	Zaire (60) Morocco (13) Canada (12) Zambia (11)

Source: Harry Magdoff, *The Age of Imperialism* (New York: Monthly Review Press, 1969), p. 52, Table XI.

One means to overcome deficiencies in raw materials is stockpiling. The United States has made use of this system—for example, oil has been stockpiled in Louisiana salt domes for the U.S. Strategic Petroleum Reserve—but it is feasible only if stockpiled materials do not deteriorate. The search for and discovery of domestic substitutes is another means of overcoming the problem of possible shortages of needed materials. Sometimes the production of substitutes develops into a major industrial pursuit, and the resulting products serve not only the purposes for which they were originally intended but completely different purposes as well. The plastics industry is an example.

Demography   A large population does not confer great power status on a country; however, a very small population precludes such a status, inasmuch as high economic development requires a good-sized labor force, an adequate number of consumers, and an extensive reserve work force to establish credible military capabilities. In general, the size of population must exceed 40 million if

Table 7.3   U.S. Crude and Product Imports by Source Country
(Including Imports to Strategic Petroleum Reserve)

Country	Oil Imports (in Thousands of Barrels per Day)		Percent Difference
	1982ᵃ	1981	
OPEC Countries			
Saudi Arabiaᵃ	548	1129	−51.5
Nigeria	505	620	−18.5
Venezuela	406	406	0
Indonesia	245	366	−33.1
Algeriaᵃ	161	311	−48.2
Iran	35	0	—
Libyaᵃ	25	319	−92.2
Other OPECᵃ	188	172	+9.3
Total OPEC	2113	3323	−36.4
Non-OPEC			
Mexico	684	522	+31.0
Canada	476	447	6.5
United Kingdom	450	375	20.0
Virgin Islands and Puerto Rico	364	389	−6.4
Other	1139	535	+112.9
Total Non-OPEC	3113	2268	+37.3
TOTAL	5042	5996	−15.9

ᵃPreliminary.

Source: U.S., Department of Energy, *Annual Energy Review 1982*, p. 57, Table 25.

a state aspires to great or even medium power status,[5] but there are exceptions. Canada, with only 24 million inhabitants, has much greater economic and military strength than has Indonesia with a population of 155.3 million. Only twenty countries exceed the power status threshold of 40 million inhabitants, as can be seen from Table 7.4.

The structure of the population is also an important factor in measuring a state's economic and military potential. A high percentage in the 15−44 age bracket is an indication of national strength. Perhaps more important than the current structure of the population is the projected future pattern, because foreign policymakers must plan for events that are yet 5, 10, or 25 years away. Their plans must take into consideration the relative size of the population at these intervals in any countries with which they plan either to collaborate or to compete. The importance of comparative projections of population can be illustrated by a historical example involving France and Germany between

Table 7.4   The Twenty Most Populous Countries in the World
(Mid-1981 Estimates)

Country	Population (Millions)
People's Republic of China	970.0
India	683.8
Soviet Union	267.6
United States	230.0
Indonesia	155.3
Brazil	127.0
Japan	117.7
Bangladesh	90.7
Pakistan	85.0
Nigeria	79.6
Mexico	74.5
West Germany	61.4
Italy	57.2
United Kingdom	55.9
France	54.0
Vietnam	53.6
Poland	49.0
Thailand	48.2
Turkey	45.5
Egypt	43.0

Source: *Information Please Almanac*, 1982, pp. 108–109.

1897 and 1940. During that period, the population of France increased by 4 million, while Germany's population grew by 27 million. Consecutive French governments viewed with alarm the much more rapid population growth rate of their neighbors to the east. Their apprehension was clearly justified: by 1940 Germany had at her disposal about 15 million men fit for military service, whereas France had only 5 million.[6]

Although large populations provide labor and military personnel, the quality of that personnel in terms of education and health is a crucial matter in assessing its contribution to the strength of a nation. A high percentage of illiteracy and low levels of education in the labor force preclude the establishment of advanced industrial plants; extensive training programs and automated production lines, however, may overcome these deficiencies in certain instances. A variety of skills and varied consumption needs are the ingredients necessary for the development of a prosperous and varied economy.

While a large labor reserve is required for a powerful military establishment, literacy plus an adequate education are needed to employ sophisticated weapons systems and to maintain tanks, missile launchers, supersonic jet planes, and electronic gear in operating condition. However, as the Israeli-

Arab War of October 1973 demonstrated, intensive training programs were able to overcome some of the educational deficiencies that plagued the Egyptian military work force during the 1950s and 1960s.

It is noteworthy that the size of population of a country does not correlate with the size of its armed forces. Despite the very large population of India, for example, the United States and the Soviet Union have more personnel under arms than does this country. In contrast, tiny Israel has military personnel of nearly 160,000 men and women and, when fully mobilized, can put nearly 300,000 soldiers in the field, almost as many as France's peacetime forces, although the population of France is twenty times as large as that of Israel.

Good health is also important if the population is to represent a factor of strength in a country. Good health assures stamina in the execution of economic and military tasks; hence higher productivity rates can be achieved and the military can obtain a better type of soldier. A healthy population is also a strong morale factor.

Finally, a few observations need to be made about the ethnic composition of a population. As already noted in Chapter 5, a racially divided population constitutes a vulnerability that can be exploited by outside forces. This does not mean that two or more races cannot live together successfully and congenially within a state; however, as every American recognizes, it requires a special effort to erase racial prejudices and to bring about a large degree of integration on the basis of full equality. Great Britain, which during the past decade has seen an influx of blacks and East Indians, has grappled with the problem of integrating the races, but so far a fully satisfactory solution has been elusive.

Religious differences can constitute serious vulnerabilities in some countries—as events in Northern Ireland and the history of Pakistan demonstrate—but in many other states, such as the Federal Republic of Germany and the United States, these differences have only very minor significance in terms of national power.

In summary, population is one factor that determines strength or weakness of a country. Such aspects of population as size, structure, quality, and composition must be assessed before a balanced judgment can be made. Comprehensive, accurate calculations and projections are often difficult, and other factors such as economic development have a bearing on demographic assessments needed by American foreign policymakers in the formulation of policies toward individual countries.

Economic Factors One of the most decisive elements of a country's strength is its economic development. In many respects, this element may have a greater bearing on its political power position than its military strength because, without a strong economic posture, it is difficult to build a powerful military establishment. Economic activities have a direct impact on the implementation of foreign policy; a government's activities to press its demands on other states, to have appeal as an ally, and to exert viable pressure on foes depends on a high level of economic development. In today's world of enormous economic interchange and giant economic entities such as multinational corporations, the line between economic and political activities is often blurred, and the name of the game is "ecopolitics."

How can we measure the economic capabilities of a country? The most common way is by comparing the national output of goods and services known as the *gross national product* (GNP). The GNP is computed in money paid for goods and services. Table 7.5 shows the GNP of selected top-ranking countries, as well as figures for selected other states, including some in the Third World. This table suggests that the United States and the Soviet Union are the top producers of goods and services. It is interesting to see, for example, that an enormous disparity exists between the GNP of the United States and that of Sweden.

It is often useful to relate GNP to the population of a country (*GNP per capita*). However, GNP per capita figures do not accurately indicate the economic benefits derived by individual citizens. For example, a country such as Kuwait with its tremendous production of oil may have a very high GNP per

Table 7.5   Measures of Economic Strength, 1979

Country	GNP ($ billion)	GNP Growth Rate (%)	National Income ($ billion)	National Income per Capita ($)
United States	2626.0	2.8	2121.4	8612
Soviet Union	1082.0	4.3	—	—
Japan	1019.5	7.8	821.8	7153
West Germany	717.7	2.4	568.8	9278
France	513.5	3.1	421.3	7908
China	517.0	4.5	—	—
Italy	394.0	3.0	173.6[a]	3076
United Kingdom	353.6	1.9	276.5	4955
Canada	228.4	3.0	177.9	8612
Brazil	207.3	6.0	175.8	1523
Spain	162.3	3.1	133.3	3625
Netherlands	143.2	2.3	118.6	4955
Poland	135.5	5.9	—	—
Australia	130.7	1.5	107.0	7515
India	126.0	1.6	93.8[a]	150
East Germany	107.6	4.8	—	—
Mexico	107.6	1.3	81.4	1244
Czechoslovakia	80.5	4.3	—	—
Sweden	98.6	1.1	76.7	9274

[a]1977 figure.

Sources: United Nations Statistical Yearbook, 1979–80; 1982 World Almanac and Book of Facts.

capita, but the benefits stemming from the high GNP flow only to a very small portion of the population.

A more refined way of looking at the strength of a nation in terms of economic development is to look at statistics for *per capita incomes*. Table 7.5 reveals that although the United States had the highest national income in 1979, West Germany and Sweden were able to surpass the United States on per capita income of their citizens. Per capita income in the Third World has remained desperately low, an aspect we will examine in detail in Chapter 12.

The degree of industrialization of a country is a meaningful element in determining its economic strength. An indicator of industrialization is the proportion of the working population engaged in nonagricultural pursuits. Table 7.6 lists most industrialized nations of the world, and it is apparent that some of the most powerful countries are ranking members of this group. Significantly, the Soviet Union is not among the top-ranking members, because it continues to employ large numbers of its population in agriculture.

Another important measure of a country's strength is its *production of electric energy* and the *per capita consumption of energy* produced by all sources, including petroleum, natural gas, and coal. Tables 7.7 and 7.8 indicate that the United States and the Soviet Union are the leading producers of electric energy, followed by Japan, West Germany, and Canada; in the per capita consumption of energy, however, Canada, Australia, and West Germany surpass the Soviet Union. While these figures refer to energy from all sources, oil supplies are a major source of energy production for all states. All economically advanced countries except the Soviet Union depend on the Third World, especially the Middle East and South America, for their supplies of oil.

Table 7.6 Percentage of Nonagricultural Civilian Employment	
United Kingdom	98.4
Belgium	96.6
United States	95.5
Canada	95.0
Sweden	95.0
Netherlands	94.0
West Germany	94.0
Luxembourg	94.0
Switzerland	92.0
Denmark	91.5
Iceland	90.0
France	88.5
Japan	88.0
Norway	83.0

Sources: 1982 World Almanac and Book of Facts.

Table 7.7   Electric Energy Production, 1980

Country	Energy Production (kilowatt hours)
United States	2,356,139
Soviet Union	1,295,000
Japan	612,040
West Germany	368,722
Canada	366,677
United Kingdom	281,752
France	257,752
Italy	186,305
Poland	121,860
East Germany	98,800

Source: U.N. Statistical Yearbook, 1979–80.

Table 7.8   Per Capital Consumption of Energy in Selected Countries, 1980

Country	Per Capita Energy Consumption (Kg Coal Consumption as Equivalent)
United States	10,410
Canada	10,241
Australia	6,032
West Germany	5,727
Soviet Union	5,595
United Kingdom	4,942
France	4,351
Japan	3,494
Italy	3,318
Mexico	1,770
Colombia	769
Brazil	761
Turkey	737
China	602
Indonesia	220
Pakistan	218
India	191
Paraguay	190
Nigeria	144
Ghana	115

Source: U.N. Statistical Yearbook, 1979–80.

Another means of measuring the economic development of a country is to make a careful *analysis of the goods and services it produces*. Some economic systems are oriented predominantly toward the welfare of their people and thereby attain a relatively high standard of living for their citizens. These systems normally emphasize production of consumer goods. Other systems are geared to increase as quickly as possible the country's productive capacity, which means that the output of factories is focused on capital goods. Finally, some countries, such as the Soviet Union, have sought to maximize their military capabilities; thus during the 1950s and 1960s, a large portion of the Soviet GNP stemmed from the production of military items and capital goods.

Savings play an important role in economic growth, as they may be the major source for the accumulation of capital, which in turn provides a major source for investment; therefore, *domestic investment* is a factor in a country's economic strength in that the higher the rate of investment, the higher the rate of increase in the nation's GNP. In the marginal economies of the Third World, expenditures on goods and services may reduce savings to an extent that economic growth is impossible.

Another category of allocation that has increased continually over the past two or three decades is the *percentage of GNP allocated to government*. Normally, this percentage is greater in Communist countries than in capitalistic countries, because the bureaucracy plays a much larger role in every aspect of society, including the provision of goods and services, in Communist countries. The share of GNP allocated to government in the United States has remained fairly steady between 1965 and 1980 (about 21 percent) but has crept up over what it was in 1958 (19 percent).

The proportion flowing into the military establishment can also be seen from the *percentage of the GNP allocated to the country's military effort*. Table 7.9 indicates that as of 1980, the United States devoted 5.2 percent of its GNP to defense expenditures amounting to $142.7 billion. A year earlier, in 1979, the Soviet Union spent between 11 and 13 percent of its GNP for that purpose. In terms of net figures, the Soviet Union expended $222 billion on defense in that year. We should stress that statistics regarding allocation of the GNP to the military establishment can be taken only as information about the level and intensity of a country's military effort; they say nothing about its quality and specific characteristics.

Finally, the share of GNP going to *foreign investment* is important, particularly if it is linked to balance-of-payments data. The ratio of imports and exports to GNP provides some insights into the strength or vulnerability of a country. The higher this ratio, the more a country is dependent for its economic posture on external factors and often on the goodwill of other countries. A low ratio suggests relative independence from external factors and conditions. An example is the United States, whose economic well-being is assured primarily by the tremendous business generated within its boundaries but whose share of exports has, nevertheless, risen from only 5 percent of GNP in the 1960s to 12

Table 7.9   Comparisons of Defense Expenditures, 1980

Country	Millions of Dollars	Dollars per Capita	Percentage of Government Expenditure	Percentage of GNP
NATO Countries				
Belgium	3,735	378	n.a.[a]	3.3
Britain	24,448	437	10.7	4.9
Canada	4,240	177	n.a.	1.7
Denmark	1,404	274	6.4	2.0
France	20,220	374	n.a.	3.9
West Germany	25,120	410	22.2	3.3
Greece	1,770	236	19.8	n.a.
Italy	6,580	n.a.	n.a.	2.4
Luxembourg	49	134	3.3	1.0
Netherlands	5,239	374	7.3	3.4
Norway	1,570	383	n.a.	3.1
Portugal	699	71	n.a.	4.1
Turkey[b]	2,591	58	15.6	9.0
United States	142,700	644	23.3	5.2
Warsaw Pact Countries				
Bulgaria	1,140	128	6.0	2.1
Czechoslovakia	3,520	229	7.6	2.8
East Germany	4,790	285	7.5	6.3
Hungary	1,080	101	3.8	2.1
Poland	4,670	131	6.0	2.4
Romania	1,470	66	4.0	1.4
Soviet Union[b]	222,000	990	n.a.	11-13

[a]Not available.
[b]1979 figure.

Source: 1982 Information Please Almanac.

percent in 1981. However, West European countries and Japan have percentages in the 20 to 40 percent range. Nonetheless, despite its high degree of self-sufficiency in raw materials, the United States must import certain essential items from abroad, and this constitutes a definite vulnerability. Indeed, the U.S. trade deficit reached a record figure in 1982, over $36 billion, and higher deficits are expected in future years.

There are other means for determining a country's economic strength, but detailed discussion of them would exceed the scope of this chapter. Suffice it to reiterate that a strong industrial economy is a very important element in the power status of a country. Not only does it produce the weapons and supplies required for modern warfare, but it also provides important international rewards that flow from the use of consumer goods and capital equipment for border-crossing trade and aid. At the same time, a strong economy offers markets for the goods of other countries. These factors help a country build a strong position of power in the global arena and, at the same time, assure a high standard of living at home with favorable implications for governmental and political stability. These various factors are significant for the formulation of American foreign policy.

Science and Technology Perhaps the most pervasive determinants of a country's strength are its capabilities in scientific research and advanced technology. These determinants can modify the impact of all other elements of power, but their direct effect is most noticeable on economic development, communications, and the offensive and defensive capabilities of the military establishment.

In the field of *economic development*, science and technology play a dramatic role in modifying the traditional factors. Many manufacturing processes have been revolutionized through the application of computer technology. Push-button manufacturing techniques may make it less essential to have a well-educated labor force, a condition that could make it possible to use uneducated laborers in less developed countries to produce sophisticated goods. Science and technology have also produced substitutes for scarce materials. In some instances, these substitute materials, such as industrial fibers and plastics, have become attractive products in their own right, serving new markets.

Radical technological advances have been made in *transportation and communications*. Supersonic planes, economically unprofitable now, may be improved and used increasingly in the future. Trains that move at speeds of 250 miles per hour or more are operating now, and faster ones are on the drawing boards. Hydrofoils and hovercrafts offer rapid transportation across waterways and, perhaps, oceans. The transmission of communications has also benefited from new technology. Pictures can be transmitted by electronic means in a matter of minutes, and space satellites offer instant and very reliable communications across vast distances.

Technological advances have improved the collection of information for intelligence purposes and have already revolutionized the traditional means of diplomacy. Sophisticated bugging devices, miniature tape recorders, and miniature cameras have given intelligence collection agencies new tools for their trade. Observation by space satellites and immediate transmission of these observations have made it very difficult for individual countries to hide military preparations.

In the *military field*, science and technology have influenced the mobility and firepower of the armed forces and thereby drastically increased military capabilities. Missiles with extraordinary destructive power can reach virtually every part of the world. Nuclear power is used to fuel ships that carry nuclear missiles over long distances. At the same time, antiballistic missiles, if they can be refined further, may bolster the defensive capabilities of countries. At present, the full military potential of space satellites and space stations cannot be foreseen, but they undoubtedly will expand the capabilities of those countries that possess them.

To appreciate the international significance of the revolution in science and technology, we must keep in mind the tendency of scientific discoveries and their engineering applications to be cumulative, to accelerate quickly, and to diffuse rapidly from the country of origin. The discovery of nuclear energy and its applications to the generation of electricity are examples. Thus, most of the important discoveries and inventions of the past 300 years are links in a chain of interrelated events. Engineering advances are made faster than individuals and governments can adjust to them. In other words, humanity may well be faced with a "runaway technology."[7] Finally, knowledge of scientific discoveries, new theories, and technological advances can be spread from country to country despite governmental efforts to prevent such movements, since much of the recently gained knowledge can be communicated in the universal language of mathematics, which can easily overcome linguistic barriers.

Countries not possessing advanced technologies may well become technologically dependent on other countries; this may impair their political independence and constitute a serious element of weakness. In turn, scientific and technological advances have become a symbol of national prestige and an indicator of status and rank in international political systems. Much depends on governmental attitude toward supporting research and development activities, and the financial capability of individual governments to extend such support. The private sector can also be a potent source of funds for research and development; subsidiaries of multinational corporations may offer smaller and weaker countries a chance to improve their R&D potential.

The Military Organization   Any evaluation of another country's capabilities must pay careful attention to its military organization. We have already discussed some components of this evaluation: the proportion of the population suitable and available for military services, a high level of economic and industrial development to furnish military material and provide financial support, a relatively large-sized allocation of the national output to the military effort, and last, but certainly not least, a high capability in scientific research and technology. What remains to be assessed in the evaluation of the military organization is the size and quality of the armed forces and the quantity, composition, and quality of military equipment.

Significant factors in assessing the quality of a country's armed forces are *training*, *military education*, and *fighting spirit*. A comprehensive school system must exist for all ranks to provide specialized education in technical matters, tactics, and strategy. To a large extent, then, the quality of a country's armed forces depends on the excellence of its military educational system—and it is no accident that militarily powerful countries present and past have outstanding educational facilities for the armed forces. The United States, Soviet Union, Great Britain, France, and Germany are good examples.

True fighting spirit can make the difference between victory and defeat when all other factors are equal. The Israelis and North Vietnamese have shown such fighting spirit and have prevailed against great odds. If the Soviet Union were to embark on a military adventure toward Western Europe, it is doubtful that the soldiers of its satellite allies in South-Central Europe—that is, Poland, Czechoslovakia, Hungary, Romania, and others—would show much fighting spirit in a protracted struggle, because their commitment to the cause of the war would be questionable.

The tools for any successful employment of the armed forces are *weapons* and the *material* necessary to use these weapons effectively. The proper composition of the arsenal for the power status of a country is at least as important as the quality of materiel. For example, the Soviet Union has a much larger number of conventional submarines than the United States, but the latter leads in ballistic missile submarines and thus has more flexibility and punch in the delivery of strategic nuclear weapons. In contrast, the Soviet Union has more land-based intercontinental ballistic missiles (ICBMs) than the United States; this has so far been balanced by the outfitting of American missiles with so-called multiple independently targetable reentry vehicles (MIRVs), meaning that each ICBM can deliver from three to ten weapons. The Soviet Union, however, has now developed MIRVs and has deployed them on many ICBMs and medium-range missiles targeted at Western Europe, a development that requires a new assessment of the balance of nuclear power between the two countries. A detailed explanation of this issue will be presented in the next chapter.

While the nuclear capabilities of the two superpowers, the United States and the Soviet Union, are indeed overwhelming, four other countries are also members of the nuclear club.* A number of other countries (e.g., Germany, Sweden, and Israel) could become members of this club if they so desired; however, to reach the sophistication of the weapons attained by the superpowers would involve a tremendous investment of funds, scientific talents, and time, which very few countries may be able to afford.

It is important to keep in mind that conventional weapons have not lost their significance. Indeed, in order to escape the dilemma of nuclear weapons and their use in Europe—a dilemma highlighted by the deployment of large numbers of Soviet "theater" nuclear weapons (SS-20s), which can hit any target in Western Europe from Soviet-controlled East European territory—it has been suggested that larger amounts of conventional weapons be secured by the NATO allies rather than introducing more powerful American medium-range weapons such as the cruise and Pershing II missiles.[8] Conventional weapons have made tremendous progress since 1945 in both firepower and range. They have also benefited from the great advances in weapons technol-

---

*The four other countries are China, France, Great Britain, and India.

ogy through the use of high electronic sophistication, and their accuracy in hitting faraway targets is astounding.

The employment of any weapons system can be successful only if the *necessary logistical means* are available. Weapons and troops must be transported to the front and ammunition delivered. Mechanized equipment, such as tanks and personnel carriers, requires gasoline and maintenance. Planes need to be serviced regularly and require large quantities of fuel. For these reasons, it is essential that the logistical system of each military establishment be carefully evaluated when a judgment is made about the strength of a country.

Governmental and Administrative Effectiveness   We will conclude our discussion of interactional variables and the comparative capabilities of third countries with a brief examination of governmental and administrative effectiveness. The degree of such effectiveness is likely to have a bearing on the exercise of a country's capabilities.

One relevant factor is the *speed of decision making*. Considerable delays occur in decisions bearing on American foreign policy. While in national security affairs the executive branch can act with great speed and decisiveness if the need arises, frequent frictions between Congress and the Executive in foreign economic and political matters have often reduced the credibility of the United States in the pursuit of its foreign policy goals.

While decisions can always be rendered quickly in dictatorships, in some parliamentary democracies the close cooperation between the legislature and the Executive makes it possible to arrive at a policy decision quickly. Such efficiency in governmental decision making as exists in Great Britain usually requires a two-party system and a high degree of party discipline. It means that the Executive, which is drawn from the ranks of the majority party, can count on the support of his or her party in most governmental decisions, including those pertaining to foreign policy. In contrast, multiparty parliamentary democracies, such as in the Netherlands and Italy, have much greater difficulty in arriving at decisions promptly, because coalition governments must bargain with the leaders of various constituent parties for support of each specific decision.

The *attitude of the people and of elites* toward a particular government in power or toward the governmental system in general also affects its performance and may raise the question of the *legitimacy of its authority*. When the population has confidence in the governmental system and accepts it as the proper decision-making unit, governmental authority is legitimized; however, in the event that large segments of the general public and of certain elites lose this confidence and refuse to accept its authority, the country is seriously weakened.

Finally, a few words need to be said about the *administrative efficiency of government*. The general style and performance of the totality of civil service in a country plays an important role in determining the strength of a country. Civil services, known for their corruptibility and inefficiencies, cast serious doubt on responsible government action. Waste of time and frequent moonlighting of civil servants, as in Italy, create unfavorable impressions on the population and reduce the power potential of a country. In contrast, a well-trained, efficient, neutral bureaucracy with a strong commitment to public service bolsters a country's strength. Great Britain and West Germany are outstanding examples of countries where this is true. While we must recognize that bureaucratic aspirations and politics play a role in all civil services, the greater the virtues of a civil service as just described and the more a civil service can reflect the objectives of the political leadership in its activities, the stronger is that country's potential power.

SYSTEMIC VARIABLES AND FOREIGN POLICY

Persistence and Change in the Politicomilitary System

The politicomilitary international system over time has assumed various constellations that have affected American foreign policy formulation. Perhaps the most significant constellation in terms of the peace of the world during the period since World War II has been *the bipolar system of nuclear deterrence* between the two superpowers. If this system were to disintegrate by either the United States or the Soviet Union gaining the capability of a first nuclear strike or making a technological breakthrough in the field the *effective* antiballistic missiles, the peace of the world would be in immediate jeopardy. In such an event, the implications for American foreign policymakers would be enormous. Even the possibility of these scenarios becoming reality casts a shadow over the policymaking process and gives rise to potent variables influencing the determination of foreign (and domestic) policies.

Another constellation of the international system with important consequences for American policymaking since the early 1970s is the *tripolar system among the United States, the Soviet Union, and the People's Republic of China* after President Nixon and Henry Kissinger opened the way for diplomatic relations with that country in 1972. It is a limited balance-of-power system in which close cooperation between China—the weakest member of the system— with either the United States or the Soviet Union would tend to restrict the other superpower in its policy discretion. The basic reason is that in such a system the capabilities of the members are more dispersed than in a bipolar system. As more states become parties in a balance-of-power system, the more dispersed are apt to be their capabilities, and the less is the likelihood that the system, especially if loosely organized, can be rapidly and radically changed by a single development.[10]

It is conceivable that the international politicomilitary system could change increasingly into a truly *polycentric system* in which additional power centers would emerge throughout the world. One such center could be Western Europe if the ten member states of the European Community* were prepared to allocate the huge amounts of money to build up British and French nuclear capabilities. However, the chances are slim that such a buildup would occur, as it would seriously upset the balance of power within the Community and thereby would offend the national sensitivities of the smaller member states. Rather, the EC countries have been content to develop the Community into a superior "civilian" power; their priority has been and is likely to continue to be to strengthen their economic development and to hold military expenditures to those necessary to assure conventional force protection, with the United States providing the nuclear umbrella.

Brazil and India might have ambitions to become regional power centers, but their economic bases, despite great progress in the Brazilian case, are likely to be insufficient to achieve adequate military power status because their nuclear weapons potential, still uncertain with respect to Brazil, could be increased only marginally. For Israel, clearly a strong regional military power, labor force is a limiting factor in the future. Hence the international system to emerge in the future may be best characterized as a *"bipolycentric"* system,[11] in which, in addition to the superpowers, other countries attain an "upper middle power" status. Some of the countries may be allied with the superpowers (e.g., the EC with the United States and East Germany with the Soviet Union), while others seek to remain basically nonaligned (e.g., India). Whatever the system that emerges, it cannot but influence American foreign policy formulation and therefore must be regarded as either an independent or an intervening variable for the explanation of policy.

The Global Economic System

The global economic system during this century has generally followed capital-istic, free-market principles. However, since the mid-1960s, the developing countries have demanded changes with increasing stridency; they would like to see the emergence of a *New International Economic Order (NIEO)* and hope to achieve this through the United Nations and associated organizations such as the U.N. Conference on Trade and Development (UNCTAD). The NIEO would replace the interplay of free-market forces, with its emphasis on supply and demand as the regulators for prices of goods and on the sanctity of private property as the basis for the international exchange of goods and capital, with a

---

*West Germany, France, Great Britain, Italy, the Benelux countries (Belgium, the Nether-lands, and Luxembourg), Ireland, Denmark, and Greece.

system that would disregard these principles in favor of whatever would promote the development of the less developed countries. This might mean mechanisms that would bring about price levels of goods at variance with supply and demand and the transfer of property such as technological know-how (patents) without compensation. In other words, the global economy would operate mainly in such ways that would enhance the interests of the Third World.*

The push for a new global economic system is a major challenge to American foreign policy and illustrates the influence that changes or potential changes in the global economic system have on American policymaking. Another example may be an increasing movement toward protectionism in international trade and away from the commitment of most countries during the post-World War II period to increased trade liberalization.

Changes in the Global Physical Environment

Finally, a few comments need to be made about the impact of changes in the global physical environment on American foreign policy formulation. American foreign policymakers addressed the problem of *lower crude oil reserves* by helping to set up and participating in the International Energy Agency (IEA). The IEA is committed to developing alternative energy sources but also has an emergency program to allocate the use of oil for industrialized countries in the event of serious shortages.

The increase in *pollution* is a worldwide problem, but the treatment of this problem varies from country to country. Air and water pollution originating in one country and entering another is a self-evident issue that foreign policymakers may have to address, but other problems are less evident. In the majority of the advanced industrialized countries, the polluter pays for the installation of antipollution equipment, which raises the cost of production and ultimately the price of the goods produced. In many Third World countries, pollution is ignored, reducing the comparative cost for production of the same goods. This discrepancy in dealing with pollution may lead to distortion of international trade, as exports of the product by a Third World country may gain price advantages in a competitive market. Hence, under such circumstances, pollution can also become an important foreign policy issue for the American government, requiring adequate policy responses. Again, it may constitute either an independent or an intervening variable and, as such, will aid in the explanation of particular U.S. foreign policies.

---

*Details of the NIEO will be examined in Chapter 12.

SUMMARY

The discussion in this chapter suggests the manifold and at times crucial influences that the international situation and specifically the comparative capabilities of states with which the United States interacts can have on the formulation of American foreign policies and perhaps on their implementation. It also points up the complexity of the proper analysis and evaluation of these capabilities—an important factor, since such assessments become part of the foreign policy decision-making process. Systemic changes also need to be evaluated continually, and their impact must be taken into account in the formulation of policy. All this compounds the difficulty of identifying independent and intervening variables as sources of explaining American foreign policy and determining the potency of individual variables.

Empirical research methods are available to measure many of the variables discussed in the preceding pages, but, as always, it is difficult to determine their particular potency, which influences the formulation of specific policies. Idiosyncratic and institutional factors clearly have an important bearing on how the different variables are evaluated by policymakers, and the outside observer can only make an informed judgment on how intensively the variables considered (or perhaps ignored) have contributed to the final policy product.

NOTES

1. William C. Vocke, *American Foreign Policy: An Analytical Approach* (New York: Free Press, 1976), p. 231, calls these variables "relational." James N. Rosenau, *The Scientific Study of Foreign Policy*, rev. and enlarged ed. (New York: Nichols, 1980), pp. 364–366, considers all international variables as "systemic."
2. *Times-Picayune* (New Orleans), September 11, 1982.
3. Rosenau, *The Scientific Study of Foreign Policy*, p. 365.
4. Sir Halford J. Mackinder, *Democratic Ideals and Reality* (New York: Holt, 1919), p. 150. An American Admiral, Alfred T. Mahan, considered sea power to be the most important determinant for national power strategy. Refer to his book, *The Influence of Sea Power upon History* (Boston: Little, Brown, 1918).
5. A.F.K. Organski, *World Politics* (New York: Alfred A. Knopf, 1958), p. 137.
6. Hans J. Morgenthau, *Politics among Nations*, 5th ed. (New York: Alfred A. Knopf, 1973), p. 126.
7. Harold Sprout and Margaret Sprout, *Foundations of International Politics* (Princeton, N.J.: Van Nostrand, 1962), p. 216.
8. *Times-Picayune* (New Orleans), September 14, 1982.
9. Morgenthau, *Politics among Nations*, p. 126.
10. Rosenau, *The Scientific Study of Foreign Policy*, p. 364.
11. John Spanier, *Games Nations Play* (New York: Praeger, 1975).

THE IMPLEMENTATION OF
FOREIGN POLICY

CHAPTER 8

The Instruments for Policy Implementation

The formulation of foreign policy goals and of appropriate courses of action regarding a particular international issue does not assure the attainment of these goals. The crucial link is implementation, which consists of a process of interaction between setting goals and actions geared to achieve these goals. As Pressman and Wildavsky put it:

> Implementation . . . is the ability to forge subsequent links in the causal chain so as to obtain the desired results.[1]

The selection of proper instruments for the implementation can be crucial for the success or failure of a particular policy. The range of instruments is large. The most common is *diplomacy*, which is carried out chiefly, but not exclusively, by foreign service officers assigned to American embassies, legations, and missions abroad backed up and guided by other officials in the Department of State. Other instruments for policy implementation are the use of (1) various *economic measures*, some friendly and others hostile, (2) *psychological warfare* means, especially propaganda, (3) *political warfare measures*, some clandestine, and (4) as a last resort, *military action*. In some instances, intergovernmental organizations may be utilized for the implementation of policies. NATO and the Organization of American States (OAS) are examples. In the aftermath of the U.S. military intervention in the Dominican Republic in April 1965, the OAS was utilized for the formation of a multinational force to soften the sting of "Yankee" interference in a Latin American

137

country.* The United Nations has also been used for various policy implementation purposes.

Most of the instruments are nonviolent. Some of the political warfare measures can be violent but may not employ organized armed forces in actual warfare. The ultimate instrument, which is violent, is the conduct of warfare, which can take several forms.

Since the appropriate choice of instruments is crucial for the success of particular foreign policies, a continuing evaluation process of policy implementation is likely to enhance the quality of American foreign policy. This evaluation must address the question of instrument selection as well as the degree of implementation effectiveness.

DIPLOMACY

Embassies as we know them now date from the middle of the fifteenth century and had their origin in northern Italy where, in 1455, the Duke of Milan announced his intention to establish the first permanent embassy abroad. The legal bases for modern diplomatic practice, including the rules for the classification of ranks, came into being with the Congress of Vienna in 1815 and were finalized in their present form by the Vienna Convention on Diplomatic Relations in 1961. They provide for three top ranks in the following order:

1. Ambassadors or papal nuncios, who represent their heads of state** and are accredited to the heads of state of the country in which they serve.
2. Ministers, envoys, and internuncios, similarly accredited.
3. Chargés d'affaires, who are the foreign service officers temporarily in charge of a diplomatic mission in the absence of the ambassador or minister.

Seniority at a capital is determined by the date of accreditation and rank, and the senior ambassador in a particular capital is known as the *doyen* or dean of the diplomatic corps.

Below the three top diplomatic ranks we find a hierarchy of lower grades and titles. Large embassies may have ministers ranking below the ambassador; this is merely a title, however, and ministers do not represent their head of state as does the ambassador. In most other embassies, legations, or missions, the highest ranking diplomat usually has the title of councillor.

The American ambassador in the capital of a particular country is the head

---

*For a complete discussion of this event, see Chapter 12.

**In the United States this is the president. In parliamentary democracies, such as Great Britain or France, this may be the monarch or the president.

of the *country team* and in this position has the responsibility for coordinating and supervising the activities of all U.S. officials stationed within the country. Even if an official of another department should have a higher comparative rank than the ambassador—for example, that of a major general in a military assistance advisory group (MAAG), it is the ambassador who is in charge and who represents the president of the United States. This arrangement has the purpose of ensuring a unified and coherent policy in a particular country. It also assigns to the State Department a dominant voice in the management of foreign affairs that may not conform to the Washington realities of power distribution with respect to foreign policymaking. Hence the theoretically sound concept of the country team has encountered difficulties in the field. Only if the ambassador in a country has high qualities of leadership and extensive knowledge in foreign affairs is he or she able to overcome the difficulties and mold the country team into an effective force.

The functions of diplomats abroad can be classified as *representation*, *observation*, and *negotiation*. In general, all functions are designed to promote the attainment of the foreign policy goals of the diplomat's government; however, representation includes a number of tasks, such as the protection of citizens in legal disputes abroad, that cannot be linked directly to the pursuit of specific foreign policy objectives.

Representation

Representational functions include many ceremonial duties, such as the American ambassador's attending in France the annual Fourteenth of July celebration of the birth of the first French republic. Chiefs of diplomatic missions and other American foreign service officers must participate in a large number of official functions of the host country, such as receptions and state dinners, and at the same time entertain high government officials and other leading personalities in the capital where they were stationed. The manner in which they entertain frequently reflects the prestige of their country. Entertainment serves also as an important means of informal intercourse among diplomats and is a convenient forum for conducting various kinds of business, including the transmission and acquisition of information, observation, and even subtle negotiation. Thus the lavish cocktail parties diplomats give and attend should not be viewed as evidence of a penchant for luxury but as performance of duty.

The function of representation also includes formal visits to the foreign ministry of the host country and perhaps even to the prime minister or president to convey information, expressions of concern, and requests of the diplomat's government. Among the information provided may be explanations of new policies initiated by Washington. At the same time, American diplomats may be called to the foreign ministries or the leaders of the host government to receive complaints or messages for their own top officials. A recent example of this is the crisis in Lebanon in the summer of 1982 when U.S. Ambassador Lewis was frequently called to Israeli Prime Minister Menachim Begin's office in Jerusalem to receive complaints about American policy statements.

In contrast, ambassadors of foreign countries may be called to the State Department or occasionally may visit the White House to provide explanations for their countries' policies or receive complaints about actions of their governments. Soviet Ambassador Dobrinyn, whose assignment to the United States goes back to the Kennedy administration, has had many occasions to talk not only to the secretary of state, but also to Presidents Kennedy, Johnson, Nixon, Ford, and Carter. Thus diplomatic representatives serve as official mouthpieces and message carriers for their governments. In the performance of these tasks, they must use a variety of techniques, such as persuasion, veiled threats, or sympathetic listening, to achieve maximum effectiveness.

Observation

Diplomats function not only as the mouthpieces of their governments but also as their eyes and ears. Observation is a major task of U.S. foreign service officers, who thereby become important cogs in the American information-gathering machinery. To introduce as much as possible professional judgment into the observation function, military, commercial, agricultural, and labor attachés are assigned to U.S. embassies and other diplomatic missions. They are civil servants of the respective services and departments. Army, air force, and naval attachés collect information about armaments, military organizations, and war planes, commercial attachés about industrial developments and economic trends, and other attachés about their own areas of specialization. They may carry out their observation functions by traveling about the country to which they are assigned—sometimes a hazardous undertaking in Communist countries—or they may pick up information by visiting ministries and industrial fairs, or by conversing at cocktail parties.

Because the reports of diplomats on their observations are often significant raw material for the production of intelligence, they normally must fill out special reporting forms that systematize their observations and include judgments as to the reliability of sources and the substance of the observations reported. Thus the diplomatic corps takes on the color of an elegant and yet sub rosa spy organization. This generally accepted practice had its origin in the Middle Ages. In fact, the purpose of the first permanent embassies of the Italian city-state was to obtain timely information about impending aggression by stronger states. Because of this mission, diplomats were often regarded as a serious liability for the receiving state when the use of embassies began to spread in Europe during the sixteenth century.

Negotiation

The most important function of diplomats is negotiation, which may pertain to formal long-term bilateral agreements or to requests for short-term support of a particular policy of the diplomat's home country. The subject of the agreements being negotiated may vary: they may be comprehensive economic treaties or tariff agreements, arrangements for cultural-exchange programs, extradition treaties, consular arrangements aimed at establishing consulates in the respective countries, the conclusion of alliances, and the like.

Short-term requests for policy support are exemplified by American endeavors in many capitals in 1971 to seek support for the U.S. policy of two Chinas, the People's Republic of China and the Republic of China on Taiwan. American ambassadors in many capitals urged the governments where they were accredited to cast a favorable vote in the United Nations General Assembly. At times, this necessitated some concessions on the part of the United States, but these were considered an acceptable quid pro quo. In the end, however, the American efforts failed; the People's Republic of China assumed the official representation of the Chinese people in the United Nations, and the Chiang Kai-shek regime was expelled.

Many books and articles have been written about the art of negotiation from the times of Machiavelli to the contemporary period.[2] Basically, negotiation involves a process in which a delicate balance is sought between giving what is asked and obtaining what is wanted.[3] The negotiation process must therefore begin with demands that are calculated to match in their excessiveness the perceived excessiveness in the opponent's position. If the process is carried out skillfully, the end result may be to "split the difference" and to conclude an agreement that is in the middle rather than one that reflects the "lowest common denominator." Somewhere a compromise must be found between the bargainer's extreme positions. Every kind of persuasion, including withholding benefits or threatening harmful actions, may be used to influence the results of the negotiations, but the last vestiges of congeniality must not be swept away, because the exchange of quid pro quos will be the basis for final agreement. Patience is therefore a great virtue, especially in negotiations with Communist countries. These negotiations are often extremely tough and drawn out, and prove a challenge for the most skillful of Western negotiators, as the Vietnam peace negotiations, the Strategic Arms Limitation Talks (SALT), and the negotiations about the Strategic Arms Reduction Talks (START) have demonstrated.[4]

Henry Kissinger, who was involved in the Vietnamese peace and SALT negotiations, characterizes his views of and approach to international negotiations as follows:

> The opening of a complicated negotiation is like the beginning of an arranged marriage. The partners know that the formalities will soon be stripped away as they discover each other's real attributes. Neither party can yet foretell at what point necessity will transform itself into acceptance; when the abstract desire for progress will leave at least residues of understanding; which disagreement will, by the act of being overcome, illuminate the as-yet undiscovered sense of community and which will lead to an impasse destined to rend the relationship forever. The future being

mercifully veiled, the parties attempt what they might not dare did they know what was ahead.

Almost invariably I spent the first session of a new negotiation in educating myself. I almost never put forward a proposal. Rather, I sought to understand the intangibles in the position of my interlocutor and to gauge the scope as well as the limits of probable concessions. And I made a considerable effort to leave no doubt about our fundamental approach. Only romantics think they can prevail in negotiations by trickery; only pedants believe in the advantage of obfuscation. In a society of sovereign states, an agreement will be maintained only if *all* partners consider it in their interest. They must have a sense of participation in the result. The art of diplomacy is not to outsmart the other side but to convince it either of common interests or of penalties if an impasse continues.[5]

Studies of U.S.-Soviet disarmament negotiations in the early 1960s have revealed a greater flexibility on the part of American than of Soviet negotiators. Eighty-two percent of the concessions made by the Americans were made during the first third of the negotiations, whereas the Soviet Union made 75 percent of its concessions in the last third.[6]

In contrast to bilateral negotiations, multilateral issues, such as international trade or disarmament, usually require special conferences or frameworks. An example is the so-called Kennedy Round of multilateral negotiations for the reduction of tariffs. These were conducted by fifty-five countries within the framework of the General Agreement on Tariffs and Trade (GATT) in Geneva, and the most influential participants were the United States and the European Economic Community—EEC, with Great Britain, Japan, and the Scandinavian countries also taking part.* These negotiations lasted from 1964 to the middle of 1967 and were characterized by very tough bargaining tactics and strategies.

The Kennedy Round negotiations had all the trappings of a high-stakes poker game, and every possible tactic—including threats of complete withdrawal from the negotiations—was used to influence their outcome. In addition to efforts by governments, nongovernmental groups were used to exercise subtle influences on similar groups in the member states sharing the same interests. For example the Crotonville Conference of nearly 100 American business executives and government leaders, held early in 1966, recommended that the American chambers of commerce be asked to appeal to their European counterparts for their vigorous support of the Kennedy Round negotiations. Private contacts were also maintained between farm groups in the United States and in the European Community, and joint meetings were held between American and European farmers on several occasions.

Similar strategies and tactics were also employed during the so-called

---

Note: Great Britain and Denmark joined the EEC in 1973 (see Chapter 11).

Tokyo Round of negotiations on tariff and nontariff barrier (NTB) reductions. Begun in 1974 following the passage of the Trade Reform Act of 1974 (signed into law in 1975), these negotiations, officially known as multilateral trade negotiations (MTN), were successfully concluded in 1979. More will be said about these negotiations later in this chapter.

Diplomatic Behavior in IGOs

With the emergence of growing numbers of IGOs, individual countries have adopted the practice of establishing diplomatic missions to these organizations, which have played increasingly larger roles on the international scene. Hence every member of the United Nations has a diplomatic mission accredited to this organization in New York, although smaller countries sometimes combine this function with their embassies in Washington. The United States has a large diplomatic mission accredited to the United Nations; moreover, the American representative to this IGO, reflecting the prestige of this assignment, enjoys cabinet rank and is at times asked to participate in National Security Council sessions. American diplomatic representatives are also assigned to the European Community, the North Atlantic Treaty Organization (NATO), the Organization for Economic Cooperation and Development (OECD), the Organization of American States (OAS), and other regional IGOs.

Diplomatic practice in these IGOs differs from that found in U.S. embassies in world capitals. While the role of a diplomat in the latter follows the tradition of straightforward representation of U.S. interests, the role of a diplomat assigned to an IGO such as the United Nations tends to be more that of a parliamentarian. Issues in the United Nations are usually decided by a vote in the General Assembly, the Security Council, or other decision-making bodies; therefore, the game is to find a majority, simple or qualified, for the attainment of U.S. foreign policy goals. As a consequence, the tactics and strategies that diplomats in the United Nations must use involve personal contacts, logrolling, and complex bargaining with payoffs for various countries willing to cosponsor or support particular resolutions. Hence, to be a good diplomat in this environment means to have the qualities of a successful parliamentary politician, because, in accordance with the U.N. Charter, it is a *vote* that decides a matter in dispute.

Another factor producing a new element in U.N. diplomacy is the easy communication among diplomatic representatives in the corridors of the United Nations building, and the many committee meetings of the General Assembly and the Economic and Social Council. Contacts between countries can be made easily and informally, and problems can be thrashed out without the constraints of traditional diplomacy. In contrast, the high visibility of statements and actions in the General Assembly and the Security Council, while pleasing to those who advocate "spotlight" or "open" diplomacy, may cause rigidity of positions and thus render delicate international problems more difficult to solve.

Conditions similar to those in the United Nations and its various specialized agencies also prevail in the frequent conferences convened under the auspices of the United Nations or by a number of states for special purposes, such as the Conference on Security and Cooperation in Europe (CSCE), which took place in Helsinki and Geneva. The stakes may be very high. An example of the latter is the U.N. Conference on the Law of the Sea (UNCLOS), which has had several sessions in different cities over a number of years. In view of the high stakes involved and the length of the conferences (several weeks), the demands on the stamina of the participating U.S. foreign service officers are severe. They may have to attend plenary sessions and various committee meetings and make the informal contacts necessary for logrolling tactics. Such "conference diplomacy" is sometimes carried out without the benefit of rapid communications with Washington, although the United States usually has embassies or consulates in the towns where conferences are held.

The Depreciation of Diplomacy

The often spectacular, brilliant, and always important role diplomats have played in the international arena in pursuit of their government's foreign policy goals began to decline following World War I and has further suffered since the end of World War II. There are two major reasons for this:

1. High-speed transportation has made it possible for chief executives and secretaries of state and defense to travel anywhere in the world in a matter of hours; therefore, bilateral personal diplomacy between these individuals and multilateral summit conferences have preempted many of the traditional activities of diplomats for the implementation of foreign policy goals.
2. High-speed communications between the leaders of governments (hot lines) and among the foreign ministries and their diplomatic representatives all over the world have often reduced ambassadors or ministers of larger countries to glorified errand runners and transmitters of routine information.

This development does not mean that the work of the diplomatic staff in the U.S. embassies has become superfluous. Many of the functions still performed by the staff require careful personal attention, and the interpersonal relations an ambassador can develop with important governmental and political leaders in the assigned country are important. However, these changes have caused a recognizable erosion of morale among foreign service officers as has the continuing tendency to make political appointments to ambassadorial posts rather than to rely on highly qualified foreign service officers for such positions.

Before frequent personal diplomacy by chief executives and foreign ministers became popular after World War II, the groundwork for this development was laid by the claim, voiced by Woodrow Wilson and other eloquent political leaders, that secret diplomacy was inherently bad. It was asserted that the secret dealings of diplomats were reponsible, at least in part, for the outbreak of World War I. Secret negotiations were an evil residue from an aristocratic world; a lasting peace could be achieved only when diplomatic negotiations were open to the scrutiny of a watchful public.

Whether this judgment is correct is uncertain. There is a widespread feeling that difficult international problems can be solved by meetings on the highest level under the fanfare of the news media, although the meetings between President Eisenhower and top Soviet, British, and French leaders in 1955, between President Johnson and Premier Kosygin in 1967, and between President Carter and Leonid Brezhnev in 1979 offer little evidence to support this contention. In contrast, the travels and activities of Henry Kissinger, often prepared and sometimes carried out in secrecy, were quite successful (although some of his "spectaculars" have been short-lived). One can conclude that summit meetings can be successful if they are prepared with care and secrecy, and the outcome is predetermined by agreements among the prospective participants.

ECONOMIC INSTRUMENTS

In view of the growing economic interdependence of the world, the economic tools for policy implementation have to be examined in some detail. These tools need not be used only to attain American foreign economic policy goals, but can also be used to achieve national security and political objectives as well. They assume special strategic importance when the export of weapons, nuclear power plants, and fissionable materials are involved. Economic instruments may be employed as rewards for favorable international actions by other states, as punishment for adverse actions, or as a means of inducing a country to adopt a different behavior. They may also be used to persuade desired behavior by multinational corporations (MNCs), either by providing incentives for foreign investment or by imposing constraints on the operations of MNC subsidiaries.

The most frequently applied economic device for policy implementation is adjustment of the *tariffs* of the United States, which stipulate the amount of duty payable for the importation of goods from foreign countries. The effect of customs duties is to raise the price of imported products. In most instances, tariffs are used to protect domestic manufacturers, but they also serve to raise revenues. If U.S. tariffs are reduced on specific items, the countries that are the leading suppliers of these items will benefit as more of these items are imported. If tariffs on particular goods are increased, the countries manufacturing these goods are apt to suffer.

Conventional Measures

From 1879 to 1934 tariffs steadily rose. Between 1913 and 1925 alone, the average percentage in duties assessed by sixteen of the leading industrial countries on the value of imported goods (*ad valorem* duties) had increased by one-third. In 1930, the Smoot-Hawley Tariff of the United States stood at a general *ad valorem* level of 41.5 percent. As a consequence, American exports, which amounted to over $2.5 billion in the first half of 1929, fell below $1 billion by the same period in 1932. Other nations, of course, had resorted to retaliatory measures, and hence, tariff walls all over the world rose higher and higher, with the result that international trade took a nose dive.

A reversal of the protectionist economic foreign policy of the United States took place in 1934 when the government committed itself to an expansion of trade through a *reciprocal trade program* aimed at lowering tariffs worldwide. This program, technically known as the Trade Agreement Act of 1934, was renewed and modified at intervals during subsequent years until 1974. It permitted the president to reduce American tariffs provided that other countries made equivalent concessions on American goods.

The Most-Favored-Nation Clause   In addition to the policy of reciprocity embedded in the American legislation, the United States based its policy also on the most-favored-nation (MFN) clause, which has been inserted increasingly into commercial agreements concluded with foreign countries. This clause provides that any reduction in duties stipulated in a commercial agreement between the United States and another country will also be made available to any third country with which the United States has MFN-type relations. The most-favored-nation clause is also known as the principle of *nondiscrimination* and has become a cornerstone of American foreign economic policy. Denial of MFN treatment to the imports from another country can be used by the United States as an expression of displeasure with an action or nonaction taken by that country. For example, the United States denied MFN treatment to the Soviet Union in the 1970s, because it disapproved Soviet policies impeding the emigration of Russian Jews.

The General Agreement on Tariffs and Trade (GATT)   The principles of *reciprocity* and *nondiscrimination* are also the foundation of the General Agreement on Tariffs and Trade (GATT), which was drafted in 1947 and put into effect in 1948. The United States was an original signatory of this international treaty, whose purpose was to remove, as far as possible, restrictions on trade between the contracting parties. Almost all non-Communist advanced countries have become members of GATT, and a number of Communist countries—including Czechoslovakia, Cuba, Poland, and Yugoslavia—participate in certain phases of the GATT machinery as well. Tariff concessions made between two parties to GATT extend to all other contracting parties as the result of the most-favored-nation principle. An important exception are customs unions and free-trade areas, within which tariffs are reduced to zero. The benefits to the participants of the customs unions and free-trade areas, which flow from the elimination of tariffs, do not have to be offered to other GATT members.*

Nontariff Barriers   A second economic tool for policy implementation is the imposition of nontariff barriers (NTBs). These barriers stem from a variety of national laws, procedures, and regulations that tend to impair or nullify the reduction in duties for imports. They include laws giving preference to national sources of supply for official purchase (e.g., the Buy American Act), labeling regulations, health standards, quantitative restrictions, licensing controls, anti-dumping measures, tax discrimination between domestic and foreign goods, and customs valuations not reflecting actual costs. In terms of inducing desired behavior on the part of a foreign country, NTBs produce effects much more quickly than do increased tariffs. Conversely, lowering or eliminating certain quantitative restrictions for the imports from a particular country can be a significant reward.

During the Tokyo Round of multilateral trade negotiations, which was carried out during the latter half of the 1970s, major emphasis was placed on the dismantlement or at least reduction of NTBs. However, success in achieving these objective was rather modest, although a comprehensive code on a number of NTBs was drawn up. It is too early to judge how well different countries including the United States will comply with this code.

In order to reduce "excessive" imports from foreign countries that might upset or injure American producers, the U.S. government has resorted to so-called *orderly marketing agreements (OMAs)*, which are bilateral international agreements in which the exporting country voluntarily restricts the flow of goods shipped to the United States. Such OMAs have been concluded with Japan regarding the import of Japanese television sets and automobiles into the United States. The West European countries exporting steel to the United States have also offered to restrict their shipments of particular steel products, but U.S. steel producers so far have not accepted this offer, claiming that the European companies are selling their products on the American market below cost ("dumping"), and acceptance of this offer would therefore not remedy the basic problem of the damaging steel imports. If the allegation of "dumping" is

---

* A number of countries in various parts of the world have taken advantage of this provision and have created regional customs unions and free-trade areas. Examples of customs unions include, of course, the European Economic Community (or European Common Market), the Central American Common Market, and the Andean Common Market along the northern and western coasts of South America. Examples of free-trade areas are the European Free Trade Association (EFTA), which has been partly dismantled with the entry of Great Britain and Denmark into the European Community, and the Latin American Free Trade Association. The original members of EFTA were Great Britain, Denmark, Norway, Sweden, Austria, Switzerland, and Portugal.

substantiated, the U.S. government can impose special duties on the imports of steel products in question, and the American steel manufacturers would be allowed to claim monetary compensation for resulting injuries to their business.

The increasing utilization of OMAs reflects a trend toward protectionism. Some American industries such as the producers of automobiles, steel, machine tools, and textiles contend that protectionist measures are a matter of survival. A poll of the Opinion Research Corporation in the spring of 1983 suggests that 69 percent of the Americans support import barriers.[7] Successive administrations have attempted to stem the protectionist tide. President Reagan has praised the virtues of free trade but has not been able to resist the accommodation of particular interests. Protectionist pressures are likely to rise as the United States moves toward presidential elections in 1984. Yet there are also very sound arguments for pursuing the free-trade route. The cost of many products increases for Americans when competition from imported goods is eliminated or curtailed. The jobs of many American workers depend on U.S. exports, which now comprise 12 percent of the GNP. If the world as a whole were to slip further into protectionism, the budding global economic recovery may become stymied, with very damaging effects for both industrially advanced and less-developed countries.

Subsidies   Another economic instrument in the promotion of foreign policy goals is the granting of subsidies to national producers to enable them to compete better on the international market. Such subsidies may take the form of outright payments, lower freight rates for the transportation of exports, higher internal taxes on foreign-produced goods, or tax credits or delays. Although these practices may violate certain provisions of the GATT, some of the GATT member states have engaged in them. For example, the Common Market has paid extraordinarily high subsidies for the exportation of wheat, impairing American wheat exports, and the United States has permitted the creation of special export companies whose tax liabilities can be deferred.

Currency Regulations and Restrictions   Currency regulations and restrictions on capital flows are also economic means of implementing foreign policy. Whenever the balance of payments of a country shows a deficit and it becomes necessary to stop the outflow of capital and other funds from that country, currency regulations and restrictions on capital movements constitute effective instruments of foreign economic policy. Because they impede the importation of goods into the country and the flow of tourists to other countries, and because capital investments abroad are reduced if not completely stopped, they have a variety of adverse effects on other countries. The United States, during the early 1970s, imposed temporary and "voluntary" restrictions on the outflow of private capital and has used the 1971 devaluation of the dollar to reverse its negative balance of payments and trade balance.

Clearly both nontariff barriers and currency regulations are much harsher instruments than changes in tariffs. Foreign manufacturers may accept a very low profit for their products to overcome a higher tariff but can do nothing against quantitative restrictions and currency regulations that prohibit their prospective customers from buying any of their goods at any price. An MNC can get around such restrictions by establishing manufacturing facilities in various countries, so that its products are treated the same as those of national manufacturing firms.

Economic Warfare Measures

Preempting and Stockpiling In times of war, it is often necessary to ensure a plentiful supply of critical materials. This can be done by preempting large quantities of the needed materials abroad before other countries can buy them. Examples are the large-scale purchases of rubber by the United States during World War II, and the purchase and stockpiling of other strategic materials.

Embargo Another economic warfare tool is the imposition of an embargo, which is the partial or total prohibition on trade with another state. American embargoes on trade with the People's Republic of China between 1949 and the early 1970s, and with Cuba, have been examples of total embargo. The American and NATO policies of prohibiting the sale of strategic goods to the Communist states in Eastern Europe constitute a partial embargo. In many instances, the effects of an embargo can be circumvented by sending prohibited goods to third countries, which then resell them to the nation against which the embargo is being enforced. This has been done in Europe to circumvent the NATO embargo and was also done in Hong Kong to mitigate the embargo against China. A more recent example of the difficulty of enforcing embargoes is the unsuccessful attempt by the Reagan administration to halt the use and export of American technology for the construction of the gas pipeline between the Soviet Union to Western Europe to which we have referred earlier.

A more subtle form of an embargo, in fact not utilizing the term at all, is the imposition of *export controls*. For example, the United States during the last few years has utilized export controls for certain agricultural commodities to assure sufficiency of these foodstuffs for the American market. At the same time, a selective imposition of these controls, either in the form of licensing or by requiring that prospective sales be reported, can become a tool of economic warfare when it is directed against certain countries. The threat of such selective imposition provides leverage against countries that may threaten or apply embargoes of raw materials against the United States, or that form price cartels for the purpose of raising the cost of resources under their control. Petroleum is of course the outstanding example of our times; the Organization of Petroleum-Exporting Countries (OPEC)* has been utilized by the oil producers in the

---

*Current members of OPEC include Algeria, Ecuador, Gabon, Indonesia, Iran, Iraq, Kuwait, Libya, Nigeria, Qatar, Saudi Arabia, the United Arab Emirates, and Venezuela.

Middle East and in other parts of the world, especially Venezuela and Nigeria, to increase the price of oil far beyond the cost of producing it. Other countries endowed with natural resources, especially minerals, have attempted to form their own price cartels and emulate the success of OPEC. For example, Jamaica, a major bauxite producer, has led the effort to form a bauxite cartel. Countries with copper resources have formed an Intergovernmental Council of Copper-Exporting Countries (CIPEC), which has attempted to devise a collective support system for the world market price of copper. Whether this kind of collaboration among countries to raise and maintain prices for these and other natural resources will be successful cannot be determined at this moment. The prevailing oil glut that has caused considerable disarry within OPEC, including lower and sometimes disparate petroleum prices, casts doubt on the efforts of bauxite and copper producers, at least for the 1980s.

Boycott   Another economic warfare measure that can be very harmful is the boycott, which is the refusal to buy goods produced in a given foreign country. Sanctions by the United Nations include boycotts, but experience has shown that the self-interest of importers in many countries is so great that they will not obey the ordered boycott. The boycott imposed by the United Nations against Rhodesia is a case in point; in fact, the United States legislated an exception on chrome shipments from that country through the so-called Byrd Amendment, which was later rescinded in 1977. The U.S. boycott of the Olympic Games in Moscow in 1980, designed to pressure the Soviet Union to withdraw its forces from Afghanistan—which it invaded in December 1979—although not a strictly economic measure, did not succeed in achieving its objective and reflects the difficulty of devising a truly effective boycott.

Penetration by MNCs   Economic warfare may also be employed in a very mild and subtle manner through the penetration of foreign markets and control of foreign strategic industries by multinational enterprises headquartered in a particular country. Penetration of West European markets and control of certain industries in some European countries by American MNCs is an example. IBM and Exxon have been in the forefront of such efforts. There may be "reverse economic penetration" as well, as indicated by the increasing establishments of European and Japanese MNC subsidiaries in the United States. Well-known examples are the manufacturing facilities built by Volkswagen and Honda. When large-scale economic interpenetration is accomplished by MNCs of one country, its government acquires political leverage on

---

*The stabilization or increase of commodity prices has also been attempted through the conclusion of *international commodity agreements (ICAs)*. Commodities that have been or are objects of ICAs include tin, rubber, coffee, cocoa, sugar, and wheat. Some of the ICAs have expired, and others are in the process of renegotiation. Their success has been limited. Some critics argue that they are inefficient and encourage waste.[8]

the penetrated countries, and can induce or perhaps even compel desired behavior. The potential exercise of this leverage may be weakened, however, by cross-penetration, as has occurred between the United States and many Western European countries. In such instances, fear of counterretaliation against subsidiaries and markets established by a country's own MNCs serves as an effective brake on unfriendly political or economic acts. Subsidiaries and markets become hostages that raise the economic and political cost to countries contemplating the employment of economic warfare against each other.

Foreign Aid

Finally, an economic tool that has been utilized by the United States since World War II is foreign aid. During the 1950s, when many Third World countries obtained their independence but were too weak to overcome the serious economic deficiencies from which they were suffering, foreign aid became a very popular way to influence them to attach their loyalty either to the Western or the Communist World. Hence foreign aid was not simply an instrument for assisting the poor countries but was a means for seeking victory in the cold war struggle. In fact, many of the newly independent countries became very adroit at playing the United States against the Soviet Union and China to obtain the highest level of foreign aid. In the late 1960s and early 1970s, the competitive factor in the dispensation of foreign aid subsided, and foreign aid is now being given by all economically advanced countries mainly to promote economic development in the Third World. Nevertheless, various political motivations, such as the maintenance of friendly relations for possible support of the donor in U.N. votes or international disputes, remain important in most foreign aid programs, including those of the United States.

Foreign aid can be divided into *economic aid* and *military assistance*. Motivations for economic assistance include subsistence and humanitarian needs as well as helping the prestige of a recipient country. Without doubt, the most successful economic aid package was the *Marshall Plan*, which received its name from General George C. Marshall, the secretary of state under President Truman, who articulated the concept of extensive aid for Europe in June 1947. Although the East European countries under Soviet control and the Soviet Union itself were considered potential aid recipients, all declined the American offer following Moscow's lead and pressure. Two reasons accounted for Soviet refusal to participate in the Marshall Plan. First, Moscow would have to disclose full information about its economy, which it was unwilling to do. Second, participation would have loosened its control over Eastern Europe, which was not completely secure in 1947. For the West European countries, including West Germany, more than $12 billion of U.S. aid was made available over a 4-year period, and this aid contributed materially to the economic recovery and the modernization of industry in Western Europe.

With respect to the Third World countries which were attaining independence in increasing numbers after World War II, President Truman initiated
the so-called *Point Four program*, which consisted mainly of massive technical
assistance. Other programs followed in the 1950s under the Mutual Security
Act and were administered by the Mutual Security Agency. American economic assistance was substantial during the early 1960s, but in terms of percentage of GNP, the volume of aid has diminished during the last two decades.

In 1962, at the beginning of the U.N.-sponsored First Development Decade of the 1960s, U.S. aid in terms of percentage of GNP stood at 0.8 percent,
whereas the developing countries wanted 1.0 percent and continue to demand
economic assistance of at least 0.7 percent of GNP from all economically
developed countries. In 1969, the U.S. percentage had fallen to 0.51 percent,
and in 1980 the figure stood at 0.27 percent, one of the lowest percentages of
the donor countries belonging to the Organization for Economic Development
and Cooperation (OECD), the club of the economically advanced countries of
the West.* Taking into consideration inflation, the net amount of aid has
likewise decreased.

Three Types of Economic Foreign Aid   Three types of governmental economic foreign aid can be distinguished: (1) outright assistance grants, (2)
government loans, and (3) technical assistance. Whereas *outright grants* were
the preferred methods during the 1950s and early 1960s, *government loans*
today play an increasingly significant role. Loans may be made in soft currency
(i.e., the currency of the recipient country) or in hard currency, which means
the repayment must be made in convertible funds. Because the repayment of
loans in soft currency may not be useful to the lending countries if they want to
apply these funds for purchases in hard-currency countries, some of these loans
actually turn out to be grants. Most loans carry a relatively low interest rate and
have very generous repayment provisions. While they are welcomed by the
developing countries, they also impose a very serious burden on them because
of the interest that must be paid, regardless of how generous the repayment
schedule is. Because of the needs of the less-developed countries, loans continue to be granted even if, in some instances, they are used simply to repay
previous loans. Mexico, Brazil, and Nigeria are current examples. At the same
time, outright grants are still made if for no other reason than to finance the
continuous deficits in budgets of many newly independent countries.

The third type of foreign aid, *technical assistance*, has assumed a greater
role during the past decade. It is a relatively inexpensive way of helping the
developing countries and often provides the training necessary to enable native
administrators, business managers, and engineers to run the more complex
factories and institutions in their country by themselves. We should note that
making available teachers and administrators is one way some former colonial

---

* Details can be found in Chapter 12 and Table 12.4.

powers continue the dependence of Third World countries on their former masters.

Bilateral versus Multilateral Aid　Foreign aid can be given either bilaterally, from one economically advanced country to a Third World country, or multilaterally through the United Nations, the World Bank, or regional organizations. From the point of view of the recipient, multilateral aid of any kind is much more desirable, because it avoids the creation of a dependency relationship with the donor country. The economically advanced states do not share this preference, however; they often use foreign aid to promote not only humanitarian goals, but also specific foreign policy objectives as well and so prefer to give aid bilaterally. Bilateral arrangements may also be more efficient than multilateral programs, although some U.N. programs seem to be gradually becoming more effective.

The United States has preferred to emphasize bilateral aid through the Mutual Security Acts from 1953 to 1961 and the Foreign Assistance Act of 1961. Since then the Agency for International Development (AID), established in the early 1960s and succeeding the Mutual Security Agency, has had the major responsibility to implement foreign economic assistance policy to Third World countries. This assistance consists of grants, loans through the Economic Support Fund (ESF) and the Import-Export Bank,[9] food aid under Public Law 480 for needy countries, and the Peace Corps. The ESF generally continues the activities of the Development Loan Fund. Loans can be used to provide immediate balance-of-payment support, to finance infrastructure and other capital projects necessary for long-term economic development, or to support smaller projects that more directly address basic human needs of the poor.[10] Table 8.1 provides some funding details for these programs in 1980 and shows comparisons for the period from 1946 to 1980.

For multilateral aid, the United States furnishes funds for international financial institutions such as the International Development Association, the International Bank for Reconstruction and Development (World Bank), and the International Monetary Fund. The percentage of this type of multilateral aid, running at about 25 percent of total aid, has increased somewhat in recent years, but the precise annual amounts are usually the subject of considerable controversy in Congress.

Military Assistance

The Mutual Security Act, which served as the legal basis for economic assistance, also served the same purpose for military assistance. In 1961, the Foreign Assistance Act provided authorization for military aid, and the military assistance program (MAP) became the principal vehicle through which recipient countries received arms, equipment, defense services, and training. This aid was in the form of grants requiring no repayment. The total amount of

Table 8.1 U.S. Foreign Economic Assistance
Breakdown and Comparative Data, 1946–1980 (millions of dollars)

Type of Assistance	Postwar Relief Period 1946–1948	Marshall Plan Period 1949–1952	Mutual Security Act Period 1953–1961	Foreign Assistance Act Period						Total FAA Period 1962–1982	Total Loans and Grants 1946–1982	Repayments and Interest 1946–1982	Total Less Repayments and Interest 1946–1982
				1962–1970	1977	1978	1979	1980	1982				
Economic Assistance—Total	12,482	18,634	24,053	63,176	5,594	6,661	7,120	7,573	8,129	105,566	157,019	26,115	130,904
Loans	5,967	2,551	5,850	26,566	2,083	2,530	1,900	1,993	1,454	37,987	50,162	26,115	24,047
Grants	6,515	16,083	18,203	36,620	3,511	4,131	5,220	5,580	6,675	67,579	106,857	—	106,857
AID and Predecessor	—	14,506	16,865	34,263	3,181	4,083	3,848	4,062	4,990	58,639	86,965	10,634	76,331
Loans	—	1,577	3,265	15,400	1,348	1,763	1,154	1,150	764	22,264	25,702	10,634	15,068
Grants	—	12,929	13,619	18,853	1,833	2,323	2,694	2,912	4,226	36,375	61,263	—	61,263
(Security Supporting Assistance)[a]	—	(348)	(8,853)	(11,291)	(1,877)	(2,221)	(1,982)	(2,183)	(2,912)	(24,555)	(32,727)	—	—
Food for Peace	—	83	6,416	19,258	1,193	1,229	1,287	1,436	1,314	27,259	32,913	8,255	24,658
Loans	—	—	2,527	10,108	705	767	746	843	690	14,664	16,357	8,255	8,102
Grants	—	83	3,390	9,150	458	462	541	593	624	12,595	16,556	—	16,556
Title I—Total[b]	—	—	3,867	12,510	735	767	746	843	690	17,066	20,099	8,255	11,844
Repay in $-loans	—	—	—	6,530	735	767	746	843	690	11,086	10,268	3,548	6,720
Pay, in foreign currency	—	—	3,867	5,980	—	—	—	—	—	5,980	9,831	4,707	5,124
Title II—Total	—	83	2,549	6,748	458	462	541	593	624	10,193	12,814	—	12,814
Economic relief, economic development, and World Food Plan	—	—	754	3,976	132	143	167	253	168	4,235	4,975	—	4,975
Volunteer relief agency	—	83	1,795	3,672	326	319	374	340	456	5,958	7,839	—	7,839
Other Economic Assistance	12,482	4,045	752	9,665	1,220	1,346	1,985	2,075	1,825	19,668	37,141	7,226	29,915
Loans	5,967	974	58	1,058	—	—	—	—	—	1,059	8,103	7,226	877
Grants	6,515	3,071	694	8,607	1,220	1,346	1,985	2,075	1,825	18,609	29,038	—	29,038
Contributions to IFT	635	—	189	5,892	931	1,104	1,632	1,478	1,262	13,284	14,108	—	14,108
Peace Corps	—	—	—	1,269	85	92	104	101	105	1,859	1,854	—	1,854
Narcotics	—	—	—	107	36	41	37	39	35	329	390	—	390
Other	5,860	3,071	505	1,339	167	110	212	450	424	3,137	12,687	—	12,687

* Includes capitalized interest on prior year loans.
a Includes peacekeeping operations.
b Includes PL 480 Title III—Food for Development.

Source: AID, U.S. Overseas Loans and Grants, and Assistance from International Organizations, 1983.

the MAP between the end of World War II and 1980 was about $54 billion. Credit financing is another way of delivering arms to Third World countries and amounted during the same period to $17 billion.[11] The basic rationale is the increase in the capabilities of friendly countries to defend themselves against threats to their national security and thereby to strengthen American security, although U.S. concern was and remains primarily defense against Soviet-backed expansionist designs and direct Soviet aggression. Once delivered, it is difficult to prevent the employment of these American arms against neighboring countries in an offensive manner. The use of American arms by Israel during the invasion of Lebanon in 1982 is a prime example.

The United States is not the largest provider of weapons to the Third World. Table 8.2 shows that in constant 1972 dollars, the Soviet Union is responsible for 26.8 percent of such arms shipments, with the United States second at 22.2 percent. However, if military construction programs, training, and spare parts are taken into consideration, the United States transfers exceed 37 percent of all transfers to the Third World countries.

Military assistance as an instrument of policy implementation also must be adjudged in connection with U.S. military sales to foreign countries and commercial exports. This topic will be examined in this chapter as a corollary to the employment of U.S. armed forces in the event of hostilities.

PSYCHOLOGICAL WARFARE

Information and Propaganda

The dissemination of information and propaganda can be a powerful instrument for foreign policy implementation and can further the political, economic, and strategic objectives of the United States. The employment of propaganda may be part of a comprehensive psychological warfare strategy that might include a number of other measures such as the creation of panic, the application of terror through bomb explosions, and causing pressures on currencies through large-scale border-crossing capital movements. Psychological warfare can be carried out during war and in times of peace. It is as old as humanity and is employed today to varying degrees by many countries of the world. The United States makes use of propaganda but rarely employs other psychological warfare measures.

Propaganda   There are many definitions of propaganda. It may be understood as the planned use of any form of public or mass-produced communications designed to affect the minds and emotions of a given group for a specific public purpose, whether economic, political, or military. In international affairs, it seeks to influence politically relevant attitudes and actions on the part of target groups in foreign countries to compel their governments to adopt policies favorable to the United States. The range of the media utilized is

Table 8.2 Arms Transfers to Third World Countries, 1972–1981[a]
($ Millions, Constant 1972 Dollars)[b]

Supplier Countries	1972	1973	1974	1975	1976	1977	1978	1979	1980	1981	Total	% of Total
U.S.S.R.	2,350	3,160	5,060	2,840	4,860	6,720	1,880	5,130	7,500	3,060	42,560	26.8
Other European Communist	200	250	560	330	710	560	410	630	480	1,550	5,780	3.6
U.S.												
Weapons	3,610	5,130	6,530	3,430	3,990	2,570	2,920	2,840	2,570	1,430	35,210	22.2
Military construction	4	990	500	3,650	4,010	260	430	750	1,020	620	12,234	7.7
Other	1,090	1,420	1,050	1,060	1,150	1,610	1,470	1,550	1,750	130	12,280	7.7
Major West European	1,000	2,040	3,250	4,070	2,010	3,340	5,630	3,960	7,350	1,930	34,580	21.8
Minor West European	140	290	370	430	580	410	250	670	1,210	450	4,800	3.0
Other	1,010	530	690	780	1,040	700	830	1,390	870	3,420	11,270	7.1
Total	9,504	13,810	18,110	16,580	18,350	16,170	13,820	16,930	22,740	12,690	158,704	

[a]"Arms" is an all-inclusive term covering the broad range of military security assistance. It includes new, used, or refurbished conventional lethal weapons (including those capable of delivering both conventional and chemical-nuclear munitions), and nonlethal military support equipment such as radar or military uniforms and accoutrements. Also included are military training, arms production or assembly facilities, and military base or fortification construction, although data on these aspects of foreign military programs are especially "soft." Because it is a uniquely large segment of American security assistance programs, U.S. military construction is shown separately. Costs of troops from a major supplier country stationed in Third World countries are excluded where it is possible to separate their costs and equipment from other military assistance.

[b]Estimate rounded to nearest $10 million except where entry is less than $10 million. Percentages may not total because of rounding. U.S. data are for fiscal year; other data are for calendar year.

Source: U.S. Department of State, Special Report No. 102, *Conventional Arms Transfers in the Third World, 1972–1981*, August 1982.

extensive. It includes radio broadcasts, television, films, loudspeakers, magazines, leaflets, libraries, information centers, scholarships, conducted tours for visitors, academic meetings, and even forgeries.

Three types of propaganda can be distinguished: (1) *white propaganda*, which is issued from an acknowledged source, usually a government or an agency of government, (2) *gray propaganda*, whose source is not clearly identified, (3) *black propaganda*, which purports to emanate from a source other than the true one. An example of the latter is radio broadcasts that claim to originate from within a particular country to obtain legitimacy, but actually come from a foreign station.

There are many reasons for the phenomenal growth in the use of political propaganda worldwide. In many countries the participation of the people in politics has increased either through extension of the voting franchise or growing membership in one or more interest groups. Public opinion is more and more recognized as important by political leaders and therefore is a very frequent target of international propagandists. The rate of literacy has risen everywhere, even in countries that formerly were very backward. At the same time communications means and techniques have improved tremendously, and their use has expanded dramatically. In most places on this earth, nearly every family owns a radio, and in many countries people carry shirtpocket radios. Finally, one country can use electronic means to inculcate its ideology systematically and subtly in the population of another.

Effective propaganda must meet certain prerequisites. It must make use of phrases that are simple and easy to understand, such as "capitalist exploiters" or "godless communism." It must stimulate interest and *avoid* the impression of "propagandizing." It must create credibility, which can be accomplished by identifying the information disseminated with an actual experience of the group toward which the propaganda is directed. To be effective, propaganda must have a high level of constancy in terms of both dissemination and the theme being propagated. Finally, good propaganda must avoid promises that may not or cannot be kept. For example, the broadcasts made under the auspices of the Office of War Information in the United States never promised a definite government to the Germans during World War II. Unfortunately, however, individual transmitting facilities attached to the armed forces in the field during the same war made all sorts of promises that could not be kept. Voice of America broadcasts in the middle 1950s may have raised expectations for a change in government in Hungary in 1956 and contributed to the ill-fated uprising there in October of that year.

Effective propaganda should avoid fabrication. No greater misconception of propaganda exists than that it is simply "the big lie." Rather, good propaganda presents facts and depends on selection and emphasis for its effectiveness. The World War II BBC broadcasts from London used facts to influence the audience to support the British was effort. Even today, BBC broadcasts are held in high regard for their reliability and truthfulness.

International propaganda, as well as all aspects of psychological warfare, must be employed in close coordination with other instruments of foreign policy. It is insufficient to define audiences as hostile, friendly, or neutral; what is required is to be precise as to the desired ends, to prepare to cope with alternative reactions from the target group, and to keep always in mind the goals of the country's foreign policy.

In addition to the spoken or written word, *actions* and *"demonstrations"* can be propaganda. Actions, such as handing out free food packages to inhabitants of areas struck by disaster or making large-scale deliveries of wheat to countries that have experienced extensive droughts and poor harvests, can have more propagandistic value than millions of words flowing from different radio transmitters. Military demonstrations, such as fleet maneuvers and jet aircraft flybys in Moscow's Red Square or the Champs-Elysées in Paris (the First of May and Fourteenth of July celebrations, respectively), are also important means of propaganda. They furnish evidence of military power that reassures allies and impresses foes.

Actions in the United Nations General Assembly by American representatives are often designed to appeal to neutral countries in the hope of attracting them to U.S. positions. Such actions thereby become tools of propaganda and have assumed increasing importance during the past two decades.

The Evolution of U.S. Information Services and Propaganda Efforts
When the United States entered World War I, the first organized effort to disseminate information to influence the governments and peoples of foreign countries was the establishment of a committee on public information that, during the period from 1917 to 1919, attempted to propagandize President Wilson's Fourteen Points.[12]

In World War II, the United States set up the Office of War Information, which was given the task of employing propaganda and psychological warfare. By the end of that war, the United States had assembled a very capable corps of psychological warfare specialists.

Following World War II, the United States reduced the activities of its propaganda machine; however, with the spreading of the cold war, the United States Information Agency (USIA) was established in 1953. Its mission was to explain United States actions and policy toward the world in a forceful and direct but not antagonistic manner. At the same time, it was to demonstrate and document the design of those forces that would threaten American security and seek to destroy freedom in general. Today, the USIA maintains nearly 300 posts in over 100 countries. It has established 200 libraries and 150 binational information centers. Each embassy and legation has at least one public information officer, who in turn may be assisted by other United States Information Service (USIS, the implementing arm of USIA) officials. In 1978, the functions of the USIA were taken over by the newly created International Communications Agency (ICA), which was also charged with carrying out the functions previously handled by the State Department's Bureau of Educational and

Cultural Affairs. In the fall of 1982, the name of the agency was changed back again to USIA, but it retained basically the same mission, which includes the dispatch of mostly university specialists to give lectures in foreign countries on various subjects to interested academic and nonacademic audiences. In addition, USIA seeks to organize the presentation of American artists, dramatists, and musicians abroad; in addition, foreign political leaders, educators, and students are given opportunities to travel in the United States to obtain firsthand knowledge about American society and politics.

The main tool for foreign broadcasts of the USIA is the Voice of America, which has very extensive foreign language programs and whose broadcasts are relayed by local stations in important parts of the world. It has been estimated that 7 to 12 million people listen to the Voice of American worldwide, and 5 to 10 million listen daily behind the iron curtain. Other broadcasting facilities supported by the United States are Radio Free Europe, Radio Liberty, and RIAS (Radio Information in the American Sector in Berlin). Radio Free Europe broadcasts are designed primarily for the satellite countries of Eastern Europe, while Radio Liberty beams its messages to the Soviet people.

There is no question that the informational and propaganda activities of the USIA are valuable instruments of policy implementation. The USIS libraries in foreign countries attract many students and other visitors; indeed, it is sometimes difficult to find a place to sit down because the libraries are so full. This applies to both developed and developing countries. American accomplishments in science and the arts are spotlighted, but problems of the complex American society are not ignored. The attainment of the broad USIA objectives of strengthening the commitment of American allies, winning the support of people in noncommitted nations, and providing news to the people behind the iron curtain appears to make progress, although specific success depends on conditions in individual countries. Sometimes overzealousness and unfulfillable promises may lead to disillusion and alienation, as the Hungarian uprisings in 1956 and empty promises to the Polish labor movement appear to suggest.

POLITICAL WARFARE

Political warfare is another instrument for policy implementation. It can be defined as any means, short of the employment of organized armed forces in actual warfare, that a state uses to weaken or exert pressure upon another state.

Subversion (Destabilization)

The best-known political warfare measure is subversion, more recently also referred to as "destabilization." This type of political warfare has ancient roots and has been utilized not only by Communist and Fascist countries but by the governments of democratic states as well. In subversion, a group allegedly loyal to the interests and values of one state is actually used to enhance the policies of another state that is intent on changing radically the political system or the policy directions of the first state.[13]

Subversion often uses *ethnic ties*. For example, according to the Hitlerian doctrines, all Germans living outside the territory of Germany were duty-bound to advance the cause of Nazism and to assist the Fatherland in every way possible. In the United States, the German-American Bund was the vehicle for propagandizing the Nazi ideology and for fostering public opinion favorable to Hitler's Germany, although its efforts were not very successful. In a similar manner, the Soviet Union has attempted to exploit Slavic populations in other countries, not only to attract them to Soviet ideology but also to use them to further Soviet policy. Again, these attempts often failed to achieve results.

More successful has been Soviet utilization of Communist parties in Western countries for the support of its policies. The *ideological ties* with these parties and other left-wing groups at times became the vehicles for the establishment of so-called front organizations, which would ally themselves with socialist parties to form "popular fronts."

Democratic countries have also attempted to use subversion to lessen the totalitarian grip of Communist governments. The United States and some of the West European countries have employed anti-Soviet emigrant groups for this purpose and, in some instances, have established governments in exile. The latter were to maintain contact with the dissatisfied elements in the Soviet Union in order to spread subversive influences in Communist countries.

Subversive penetration is not an end in itself, but it often serves to prepare the ground for coups d'état (the overthrow of governments) and possible annexation. Coups d'état are the result of and illustrate the effectiveness of destabilization measures.

The United States has undertaken successful attempts at coups d'état in foreign countries, although subversion in the narrow sense may have played only a minor role. For example, with covert U.S. backing, a 1954 revolt was led against President Arbenz of Guatemala, who had won the presidential election in 1950 but displayed communist leanings. In 1953 the Iranian Prime Minister Mohammed Mossadegh was ousted and sent to jail for 3 years, and it has been assumed that U.S. covert operations played a role in his ouster. In 1966, Western subversion efforts contributed to the overthrow of President Sukarno in Indonesia and the installation of General Suharto as his successor. Led by Muslim students, Indonesian masses engaged in an anticommunist campaign that eventually forced Sukarno to yield power to Suharto in March of that year. During the early 1970s, the CIA expended several million dollars to "destabilize" the socialist government of Allende in Chile by supporting groups and newspapers opposed to him. His final overthrow may well have been caused in part by these U.S. activities.

Miscellaneous Activities

Armed demonstrations may also be utilized as a political warfare device. For example, the United States in 1980 sent naval units to the Indian Ocean area close to Iran, signaling its resolve to protect the oil-producing countries rimming the southern shores of the Persian Gulf and oppose any Soviet move toward the gulf. Those "demonstrations" were backed up by another "demonstration," namely, maneuvers in Egypt carried out by U.S. ground and air forces in cooperation with the Egyptian military. Finally, the use or threat of use of explosives, singly or multiply in various patterns, and other terrorist acts can be a potent measure in political warfare. Assassination and kidnapping of political leaders also fall into this category. There is no clear-cut evidence that the United States engages in this type of political warfare, although suspicions have been voiced that assassination attempts were undertaken against Cuba's Castro and Patrice Lumumba, a former leader of the Congo government, a country now called Zaire.

Political warfare in the United States during World War II was conducted by the Office of Strategic Services. Later the CIA became involved in these activities and participated in the Iranian, Guatemalan, Chilean, and most likely Indonesian actions related above. It appears that in some instances CIA personnel carry out political warfare operations directly, whereas in other instances they are the guiding hand of indigenous forces or refugees, as seems to have been true during the 1961 abortive invasion of Cuba. To carry out their assignments, CIA personnel have had to learn how to gain control of civilian populations and to apply the principles and techniques of guerrilla warfare.*

Political warfare does not end with the outbreak of military conflict but normally continues and supports the military objectives of a country at war. Of course, it is war itself that is the ultimate tool of foreign policy implementation; it is the tool that we will discuss next.

MILITARY ACTION

Karl von Clausewitz, in his study on war, declared that "war is . . . a continuation of policy by other means. It is not only merely a political act, but a real political instrument, a continuation of political intercourse, a conduct of political intercourse by other means."[14] War is a means for maximizing the power of a state if other means have failed; of course it can also be a defensive tool for survival if a state is attacked by another country, or if overwhelming political and strategic pressures by one state on another necessitate a preemptive attack.

Guerrilla is a Spanish word meaning "the small war." Guerrilla tactics were first used in Spain at the beginning of the nineteenth century when small units offered continuous resistance to the overwhelming power of Napoleon's invasion forces.

If the Soviet Union had not withdrawn the nuclear weapons that it installed in Cuba in 1962 and had in fact attempted to strengthen these forces with additional offensive nuclear missiles, the United States might have had to consider the preemptive use of its armed forces. United States survival was at stake.[15]

It is difficult to define what constitutes an international war. It requires as a minimum two or more opposing states. In addition, more than occasional hostilities must occur. Singer and Small consider a war to exist when hostilities involving one or more states lead to a minimum of 1000 battle fatalities among all participants. Any individual state could qualify as a participant by having a minimum of 100 fatalities. However, if under certain circumstances this figure is not reached, the 1000 figure for total battle losses qualifies a country as long as it engages with armed personnel in an act of combat.[16] Singer and Small have carefully analyzed all of the wars fought between 1816 and 1965. Using their definition, they list 93 international wars with the two most violent being World Wars I and II, with 9 and 15 million battle deaths, respectively.[17]

We can distinguish among conventional wars, nuclear wars, and unconventional wars. Conventional war is the type of warfare developed over the past four centuries and excludes the use of nuclear weapons.

Conventional War

During the past four centuries, the size of the armies has grown enormously. During the Thirty Years' War, the normal size of an army was 19,000 soldiers. During the seventeenth century, it occasionally reached 30,000 soldiers. During the eighteenth century, the average army grew to between 40,000 and 50,000 soldiers, although in exceptional cases it may have reached 90,000. With the advent of the people's armies, Napoleon commanded as many as 200,000 soldiers in some battles. By the end of the nineteenth century, the standing armies of the major powers in Europe averaged 500,000 soldiers each; furthermore, by the outbreak of World War I, the number of soldiers in these armies was even greater. Present-day standing forces of the United States, the Soviet Union, and China are between 2 and 3 million.

During wartime, widespread conscription expanded the armed forces tremendously. During Napoleonic times, France had about 800,000 soldiers under arms. During World War I, the United States had 4.7 million under arms, Germany had 11 million, and Russia 12 million. During World War II, these figures were 16.1 million for the United States and 20 million for Germany.

The range, accuracy, and destructive power of conventional weapons has increased tremendously during the last 400 years, and their level of sophistication has risen remarkably as the result of the miniaturization of electronic components. American capabilities in terms of conventional weapons are impressive, but the number of tanks, antitank weapons, armored vehicles, and heavy artillery is well below those possessed by the Soviet Union. Even if the weapons and equipment of our NATO allies are added to those of the United States and then are compared with those of the Warsaw Pact forces, which include the Soviet Union, Poland, Czechoslovakia, Hungary, Romania, East Germany, and Bulgaria, we find a heavy preponderance of weapons and soldiers in favor of the Warsaw Pact, as Figure 8.1 illustrates.* Only in helicopters does NATO have a slight edge. As far as naval vessels are concerned, NATO has considerably more surface vessels, but the Warsaw Pact's submarines are somewhat more numerous. The number of combat planes is difficult to compare, since both the United States and the Soviet Union have military responsibilities in other parts of the world than Europe, and many planes are stationed outside the European region.[18]

Of course it is not just quantity of personnel and materiel that counts but also their quality. The enormous numbers of Soviet-built fighter planes piloted by Syrian air force officers shot down by American-built fighters flown by Israelis in the Lebanon war of 1982, the inability of Soviet-produced SAM (surface-to-air) antiaircraft missiles to down large numbers of Israeli aircraft, and the very sophisticated American antitank projectiles suggest superior quality of some of the U.S. equipment and, to some degree, reduces the significance of the Warsaw Pact preponderance in tanks. Moreover, the larger number of Soviet divisions is somewhat misleading, because U.S. divisions average about 18,300 soldiers to 11,000 of the Soviet divisions. Finally, there is always the nagging question of how well the armies and air forces of the East European Communist satellites will fight. Opposition to Soviet direct or indirect oppression in Hungary (1956), Czechoslovakia (1968), and Poland (1981), as well as the often demonstrated independent spirit of Romania augur unfavorably for the armed forces of these countries to support enthusiastically any Soviet military action against Western Europe and the United States.

All this does not mean that the U.S. and NATO security is assured and that a conventional war between the two antagonist camps can be won without difficulty by NATO. However, how much American conventional forces and those of other NATO countries should be built up to increase the margin of a potential victory is a highly controversial issue grounded in both questions of appropriate strategic doctrines and domestic politics in the NATO member states. In addition, what may be the best strategic doctrine is closely intertwined with the effectiveness of nuclear weapons and the complexity of nuclear war.

---

* Comparative data on weapons vary from source to source. That the data in Figure 8.1 come from NATO suggests a consensus among the allies that I found quite persuasive.

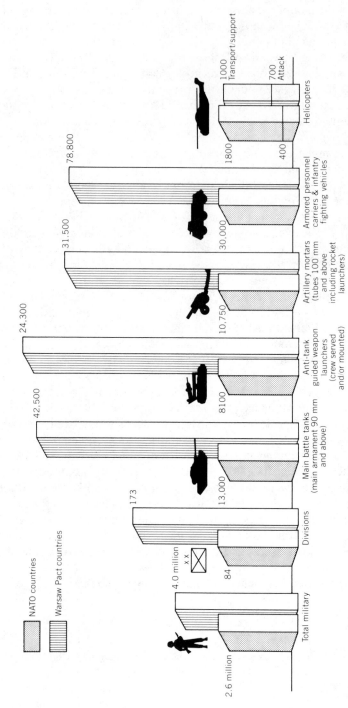

Figure 8.1 NATO-Warsaw Pact force comparison (in place in Europe). Warsaw pact divisions normally consist of fewer personnel than many NATO divisions but contain more tanks and artillery, thereby obtaining similar combat power. Forces shown are those in place in NATO Europe, Warsaw Pact forces as far east as but excluding the three Western military districts in western Russia (Moscow, Volga & Ural military districts).

Source: NATO and the Warsaw Pact, p. 11.

Nuclear War

The curtain was raised on nuclear war in 1945 when American bombers dropped atomic bombs on Hiroshima and Nagasaki in Japan. Since that time no country has resorted to nuclear weapons, even though more than fifteen international wars have been fought.

Although the nuclear club at present includes six states, only the United States and the Soviet Union have the kind of nuclear weapons arsenal to make nuclear war a sophisticated instrument of policy implementation. Both of these countries have a variety of tactical and strategic nuclear weapons, which increases the chances that at first low-yield tactical nuclear weapons may be utilized and escalation of the nuclear conflict may be controlled, depending on what kind of counterweapon is used against a nuclear attack. For many years, both the United States and the Soviet Union seemed anxious to adhere to a "no-first-use clause" for tactical nuclear weapons; however, the Reagan administration has objected to making a formal declaration to this effect. Indeed, whether such a condition could be maintained in a conflict where one country found itself weaker in the total number of nuclear weapons than the other is very difficult to judge.

During the first decade of the nuclear era, the United States tended to rely for its security mainly on the deterrent effect of threatening to use nuclear weapons. Instant and *massive retaliation* with nuclear weapons against the population of the aggressor (called "countervalue") by means and at places of our own choosing in the event of attack by an enemy country was seen as providing substantial security at relatively low cost.

It was Henry Kissinger's famous book, *Nuclear Weapons and Foreign Policy*,[19] that changed the strategic thinking of the United States. Kissinger pointed out that it was a very shortsighted strategy that would rely only on long-range, powerful nuclear weapons. It would deprive the United States of the needed flexibility to react with its armed forces successfully against limited brushfire wars, which were likely to be much more frequent than a challenge by the Soviet Union. Kissinger intimated that the reliance on what Secretary of State John Foster Dulles of the Eisenhower years called massive nuclear retaliation alone provided few options and basically implied an all-or-nothing response. Kissinger therefore argued for an expansion of conventional armed forces to fight limited wars and to avoid future situations such as the invasion of South Korea by the North Korean Communists in 1950. Even though the United States had a virtual nuclear monopoly when the Korean War broke out, the government was not prepared to use nuclear weapons at that time and had to rebuild quickly its army and air force to stave off defeat on the battlefield.

Closely related to the question of the size and composition of the armed forces was the very important issue of how to employ these forces and their weapons, which ranged from conventional arms to tactical and finally strategic nuclear weapons. Until 1961, the United States remained committed to a strategy of massive nuclear retaliation. This strategy was seen by all NATO allies as the most credible means to deter Soviet aggression. Thus the threshold at which powerful nuclear weapons were to be introduced was low. Conventional forces were designed only to stop minor incursions. Conventional NATO forces in the European theater were to serve as a trip wire that would trigger a strategic strike by the American nuclear deterrent.

The Kennedy administration brought to power a group of defense planners, including Secretary of Defense Robert McNamara, who were determined to reduce NATO's dependence on nuclear weapons and to emphasize instead the conventional aspect of the defense of Western Europe. As a result of their efforts, the official strategy of NATO was changed in 1967 to the policy of *flexible or graduated response.* Stripped to its bare essentials, this policy or strategy as developed by the Kennedy and Johnson administrations called for a distinct "firebreak" between the conventional and nuclear phases of combat. To maintain the firebreak, tactical nuclear weapons were given a primary deterrence role to prevent Soviet use of similar weapons. They were to provide a backstop if conventional defenses failed. Nuclear weapons were to be employed only after the conventional battle had actually been lost. Any escalation of conflict was to be very deliberate, because there was the fear that, once the level of using strategic nuclear weapons was reached, a worldwide nuclear holocaust would become inevitable. To reduce this prospect, American nuclear weapons were targeted not only against population centers (*countervalue*) but also on military installations (*counterforce*). The latter would be the first targets, but eventually, population centers would be attacked as well if necessary to prevent a Soviet victory. Thus "no potential adversary could ever conclude that the fruits of his aggression would be worth his own costs."[20]

An analysis of this flexible response strategy reveals advantages as well as drawbacks. Effective implementation of this strategy in Europe requires the maintenance of large troop contingents that must be kept in a state of high military preparedness to defend NATO's eastern boundaries successfully. Moreover, this strategy must be able to cope with military actions of all kinds, ranging from a minor and perhaps nonrecurring probe of NATO defense sectors to a full-scale nuclear attack against the West.

Obviously, the success of the flexible response doctrine depends on the careful management of the military conflict. Political leaders are given time to communicate, perhaps through the hot line between Washington and Moscow, or through other facilities, to prevent an all-out nuclear holocaust. It opens up the possibility of setting limits to the war in terms of the geographical area involved and in terms of the weapons employed, although serious difficulties experienced by one side or the other can change this situation rapidly. When such change may occur is very uncertain and adds a highly speculative dimension to flexible response. At what point would the U.S. government decide to use its strategic nuclear weapons against an enemy? Would the United States be willing to risk destruction of its own territory to defend secondary cities in

West Germany or France that are about to fall to Soviet ground forces? The European NATO partners are aware of the dilemmas that the flexible response doctrine can create, and some responsible Europeans have argued for a return to the massive retaliation strategy, which in their view would assure greater security for all of NATO.

Any of the strategic considerations discussed above may of course be changed if one or the other nuclear power should pursue efforts to acquire an overwhelming first-strike capability. A large first nuclear strike must be able to destroy or neutralize all of the opponent's nuclear counterforces and anti-ballistic missiles (ABMs). Full success would also require a large ABM system designed to shoot down any enemy missiles that survived the first attack. Any country that acquired such capability could bring to its knees other nuclear powers if they became convinced of this extraordinary capability. If other nuclear powers did not acknowledge this superiority, the first country might consider the actual employment of a first strike as opportune and beneficial. So far, neither the United States nor the Soviet Union has pursued this strategy; despite the SALT agreements, however, apprehension continues to exist in some quarters in the United States and Western Europe that the Soviet Union may develop delivery vehicles for nuclear weapons that are powerful enough to give it a decisive first-strike capability.

First Strike A first-strike capability would undermine the concept of deterrence, which is based on mutually assured destruction (MAD) of both superpowers in the event of an intercontinental nuclear conflict. The United States, under the Reagan administration, has expressed serious concern about its strategic forces (long-range nuclear system) becoming inferior to those of the Soviet Union. Figure 8.2 demonstrates that the Soviet Union has larger numbers of intercontinental ballistic missiles (ICBMs)—1398 versus 1054 U.S. ICBMs—and more submarine-launched ballistic missiles (SLBMs) than the United States, and this advantage is further enhanced by greater throw-weight, very high-yield warheads, and increased accuracy. This gives the Soviet Union the ability to kill hard targets, meaning that the U.S. silos containing ICBMs have become vulnerable to destruction before American ICBMs might be launched. This clear and growing advantage is bolstered further by the only currently operational antiballistic missile network deployed around Moscow, the only antisatellite system possessed by the Soviet Union, and an extensive civil defense program.[21]

In terms of *individual* nuclear weapons, however, the United States continues to enjoy an advantage, because its number of multiple independently targetable reentry vehicles (MIRVs) attached to U.S. strategic missiles is slightly larger than those of the Soviet Union. This advantage is likely to continue during the 1980s, as both countries will seek to increase the number of MIRVs on existing missiles and new American missiles are built.[22] To remedy the growing vulnerability of the current ICBM force and to increase the

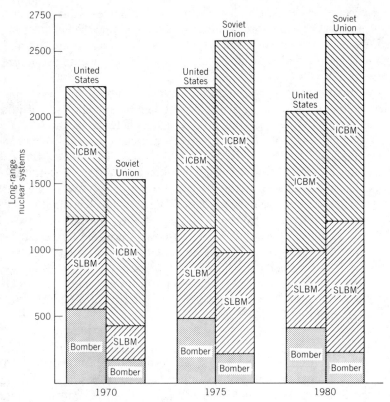

Figure 8.2   U.S. and Soviet Strategic forces compared. (Includes Backfire and FB-111.)

Source: David C. Jones, *United States Military Posture for FY 1982*, Supplement, p. 24.

credibility of strategic deterrent, the MX missile is being developed, of which 100 are expected to become operational in 1987, and which will be extremely accurate and very lethal. The Trident, a new SLBM with MIRVs, will be the standard nuclear strategic weapon for American nuclear submarines and will be able to destroy hardened missile silos for the first time. Finally, the air-launched cruise missile (ALCM) has become operational and can be employed through the B-52 bomber and perhaps later by the B-1 bomber when it joins the U.S. Air Force.[23]

Opinions expressed by a number of knowledgeable persons, such as former defense secretaries Robert McNamara and Harold Brown in the United States, dispute the Reagan administration claims of U.S. current or future strategic inferiority vis-à-vis the Soviet Union. However, Congress has approved most of the administration's plans for a military buildup. The goal is, as stated by the *United States Government Budget for Fiscal Year 1983*, to implement U.S. defense policies that "ensure our preparedness to respond to and, if necessary, successfully fight either conventional or nuclear war."[24]

In the event of a nuclear attack, the consequences for the target area would be almost beyond comprehension. If a full-scale attack were made on the United States with 263 megaton bombs, which would be equivalent to 1.5 billion tons of TNT, and 224 cities, military installations, and other targets were hit, 50 million deaths and 20 million additional casualties would result on the first day. Such a catastrophe, which would transform organized society into a dazed mob, would tax the discipline of a people to the utmost. Therefore, the nature and extent of civil defense and other disaster organizations might hold the key to survival of a country as an operating unit of the community of states. However, the tasks of any civil defense organization are awesome and, if possible at all, extremely difficult to carry through. They include giving first aid, providing *uncontaminated* food and water, furnishing transportation, ensuring the continuity of government, and burying the millions of dead. It is a tremendous challenge, one that only the civil defense organization in the Soviet Union has attempted to meet. In other countries, including the United States, civil defense has very limited capabilities, perhaps because the realistic prospects for any success are so dim.

It may be that ABMs may reduce the horrible prospect described, but whether they can be perfected sufficiently to lower the risk of nuclear attack is far from certain. It is equally questionable whether "space-based" missile defenses, as called for by President Reagan in the spring of 1983, can be produced in the near future to prevent incoming Soviet missiles from devastating the United States. An arms race in space would be not only very expensive but also extremely dangerous, because it could be an inducement for the Soviets to launch a first strike. Moreover, the development of such a missile defense system would undermine the very foundation of strategic stability—the concept of MAD, which has often been modified but never abandoned. Hence *if they wished to accept the cost*, both the Soviet Union and the United States can mount attacks with about 20,000 megatons of nuclear power that would perhaps kill 95 percent of the American people. In the Soviet Union, the percentage of casualties might be considerably lower, because the population and industrial plants are more dispersed and civil defense agencies are more effective.[25]

Nuclear Weapons in Europe   American nuclear weapons are also deployed in Western Europe. They are known as tactical nuclear weapons, and most of the 6000 weapons have only a short range and would be employed primarily on the battlefield. During the 1970s, the Soviet Union began deploying long-range theater nuclear forces (LRTNF)—the *SS-20 missile*—which are much more potent than the older SS-4 and SS-5 missiles and can reach every part of Western Europe. Nuclear attacks on Soviet territory can be carried out from Western Europe at present only by 162 British and French nuclear weapons and NATO aircraft carrying such weapons. In order to counter the installation of the SS-20s, the United States has pledged to deploy, under

NATO auspices, 108 *Pershing II ballistic missiles* and 464 *ground-launched cruise missiles (GLCMs)* during 1983 and 1984. These missiles will have an operational range of about 1500 miles and have a high degree of accuracy that will challenge the hardest enemy targets.[26]

The deployment of the Pershing II and GLCMs has aroused sharp controversy in Western Europe about the direction of NATO strategy toward the Soviet Union. Some prominent American scholars and high former officials have advocated the renunciation of the first use of nuclear weapons—rejected by the Reagan administration as noted earlier—and a greater buildup of conventional forces in Western Europe.[27] However, this concept has also aroused opposition in some quarters in Western Europe on the basis of two principal arguments. First, the promise by NATO not to make the first use of nuclear weapons would make it much easier for the Soviet Union to calculate how to wage war against Western Europe. Second, there would be a massive deployment of conventional NATO forces in West Germany, transforming that country into a gigantic military camp.[28] We will return to this subject in Chapter 11. Meanwhile, the U.S. strategic doctrine retains the possible first use of nuclear weapons as the ultimate means of West European and American protection.

Unconventional Warfare

The conventional tactics of employing large formations of personnel and firepower to overcome and defeat the enemy normally have favored stronger over weaker states; however, special unconventional tactics of rapidly moving small groups of men and weapons, quickly attacking violently under cover of stealth and with surprise and ruses, and then withdrawing just as quickly may offer weaker states military capabilities somewhat offsetting their lack of personnel and a broad arsenal.

Unconventional warfare can be as costly in battle losses as some conventional wars. In general, the state engaged in unconventional and especially guerrilla warfare minimizes direct military confrontation which may subject its forces to quick annihilation. States using this type of warfare cannot count on a quick knockout of the enemy. They must be patient, and indeed it is this attribute that marks the national character of countries that employ these tactics. North Vietnam is an excellent example. The fact that unconventional warfare is a slow tool for fighting an opponent does not alter its ultimate effectiveness, as the Vietnam War illustrates. The United States suffered large casualties and, for a variety of reasons, finally had to disengage itself from the conflict.

The United States is unlikely to use unconventional war as an instrument of policy in a major dispute with other countries, but it has employed unconventional warfare measures on occasion. An example is American involvement in Laos, where over 30,000 tribesmen were organized into a kind of private CIA army.[29] However, although the United States is not apt to initiate an unconventional war with its own military forces, it must be prepared to fight in such a war. Countering guerrilla forces is a very difficult task, and—despite training of U.S. ground and air forces in counterinsurgency tactics—success is often elusive, as again the Vietnam War has demonstrated.

War and Communication

Although the normal traditional practice during war has been a complete rupture of communications and diplomatic relations between the warring states when hostilities broke out, this practice is being modified. Some indirect communications were carried out between the United States government and North Vietnam during the war through various unofficial intermediaries, and these were supplemented by trips to Hanoi by "peace" group representatives. In the event of a nuclear war, instant communications between the opponents may be of critical significance, and it is hoped that the hot line connecting the Kremlin with the White House would continue to operate in such a calamity to transmit clear signals of intentions on the part of the governments. Of course, third governments may also be used as intermediaries for message transmission. The International Red Cross has certain functions that touch warring nations but cannot be used to relay governmental messages regarding strategic decisions of opponents.

Foreign Military Sales

An important complement to the conduct of war is supporting action on the part of allies and friendly nations. Military assistance to such nations may provide some assurance in this respect. As a minimum, it strengthens the capabilities of American allies and friendly countries to defend themselves.

The military assistance program (MAP) to Third World countries includes the transfer of substantial amounts of weapons and equipment to them. However, exports of weapons are also made on cash or credit bases to foreign countries, and these are known as foreign military sales (FMS).

FMS have been substantially greater than the MAP shipments beginning with 1964, and indeed, there was hope at that time that MAP could be phased out completely. However, rapidly rising energy costs during the post-1973 oil crunch, and the global recession of the late 1970s and early 1980s made it imprudent to discontinue MAP, as even some NATO allies (Turkey and Portugal) found it very burdensome to make even deferred payments for American weapons and equipment.[30] The trend of FMS worldwide sales agreements from 1978 to 1982 shows an increase from $6.4 billion in 1978 to $8.9 billion in 1982. During the same period, MAP grants were much smaller, rising from $218 to $391 million. For details, see Table 8.3.

Table 8.3   Foreign Military Sales and Military Assistance Program, 1977–1981
(Dollars in Thousands)

	FY 1978	FY 1979	FY 1980	FY 1981	FY 1982
Foreign Military Sales					
Worldwide	6,413,002	6,873,921	5,876,086	7,718,530	8,948,143
East Asia and Pacific	886,637	948,161	1,075,532	1,921,656	1,319,084
Near East and South Asia	4,404,347	4,345,837	2,407,692	3,097,345	4,353,227
Europe and Canada	925,524	2,223,409	2,223,409	450,875	2,781,650
Military Assistance					
Worldwide	217,593	229,229	278,464	269,057	391,102
East Asia and Pacific	41,070	30,188	160,518	125,598	135,164
Near East and South Asia	55,218	41,741	28,220	1,302	1,307
Europe and Canada	73,151	109,311	37,907	56,162	78,079

Source: Foreign Military Sales and Military Assistance Facts 1982

President Carter was anxious to reduce arms transfer to foreign countries. He considered it immoral for the United States to be at the same time an advocate of peace and one of the world's largest suppliers of arms. However, the realities of world politics and American interests made it impossible for Carter to realize his good intentions. Moreover, opponents of Carter's intention regarding arms sales pointed out that a good record of adequate U.S. support, as perceived by American allies and friends, either through FMS or MAP, would greatly aid in building and maintaining attitudes backing U.S. views and objectives. In addition, economic arguments for continuing a high level of arms sales can be advanced. They help maintain high employment in key industries, assure that defense production remains geared up and large enough to benefit from mass production, and, finally, have a favorable impact on the U.S. balance of payments. Of course, there are also risks that were mentioned earlier. Recipient countries may use American weapons against their neighbors rather than for their defense, and American high technology employed in certain weapons such as sophisticated planes may fall into the hands of hostile governments in cases of revolution, as the history of Iran has demonstrated. There seems little doubt, however, that the Reagan administration and other subsequent administrations will continue to follow the American practice of arms sales and consider both FMS and MAP as useful instruments of foreign policy.

THE CHOICE OF INSTRUMENTS AND EFFECTIVE POLICY IMPLEMENTATION

The discussion so far demonstrates the wide range of instruments available for the implementation of American foreign policy. The choice of instruments is crucial for achieving the goals of particular policies. If the proper instruments are not selected or the implementation process lacks effectiveness, the outcome of these policies may be the opposite of what had been intended. Reviewing the Reagan administration's record on foreign policy during the first 20 months in office, the distinguished columnist of the *New York Times*, James Reston, has the following to say about Reagan's declared objectives and implementation outcomes in the international arena:

> He came to office promising to unify the Atlantic alliance but has divided it over trade with the Soviet Union more seriously than at any time since World War II. He wanted to increase the defenses of Western Europe with modern missiles, but the Allies are reducing their defense budgets. Even the Senate Appropriations Committee has voted to reduce U.S. forces in Europe, and in the confusion Chancellor Helmut Schmidt of West Germany, Secretary Shultz's best friend in the alliance, is in deep trouble.
>
> Accordingly, it's not unreasonable to ask whether the president's policies are achieving his objectives or opposing them. He wanted to keep China and the Soviet Union apart, but by his ambiguous policy about providing arms to Taiwan he may be encouraging them to get together.[31]

Of course, the last word has not been written on the above policy endeavors, and some of President Reagan's foreign and security policies may bear ultimate fruit. The increases in American defense capabilities may have the desired effects on Soviet behavior in the long run, and his strong commitment to finding a solution for the Mid-East troubles may ultimately produce a compromise acceptable to all parties, including Israel and the Palestinians.

Looking at the implementation success of American foreign policy before the Reagan administration, the record clearly is mixed. Mutual nuclear deterrence has kept the peace since World War II; in addition, NATO, in spite of recurring frictions among the allies, has materially contributed to the maintenance of peace in Europe. In Korea the territorial status quo was retained, and thereby the limited goal of U.S. policy was achieved. We have already referred to the fiasco of the attempted Bay of Pigs invasion, a failure in both foreign policy formulation and implementation. The opposite is true about the Cuban missile crisis, during which stated goals were attained through capable policy implementation. In contrast, the conduct of the war in Vietnam turned out to be a failure with far-reaching negative consequences for U.S. policies. Although during the Carter years the Camp David agreement must be adjudged as a qualified success, subsequent implementation was impossible to achieve in all respects. The planned rescue of the American hostages from Iran was a clear example of implementation failure.

In economic foreign policy, two examples of policy implementation show very different outcomes. As already noted, the Marshall Plan for aid to Western Europe was quite successful. However, the Alliance for Progress initiated and planned under the Kennedy administration to help Latin America lacked the proper implementation and therefore slowly disintegrated. More will be said about the Alliance for Progress in Chapter 12.

While these examples indicate that the choice of instruments may have been ill-advised as in the cases of President Reagan's imposition of pipeline sanctions jeopardizing his meritorious goals of unifying the Atlantic Alliance or President Kennedy's employment of anti-Castro Cubans and Central Americans with CIA help to topple Fidel Castro in the disastrous Bay of Pigs invasion, the *process of implementation* may also be flawed and therefore result in unintended outcomes. The aborted rescue attempt of the American hostages in Iran may be an instance of both a poor choice of instrument and inept implementation. The latter may also have been an important reason for the eventual failure of the Alliance for Progress in Latin America.

In some cases, the *content of policy as formulated* may lead to the inappropriate choice of instruments and eventual implementation misfire. The difficulties of the Vietnam War and ultimate U.S. defeat may be traced back to policy formulations under Presidents Eisenhower, Kennedy, Johnson, and Nixon, with the latter finally drawing the proper conclusion of ending American involvement.

Finally, the *assumptions* underlying the formulation of policies may not be consistent with reality and thus lead to ill-advised and nonsupportable policies, which in turn may result in the improper choice of instruments. Washington's frictions with the European NATO allies during the Carter and Reagan administrations may have been caused by unrealistic assumptions with their unfortunate consequences.

All this points up the need of continuous evaluation of the policy implementation process, including the choice of instruments by the participants in foreign policymaking. *Variables leading to the adoption of particular policies*, with special attention to international situational variables, need to be researched and analyzed to determine the reasons for deviations from intended policy outcomes.[32] As shown in domestic contexts, public policy evaluation is a difficult undertaking, but considering the importance of making American foreign policy as successful as possible considering the high stakes involved, foreign policy implementation evaluation is essential for better formulation of policy as well as the choice of proper instruments.

SUMMARY

The *choice of the instrument* for the implementation of a particular American foreign policy has an important bearing on the success or failure of this policy. An extensive number of implementing instruments are available to the policymaker. The majority of them assume an underlying friendly relationship, but some instruments have an antagonistic nature and a few may involve violence of different degrees. War is the most violent instrument.

The best-known instrument for policy implementation is *diplomacy*, which is carried out by foreign service officers through American embassies, legations, and missions in the capitals of the world. The American ambassador in a particular country is the head of a *country team*, which consists of all U.S. officials assigned by the State Department and other agencies to that country.

The main functions of diplomats are *representation*, *observation*, and *negotiation*. Different methods are used for *bilateral* or *multilateral* negotiations. Diplomatic practice in IGOs has special features; the role of the foreign service officer in IGOs resembles that of a *parliamentarian*. Since World War II, the art of diplomacy has been depreciated by high-speed transportation, high-speed communication, and summit meetings.

The chief economic instruments for policy implementation are the *adjustment of tariffs*, which in the United States has been carried out through the *reciprocal trade program* and the imposition or lifting of *nontariff barriers*. The main principles underlying U.S. trade policy are *reciprocity* and *nondiscrimination* (the *most-favored-nation clause*). These principles are also the core of the General Agreement on Tariffs and Trade (GATT). Orderly marketing agreements (OMAs) have been used by the United States to curb imports of certain products. *Subsidies* and *currency regulation* are also economic policy measures toward foreign countries.

Economic warfare measures are *preempting* and *stockpiling*, *embargoes*, *boycotts*, and *penetration by multinational corporations*.

Foreign aid has developed into an important instrument of foreign policy implementation. It can be divided into *economic* and *military assistance*. Economic aid is dispensed through *outright assistance grants*, *government loans*, and *technical assistance*. Aid can be given on a *bilateral* or a *multilateral* basis. The United States prefers the former; the Agency for International Development (AID) is in charge of implementation. For multilateral aid, the U.S. government furnishes funds to the World Bank and the International Monetary Fund. Military assistance is given through the military assistance program (MAP). The funds provided by MAP to foreign countries are very high.

An increasingly important instrument of foreign policy implementation is the *dissemination of information and propaganda*. The purpose of propaganda is to affect the minds and emotions of a given group through public communications. In terms of its source, propaganda can be identified as *white*, *gray*, or *black*. To be effective, propaganda must meet certain prerequisites such as the use of simple phrases, the establishment of credibility, and the avoidance of fabrication. Propaganda can also be carried out through actions and "demonstrations."

The USIA is in charge of the American information and propaganda efforts. Important tools of the USIA are the Voice of America and the libraries of the U.S. Information Service (USIS) in many countries of the world.

Political warfare as an instrument of policy implementation has been employed by the United States on various occasions, but not always with success. This instrument can be used in a nonviolent or violent manner. A nonviolent measure is *subversion* or *"destabilization"* of an existing political system. *Ethnic* and *ideological ties* are utilized to promote destabilization. Coups d'état are the result if destabilization measures were effective. Armed demonstrations have also been employed by the U.S. government for political warfare purposes. Violent measures such as assassinations and terrorist acts seem to have attempted by the United States (the CIA), but their extent and success are shrouded in secrecy.

Three kinds of major military actions, the ultimate instrument of policy implementation, can be distinguished: conventional, nuclear, and unconventional war. The size and quality of the armed forces and the range, accuracy, destructive power, and number of nonnuclear weapons determine the capabilities of the United States to engage successfully in *conventional* war. Similar considerations apply to America's NATO allies and the opposing Soviet forces and their East European allies, who in sheer numbers at present exceed NATO capabilities. For a *nuclear war*, U.S. strategy has shifted from *massive retaliation* against nuclear attack or in the event of impending defeat in a conventional war to a *flexible response*. This strategy implies an initial use of small tactical nuclear weapons to remedy losses in conventional warfare and a gradual escalation toward the employment of large strategic nuclear missiles. In the targeting of strategic weapons, a distinction is made between *countervalue* (population centers) and *counterforce* (missile and other military installations) targets. The basic concept to deter either side from attack is "mutually assured destruction (MAD). The soundness of this concept is placed into jeopardy by the development of antiballistic missiles (ABMs), regardless of whether they are ground-based or "space"-based weapons. If the MAD concept were to lose its potency, a successful *"first strike"* by either the Soviet Union or the United States may be considered by either side.

The deployment of long-range theater nuclear forces (LRTNF) in Europe by the Soviet Union (*SS-20*) and NATO's prospective response in the form of the deployment of *American Pershing II* and *ground-launched cruise missiles (GLCMs)* has introduced additional problems in the nuclear equations between Washington and Moscow.

Unconventional warfare consists of tactics employing rapidly moving small groups of men and weapons, quickly attacking violently, and then withdrawing just as quickly. The United States has used unconventional warfare only on occasion.

A corollary to military action is the sale of weapons and equipment for cash or credit to allies and friendly countries. These transactions are known as foreign military sales (FMS); while they complement the MAP to Third World countries, their volume is at present much larger.

Finally, the choice of implementing instruments is crucial. If the proper instruments are not selected, the outcome of particular policies may be quite different from what was intended.

NOTES

1. Jeffrey L. Pressman and Aaron B. Wildavsky, *Implementation* (Berkeley, Calif.: University of California Press, 1974), p. xv.
2. Niccolo Machiavelli, *The Prince* (1531), reproduced by Modern Library (New York: Random House, 1950); Jules Cambon, *Le Diplomate* (Paris: Hachette, 1926); Adm. C. Turner Joy, *How Communists Negotiate* (New York: Macmillan, 1955); Raymond Dennett and J.E. Johnson (eds.), *Negotiating with the Russians* (Boston: World Peace Foundation, 1951); Fred C. Ickle, *How Nations Negotiate* (New York: Harper & Row, 1964).
3. Frederick H. Hartmann, *The Relations of Nations*, 4th ed. (New York: Macmillan, 1973), p. 97.
4. See Joy, *How Communists Negotiate*, p.170.
5. Henry Kissinger, *Years of Upheaval* (Boston: Little, Brown, 1982), p. 214.
6. Lloyd Jensen, "Soviet-American Bargaining Behavior in the Postwar Disarmament Negotiations," *Journal of Conflict Resolution* 7 (September 1973), pp. 522–541.
7. *Time*, May 30, 1983, p. 66.
8. Joan E. Spero, *The Politics of International Economic Relations*, 2nd ed. (New York: St. Martin's Press, 1981), pp. 211–212.
9. For details on loan procedures see Robert E. Asher, *Grants, Loans, and Local Currencies* (Washington, D.C.: Brookings Institution, 1971), pp. 17–53.
10. For a brief history including many organizational changes of U.S. foreign aid, see Burton M. Sapin, *The Making of United States Foreign Policy* (New York: Praeger, 1966), pp. 188–202.
11. International Development Cooperation Agency, *1981 Annual Report of the Chairman of the Development Coordination Committee.*
12. See *Selected Addresses and Public Papers of Woodrow Wilson*, edited by Albert Bushnell Hart (New York: Boni & Liveright, 1918), pp. 247–248.
13. Ernst B. Haas and Allen Whiting, *Dynamics of International Politics* (New York: McGraw-Hill, 1956), p. 200.
14. Karl von Clausewitz, *War, Politics, and Power* (*On War*) (Chicago: Henry Regnery, 1962), p. 83.
15. For details see Graham Allison, *Essence of Decision: Explaining the Cuban Missile Crisis* (Boston: Little, Brown, 1971), passim.
16. J. David Singer and Melvin Small, *The Wages of War, 1816–1965: A Statistical Handbook* (New York: John Wiley & Sons, 1972), pp. 35 and 36.
17. Ibid., pp. 59–70. Battle deaths during Korea and Vietnam were 33,629 and 45,501, respectively. (See *Information Please Almanac*, 1972, p. 701.)
18. See *NATO and the Warsaw Pact—Force Comparisons*, pp. 1–26.
19. Henry Kissinger, *Nuclear Weapons and Foreign Policy* (New York: Harper & Row, 1957).
20. U.S., Department of Defense, *Annual Report, FY 1982*, pp. 39–40.
21. David C. Jones, chairman of the Joint Chiefs of Staff, *United States Military Posture for FY 1982*, Supplement, pp. 24–25.
22. Ibid., pp. 25–27.
23. Ibid., pp. 69–71; and *The Defense Monitor* 11, 6 (1982), p. 7.
24. Quoted in Jones, *United States Military Posture*, p. 19.

25. Donald G. Brennan, "When the SALT Hit the Fan," in *Great Issues of International Politics*, 2nd ed., edited by Morton A. Kaplan (Chicago: Aldine, 1974), pp. 548–564, on p. 562.
26. Jones, *United States Military Posture*, p. 77.
27. McGeorge Bundy, George F. Kennan, Robert S. McNamara, and Gerard Smith, "Nuclear Weapons and the Atlantic Alliance," *Foreign Affairs* 60, 4 (Spring 1982), pp. 853–868.
28. *Stuttgarter Zeitung*, June 24, 1982.
29. Charles W. Kegley and Eugene R. Wittkopf, *American Foreign Policy*, 2nd ed. (New York: St. Martin's Press, 1982), p. 113.
30. Jones, *United States Military Posture*, p. 66.
31. *Times-Picayune* (New Orleans), October 1, 1982.
32. See the applicable and useful contributions to Kenneth M. Dolbeare (ed.), *Public Policy Evaluation* (Beverly Hills, Calif.: Sage Publications, 1975).

THE CONTENT OF AMERICAN FOREIGN POLICIES

9

Policies toward
the Soviet Union

THE INITIATION OF THE CONTAINMENT POLICY

During World War II, the highest-priority goals of the U.S. government were the defeat of Germany and Japan. The Soviet Union was allied with the United States, Great Britain, and later the Free French Forces under General de Gaulle in the struggle against Hitler.

The treatment of Germany in the immediate postwar period played a pivotal role in the relationship between the United States and the Soviet Union. Six months after the Germans had invaded the Soviet Union in June 1941, Stalin made known his war aims with regard to Germany in a conversation with British Foreign Secretary Anthony Eden in Moscow. It was the first statement of purpose concerning Germany that any of the leaders of the Big Three Powers (the United States, Great Britain, and the Soviet Union) made. Stalin stated his aims as follows: independence of Austria, detachment of the Rhineland from Germany and establishment of this territory as an independent state or protectorate, independent status for Bavaria, and reparations in kind, especially machine tools. There was no demand that the capitalistic system should be overthrown, which was not surprising, since Stalin was allied with two capitalistic powers in his desperate and critical fight against the Germans. Nor was there any indication at that time that Stalin had designs for controlling Germany after her defeat.[1]

Although the end of the war was not in sight, the problem of the occupation of Germany was given serious consideration in 1943. During the Foreign

Ministers' Conference held in October of that year in Moscow and attended by U.S. Secretary of State Cordell Hull, Anthony Eden, and Soviet Foreign Minister Molotov, agreement was reached in principle on joint responsibility for and joint occupation of defeated Germany. A European Advisory Commission was created and was assigned the tasks of determining the terms of surrender to be imposed on Germany and of suggesting machinery to ensure the fulfillment of these terms.[2]

The European Advisory Commission, in its Protocol of September 12, 1944, set forth (1) the boundaries of the zones to be occupied by the United States, Great Britain, and the Soviet Union, (2) the sectors of Berlin to be occupied by each of the powers, and (3) the joint administration of Berlin by a common authority, later called *Kommandatura*. In November 1944, the European Advisory Commission also reached agreement on the establishment of the Allied Control Council, which was to function as the government of Germany for the interim period until an indigenous German government could be established.[3] During the Yalta conference of February 1945, Stalin was persuaded to enter the war against Japan 2 to 3 months after the war in Europe had been terminated and "free elections" were promised for Poland and other East European countries. The conference generally confirmed the agreements reached by the European Advisory Commission regarding the occupation of Germany, but amended them by assigning to France a separate zone of occupation together with a sector of Berlin, and France was made a member of the Allied Control Council.[4]

By the end of the war in Europe on May 8, 1945, the Soviet armed forces had seized all of Berlin, while at the same time American forces were deep in territory designated as the Soviet Zone. On assuming supreme authority over defeated Germany on June 5, 1945, and after Western forces had been admitted to Berlin, the commanders of the victorious Four Powers implemented the agreement of the European Advisory Commission and moved their forces into their respective zones. Later, on June 29, 1945, arrangements were made between representatives of the United States and the Soviet Union for Western access to Berlin, consisting of one main highway, one rail line, and two air corridors, which were increased to three in November of that year.

During the Potsdam conference in July and August 1945, both President Truman and Prime Minister Churchill agreed to support the Soviet claims to Königsberg in an eventual peace conference. Soviet demands for the recognition of the transfer of all German lands east of the Oder-Neisse Line to Poland were rejected by the United States and Britain. It was decided, however, to let Poland administer these territories pending a final decision of a future peace conference.[5] Stalin's demands for reparations were met only to the degree that he should receive no more than 25 percent of what was determined as West German surplus, part of which the Soviet Union would pay for, plus reparations that the Soviet Union would extract from her own zone.[6] Soviet attempts to create a separate state in the Ruhr and the Rhineland under Four-Power control were refused. Agreement was reached in Potsdam on the preservation of the economic unity of the country, on control of a large part of German industry, and on a gradual political revival of Germany. Further, the Allied Control Council was assigned the mission of the "four D'S"—denazification, democratization, demilitarization, and deconcentration of German political and economic life.

Soviet policy toward Germany until 1949 consisted of efforts to exploit German economic resources to the limit and of attempts to establish a Soviet-oriented government in Germany. In view of the tremendous war losses suffered by the Soviet Union, the fulfillment of Soviet economic requirements was given undisputed priority over the political policy of winning over the Germans to the Soviet side.[7]

Reparations obtained from the Western Zone were primarily in the form of equipment from dismantled plants that were shipped either by sea or by rail to the Soviet Union. Reparations in the Soviet Zone were exacted by several conventional and unconventional methods: dismantling of plants and shipment to the Soviet Union, removal from current industrial production, conscription of labor including inmates of concentration camps, establishment of Soviet corporations to which would be transferred title of plants formerly owned by the German state, the Nazi party, or Germany's wartime allies, and export of German production on Soviet account.[8] At the same time, the Soviet Union initiated in the Soviet Zone of Germany a policy of partial communization of agriculture and industry, the development of a planned economy, and the nationalization of factories owned by former Nazis.

As early as 1945, the Soviet Union began to make efforts to appear as the only sincere advocate of rapid political unification of Germany. This lip service to German unity and, at the same time, the effective prevention of this unity unless unification would result in a Germany oriented toward the Soviet Union, seem to have been the basic guides of Soviet foreign policy toward both Germanies for about 20 years following the end of World War II.[9] A long-term Four-Power treaty that would have guaranteed the continued demilitarization of Germany was proposed by James F. Byrnes, then secretary of state, at the end of 1945, but was rejected by the Soviet government.[10]

It is interesting to note that during the 1943–1944 period, U.S. postwar planners were determined to base postwar policies on a firm agreement with the Soviet Union and the construction of cooperation with that country. Another pillar of postwar policy was to be a reliance on an *effective* United Nations to maintain a peaceful world.[11] However, positions on Germany hardened in 1946; Stalin declared that communism and capitalism were incompatible and that true peace was impossible until capitalism had given way to communism.[12] At the same time, Winston Churchill made his famous iron curtain speech in which he contended that while the Soviet government may not want war, it desires "the fruits of war and the indefinite expansion of their power and doctrines."[13]

When early in 1947 Great Britain became unable to continue economic and military assistance to either Greece or Turkey, this development produced conditions that seriously aggravated further the already tenuous relationship between Washington and Moscow. In Greece, strong communist pressure was exerted through widespread guerrilla warfare that originated in Yugoslavia and was aided by guerrillas from Albania and Bulgaria. Greece, exhausted by 4 years of occupation by German and Italian forces, did not have the capability to mount a strong defense. In Turkey, the Soviet Union demanded the secession of several areas located on the Turkish-Soviet border and requested the revision of the basically neutral Montreux Convention, which governs ship traffic through the Straits of the Dardanelles, to favor a system to be administered jointly by the Soviet Union and Turkey. In addition, Moscow wanted Turkey to sever its ties with Great Britain and sign a treaty making this country a Soviet satellite. The United States, which Moscow had asked to acquiesce to a new regime of the Dardanelles to be controlled undoubtedly by the Soviet Union, responded in the negative.

To respond adequately to these Soviet challenges required an analysis of Soviet foreign policy motivations. George Kennan, historian and a foremost expert on the Soviet Union, provided in 1947 the needed analysis in a famous article in *Foreign Affairs* written under the pseudonym X.[14] This analysis reflected thoughts and advice to the State Department that Kennan had conveyed in an 8000-word telegram dated February 22, 1946,[15] while he was chargé d' affaires at the American Embassy in Moscow. Kennan stated in his article:

> The Kremlin is under no ideological compulsion to accomplish its purposes in a hurry. Like the Church, it is dealing in ideological concepts which are of a long-term validity, and it can afford to be patient. It has no right to risk the existing achievements of the revolution for the sake of vain baubles of the future. The very teachings of Lenin himself require great caution and flexibility in the pursuit of Communist purposes. Again, these precepts are fortified by the lessons of Russian history: of centuries of obscure battles between nomadic forces over the stretches of a vast unfortified plain. Here caution, circumspection, flexibility, and deception are the valuable qualities; . . . Thus the Kremlin has no compunction about retreating in the face of superior force. And being under the compulsion of no timetable, it does not get panicky under the necessity of such a retreat. Its political action is a fluid stream of moves constantly, wherever it is permitted to move, toward a given goal. . . . The main thing is that there should always be pressure, increasing constant pressure, toward the desired goal.

It should be noted that Kennan has not always maintained the views expressed in the 1947 article. Indeed, he has vacillated between more hawkish and dovish opinions regarding Soviet foreign policy and what policy stand the United States should take. In his *Memoirs* (1925–1950) he downplayed the significance of the 1946 telegram (and implicitly the *Foreign Affairs* article) and, in retrospect, revised his opinion about Soviet expansionist intentions.[16] Nevertheless, in 1947 the U.S. government took Kennan's analysis very seriously, and President Truman decided to meet the Soviet challenge in Greece and Turkey with specific policy that became known as the containment policy or the Truman Doctrine.

The core of this new policy was the assumption that the United States could survive only in a world in which democracy could flourish. Hence, to realize this objective, Truman declared before a joint session of Congress on March 12, 1947, that we must be

> willing to help free peoples to maintain their institutions and their national integrity against aggressive movements that seek to impose upon them totalitarian regimes. This is no more than a frank recognition that totalitarian regimes imposed on free peoples, by direct or indirect aggression, undermine the foundations of international peace and hence the security of the United States.
>
> The peoples of a number of countries of the world have recently had totalitarian regimes forced upon them against their will. The Government of the United States has made frequent protests against coercion and intimidation, in violation of the Yalta agreement, in Poland, Romania, and Bulgaria. I must also state that in a number of other countries there have been similar developments. . . .
>
> One way of life is based upon the will of the majority, and is distinguished by free institutions, representative government, free elections, guarantees of individual liberty, freedom of speech and religion, and freedom from political oppression.
>
> The second way of life is based upon the will of a minority forcibly imposed upon the majority. It relies upon terror and oppression, a controlled press and radio, fixed elections, and the suppression of personal freedoms.
>
> I believe it must be the policy of the United States to support free peoples who are resisting attempted subjugations by armed minorities or by outside pressure.[17]

To carry out the new policy, Truman asked Congress to appropriate $400 million for economic assistance and military aid for Greece and Turkey and to permit American civilian and military personnel to be sent to the two countries for the purpose of helping in economic reconstruction and providing military training and instruction. After an extended debate, Congress approved the appropriation in May 1947 with a wide margin in both houses. It was a very significant vote because it gave birth to the principle of containment, which remains a major American foreign policy goal to this day.

In spite of the fact that public opinion polls throughout 1946 indicated a low interest of the Americans in foreign policy problems (less than 25 percent), there was no major public outcry against the containment policy. Containment was most likely seen as being within the limits allowed by public opinion. Although a number of liberal Democrats continued to advocate a policy of conciliation with the Soviet Union including continued negotiation, they were ignored by Truman. Henry Wallace, the secretary of commerce and a former vice-president under Roosevelt, who was a leading figure among those liberals, was dismissed by Truman. At the time of its promulgation, containment was directed only at the Soviet Union. During the 1950s and 1960s, however, this policy assumed a broader scope and was applied against all communist expansionism, a notion that currently prevails.

Explanatory Variables

In terms of variables explaining the containment policy, we can identify interactional, societal, and idiosyncratic sources of explanation.

Interactional Variables   A major interactional variable stemming from apparent changes in the international situation was the perception of American foreign policymakers that the Soviet Union was not interested in the continuation of the World War II alliance with the United States and was returning to the pursuit of communist expansionist designs. Evidence for such intentions consisted of not only direct and indirect Soviet pressures on Turkey and Greece, but also the installation of a Communist regime in Poland (the Lubin group rather than the Western-oriented government-in-exile in London), which was seen as a clear violation of the Yalta agreements on Poland. The tight control over other East European countries on which Moscow insisted and its imposition of a communist economic and political system[18] were additional actions that rendered imperative a tough American response in the Truman administration's view. Clearly, the hopes of Roosevelt in 1943–1944 for a peaceful world anchored in U.S.-Soviet collaboration and the United Nations had been disappointed.

From a systemic point of view, if thought were given by American foreign policymakers to a future balance of powers, the containment policy was a necessary beginning to establishing a countervailing force to Soviet influence in Europe, although at that time the United States still possessed strong military superiority as the result of its atomic weapons capability.

Societal Variables   In terms of societal variables, general American commitment to democracy and the capitalist system, inherent widespread anti-communist sentiments, and basic distrust of the Soviet Union provided supporting elements of the containment policy. Nor was the majority of public opinion opposed to such a policy; rather, this policy was well within the limits that public opinion would tolerate.

Idiosyncratic Factors   As far as idiosyncratic factors explaining the containment policy is concerned, there is little doubt that Truman's combative, tough, and decisive nature, his courage and forthrightness, and his readiness to meet challenges adroitly and forcefully played important roles in adopting the containment policy. Truman's hard line vis-à-vis the Soviet Union began to be formed shortly after he assumed office, when it became obvious that Moscow was to flout the Yalta agreement. This trend in Truman's attitude toward the Kremlin was further strengthened during the Potsdam conference, which convinced him that any concessions to Moscow had to be matched by equal concessions on the part of the Soviet government.[19]

Dean G. Acheson, who served both as undersecretary and secretary of state in the Truman administration, advised and supported Truman in the formulation of the containment policy. His image and view of Soviet expansionist designs were similar to those of Truman; he looked at communism as the subtle spearhead of Soviet imperialism that had to be stopped.

His views were clearly expressed in a discussion with U.S. senators before the adoption of the containment policy:

> Soviet pressure . . . on northern Greece had brought the Balkans to the point where a highly possible Soviet breakthrough might open three continents to Soviet penetration. Like apples in a barrel infected by one rotten one, the corruption of Greece would infect Iran and all to the east. It would also carry infection to Africa through Asia Minor and Egypt, and to Europe through Italy and France, already threatened by the strongest domestic Communist parties in Western Europe. The Soviet Union was playing one of the greatest gambles in history at minimal cost. It did not need to win all the possibilities. Even one or two offered immense gains.[20]

A forceful and influential individual, Acheson was highly persuasive in convincing Congress of the merit and need of Soviet containment.

Collaterals for the Containment Policy

The initial instrument of the containment policy, the $400 million program for Greece and Turkey providing economic and military aid, proved to be effective. American military advisors sent to Greece helped to defeat the communist guerrilla forces that had infiltrated from Yugoslavia and were aided by an indigenous Greek Communist movement. As a consequence, any communist seizure of the Greek government was averted. In fact, Yugoslavia, under Tito's leadership, began to pull out of the Soviet satellite system in 1948, although it retained a socialist regime. Turkey was also able to maintain its independence, and Soviet pressure relaxed.

Although the successes in Greece and Turkey were gratifying, the Truman Doctrine of containment had a broader objective, namely, to help free people all over the world to maintain their democratic way of life against encroachment by Soviet expansionist forces. This required the formulation of collateral American policies, especially for the protection of Western Europe, which was regarded as a crucial region for American security. Two major policies were developed for this purpose: the Marshall Plan and the establishment of the North Atlantic Treaty Organization (NATO).

The Marshall Plan   The ravages of World War II had created havoc with the economies of Western Europe. Factories were destroyed, food was in short supply, highways and railroad tracks and rolling stock had been seriously damaged. An exceptionally severe winter in 1946−1947 diminished the production of coal and reduced further an already low level of industrial production. These were conditions likely to produce economic and social chaos, which could easily be exploited by subversive communist activities and eventually lead to Communist regimes in some West European countries. In France and Italy, serious governments crises were imminent, with the Communists parties the immediate beneficiaries. In defeated Germany, the reparations demanded by the Soviet Union for the losses suffered during the war led to wholesale transfers of the machinery of entire plants to Russia; industrial production in early 1947 had fallen to less than 30 percent of the prewar levels.[21]

To remedy a rapidly deteriorating economic situation in Western Europe that was seen as having grave implications for U.S. security, General George C. Marshall, former chairman of the Joint Chiefs of Staff during World War II and in 1947 secretary of state, proposed a multibillion-dollar plan in June of that year to speed the recovery of West European economies. This plan, which was to carry his name and was officially known as the European Recovery Program (ERP), was not only a vehicle for the transfer of badly needed funds from the United States to Europe, thereby strengthening West European democracy, but also an initial blueprint for European economic integration. The Europeans were required to establish a structure whose purpose was to liberalize trade within Europe and that was to distribute the funds received from the United States.

It is noteworthy that the original Marshall Plan envisaged the participation of all European states including the Soviet Union, an apparent inconsistency with the Truman Doctrine.[22] However, the American conditions attached to the plan were such that they were found unacceptable by the Soviet Union, and it therefore declined to participate. Eight other East European states controlled directly or indirectly by Moscow, which included Finland and Yugoslavia, and which had shown varying interest in participation (especially Czechoslovakia) were forced to decline involvement in the plan. This was perhaps fortunate, because it is far from sure that, under such circumstances, Congress would have voted the necessary funds for the plan. As it was, the plan generated considerable controversy in Congress, some charging that the $17 billion requested by President Truman over a period of 51 months was too much money to be poured into the pockets of ungrateful Europeans, and a few others, including Henry A. Wallace, claiming that the plan reflected "dollar imperialism."[23]

Spurred most likely by the Communist coup in Czechoslovakia in February 1948, Congress ended the lengthy debate with an initial appropriation of approximately $6.1 billion for the first 12 months. By the end of the ERP in 1951, more than $12 billion had been appropriated by Congress, and it was obvious that the program had achieved its purpose, with West European production having either reached or surpassed prewar levels.

The European structure, which Washington required to be set up for the distribution of U.S. funds in West Europe, and the liberalization of intra-regional trade, was the Organization of European Economic Cooperation (OEEC). Sixteen countries were members: Great Britain, France, Italy, Belgium, Denmark, Ireland, Iceland, Greece, The Netherlands, Denmark, Norway, Luxembourg, Portugal, Switzerland, Sweden, and Turkey. The OEEC became an important factor in U.S. policy developments toward Western Europe.

NATO: Genesis The basic motivation for the American policy decision to participate in an alliance of West European countries and Canada was the assurance of U.S. security, which was seen as depending on the successful defense of Western Europe against a potential attack by powerful Soviet armed forces. The threat by the Soviet Union, which began with attempts of a Communist takeover in Greece and increased with the Communist coup and seizure of governmental power in Czechoslovakia in 1948, continued with heavy political pressure on Norway and Finland, efforts by indigenous Communist parties to disrupt the economic reconstruction of West Europe, and the blockade of Western road and rail access to Berlin in the fall of 1948.[24]

In Western Europe the first organizational arrangements for the enhancement of security after the end of World War II were made by Great Britain and France, which signed the Dunkirk Treaty in March 1947. However, this treaty was directed primarily toward providing mutual aid in the event of a renewal of German aggression. It also aimed at economic cooperation, and therefore a longer-range goal was to bring in the Benelux countries (Belgium, the Netherlands, and Luxembourg) and perhaps later other West European nations. Alarmed by the expansion and consolidation of Soviet influence in Eastern Europe and the Balkans, the British government in January 1948 called for a "Western union," which was followed up by preliminary negotiations with the Benelux states aiming chiefly at a military alliance, but also seeking greater economic, social, and cultural cooperation. A treaty to this effect was signed in Brussels on March 17, 1948. This so-called Brussels Treaty made reference to Article 51 of the United Nations Charter, which authorized collective self-defense and stipulated that in the event of an armed attack on one of the signatories the other parties to the treaty would come to the aid of the victim of aggression. The treaty mentioned Germany as a potential aggressor; the Soviet Union was not named as such but was evidently very much on the minds of the alliance partners.[25]

The principal policy organ of what came to be called the Brussels Treaty Organization (BTO) was the Consultative Council, which consisted of the foreign ministers of the five member states and which met several times. Between meetings, policy was determined by a permanent commission located in London and administration matters were handled by a secretariat, also set up in London. A unified defense force was established in Fontainbleau, France, under Field Marshal Lord Montgomery, but in fact he had very few troops to command.[26]

To the British government it soon became clear, however, that the BTO would not be sufficiently strong to deal with joint pressures, although Washington had promised to aid that organization in a way yet to be specified.[27] Ernest Bevin, British foreign secretary, was particularly concerned about Norway becoming subservient to Soviet wishes, which might result in the collapse of the whole of Scandinavia and which "in turn prejudiced our chance of calling any halt to the relentless advance of Russia into Western Europe."[28]

Bevin perceived two threats: an extension of the Soviet Union's sphere to the Atlantic and a political threat to destroy all the efforts made (with U.S. approval) to build up a Western union. He therefore strongly recommended to the United States a regional Atlantic pact in which all states directly threatened by a Soviet move to the Atlantic could participate, and these were to include the United States, Britain, Canada, Ireland, Iceland, Norway, Denmark, Portugal, France, the Benelux countries, and Spain when it had again a democratic form of government.[29] For the Mediterranean, he envisaged a separate system, with Italy playing a major role.

The United States' response to the British proposals was given promptly by General George C. Marshall, then secretary of state. He suggested that joint discussions on the establishment of an Atlantic security system should be undertaken at once. The initial discussions began in Washington on March 22, 1948, and revealed a number of uncertainties in the British proposals regarding prospective membership and the geographical area to which the system was to apply. There seemed to be an increasing need to include Italy, Greece, and perhaps Turkey in the membership list, but the acceptability of the western zones of Germany as a member seemed at that time doubtful, because it had been the enemy of most of the prospective members during World War II, terminated only 3 years earlier.[30]

For the U.S. government to join any kind of alliance raised fundamental questions. First, the United States had at that time potential capabilities and resources that might have been perceived by policymakers and the public as adequate for a successful defense of its territory and people. However, doubt may have been cast on such a judgment by the enormous advances in military technology that had been made by 1948 and could be expected to go even further in the years to come, and by the extraordinary destructiveness of nuclear warfare—as was seen in the Nagasaki and Hiroshima attacks. Second, George Washington's warning against "entangling alliances" was known to every American and was often reiterated in political oratory. With 1948 being an election year and the political power divided between a Democratic president and a Republican Congress, this was a most difficult time to move beyond Washington's warning into the uncharted territory of peacetime international politics.

The initial reaction of Secretary Marshall to the British proposal was cautious and somewhat negative. On the one hand, he considered U.S. participation in a military guarantee as impossible; U.S. aid would have to be confined to supplying material assistance to the members of the West European security pact. On the other hand, the directors of the Office of European Affairs and of the Division of West European Affairs strongly advocated a North Atlantic treaty and alliance.

During the spring of 1948, the State Department, reacting to the Soviet coup in Czechoslovakia and the continued pressure on Norway, began to commit itself to the treaty; in April the National Security Council approved a State Department recommendation that President Truman announce U.S. preparedness to negotiate a collective defense agreement with the Brussels Treaty members and with Norway, Denmark, Sweden, Iceland, and Italy. Pending the conclusion of such an agreement, the United States would regard an armed attack against any member of the Brussels Treaty as an armed attack against itself.[31]

NATO: Shaping the Treaty   Since ratification of this proposed agreement would require Senate approval and it was a Democratic president who needed consent from a Republican-controlled Senate, a bipartisan approach was essential. As a form of senatorial "advice" to the president, Senator Arthur Vandenberg, the Republican chairman of the Senate Foreign Relations Committee, introduced a resolution that was adopted by the Senate in an overwhelming vote on June 11, 1948. The resolution advocated progressive development of regional and other collective arrangements for individual and collective self-defense in accordance with the U.N. Charter and specifically referred to the right of collective self-defense under Article 51 of the charter. It also approved U.S. association with such arrangements "as are based on continuous and effective self-help and mutual aid, and as it affects national security."[32]

The so-called Vandenberg Resolution opened the way to negotiation for a North Atlantic treaty, which included regular meetings with the Senate Foreign Relations Committee and its staff to discuss actual treaty language. There were basic differences in the negotiations, because the Western Europeans, especially the French, wanted as binding and as long a commitment as possible, and the Americans—while agreeing in principle—were constrained by what the administration believed Senator Vandenberg would accept.[33]

Disparities of views between the United States and other prospective alliance members about the substance of the treaty under consideration were not surprising in view of the large gap in the capabilities and resources of the individual states involved in the negotiations. France wanted to accept an Atlantic security pact only if unity of command of the armed forces of the allies were to be achieved at once, and U.S. military personnel and supplies were to be moved to France immediately. For Norway, the matter was also urgent because of Soviet pressure for a pact similar to the Soviet-Finnish agreements, which could result in concessions to Soviet demands for domination or, if rejected, could trigger a Soviet attack on Norway *and* Sweden. Canada also strongly advocated an effective treaty and was concerned that, as a result of discussions in the Senate, the treaty might be watered down so that it would not be much more than a Kellogg-Briand Pact. Belgium was apprehensive about the provocative effect that any North Atlantic security treaty might have on the Soviet Union. While the Belgians were anxious to obtain immediate help from the United States, they floated ideas about the "armed neutrality" of Western Europe as perhaps being preferable to a formal Atlantic treaty relationship.[34]

With respect to the prospective members' obligations, the most controversial provision was the exact nature of the commitment to respond to armed attack on a treaty member state. The United States could not be obliged to use its armed forces automatically to aid a victim of an attack, because the U.S. Constitution stipulates that only Congress can declare war. After many negotiating sessions and consultations with the foreign ministries of the prospective members and the Senate Foreign Relations Committee, the crucial Article 5 of the North Atlantic Treaty was to read as follows:

> The Parties agree that an armed attack against one or more of them in Europe or North America shall be considered an attack against them all, and consequently they agree that, if such an armed attack occurs, each of them, in exercise of the right of individual or collective self-defense recognized by Article 51 of the Charter of the United Nations, will assist the Party or Parties so attacked by taking forthwith, individually and in concert with the other Parties, such action as it deems necessary, including the use of armed force, to restore and maintain the security of the North Atlantic area.
>
> Any such armed attack and all measures taken as a result thereof shall immediately be reported to the Security Council. Such measures shall be terminated when the Security Council has taken the measures necessary to restore and maintain international peace and security.[35]

In spite of the qualifying words, it was believed that Congress could be counted on to back up the president with a declaration of war, particularly if the armed attack was not just an incident but a full-fledged initiation of extensive hostilities.

For the southern boundary of the territorial coverage of the treaty, the Tropic of Cancer was adopted (Article 6). This avoided involving most parts of Africa or any states of Latin America as areas where an armed attack would constitute a casus belli. However, *consultation* on threats of or actual attack anywhere in the world was not restricted by the geographical parameters specified in the treaty. Indeed, consultations on possible threats is a major obligation of the member governments (Article 4). Although some European governments had insisted on a treaty duration of 50 years, the final agreement reached was limited to 20 years. It was doubtful that the U.S. Senate would have accepted a longer duration.

It should be noted that the treaty has an economic dimension. Article 2 emphasizes the elimination of conflict between the international economic policies of the member states and encouragement of economic collaboration between "any or all of them." However, these provisions have been used only rarely—for example, when the NATO members states pledged contributions to an assistance program for Turkey, which faced serious economic difficulties in the late 1970s.

It is noteworthy that the treaty negotiators did not spell out institutional and organizational details for the implementation of the agreement beyond stipulating the establishment of a council and a committee, giving these organs the mandate to set up subsidiary bodies, including a defense committee, now called military committee. No mention was made of voting procedures, but the basic rule developed in the council was that no government could be forced to take action against its will; conversely, however, no government could prevent other governments from taking such collective action as they agreed to take.[36]

NATO: The Structure   As evolved over the years, the NATO structure is divided into a civilian and military segment. The civilian segment is predominant in the decision making; its highest organ is the council, which meets twice a year and is attended by the foreign and defense ministers of the member states. In between these meetings, the council convenes monthly on a deputy level, composed mostly of the ambassadors of the NATO member states. Numerous subordinate committees have been set up, as can be seen from Figure 9.1. An international secretariat headed by a secretary general provides administrative and logistical support.

The military segment, under the military committee, operates through three major commands: Atlantic, Europe, and Channel. These are coordinated by the Supreme Allied Commander Europe (SACEUR). An international military staff provides administrative support (see Figure 9.1), and a

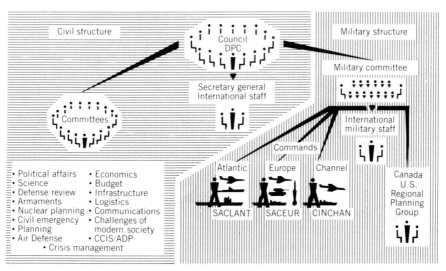

Figure 9.1   Civil and military structure of NATO.
Source: NATO Handbook 1982, p. 30.

number of logistics facilities in support of NATO have been established. However, it should be noted that whatever armed forces are assigned to NATO by the member states, they remain under national control. Only a very few fully integrated operational NATO units exist at present; a situation that would of course change in the event of hostilities, when all armed forces assigned to NATO would operate under an integrated command structure.

Finally, if NATO were to be expanded, unanimous agreement is necessary to invite any other state to accede to the North Atlantic Treaty. However, only those states in a position to further the principles of the treaty and to contribute to the security of the North Atlantic area may be invited (Article 10). West Germany's accession to NATO membership in 1955 and that of Spain in 1982 are cases in point.

Explanatory Variables

As with the containment policy, the geneses of the Marshall Plan and NATO were mainly stimuli from the international situation. Hence international variables such as successful Soviet attempts to consolidate their positions of power in Eastern Europe, difficulties of Greece and Turkey in withstanding Soviet pressures and subversion, perceived potential Soviet expansionist designs on Western Europe (all interactional variables), as well as concerns with establishing a bipolar balance-of-power system between the United States and the Soviet Union (systemic variable), accounted for the policies creating the Marshall Plan and establishing NATO.

Institutional variables, however, also played important parts in the formulation of these policies. While the Marshall Plan had general support in the U.S. State Department, some members of Congress voiced their opposition to the large expenditure of funds. However, the forthright leadership of President Truman and his secretary of state, aided by further evidence of communist expansionism in Czechoslovakia, eventually overcame congressional opponents. Economic interest groups also favored the ERP, since it was anticipated that putting Western Europe back on its economic feet would expand American exports to that region of the world.

For the establishment of NATO, the major problem was the historically understandable reluctance on the part of the United States to enter an "entangling" alliance for military purposes. This reluctance was apparent in the State Department and in Congress. The Soviet coup in Czechoslovakia prompted a positive attitude toward NATO by Secretary Marshall, and the bipartisan approach in the Senate promoted by the Vandenberg Resolution was a powerful factor in support of the initiation of the negotiations for NATO and its final Senate approval.

Idiosyncratic variables also serve as sources of explanation for both policies. Truman's fighting spirit and strong anti-Moscow attitude, seconded by

Marshall's and Acheson's diplomatic and political skills, played important roles in the successful policy formulations. However, without Senator Vandenberg's leadership and political ability in guiding the bipartisan resolution through the Senate, the establishment of NATO may well have been in jeopardy.

NUCLEAR DETERRENCE POLICIES

The containment policy put in place during the Truman administration, bolstered by the Marshall Plan and NATO, was insufficient to assure the security of the United States in the face of the nuclear capability acquired by the Soviet Union in 1949. This capability was expanded substantially as delivery vehicles were developed during the 1950s and the Soviet nuclear stockpile grew. Meanwhile, the United States had lost its nuclear monopoly, and policies had to be formulated to counter a growing Soviet threat of an attack on Western Europe and eventually on U.S. territory itself.

Changing Capabilities and Policies

To forestall Soviet nuclear attacks against the United States and aggression by conventional or nuclear forces against Western Europe, the U.S. government formulated the policy of massive retaliation with U.S. nuclear weapons. President Eisenhower approved plans to use nuclear weapons, tactical as well as strategic (intercontinental), whenever their use would be needed for military purposes.[37] Massive nuclear retaliation rather than the deployment of conventional ground and air forces became the major deterrent against possible Soviet aggression. This new concept of U.S. policy was characterized by Secretary of State John Foster Dulles in a famous speech to the Council on Foreign Relations in January 1954 as "the way to deter aggression . . . for the free community . . . willing and able to respond vigorously at places and with means of its own choosing."[38]

American nuclear superiority during the 1950s was an important factor feeding Dulles' declared commitment to "brinksmanship" in foreign policy. Brinksmanship denoted foreign policy behavior of going to the brink of war through strong action, but without getting into war.[39] Dulles hoped to use brinksmanship to compel the Soviet Union to conform to American wishes through the threat of nuclear superiority. He also hoped to roll back Soviet control of Eastern Europe and to liberate some of the communist-dominated countries in that region. However, in spite of opportunities created for a rollback in Eastern Europe when East Germans staged riots in 1953 and Poles and Hungarians revolted against their Communist masters in 1956, no concrete American moves were undertaken by the Eisenhower administration to attempt a "rollback," regardless of Dulles' high-sounding rhetoric.

While in terms of Soviet containment massive retaliation was a generally successful policy, a number of questions were raised about its long-term efficacy. We already mentioned Kissinger's book, *Nuclear Weapons and Foreign Policy*,[40] in which he criticized massive retaliation as an all-or-nothing strategy that allowed Moscow to nibble away the status quo bit by bit and impose a series of piecemeal defeats on the West. Kissinger contended that if the Soviet Union could present its challenges in less than all-out form, it may gain important advantages. Such moves would pose serious dilemmas to the U.S. leaders: were they willing to accept the destruction of major American cities with enormous casualties to prevent Soviet encroachment in Western Europe or elsewhere, encroachments that by themselves may not threaten vital American interests?

Similar concerns were also expressed by our European NATO allies. Moreover, would not the employment of massive nuclear weapons in Western Europe lead to enormous devastation given the high density of population and closeness of cities? For Kissinger, the answer was a buildup and greater deployment of conventional armed forces and the use of small tactical nuclear weapons that would extract the U.S. leadership from the all-or-nothing nuclear dilemma, while making it possible to reject the notion of "peace at any price."

The Kennedy administration was sympathetic to a change in nuclear strategy generally along the lines suggested earlier by Kissinger. President Kennedy and his secretary of defense sponsored efforts within the Department of Defense to develop a more diversified military capability that would make it possible for the United States to fight limited wars and employ only nonnuclear weapons to deter or meet Soviet aggression.[41] However, while in case of a Soviet attack with conventional forces the immediate response by the United States and its NATO allies would be conventional, it did not exclude the employment of tactical nuclear forces to support conventional defenses and the eventual use of strategic nuclear weapons as the ultimate sanction and defense against a Soviet attack. This is the heart of the "flexible response" doctrine that was accepted by NATO in 1967 in spite of some reservations by Europeans who feared that this doctrine would ensure any nuclear war to be fought in Western Europe and save the United States from the horrors of nuclear devastation. These Europeans would have preferred the retention of "massive retaliation" as the proper deterrent of Moscow.

As far as U.S. global security policy was concerned, the planned increase in conventional war capabilities was to make it possible to fight two and a half wars at the same time. Hence the United States would be enabled to engage simultaneously in a conventional war in Europe with the Soviet Union, a Southeast Asian war, and a smaller conflict somewhere else. Under the Nixon administration, U.S. capability was reduced to a one and a half-war capability—the Vietnam conflict was at an end—but, under President Reagan, the two and a half-war strategy has been resumed.

Limitations on Strategic Nuclear Weapons

The basic American expectation underlying both the massive retaliation and flexible response strategies was the full comprehension by the Soviet leadership that any military attack against U.S. interests would lead to such powerful nuclear retaliation as to produce unacceptable devastation of Soviet cities, population, and military facilities. Indeed it was the concept of mutually assured destruction (MAD) that was trusted to maintain the peace between the two superpowers. However, in the 1960s and the early 1970s, military technology began to make new and rapid advances that raised questions about the continued application of the MAD principle. Antiballistic missiles (ABMs) were developed that, if effective, could undermine this principle, as they might be able to destroy incoming intercontinental ballistic missiles (ICBMs) fired either as a first strike or in retaliation by either the Soviet Union or the United States. At the same time, the Multiple Independently Targetable Reentry Vehicles (MIRVs) were beginning to be produced in the United States, which made it possible for ICBMs to carry multiple warheads that could separate in flight, change trajectory, and hit specifically assigned and dispersed targets. Hence subsequent generations of American ICBMs were expected to carry as many as ten individual warheads, but this initial U.S. advantage in technology was likely to be matched in the future by similar Soviet achievements, which did in fact happen. At the same time, the Soviets began to build heavier missiles (SS-9s) than those used by the United States; these missiles were able to carry one 25-megaton warhead or three 5-megaton warheads and were seen by Washington as "first-strike" weapons that could seriously damage American land-based ICBMs such as the Minuteman, thereby weakening U.S. retaliatory capabilities.

Perhaps with these future developments in mind and anxious to maintain MAD stability, President Johnson put forth feelers to Moscow in early 1967 for an agreement on limiting strategic nuclear weapons. Although the Soviet Union expressed some interest in Johnson's initiatives, nothing happened until after the inauguration of President Nixon, when the Soviet government declared a definite desire to enter into negotiations on limiting nuclear weapons. Following preliminary talks in November 1969, substantive discussion began in April 1970 on strategic arms limitations. The United States' chief delegate was Gerard C. Smith, the director of the Arms Control and Disarmament Agency,[42] a middle-of-the-road Republican with a balanced judgment and extensive knowledge of international affairs.[43]

After considerable effort and time expended by the negotiators, agreement was reached and SALT I was signed in May 1972 at the Nixon-Brezhnev summit conference held in Moscow. Agreements were signed also between the two superpowers at that time on other subjects including joint space exploration, scientific and technical cooperation, and the creation of a joint American-

Soviet trade commission. SALT I, which consisted of an Anti-Ballistic Missile Treaty and an Offensive Strategic Weapons Agreement, received Senate approval in August and September 1972.

The content of the SALT I agreements reflected the objectives the Nixon administration had set when it entered into the negotiations for this accord. They were to (1) enhance the stability of the U.S.-Soviet strategic relationship, (2) halt the upward spiraling of nuclear weapons arsenals, and (3) strengthen American security by lessening the risks of nuclear war. The Anti-Ballistic Missile Treaty limited both superpowers to two ABM complexes each, one for their capitals and the other for the protection of one ICBM site. Each protected area was allowed 100 ABMs. While the Soviet Union maintains an active, though limited, ABM system around Moscow, the United States has only a limited installation at Grand Forks, North Dakota, to protect a Minuteman complex in that area.

The Offensive Strategic Weapons Agreement must be appraised in the light of the guidance given to the U.S. negotiating team by President Nixon, who sought to ensure "sufficiency" in the nuclear force levels to protect the United States and its allies.[44] The limitations imposed by the agreement were for the Soviet Union to maintain 1618 operational ICBMs including 313 large SS-9 missiles, while the ceiling for the United States was 1054 operational ICBMs (1000 Minuteman and 54 Titan missiles). As for submarines, the Soviets were allowed to maintain 950 ballistic missile launchers (SLBMs) on 62 nuclear-powered submarines; the figures for the United States were 710 launchers on 62 submarines.[45]

No limitations were placed by the SALT agreements on qualitative improvements. Hence each signatory could increase the number of warheads for each missile and improve the guidance system and penetration capabilities. By the end of 1972, the United States possessed 5700 nuclear warheads spread on U.S. territory, while the Soviet Union had only 2500. American strategic bombers also outnumbered those of the Soviet Union by better than three to one. No on-site verification of compliance was included in SALT I, but the parties were not to interfere with electronic satellite monitoring efforts.

Two subsequent changes to SALT I must be noted. In July 1974, a Treaty for Limited ABM Deployment was signed that reduced the number of permissible ABM sites to one for each signatory. In November of that year, President Ford and Brezhnev met in Vladivostok, a Soviet port city on the Sea of Japan, and agreed to limit their offensive nuclear weapons (ICBMs, SLBMs, and long-range bombers) to 2400 delivery vehicles. No more than 1320 ICBMs and SLBMs could be equipped with MIRVs, but each government could decide which of the delivery vehicles was to be MIRVed.

Although the limits of the Vladivostok agreements were to be applicable until 1985, the accord also expressed the need for further negotiations to reduce the ceilings for strategic weapons further. President Carter shared the desire for further reduction in the number of nuclear strategic arms. SALT II got under way in March 1977, with Washington presenting a comprehensive proposal to Moscow for new reductions on the number of weapons and other provisions. This proposal included (1) lowering the Vladivostok ceilings from 2400 to 2000 launchers and the number of launchers allowed to have MIRVs from 1320 to 1100, and (2) prohibiting qualitative improvements on existing missiles, the testing of new strategic weapons, and the development of mobile ICBM launchers. Cruise missiles would be permitted as long as their range did not exceed 300 miles.[46]

The Soviet government rejected the Carter proposals, but this rejection did not end the negotiating process. After prolonged, very complex, and at times excruciatingly difficult negotiations, an agreement was reached and signed by Carter and Brezhnev in 1979. It stipulated a gradual reduction of the ceiling of 2400 to 2250 delivery vehicles and set a limit of 1320 on MIRVed ICBMs, SLBMs, and aircraft with long-range cruise missiles, with 1200 the ceiling of MIRVed missiles and 820 the limit of MIRVed ICBMs. Although some selected constraints were placed on the improvements of the signatories' weapon systems, for example their throw-weight, all technological advances were not excluded. At the same time, the Soviets were allowed to retain some of their heavy launchers (SS-18s), and the Soviet Backfire bomber, which is capable of striking some targets in the United States, was not included in the agreement. It should be noted that when the Backfire bomber is included in a comparison of U.S. and Soviet bombing planes, Figure 8.2 (Chapter 8) indicates a substantial American advantage.

Opposition against the ratification of any SALT II agreement surfaced early during the Carter administration and was fed by the strong military buildup in which the Soviet Union had been engaged since 1962 (Table 9.1) and

Table 9.1   U.S. and Soviet Strategic Weapons Inventory, 1962–1977 (Midyear)

	1962	1965	1970	1971	1972	1974	1975	1977
United States								
ICBM[a]	294	894	1054	1054	1054	1054	1054	1054
SLBM	144	496	656	656	656	656	656	656
Long-range bombers[b]	600	630	550	505	455	437	432	441
Soviet Union								
ICBM	75	270	1300	1510[c]	1527[c]	1575	1618	1477
SLBM	Some	120	280	440	560	720	784	909
Long-range bombers	190	190	150	140	140	140	135	135

[a]ICBM range = 4000+ miles.
[b]Long-range bomber = maximum range of 6000+ miles; medium-range bomber = maximum range of 3500 to 6000 miles, primarily designed for bombing missions. Backfire is classified as a medium-range bomber on the basis of reported range characteristics.
[c]A version of the SS-11 with three MIRVs replacing some of the single-warhead versions in the SS-11 force.

Source: International Institute of Strategic Studies, *The Military Balance 1975–76*, p. 73.

which resulted in what many observers considered Soviet military superiority vis-à-vis the United States (see Figure 8.2, Chapter 8). Contributing to this attitude was the increased accuracy of Soviet ICBMs and their enormous destructive power, which placed into question American deterrent capability if Soviet missiles were able to incapacitate large numbers of U.S. land-based ICBMs. At the same time, American SLBMs did not have the accuracy to be a credible counterthreat to Soviet military targets.

In the forefront of the opposition was the Committee for the Present Danger under the leadership of Eugene V. Rostow, a former law professor at Yale University and later the director of ACDA. Its numerous pamphlets argued that the proposed SALT II accord had many flaws, but most importantly, its ratification would lull the people of the United States into a false sense of security with the result of a likely neglect of an urgently needed increase in the strength of U.S. military capabilities.

While it is difficult to determine the exact motivations of the Soviet arms buildup, the 1962 Cuban missile crisis may well have been a major contributing factor. In the fall of 1962, U.S. intelligence discovered that the Soviets were building launching sites in Cuba for about seventy medium- and intermediate-range ballistic missiles (MRBs and IMRBs). Nikita Khrushchev, then secretary-general of the Soviet Communist party and premier of the Soviet Union, had dared to move these missile sites so near to the United States, anticipating apparently no counteraction beyond diplomatic protests. However, this was a miscalculation. President Kennedy was determined that these missile sites were to be dismantled and that whatever missiles had been installed were to be removed. Kennedy ordered a naval blockade to show its resolve in this confrontation. It was an "eyeball-to-eyeball" situation, and Moscow backed down in the face of superior U.S. strategic power. This incident led to Khrushchev's dismissal in 1964 and most likely represented to the Soviet leaders evidence of weakness that was not to be tolerated again.[47]

Whatever the motivations for the Soviet buildup of its nuclear arsenal, U.S. foreign policymakers felt compelled to expand American military forces as well. In the last year of his presidency, President Carter, partially in response to the Soviet invasion of Afghanistan, ordered an increase in defense expenditures including the construction of a mobile land-based missile system, the MX. Afghanistan was also the immediate cause for Carter's withdrawal of the SALT II agreement from any further Senate consideration. President Reagan expanded the process of rebuilding U.S. armed forces by heavy infusion of funds. The Pentagon budget was to be increased by an annual rise of 7 percent in "real" dollars, adjusted for inflation, over several years. The MX missile with ten independently targeted warheads is to be built, but instead of being a mobile system, it will be placed into hardened silos that earlier contained Minuteman missiles. A smaller mobile missile with one warhead, the Midgetman, is expected to be built and deployed in the early 1990s. Meanwhile, it was hoped that American increased nuclear strength would bring new viability to the principle of mutual deterrence and close, to use Reagan's phrase, "the window of vulnerability." It would also help in inducing a meaningful and concessionary Soviet approach to negotiations on arms control, which—according to Reagan—was to aim at a *reduction* of the nuclear arsenals held by the superpowers rather than simply a limitation. Hence the U.S. government began in 1982 to talk about START (Strategic Arms Reduction Talks) instead of SALT negotiations, and START commenced in the summer of that year.[48] Finally, there was the expectation that "negotiating from strength" may not only lead to Soviet concessions and acceptable compromise on nuclear weapons, but eventually could bring changes in Soviet behavior in the international arena, since the United States may be much less acquiescent to Moscow's interventions as carried out, sometimes with surrogate forces, in Angola, Ethiopia, and perhaps even Afghanistan. Reagan's often tough rhetoric was at times punctuated by appeals for peace and for better relations with the Soviet Union,[49] but the drive for increased U.S. armament continued relentlessly. Meanwhile, rather interestingly, both countries promised to comply with the provisions of the unratified SALT II agreement.

The death of Leonid Brezhnev and the appointment of Yuri Andropov as general secretary of the Soviet Communist party is unlikely to change materially the relationship between the United States and the Soviet Union in the short term. Andropov's views of the world and of Soviet security needs seem to be similar to those held by his predecessor.[50] However, depending on economic factors, especially in the Soviet Union, the attitudes of the Soviet leadership may be modified and the START negotiations may assume a more conciliatory tone in the years to come.

Explanatory Variables

When assessing the sources of explanation for U.S. deterrence policy, it is quite obvious that international variables have played a major part in the formulation and reformulation of this policy. Interactional variables are reflected in both U.S. and Soviet initiatives, actions, and reactions. The initial nuclear superiority of the United States prompted a major Soviet effort over two to three decades to catch up, and once the Soviets had reached parity or perhaps superiority, U.S. policy responded with a major buildup of its own to wipe out perceived inferiority. Thus we witness a continued escalation in the expansion of nuclear arsenals on the part of both superpowers and a failure of the Carter administration to bring about an immediate reduction of launchers and warheads.

In addition to the interactional variables, systemic variables are also influential in explaining the U.S. policy of maintaining the credibility of the deterrence or MAD principle. A powerful bipolar strategic system has evolved following World War II that dominates the U.S.-Soviet relationship. This system consists of two alliances, NATO and the Warsaw Pact, whose members are organized around the United States and the Soviet Union, respectively. For both superpowers, their respective alliances provide added strength as well as increased responsibility for the combined security of each bloc. It is the continuously growing security concerns that drive the nuclear escalation process. The bipolar system may have been somewhat modified by the emergence of the People's Republic of China as a major international actor and may in due time produce a viable triangular strategic system, but at present there is little doubt that the dynamics of the bipolar system predominate the systemic landscape in terms of explaining U.S. deterrence and rearmament policy.

Idiosyncratic variables generally have accounted only for minor modifications in the formulation of deterrence policy toward the Soviet Union. All presidents since 1945 fully supported a viable deterrence policy, but three presidents seemed determined to break the upward spiral. As mentioned earlier, President Nixon introduced the notion of "sufficiency" and appeared to take a more pragmatic and broader view of parity in nuclear weapons between the two superpowers. The result was SALT I. President Ford, formulating policy under the guidance of the same secretary of state as Nixon, namely Kissinger, was successful in arranging for limits to nuclear weapons. As we have seen, Carter, who had a very strong personal and religious commitment to peace, failed in lowering these limits. For Reagan, a strong conservative with a hawkish orientation, any apparent nuclear inferiority vis-à-vis the Soviet Union was unthinkable (although many experts question any supposed inferiority), and therefore a major U.S. buildup of the nuclear arsenal continues.

It is important to note that the idiosyncrasies of some of the presidents are often reflected by those of their secretaries of state or defense, and the chief negotiators in the negotiations about strategic weapons. Nixon and Kissinger both were realists and pragmatists, and Gerard Smith who negotiated SALT I fell into the same mold. Carter and Secretary Vance were idealists, and Paul Warnke, the chief negotiator for SALT II, was a liberal whose hope it was to persuade the Soviet government of the benefits of lowering their nuclear stockpile as a boon to humanity. Reagan and his secretary of defense view the Soviet Union as a growing threat to the United States and see the solution to peace in an ever-growing buildup of nuclear weapons. Both Eugene Rostow, the former director of ACDA, and Paul Nitze, the chief negotiator, exhibit the same attitudinal characteristics.

A third cluster of variables likely to have affected and promoted a strong deterrence policy is the institutional category. The organizational goals of the Defense Department are enhanced when the military forces are expanded; ensuring a credible deterrence posture requires first the maintenance and later an increase of the nuclear arsenal and supporting military forces. Hence it is fair to assume that the Pentagon wielded considerable influence on the formulation of pertinent policies and that defense contractors and their associations bolstered the effectiveness of this influence through lobbying Congress and relevant executive departments.

There is a peculiar interplay between the goals of defense departments in both the United States and the Soviet Union. As the Soviet counterpart of the Pentagon clamors for stronger nuclear armament and these requests are accommodated by the Soviet leadership, justification is provided for the American military top echelon to demand increases in U.S. defense capabilities. Thus there exists an invisible partnership between the defense estalishments of the two countries that, though ominous, is not a conspiracy but part and parcel of the strategic bipolar system characterizing the relationship between the two countries.

Finally, public opinion—a societal variable—gave its permissive support to the deterrence policy, especially since the middle of the 1970s. Massive retaliation was seen as the needed protector during the 1950s and early 1960s in the event of Soviet aggression particularly in Europe, and the switch to the flexible doctrine aroused little opposition in the United States. In the turmoil of the Vietnam War, the deterrence principle was seen as a viable insurance policy against involvement by the Soviet Union.

Public support for strengthening American defense became visible in opinion surveys in 1969, and this support for greater expenditures for this purpose and a greater commitment to NATO rose steadily until the end of 1981 (see Table 9.2). However, in 1982, a slight decline in this support could be discerned. Whether this indicates a basic change in support for increased American military strength cannot be judged at this time. It may reflect the influence of the peace movement that spread across the United States during 1982, or it may suggest nothing more than a pause for reflection about the extraordinary devastation that would follow a nuclear exchange between the superpowers.

Table 9.2   Defense Spending Priorities and Commitment to NATO

	Too Little	Too much	About Right	No Opinion
Defense Spending				
1982	19%	36%	36%	9%
1981	51	15	22	12
1976	22	36	32	10
1973	13	46	30	11
1971	11	50	31	8
1969	8	52	31	9
	Increase	Keep Same	Decrease	Withdraw
Increase of Commitment to NATO				
1980	21%	44%	7%	7%
1978	9	59	9	n.a.[a]
1974	4	51	13	7

[a]Not available.

Sources: Gallup Organization Poll, October 1980; Gallup Survey 191-G (Q. 10) 1982; and Werner J. Feld and John K. Wildgen, *NATO and the Atlantic Defense* (New York: Praeger, 1982), p. 80.

U.S.-SOVIET COOPERATIVE TREATIES AND DETENTE

Despite the often confrontational and conflictual character of U.S. foreign policy toward the Soviet Union, there have also been significant aspects of cooperation. These aspects were reflected by a number of treaties and agreements concluded by the two countries, most of which relate to nuclear weapons and the avoidance of conflicts.

A brief summary of these agreements is instructive and suggests that when common interests are clearly definable, prolonged cooperation is feasible. We have, of course, discussed already the most significant set of agreements, SALT, which basically remains in force today. The other agreements also continue to be valid, although their significance may have been altered as the result of changed conditions surrounding the U.S.-Soviet relationship.

• The *Antarctic Treaty* of December 1959 was designed to prohibit the establishment of military bases and the testing of weapons in Antarctica. It provides for on-site inspections, and the United States has carried out several inspections of Soviet installations. Sixteen other states have acceded to this treaty.

• The *Direct Communications Agreement* of 1963, better known as the hot line, provides two direct communications circuits for immediate contact between Washington and Moscow. The hot line was used during the 1967 Middle East War and has been modernized in the early 1970s by using space satellites communications systems to assure improved reliability. It is tested hourly to maintain the highest degree of effectiveness.

• The *Limited Nuclear Test Ban Treaty*, also concluded in 1963, prohibits atmospheric tests of nuclear weapons and has been adopted by 113 countries, including the United States; however, France and the People's Republic of China, both nuclear powers, have refused to sign or to be bound by this treaty. Underground tests remained permissible.

• The *Outer Space Treaty* of 1967 requires the United States and the Soviet Union not to place in orbit around the earth any objects carrying nuclear weapons or any other kind of weapons of mass destruction, or to install such weapons on satellite bodies and outer space stations. However, the Soviet Union may have developed satellite "killers" that, operating from ground facilities, could play havoc with U.S. military satellite communications and prompt the American government to build similar devices including space-based ABM systems with laser- and particle-beam technology.

• The *Nuclear Non-Proliferation Treaty* of 1968 obligates the signatories not to transfer nuclear weapons or supply weapons technology to any non-nuclear weapons state, and it requires nonnuclear weapons states not to receive such weapons. In addition, nonnuclear countries agreed to inspections by the International Atomic Energy Agency (IAEA) as a means to prevent diversion of nuclear material from peaceful to military purposes. More than a hundred states have acceded to this treaty, including the United States, the Soviet Union, and Great Britain. France and the People's Republic of China are again notable exceptions, and so are Israel, South Africa, Brazil, and Pakistan.

• The *Seabed Arms Control Treaty* of 1971 prohibits placing nuclear weapons or other weapons of mass destruction beyond a 12-mile coastal seabed zone. Inspection may be carried out to ensure compliance. Besides the United States and the Soviet Union, seventeen other states are signatories to this agreement.

• A *U.S.-Soviet Trade Agreement* signed at the same time as SALT I in 1972 set up the joint U.S.-Soviet Trade Commission mentioned earlier and was to pave the way for the Soviet Union and East European satellites to be granted the benefits of the most-favored-nation clause. However, when the U.S. Trade Reform Act of 1974 was passed, a congressional amendment proposed by Senator Jackson and Congressman Vanik was accepted that made granting this clause contingent on freer emigration of Jews from the Soviet Union. The imposition of these conditions was considered a violation of the 1972 trade agreement and rejected. As a result, trade expansion between the two countries made little progress; however, U.S. grain sales to the Soviet Union have continued except for the period of the embargo put in place by President Carter as sanction against the invasion of Afghanistan.

• The *Treaty on the Limitation of Underground Nuclear Weapons Tests* of 1974 prohibits tests having a yield exceeding 150 kilotons.

• The *Peaceful Nuclear Explosions Treaty* of 1976 imposed the same limit of 150-kiloton size on tests of nuclear explosions for peaceful purposes. Moreover, and most significantly, both the United States and the Soviet Union permitted observers to monitor all nuclear explosions carried out on the territory of the other country when the explosion was to exceed the 150-kiloton limit. This was seen as a milestone for on-site inspections, which was a major goal for U.S. policy in all arms control negotiations.[51]

Detente a Viable Policy?

The question may be raised whether the above list of cooperative agreements between Washington and Moscow reflects a genuine relaxation of tension (detente) between the superpowers or merely occasional manifestations of common interests transcending a usually confrontational climate. More specifically, has detente been regarded as a viable U.S. policy vis-à-vis the Soviet Union in the past? How is it viewed by the Reagan administration? How does it relate to the policies of containment and deterrence?

As for Soviet interest in detente—a possible stimulus for U.S. foreign policy to respond either positively or negatively—it needs to be pointed out that as early as 1925 Stalin announced a period of "peaceful coexistence," when he perceived the revolutionary movement ebbing and capitalism achieving a temporary stabilization. However, Stalin did not consider peaceful coexistence to be permanent; it was a convenient tactic that did not preclude a simultaneous call to the international Communist parties to prepare for attack.[52]

The first major peace offensive after World War II was launched by the Soviet Union in March 1952. It proposed talks with the United States, Great Britain, and France on a German peace treaty, possible German reunification, and rearmament, although a rearmed Germany would have to be neutralized. In addition, the Soviet government held out the prospect for a 50-year European security treaty. Perhaps significantly, this proposal, articulated before Stalin's death in 1953, was made during a period of United States' overwhelming strategic superiority over the Soviet Union. When a foreign ministers' conference of the Four Powers was finally held in early 1954, the Soviet Union backed away from a unified but neutralized Germany.[53] In 1953, it had mastered the technology of the hydrogen bomb and was pressing forward with its nuclear buildup. A summit conference of the Four Powers held in Geneva in 1955, which was attended by President Eisenhower and Soviet Premier Bulganin and which earlier had been very much desired by the Soviet leadership, turned out to be a relaxed get-together, but made little progress in solving any major problems between East and West.

Nevertheless, the Geneva summit of 1955 was seen by many as the first step toward detente. It was followed in 1959 by the visit of Nikita Khrushchev, first secretary of the Soviet Communist party and Soviet premier (chairman of the Council of Ministers) to Camp David for consultations with Eisenhower. Khrushchev's trip to the United States was remarkable, including lunches with film stars, a visit to Eisenhower's farm at Gettysburg, and a farewell address to the American people on television. Hopes were high that the confrontational period between the two superpowers was coming to an end. However, while Khrushchev was clearly committed to "peaceful coexistence," it did not mean the abandonment of basic Soviet foreign policy goals or an end to the ideological and economic struggle between the Soviet Union and the Western democracies. The primary concern was the repudiation of war as a means of solving controversial issues.[54]

What had been dubbed the "spirit of Camp David" did not last long. Both Eisenhower and Khrushchev had agreed to meet again in May 1960 in Paris for another summit of the Big Four powers and later in Moscow. Problems with Western access to Berlin and the Soviet threat of signing a peace treaty with its East German satellite darkened the prospect for continuing on the path of detente. However, it was the downing of an American U-2 spy plane within the Soviet Union that scuttled the meeting of Eisenhower and Khrushchev in Paris, although both leaders had actually traveled to that city. Khrushchev demanded an apology from Eisenhower for the overflight, which the latter was unwilling to extend.[55] Although it is far from sure whether any benefits for peace and for a better relationship between the superpowers could have been derived from the Paris meeting, as things turned out, it was not surprising that the confrontational climate reemerged. Containment of the Soviet Union remained the primary preoccupation of U.S. policymakers.

Whereas U.S. and Soviet cooperative behavior was manifested in the Antarctica and Limited Nuclear Test Ban treaties as well as in the establishment of the "hot line," in-depth consideration of detente policy did not surface until 1967.

U.S. Acquiescence to Detente

Pressures for improved relations between the West and Soviet Union emanating from European elites such as the Action Committee for the United States of Europe found only a cautious response from President Kennedy, who declared in July 1963, "In time the unity of the West can lead to the unity of East and West."[56] In 1966, President Johnson followed this line of thought guardedly when he stated that NATO, the Atlantic Alliance, must adapt to changing conditions including quickening the progress in East-West relations.[57]

NATO became indeed the forum within which the basis for a joint U.S.-West European detente policy was placed. At the December 1967 meeting of the NATO Council, the so-called Harmel Report was approved—Pierre Harmel was the Belgian foreign minister. This report declared:

> Military security and a policy of detente are not contradictory but complementary. . . . Each Ally should play its full part in promoting an improvement in relations with the Soviet Union and the countries of Eastern Europe, bearing in mind that the pursuit of detente must not be allowed to split the Alliance. . . . The relaxation of tensions is not the final goal but is part of a long-term process to promote better relations. . . . The ultimate political purpose of the Alliance is to achieve a just and lasting peaceful order in Europe accompanied by appropriate security guarantees.[58]

The Soviet invasion of Czechoslovakia in 1968 to suppress by armed force an indigenous movement toward political liberalization quickly dispelled in Western Europe much of the euphoria surrounding the Harmel-inspired detente initiative. However, this reaction did not last long, and within a few months the pursuit of detente resumed in Western Europe, although the United States remained much more lukewarm toward this effort.

The Harmel Report spawned another initiative with potentially significant implications for detente to end the arms spiral. An attempt was undertaken to reduce the conventional forces of NATO and the Warsaw Pact countries in a mutual and balanced manner. Negotiations on Mutual and Balanced Force

Reductions (MBFR) began in Vienna in 1973 and are still in progress. All members of NATO except France, Portugal, and Iceland are participants.

In response to repeated Soviet requests, NATO set up machinery beginning in 1970 to coordinate the views of the NATO allies for preparatory meetings on European security and cooperations to be held in Helsinki in 1972 and later in Geneva in 1973 for substantive discussions. Various NATO committees dealing with issues that might come up in the first multilateral contacts between East and West met very frequently and were successful in harmonizing the NATO members' positions. Although the United States initially wanted to link these negotiations with positive results in the MBFR talks, it later abandoned this attempt at linkage. The results of the Conference on Security and Cooperation in Europe (CSCE), as stipulated in the Final Act signed August 1, 1975, in Helsinki, contained confidence-building measures based on exchanges of information about military activities such as impending maneuvers, agreements dealing with economic cooperation, and a chapter concerning humanitarian issues and freedom of information.

To monitor the implementation of CSCE a follow-up meeting took place in Belgrade between October 1977 and March 1978. Although there was much controversy during that meeting about what if any progress was achieved, a decision was taken to continue the CSCE process and to hold another follow-up meeting in Madrid, which began in November 1980 and, after a long adjournment in 1981, was resumed in 1982. Events in Poland after the declaration of martial law in December 1981 have focused attention on violations of the Helsinki agreement in Eastern Europe and have cast a pall of gloom and disappointment over this phase of detente, especially in the United States.

Continued Doubt about the Value of Detente

Many Americans have been suspicious of detente as being a tactic through which the Soviet Union is gaining considerably more advantages than the West, advantages that could not be achieved through other, especially Soviet, economic and technological resources. In very conservative quarters, a tough, confrontational stance toward the Soviet Union is seen as the only means to deal with Moscow and obtain concessions. Indeed, when during the Republican presidential primaries in 1976 Ronald Reagan challenged President Ford's foreign policies toward the Soviet Union as not being tough enough, the latter ordered his campaign organization to drop the word "detente" from the description of his foreign policies.

For President Nixon and Secretary of State Kissinger, however, detente was an important part of U.S. foreign policy. They considered detente to be based on strict reciprocity in the national interest.[59] For Kissinger, "detente could never replace a balance of power; it would be the result of equilibrium, not a substitute for it."[60] Yet, Kissinger acknowledged that the quest for detente or peaceful coexistence had its perils, but it did not follow from this that a "crusading policy of confrontation would prove more successful. The former might sap our vigilance; the latter would risk our national cohesion and our alliance as our government would be denounced with increasing vehemence as the cause of international tensions."[61] According to Kissinger, the American strategy of detente required the provision of incentives and penalties in order to restrain the Soviets from the temptation of expansionism.[62] In other words, U.S. resistance to expansionism was to be linked to reciprocal cooperation with Moscow.

To a certain extent, these words were prophetic. As President Carter's proposals for a SALT II agreement with lowered limits on strategic nuclear weapons were rejected by Moscow and the prospects for a less ambitious agreement faded away in the wake of the invasion of Afghanistan, the level of superpower confrontation rose rapidly; moreover, this trend accelerated further under President Reagan. His characterization of the Soviet Union as engaging in immoral, underhanded practices and duplicity in international politics, his repeated assertions—though most likely correct—that the Soviet Union is in deep economic difficulty and that "the march of freedom and democracy . . . will leave Marxism-Leninism on the ash heap of history,"[63] and the continued drive for extensive rearmament accompanied by warlike rhetoric have created a high degree of uneasiness among our NATO allies. The widespread peace demonstrations in many parts of Western Europe against U.S. strategic and regional nuclear policies during 1981 and 1982 have underscored the deepening rift in the alliance. Finally, the imposition of U.S. sanctions against the construction of the Soviet gas pipeline to Western Europe upset both West European governments and peoples, who see in detente and maximum trade with Eastern Europe the solution for domestic economic problems and for bridging East-West differences.

Of course, there have been calls for "constructive East-West relations" by the Reagan administration, and they were voiced again after Breshnev's death, but they were said to depend on "constructive Soviet behavior."[64] Such behavior in the near future may be doubted when one reads the first speech of Breshnev's successor, Yuri Andropov, who stated: "We know full well that the imperialists will never meet one's pleas for peace. It can be upheld only resting upon the invincible might of the Soviet armed forces."[65]

For all practical purposes, detente as a U.S. policy is dead at present, in spite of the fact that the Soviet government has shown some restraint since Afghanistan and has not undertaken new expansionist interventions. It is impossible to foresee whether the Reagan administration will come up with any new initiatives with respect to East-West relations. Basically, what is evident today is a complete return to containment policy whose aims in fact are stronger now than at any time since 1947.

However, Reagan has the same kind of political credentials to change the U.S.-Soviet relationship as Nixon had for the reversal of the U.S.-China relations. If that were to happen, Reagan would have to make clear what quid pro quo the United States is prepared to offer for particular Soviet "constructive" actions.

Explanatory Variables

As with other U.S. policies toward the Soviet Union, detente, which as a policy was pursued from about 1967 to 1979, has its mainsprings in the international arena. However, interactional variables in this case have sprung more from America's interactions with its NATO allies than the Soviet Union. It is somewhat doubtful whether the United States would have responded favorably to Soviet demands for a European security treaty if it had not been for the pleas of major West European allies such as the Federal Republic of Germany. Indeed, the Soviet Union initially wanted to exclude Washington from European security talks, but Moscow was persuaded to include the United States and Canada because the West Europeans rejected the Soviet overtures for such talks without the Americans and Canadians.

It is interesting to note the concept of detente advanced by Kissinger that relaxation of tensions in East-West relations should be seen as part of the balance of power between the superpowers. Considering that the bipolar balance-of-power relationship includes the respective allies of the two superpowers and that the allies have a measure of influence on the attitudes of the superpowers, this relationship has to be regarded as a systemic variable that affects the nature and magnitude of detente in U.S. policy. From this perspective, detente would take its place with containment as measures to control and influence Soviet behavior—which, after all, is the fundamental rationale for all U.S. policies toward the Soviet Union.

What is the explanation for the cooperative agreements concluded between Washington and Moscow? They are manifestations of recurring commonalities of interest of the two superpowers that can be seen as interactional variables motivating cooperation when it benefits both countries. They confirm the soundness of a U.S. detente strategy based on the concept of reciprocal cooperation with the Soviet Union.

Idiosyncratic variables also have influenced the formulation and demise of detente policy. Nixon and Ford, with guidance by Kissinger, had the foreign policy experiences and balanced judgments to see merit in detente. The intellectual basis was provided by Henry Kissinger, whose penchant for the intricacies of the balance-of-power game was of long standing. In spite of the fact that Ford had to denounce the use of the term "detente," the policy thrust was not changed. Carter's sincere wishes to produce a rapid reduction in the nuclear arsenals of the two superpowers, coupled with his religious commitment, were a strong motivation to pursue detente until his deep disappointment with the Soviet invasion of Afghanistan.

From the institutional point of view, it is fair to assume that the Departments of State, Commerce, and Agriculture were by and large supporters of detente. Most State Department officials prefer political solutions to East-West problems, and this implies cooperation rather than confrontation. Important constituencies of the Departments of Commerce and Agriculture benefit from trade with the Soviet Union and Eastern Europe, and therefore have substantial interests in relatively harmonious relations with Moscow. These constituencies include manufacturers of heavy machinery and electrical products as well as producers and exporters of grain. Officials of the two departments usually are responsive to the interests of these groups and therefore seek to promote conditions conducive to the satisfaction of these interests. However, the Defense Department and its contractors are likely to oppose the pursuit of a detente policy. Their interests generally are aided by a confrontational climate in East-West relations, and their distrust of Soviet intentions, for whatever reasons, is usually high.

In terms of societal variables, the widespread anticommunist sentiments and the often-voiced distrust of the Soviet Union do not augur well for a sustained detente policy, no matter how it is packaged. It is noteworthy, however, that public opinion does not appear to have set any limits on the initiation or pursuit of a detente policy in spite of the fact that beginning with 1971 there has been growing support for increased defense expenditures, as shown in Table 3.2. As this table shows, however, support for increases in defense costs may be waning, and in 1982 there was strong support by the U.S. public (77 percent) and elites (96 percent) for the negotiation of arms control agreements between the two superpowers and for joint efforts with the Soviet Union to solve energy problems (64 and 78 percent, respectively).[65] Thus, it seems that the American public may well accept detente as a policy if it were offered by the present or future administration. Indeed, the increasing realization of the enormous disaster that would follow a nuclear exchange, also reflected in a growing American peace movement, might make such a policy welcome.

SUMMARY

American foreign policy toward the Soviet Union has been characterized by a persistent theme: *containment* of Soviet expansionist designs. Shortly after the adoption of the containment policy in 1947, two collateral policies were formulated and implemented. One was the creation of the *Marshall Plan*, designed to achieve West European economic recovery, also known as the *European Recovery Program (ERP)*. It was a very successful policy. The other was the establishment of the *NATO alliance*, which, despite having been plagued by occasional controversies, has retained most of its effectiveness until now.

Although the NATO alliance strengthened U.S. security, the possibility of Soviet aggression in Europe with overwhelming conventional forces or nuclear weapons was seen as requiring an American nuclear response. The initial U.S. policy response was the strategy of *massive retaliation*, which became the major deterrent against possible Soviet attack.

This strategy was placed into question when it appeared the Soviet challenges might be cast in less than all-out form and Soviet encroachments in Western Europe by themselves may not threaten U.S. vital interests. The result was the adoption of a different strategy called *flexible response*, through which nuclear escalation was hoped to be controlled.

To maintain the peace between the United States and the Soviet Union in face of a growing nuclear arsenal on both sides, the concept of *"mutually assured destruction" (MAD)* was developed, which was hoped would deter either side from an attack on the other. At the same time, much effort and time was expended to reach an agreement on the limitation of strategic arms, all nuclear weapons. The result in 1972 was *SALT I*, which limited both the deployment of antiballistic missiles (ABMs) and put a ceiling on the number of permissible offensive weapons.

In 1974 an additional agreement was reached in Vladivostok to limit further the number of delivery vehicles to 2400 and those that could have multiple warheads (MIRVs) to 1320. A further round of strategic arms limitations talks (*SALT II*) was concluded and signed in 1979, but not ratified by the U.S. Senate.

A number of U.S.-Soviet cooperation treaties dealing with nuclear and economic matters were concluded beginning in 1959, and in the second half of the 1960s, the United States gave serious consideration to a policy of *detente* (relaxation of tensions). As a consequence, NATO became a forum in which details of a detente policy toward the Soviet Union were elaborated. Although troubled by reservations, the United States signed the Final Act of the *Conference on Security and Cooperation in Europe (CSCE)*, perhaps so far the high point of American detente policy.

The future of American detente policy is very clouded. American support for such a policy, according to the Reagan administration, depends on Moscow's "constructive behavior." For many Americans, the past era of detente was used by the Soviet Union for a strong and sustained buildup of its nuclear arsenal, making the Soviet nuclear might superior to that of the United States.

NOTES

1. John L. Snell, *Wartime Origins of the East-West Dilemma over Germany* (New Orleans: Hauser Press, 1949), pp. 38 and 39.
2. Ibid., p. 44.
3. Karl Lowenstein, "The Allied Presence in Berlin: Legal Basis," *Foreign Policy Bulletin* (February 15, 1959), pp. 81 ff.
4. Ibid., p. 82.

5. For a careful discussion of the Oder-Neisse Line problem, see Z.M. Szaz, *Germany's Eastern Frontiers, The Problem of the Oder-Neisse Line* (Chicago: Henry Regnery, 1960); W.M. Drzewieniecki, *The German-Polish Frontier* (Chicago: Polish Western Association of America, 1959); and Elizabeth Wiskemann, *Germany's Eastern Neighbors* (London: Oxford University Press, 1956).

6. U.S. Department of State, *The Axis in Defeat*, pp. 15 and 16 Washington, D.C., 1945; James F. Byrnes, *Speaking Frankly* (New York: Harper, 1947), p. 85.

7. Robert Slusser (ed.), *Soviet Economic Policy in Postwar Germany* (New York: Research Program on the U.S.S.R., 1953), p. x.

8. J.P. Nettle, *The Eastern Zone and Soviet Policy in Germany 1945−50* (London: Oxford University Press, 1951), pp. 219 ff.

9. Snell, *Wartime Origins*, p. 223; Slusser (ed.), *Soviet Economic Policy*, p. xix.

10. Byrnes, *Speaking Frankly*, pp. 171−198.

11. See Max Beloff, *The United States and the Unity of Europe* (New York: Vantage Books, 1963), pp. 5−10.

12. John L. Gaddis, *The United States and the Origins of the Cold War* (New York: Columbia University Press, 1972), pp. 299−300.

13. Winston Churchill, "The Sinews of Peace," *Vital Speeches of the Day* 12 (March 15, 1946), p. 332.

14. "The Sources of Soviet Conduct," *Foreign Affairs* 25 (July 1947), pp. 566−582.

15. See George Kennan, *Memoirs* (Boston: Little, Brown, 1967), pp. 547−559.

16. Ibid., p. 294. "It reads like one of those primers . . . to arouse the citizenry to the dangers of the Communist conspiracy."

17. Harry S. Truman, "The Truman Doctrine: Special Message to the Congress on Greece and Turkey," March 12, 1947, in *Public Papers of the Presidents of the United States: Harry S. Truman, 1947* (Washington, D.C.), p. 178.

18. For details see Ronald Steel, "Did Anybody Start the Cold War?" *New York Review* 26 (September 2, 1971), p. 26.

19. Harry S. Truman, *Memoirs*, Vol. 1 (Garden City, N.Y.: Doubleday, 1955), p. 71. See also Robert J. Donavan, *Tumultuous Years* (New York: W.W. Norton, 1982), pp. 14−15.

20. For more details on Acheson's view, see Dean G. Acheson, *Present at the Creation* (New York: W.W. Norton, 1969), p. 293, and also all of Chapter 22.

21. For details see Slusser, *Soviet Economic Policy*.

22. For an explanation of this inconsistency and the strategy for "self-exclusion" of the Soviet Union, see Beloff, *United States and the Unity of Europe*, pp. 29−40.

23. Thomas A. Bailey, *A Diplomatic History of the American People*, 6th ed. (New York: Appleton-Century-Crofts, 1958), p. 800.

24. For a detailed study of this period of postwar history, see Ernst H. Van der Beuge, *From Marshall Aid to Atlantic Partnership* (New York: Elsevier, 1966).

25. Eric Stein and Peter Hay, *Law and Institutions in the Atlantic Area* (Indianapolis: Bobbs-Merrill, 1967), p. 1032. For a survey of the founding of the institutions of NATO as well as the conclusion of the North Atlantic Treaty, see Robert S. Jordan, *The NATO International Staff/Secretariat 1952−1957: A Study in International Administration* (New York: Oxford University Press, 1967).

26. Stein and Hay, *Law and Institutions*.

27. See Theodore C. Achilles, "U.S. Role in Negotiations that led to Atlantic Alliance," *NATO Review* 27 (August 1979), pp. 11−14.

28. Quoted in Alexander Rendel, "The Alliance's Anxious Birth," *NATO Review* 27 (June 1979), pp. 15−20, on p. 16.

29. Ibid., p. 17.

30. For a full discussion of these problems see ibid., pp. 17−20. See also Robert Strausz-Hupe, James E. Dougherty, and William R. Kintner, *Building the Atlantic World* (New York: Harper & Row, 1963), passim.

31. Achilles, "U.S. Role in Negotiations," pp. 12–13.
32. Paragraph 3 of Senate Resolution 239, June 11, 1948, 94 Congressional Record 7791, 7846.
33. Achilles, "U.S. Role in Negotiations," p. 14. See also Edwin H. Fedder, *NATO, The Dynamics of Alliance in the Postwar World* (New York: Dodd, Mead, 1973).
34. For additional details see Endicott Reid, "The Miraculous Birth of the North Atlantic Alliance," *NATO Review* 28 (December 1980), pp. 12–18, esp. pp. 14–17.
35. Quoted in Theodore C. Achilles, "U.S. Role in Negotiations that Led to Atlantic Alliance," Part 2, *NATO Review* 27 (October 1979), pp. 16–19, on p. 18.
36. *New York Times*, May 15, 1947. For a survey of how the treaty provisions were applied in the first 20 years, see Robert S. Jordan, *Political Leadership in NATO: A Study in Multinational Diplomacy* (Boulder, Colo.: Westview Press, 1979).
37. Glen H. Snyder, "The New Look of 1953," in *Strategy, Politics, and Defense Budgets*, edited by Warner Schilling, Paul G. Hainsmond, and Glen H. Snyder (New York: Columbia University Press, 1962), p. 436.
38. John Foster Dulles, "The Evolution of Foreign Policy," *Department of State Bulletin* 30, 761 (January 25, 1954), p. 108.
39. See John Foster Dulles, "A Policy of Liberation," *Life* (May 19, 1952), pp. 19 ff.
40. Henry Kissinger, *Nuclear Weapons and Foreign Policy* (New York: Harper & Row, 1957).
41. See McNamara's speech at the University of Michigan, June 16, 1962, *Department of State Bulletin* (July 9, 1962), pp. 64–69.
42. Henry T. Nash, *American Foreign Policy: Changing Perspectives on National Security*, rev. ed. (Homewood, Ill.: The Dorsey Press, 1978), p. 266.
43. This appraisal is based on the author's conversation with Smith.
44. For details see U.S. Arms Control and Disarmament Agency, *Tenth Annual Report to Congress* (Washington, D.C., January 1, 1970–December 31, 1970).
45. Nash, *American Foreign Policy*, p. 277. Nash provides an excellent account and analysis of the SALT I negotiations and results on pp. 267–283. See also Mason Willrich and John B. Rhinelander (eds.), *SALT, The Moscow Agreements and Beyond* (New York: Free Press, 1974).
46. Nash, *American Foreign Policy*, p. 292.
47. For a detailed account of the Cuban missile crisis, see Graham T. Allison, *Essence of Decision: Explaining the Cuban Missile Crisis* (Boston: Little, Brown, 1971).
48. For details, see Alexander Haig's statement, when secretary of state, to the Senate Foreign Relations Committee on May 11, 1982, reprinted in U.S., Department of State, Bureau of Public Affairs, *Current Policy No. 389*.
49. For example, in his news conference on November 10, 1982, published in *Times-Picayune* (New Orleans), November 11, 1982.
50. See his statement on November 12, 1982, published in *Times-Picayune* (New Orleans), November 13, 1982.
51. *Arms Control Report*, ACDA, Publication 89 (July 1976), p. 75.
52. For details and citations see Werner Feld, *Reunification and West German-Soviet Relations* (The Hague: Martinus Nijhoff, 1963), pp. 87–88.
53. Ibid., pp. 106, 107, 132–135. See also Adam Ulam, *Expansion and Coexistence: Soviet Foreign Policy 1917–1973*, rev. ed. (New York: Praeger, 1973), pp. 535–540.
54. For additional details, see Richard C. Gripp, *Patterns of Soviet Politics* (Homewood, Ill.: The Dorsey Press, 1963), pp. 295–297.
55. Details are found in Dwight D. Eisenhower, *Waging Peace* (Garden City, N.Y.: Doubleday, 1965), pp. 546–558.
56. Quoted in Elliot R. Goodman, *The Fate of the Atlantic Community* (New York: Praeger, 1975), p. 298.
57. Address by President Lyndon B. Johnson at New York, October 7, 1966, *Department of State Bulletin* 55, 1426, pp. 623–624.

58. *NATO Handbook* (February 1976), p. 64.
59. Henry Kissinger, *White House Years* (Boston: Little, Brown, 1979), p. 949.
60. Ibid., p. 1143.
61. Ibid., p. 1256.
62. Ibid., p. 1144.
63. U.S., Department of State, Bureau of Public Affairs, *Promoting Democracy and Peace* (Current Policy No. 399, June 8, 1982).
64. *Times-Picayune* (New Orleans), November 15, 1982; see also William G. Hyland, "U.S.-Soviet Relations: The Long Road Back," *Foreign Affairs* 60, 3 (Winter 1981), pp. 525−550.
65. *Times-Picayune* (New Orleans), November 13, 1982.
66. John E. Rielly (ed.), *American Public Opinion and U.S. Foreign Policy, 1983* (Chicago: Chicago Council on Foreign Relations, 1983), p. 15 (Table II-5).

10

Policies toward
Communist Asia

THE PEOPLE'S REPUBLIC OF CHINA

Post-World War II China was characterized by a severe struggle between the Nationalist government of Chiang Kai-shek and the Communists under Mao Zedong. During World War II, both the Nationalists and the Communists fought to defeat the Japanese who, during the 1930s, at first invaded Manchuria where they set up a puppet government in 1934, and moved into China's northern provinces in 1937.

Chiang Kai-shek, who in the late 1920s had emerged as the leader of the Kuomintang party, subscribed to the concept of democracy and was anxious to modernize China. However, Chiang's government was opposed by Mao's Communist party, and, in the early 1930s, an internal political contest ensued that, although drowned out during World War II because of the common struggle against the Japanese enemy and the U.S.-Chinese military cooperation, broke out again soon after Japan was defeated. During the war, Chiang did not fully commit his forces against the Japanese in order to save them for a later fight with Mao. Consequently, the Communist forces by their very vigorous combat against the Japanese gained the support of the Chinese peasants.

The United States attempted to mediate between Chiang and Mao. General George C. Marshall traveled to China in December 1945 and succeeded in arranging a cease-fire between the two opposing forces in February 1946.

However, the cease-fire did not hold, and in April 1946 fighting resumed. The United States spent over $2 billion for the transportation of Chiang's troops to North China, the stronghold of the Communist forces, and for American military advisors to assist the Nationalists' field commanders. The Soviet Union aided Mao with large quantities of captured Japanese weapons, as Soviet forces withdrew from Manchuria occupied earlier by Japan.[1]

It became clear in 1947 that Chiang would be unable to defeat the Communist forces. Corruption and inefficiency were widespread in Chiang's administration. Inflation was rampant, and as a consequence, the economic base of Nationalist China deteriorated. Chiang's troops suffered defeat after defeat by the Communists, while at the same time Chiang's government resorted increasingly to police-state methods including outright terrorism.

In the summer of that year, the U.S. government sent General Albert Wedemeyer on a fact-finding tour to China in order to come up with an assessment whether additional assistance could turn around the deteriorating situation. Wedemeyer's report was pessimistic; it stated that only far-reaching economic and administrative reforms could produce a real and lasting improvement. Nevertheless, the United States offered an additional $300 million in economic assistance for 1948, but the decline of the Nationalist military situation continued with more and more territory falling into Communist hands.

By the end of 1948, the Truman administration had come to the conclusion that the Nationalist government in China could only be saved by the direct intervention of American forces. Chiang's major problems on the battle field were seen as lack of effective leadership and other morale-destroying factors, as well as loss of political and popular support.[2] However, Secretary of State Marshall advised against such U.S. intervention.

During the early part of 1949, Chinese Communist forces spread out toward the south of China, and the Nationalist government was compelled to move from Nanking to Canton. Finally, defeated in one battle after another, Chiang was forced to flee the mainland and set up a government-in-exile on the island of Taiwan, formerly Formosa. The new regime was given the name of the "Republic of China," whereas Mao inaugurated his Communist government in Peking on October 1, 1949 and proclaimed it the "People's Republic of China."

The Period of Nonrecognition

Unable to produce a satisfactory solution on the Chinese mainland and accused by many Republicans and some conservative Democrats of having lost China to the Communists, the Truman administration declined on the one hand to extend diplomatic recognition to the regime of Mao Zedong and broke off all contacts including trade with the Chinese mainland. On the other hand,

Washington barred further military aid to Chiang on Taiwan but extended limited economic assistance under the general foreign aid program. Meanwhile, the Soviet Union signed a 30-year mutual aid pact with Peking that obligated each signatory to come to the aid of the other if attacked by Japan or the Western allies.[3]

In a somewhat prophetic assessment of future developments in China, Dean Acheson predicted in 1949 that despite the basically common ideology of the Soviet Union and the PRC, they would eventually clash with one another. Concerned with preserving their national interest, the PRC would resist Soviet penetration. Hence the United States should avoid raising the anger and hatred of the Chinese people on the mainland that would follow a strong support of Chiang on Taiwan.[4] At the same time, the administration published a white paper arguing that the Nationalists had lost control of the mainland in spite of adequate U.S. military and economic aid.[5] Indeed, it was generally expected that Taiwan would fall soon to the Communists. In terms of U.S. containment of the Soviet Union, Chiang was seen as having failed in this task.

The Korean War

The perceptions and attitude of the U.S. government toward the PRC and Chiang began to change when, on June 24, 1950, North Korean forces supported by more than 100 Soviet-built tanks invaded South Korea by crossing the thirty-eighth parallel, the boundary between North and South Korea. The U.S. response was quick and decisive. American air and naval units were ordered into action by President Truman on June 26 to provide assistance to South Korea. The U.N. Security Council was asked to meet, and it passed a resolution on June 27 recommending that the member states provide assistance to South Korea. The resolution was not vetoed by the Soviet Union, because its representative was absent during the crucial meeting, the result of a protracted Soviet boycott of any Security Council session. The outcome of all this was that the command and deployment of U.N. forces in Korea were totally under U.S. control, and any military units of U.N. member states assigned to these efforts were to operate under General Douglas MacArthur, as the U.S. top commander.

Although there was no evidence that the leadership of the PRC had instigated the North Korean attack, it was clear that a North Korean victory would benefit the Chinese Communists. Moreover, such an event might prompt a PRC attack on Taiwan. To make sure that such an attack would not be provoked otherwise, Truman asked Chiang to halt all military actions against the mainland, and he declined Chiang's offer, supported by MacArthur, of 30,000 Nationalist troops.

Domestic politics also played a part in generating a stronger anti-PRC stance of the Truman administration. The administration was attacked by conservatives for its unwillingness to commit U.S. forces in defense of Chiang and the failure of adequately containing communism in Asia. These criticisms found ready support by a vocal and often very influential group of organizations and individuals that was referred to generally as the China lobby and that carried on very successful propaganda operations to prevent any improvement of U.S. relations with the PRC. These lobbying activities were bolstered and sometimes coordinated by the Chinese government in Formosa and resulted in large amounts of economic and military aid to the Chiang regime, totaling $5.82 billion between 1946 and 1980.[6] Even today, the political clout of what is essentially now the Taiwan lobby is awesome.

Any thought of improving U.S. relations with the Mao government vanished when the PRC intervened in the Korean conflict late in 1950. Following a brilliantly conceived and executed behind-the-enemy-lines landing of American troops at the port city of Inchon in September 1950 and the virtual defeat of the North Korean army, MacArthur planned to move up the west coast of Korea to the Yalu River, the boundary between North Korea and the PRC. This plan, if successful, would go beyond containment and embark on a path of "liberating" the people of North Korea from the Communist regime. Truman consented to this plan, undoubtedly motivated in part by domestic political considerations in view of the upcoming 1952 presidential election. This was the likely reason that he ignored Chinese and Soviet feelers for a political settlement in October 1950.

In spite of clear warnings by the leadership of the PRC in October against moving U.S. troops toward the Yalu River,[7] MacArthur pressed his offensive. By early November, U.S. forces became engaged heavily in combat with PRC troops that had crossed the Yalu River. Although American planes bombed the Yalu River bridges, six PRC armies went on the offensive at the end of that month and inflicted a serious defeat on American and South Korean forces compelling them to retreat rapidly. By the end of December, North Korea was evacuated, and the U.N. forces were deployed along the thirty-eighth parallel.

The Korean War pointed up the problems of formulating security and foreign policy aimed at a limited objective about which disagreements existed between the civilian leadership (the president) and the top-level field commander (General MacArthur). With the idiosyncrasies of the two leaders sharply diverging,[8] misunderstandings (both purposeful as well as inadvertent) became almost inevitable. This divergence was compounded by their profound differences of priorities based on their very disparate images of the world. MacArthur felt that the United States should fight the Communists everywhere; he hoped to use Chiang's forces in the war but underestimated the PRC reaction. Truman, on the other hand, wanted to keep the Chinese Communists and the Soviet Union out of the Korean conflict, because his main concern was to prevent a Soviet attack on Western Europe, and therefore he wanted to limit the struggle in Korea. MacArthur, on the other hand, was convinced that without the constraints imposed on him by Washington, including the prohibition to bomb north of the Yalu River, he could have defeated the PRC forces.[9]

General MacArthur was relieved of his command on April 11, 1951, and the Korean struggle continued inconclusively until 1953 when, on July 27, an armistice was signed between the belligerents. Ending the war in Korea had been one of the goals that President Eisenhower had set for himself in his election campaign for the presidency, and during his promised visit to Korea carried out in December 1952, he became convinced that further offensive military action would be extremely costly in view of the very strong defensive positions occupied by the North Koreans and Chinese. However, to obtain an acceptable agreement, Eisenhower had to threaten privately the employment of nuclear weapons and to bomb hydroelectric and irrigation dams on and near the Yalu River.[10] For most Americans, fighting and concluding a limited war was a new and somewhat unsettling experience. It meant fighting with one hand forced behind their backs; clearly MacArthur's maxim "In war, there is no substitute for victory" was more appealing.[11]

For nearly two decades following the hostilities in Korea in 1953, the U.S. policy of diplomatic nonrecognition of the PRC continued. American official enmity toward the PRC received support by the public at large, which looked on the Mao regime as part of the "Communist global conspiracy." These sentiments appeared to be confirmed, if not strengthened, by the Formosa Strait crises in 1954 and 1955, when the Communists began shelling the Nationalist islands of Quemoy and Matsu located less than 10 miles from the Chinese mainland. The United States pledged to defend these islands if attacked, and when in 1958 the Communists again shelled the islands quite heavily, the U.S. Seventh Fleet escorted Nationalist supply vessels within 3 miles of the beleaguered islands. Attempts by the PRC air force to gain air supremacy over the islands also failed because of strong opposition by Nationalist planes equipped with U.S. air-to-air missiles. However, Chiang Kai-shek's calls for a reconquest of the mainland did not find support by the United States, signaling that the United States acknowledged the Chinese Communist government as being in de facto control of the mainland.[12]

Another major flashpoint of conflicting U.S. and PRC foreign policies was Vietnam. Peking supplied vital military materiel, economic aid, and diplomatic support to North Vietnam, and it had close ties with the Viet Cong forces. In addition, it aided the *Pathet Lao* and other insurgent forces in Laos and Cambodia. Finally, when negotiations to end the war in Vietnam began in 1968, North Vietnam's reticence to pursue these negotiations with some vigor may well have been caused by Peking's tough positions vis-à-vis the United States and its desire to keep the "revolutionary movement" in Vietnam at a high pitch. For this reason, Communist Chinese assistance was also given to insurgent movements in other parts of Southeast Asia, especially Thailand, Burma, and Malaysia.

A New Beginning

A radical change in the relationship between the United States and PRC and in their foreign policies toward each other took place in 1971 when Henry

Kissinger, following a Peking invitation to President Nixon to send a personal envoy, traveled to the capital of the PRC.

The invitation from PRC premiere Chou en Lai was transmitted through Pakistan's President Yahya Khan. The pertinent part of the invitation read as follows:

> If the relations between China and the USA are to be restored fundamentally, the US must withdraw all its Armed forces from China's Taiwan and Taiwan Straits area. A solution to this crucial question can be found only through direct discussions between high level responsible persons of the two countries. Therefore, the Chinese Govt reaffirms its willingness to receive publically (sic) in Peking a special envoy of the President of the US (for instance, Mr Kissinger) or the US Secy of State or even the President of the US himself for a direct meeting and discussions. Of course, if the US President considers that the time is not yet ripe, the matter may be deferred to a later date.[13]

Kissinger arrived in Peking July 9, 1971, after enormous efforts were made to shroud the trip in secrecy. Although during the 2 days of talks controversial issues such as Taiwan and the negotiations with North Vietnamese in Paris could not be settled, the groundwork was laid to turn a page in history.[14] This was obvious when President Nixon announced Kissinger's concluded visit to Peking to the American people. The announcement stated:

> Premier Chou En-lai and Dr. Henry Kissinger, President Nixon's Assistant for National Security Affairs, held talks in Peking from July 9 to 11, 1981. Knowing of President Nixon's expressed desire to visit the People's Republic of China, Premier Chou En-lai, on behalf of the Government of the People's Republic of China, has extended an invitation to President Nixon to visit China at an appropriate date before May 1972. President Nixon has accepted the invitation with pleasure.
>
> The meeting between the leaders of China and the United States is to seek the normalization of relations between the two countries and also to exchange views on questions of concern to the two sides.
>
> In anticipation of the inevitable speculation which will follow this announcement, I want to put our policy in the clearest possible context.
>
> Our action in seeking a new relationship with the People's Republic of China will not be at the expense of our old friends. It is not directed against any other nation. We seek friendly relations with all nations. Any nation can be our friend without being any other nation's enemy.
>
> I have taken this action because of my profound conviction that all nations will gain from a reduction of tensions and a better relationship between the United States and the People's Republic of China.
>
> It is in this spirit that I will undertake what I deeply hope will become a journey for peace, peace not just for our generation but for future generations on this earth we share together.[15]

Although the announcement electrified the world, preparations for an opening between the United States and the PRC had been under way for about 2 years.

Indirect contacts had been established in Europe, mainly in Warsaw between the U.S. and Chinese chief diplomats who met more than a hundred times. Person-to-person relationships were also generated through a trip by an American table tennis team to China in the spring of 1971.[16]

For the Chinese leadership in Peking, an important motivation for the opening toward the United States undoubtedly lay in the deterioration of the Sino-Soviet relations. This deterioration was caused by conflicting territorial claims along the 4500-mile border between the two countries, which created especially tense relations on the frontier of China's westernmost province of Sinkiang and the disputed Amur River district of Manchuria. Another cause for the Sino-Soviet split was a different perception of communism on the part of the two countries and Mao's claim to the ideological leadership of world communism, with Peking's insistence that the revolutionary struggle must be intensified and continued, even if it would lead to nuclear war. Moscow, in contrast, pushed for peaceful coexistence. In any event, with a continuing Soviet military buildup along the extensive common border, the PRC became anxious to reduce the number of adversaries and obtain a counterweight to Soviet pressure. Hence the signals from Peking to Washington for a change of course corresponded to their perceptions of what would best serve Chinese national interests.

An immediate task after Kissinger's return from Peking was to shift U.S. policy on Chinese representation in the United Nations. The stance assumed by the Nixon administration (after some internal controversy) was dual representation by the PRC and Taiwan, with Peking occupying the seat in the Security Council, giving it the right of the veto. In order to assure this outcome, the U.S. embassies all over the world were instructed to lobby intensively the governments in those countries where they were located to support the U.S. position. However, the lobbying efforts were not successful. When the General Assembly voted on October 25, 1971, Peking was granted the sole representation of China in all bodies of the United Nations, and Taiwan, for all practical purposes, was expelled.[17]

American policy toward the PRC was shaped further by Nixon's visit to China in February 1972. After many talks held by Nixon and his entourage with the Chinese leadership, the evidence of a newly emerging relationship between Washington and Peking was reflected in the famous Shanghai Communique. The Chinese, motivated by fear of Soviet expansionism, and the United States, interested in some kinds of triangular diplomacy and international equilibrium, came up with agreements on a number of points. However, as Kissinger points out, U.S. interests and goals were somewhat different from those of the PRC with respect to the Soviet Union.

> We had no vested interest in permanent hostility with Moscow unless Moscow challenged the international equilibrium. As nuclear superpowers, we had indeed an obligation to reduce the threat of nuclear confrontation. Peking would no doubt

have preferred a simpler pattern of overt hostility between Washington and Moscow. This would have eased its calculations and improved its bargaining position. Our necessities were more complicated. Peking's domestic imperatives pushed it toward confrontation; our imperative was to demonstrate to our public and to our allies that we were not the cause of conflict, or else the Congress would dismantle our defenses and our allies would dissociate from us. Only from a conciliatory platform could we rally support for firm action in a crisis. We were prepared to confront Soviet expansion. But we were not willing to foreclose the option of a genuine easing of tensions with Moscow if that could in time be achieved. Thus we had to make sure that China understood our purposes and would not be surprised by our actions. We kept Peking assiduously informed of our moves. We sought to avoid any implication of condominium. What we could not do was to give Peking a veto over our relationship with Moscow any more than we would give a veto to the Soviets over our relations with China. It was a three-dimensional game, but any simplification had the makings of catastrophe. If we appeared irresolute or leaning toward Moscow, Peking would be driven to accommodation with the Soviet Union. If we adopted the Chinese attitude, however, we might not even help Peking; we might, in fact, tempt a Soviet preemptive attack on China and thus be faced with decisions of enormous danger.[18]

In the Shanghai Communique, the two countries renounced the use of force for the settlement of disputes between each other. They agreed not to enter into any agreements aimed at the other and declared their common opposition to "hegemonic" aspirations of others. They undertook to expand mutual trade and exchanges, but these were of secondary importance to both sides. Liaison offices were to be set up in 1973 in each other's capitals, which were almost de facto embassies and which had as their tasks to promote expanded economic, cultural, and people-to-people exchanges.

Understandably, the most difficult problem was Taiwan. The United States acknowledged that Taiwan was part of China and reaffirmed its interest in a peaceful settlement of the Taiwan question by the Chinese themselves. The United States also stated that as an ultimate objective linked to the peaceful settlement of the Taiwan issue, it agreed to the principle of total withdrawal of American military forces from the island. However, the number of such forces on Taiwan was small, consisting mostly of communications personnel. Rather, the real U.S. security role in support of Taiwan was stipulated in the Mutual Defense Treaty of 1955, which remained in force and was reaffirmed by Kissinger.[19]

Without doubt, the credit for the basic formulation and initiation of this extraordinary change in U.S. policy must go to Richard Nixon. His well-known "anticommunist" credentials and his farsighted understanding of international politics were the essential ingredients to make this new and courageous direction in American policy possible.

Diplomatic Relations

The foreign policy thrust toward the PRC initiated by Nixon continued under the Ford and Carter administrations. A major upgrading of U.S.-PRC relations took place January 1, 1979 when the two countries established full diplomatic relations. At the same time, the U.S. government withdrew recognition of Taiwan and broke diplomatic relations with Taipei. It gave notice under Article X of the Mutual Defense Treaty with Taiwan to terminate that treaty effective January 1, 1980. However, while the United States imposed a 1-year moratorium on new commitments, previous commitments under that treaty for arms deliveries were to be honored. At the same time, the PRC declared that it would respect the "status quo on Taiwan in settling the question of reunification" and that "all military confrontation should be ended" between the government of the PRC and the Taiwan authorities.[20]

The U.S. embassy in Peking (now called Beijing) and the PRC embassy in Washington opened on March 1, 1979, while the U.S. and "Republic of China" embassies closed in the respective capitals. Two weeks earlier, Taiwan established the Coordination Council for North American Affairs (CCNAA) to carry out unofficial relations with the people of the United States, while the United States set up the American Institute in Taiwan (AIT) to handle unofficial relations with the people of Taiwan. During this period, Congress passed the Taiwan Relations Act in spite of formal protests by the PRC government. The law was signed by President Carter on April 10, 1979, with statements that it would be implemented consistent with earlier U.S. commitments made to Beijing.

Despite declarations by high PRC officials that the Taiwan Relations Act would undermine the normalization of U.S.-China relations, this relationship moved forward on many fronts. Consulates were established in China and the United States by the respective governments, and progress was made in several international trade sectors: the most-favored-nation clause for the PRC was approved by Congress, technology transfers and sales of some military support equipment to China were discussed, and agreement was reached on U.S. financial claims against China.

However, there also were some difficulties. In January 1980, the United States announced new arms sales to Taiwan, which aroused immediate PRC protests as being contrary to U.S. commitments made to Beijing. A U.S. federal judge ruled that the termination of the U.S.-Taiwan Mutual Defense Treaty required congressional approval, but this ruling was overturned by both the court of appeals and the Supreme Court, and the treaty expired at the end of 1979.[21]

For the Carter administration, playing the "China card" to moderate Soviet behavior was very important. Hence there was a seemingly unending stream of high U.S. officials visiting the PRC, including Defense Secretary Harold Brown and Vice-President Mondale during 1979 and 1980. During the same period, many Chinese officials toured the United States and held conversations with their American counterparts. In the White House itself, a practice of regular strategic consultation with the Chinese was developed, involving the exchange of mutually beneficial and sometimes sensitive information.[22] On a lower level, thousands of young Chinese have begun to study in American institutions.

When Reagan assumed the presidency in January 1981, his administration basically maintained the friendly relations with the PRC established by his predecessors. However, Reagan and his conservative constituencies had a much deeper commitment to Taiwan than Carter had. As presidential candidate, Reagan had favored restoring official relations with Taiwan, which was of course anathema to the PRC leadership. Indeed, after Reagan's election, the Chinese Ministry of Foreign Affairs issued a statement in which it expressed hope and expectation that the new U.S. administration will adhere to the principles set forth in the Shanghai Communique and those underlying the establishment of diplomatic relations between the two governments so that Sino-American relations may continue to progress and grow stronger.[23]

To play the "China card" had its attraction also for the Reagan administration. In the spring of 1981, the Secretary of Defense Caspar Weinberger threatened to sell arms to the PRC if Soviet armed forces were to intervene in Poland. Indeed, later in the year, the Reagan administration did lift restrictions on the sale of arms to the PRC, but this action may well have been tied to its intention of arms sales to Taiwan, which had aroused extreme displeasure in Beijing.

Throughout the second half of 1981 and much of 1982, the issue of selling arms to Taiwan produced much controversy and displeasure on the part of the PRC leadership. During the discussions between the United States and the PRC leading to the normalization of relations between the two countries, Beijing had demanded that arms sales to Taiwan be terminated; however, Washington refused because of previous commitments. Although the negotiations over normalization almost foundered over this issue, the PRC decided to proceed with normalization but reserved the right to raise this very sensitive issue again.

When this issue became again a matter for discussion, the Taiwan Relations Act of 1979 had been passed, which committed the United States to sell to Taiwan arms necessary to maintain a sufficient self-defense capability. Earlier the PRC had promised to employ only peaceful means to resolve the long-standing dispute between the mainland and Taiwan and had issued a nine-point reunification proposal in September 1981. Since this proposal included a commitment that Taiwan could retain its present social and economic system as well as its armed forces if it rejoined the mainland,[24] it was reasonable to assume that in view of this promise U.S. arms sales could be eventually terminated. This was the PRC position, which considered the arms sales as an interference in its internal affairs. Hence it wanted a U.S. commitment to this effect. However, the Reagan administration declined to make such a commitment, which might be seen as in conflict with the principles embodied in the Taiwan Relations Act. Yet a compromise was found. Assuming that the military threat to Taiwan from the PRC has been lowered if not eliminated by the announced policy of the PRC leadership, the United States declared that it would gradually reduce arms sales to Taiwan and that in quality and quantity these sales would not go beyond levels established since normalization, that is, the establishment of diplomatic relations. This compromise is part of the U.S.-China Joint Communique of August 17, 1982. Its pertinent parts follow:

4. The Chinese Government reiterates that the question of Taiwan is China's internal affair. The Message to Compatriots in Taiwan issued by China on January 1, 1979 promulgated a fundamental policy of striving for peaceful reunification of the Motherland. The Nine-Point Proposal put forward by China on September 30, 1981 represented a further major effort under this fundamental policy to strive for a peaceful solution to the Taiwan question.

5. The United States Government attaches great importance to its relations with China, and reiterates that it has no intention of infringing on Chinese sovereignty and territorial integrity, or interfering in China's internal affairs, or pursuing a policy of "two Chinas" or "one China, one Taiwan." The United States Government understands and appreciates the Chinese policy of striving for a peaceful resolution of the Taiwan question. . . .

6. Having in mind the foregoing statements of both sides, the United States Government states that it does not seek to carry out a long-term policy of arms sales to Taiwan, that its arms sales to Taiwan will not exceed, either in qualitative or in quantitative terms, the level of those supplied in recent years since the establishment of diplomatic relations between the United States and China, and that it intends to reduce gradually its sales of arms to Taiwan, leading over a period of time to a final resolution. In so stating, the United States acknowledges China's consistent position regarding thorough settlement of this issue.[24]

If this communique were to remove the arms question as a serious issue in U.S.-PRC relations, a giant step forward would have been taken in the cooperation on the attainment of mutual foreign policy objectives such as the containment of the Soviet Union, deterring Soviet aggression in East Asia, and removal of Vietnamese troops from Kampuchea (to be discussed later in this chapter). However, the PRC seems to have some doubts about the consequences of what has been agreed on in the communique, especially about the types of airplanes and other weapons that might be sold to Taiwan. These doubts may have been increased by a statement that Reagan made in connection with the issuance of the communique. While acknowledging that a "strong and lasting relationship with China has been an important foreign policy goal of four consecutive administrations," and that such a relationship is "vital to our long-term national security interests" and therefore needs to be advanced, he also made the following comments:

> In working toward this successful outcome we have paid particular attention to the needs and interests of the people of Taiwan. My longstanding personal friendship and deep concern for their well-being is steadfast and unchanged. I am committed to maintaining the full range of contacts between the people of the United States and the people of Taiwan—cultural, commercial, and people-to-people contacts—which are compatible with our unofficial relationship. Such contacts will continue to grow and prosper and will be conducted with the dignity and honor befitting old friends.[25]

Reagan's statement reflects a measure of ambiguity in American policy, a continued very warm feeling toward Taiwan, motivated in part by domestic political considerations, and a subtle hesitation to engage the PRC leadership genuinely in U.S. strategic plans. Moreover, the momentum established by the Carter administration in U.S. relations with the PRC has not been kept up. This somewhat ambiguous and possibly subtly changing U.S. behavior has not escaped Soviet attention and has led to attempts by Moscow to reestablish normal relations with Beijing, thereby reducing tensions along the southern frontier of the Soviet Union. The Chinese have indicated an interest in these reconciliation efforts, which may cover political issues such as Soviet concessions on Vietnam and Kampuchea as well as Afghanistan, some Soviet force reduction along the Sino-Soviet border, and perhaps some ideological accommodations. During the Breshnev funeral in November 1982, long talks were held between high Soviet officials and Chinese foreign minister Hua Huang who, for whatever reasons, was dismissed after his return to Beijing.

While it is impossible to predict the evolution of the Sino-Soviet relationship, it would be tragic if the ongoing process of normalization between the United States and the PRC were to be permitted to erode and thereby undermine the triangular balance-of-power system that provides important leverage to U.S. foreign policy. A deterioration in the relations with the PRC must also be a major strategic concern for our policymakers from another perspective. It would put the United States in a disadvantageous position compared to other Western countries with which we are competing for trade with the PRC, and it would coincide with already existing weakened and conflictual relationships with America's NATO allies. A visit by Secretary of State George P. Shultz to Beijing in February 1983 has not ameliorated the situation between Washington and Beijing. In fact, a few weeks after the visit the PRC accused the Reagan administration of "trampling" on the 1982 (August) communique because of the persistent political support of Taiwan and continuing American arms sales to Thailand.[26]

Explanatory Variables

For the examination of the variables that might have played the major part in the formulation of U.S. policies toward China, it is useful to distinguish between the periods from 1949 to 1970 and from that time to now. As in our preceding efforts to explain the sources of American foreign policies, international variables appear to have particular potency. American inability in the years immediately following World War II to create a government in China that would have been based on collaboration between Mao and Chiang, and the increasing view in Washington that a global Communist conspiracy was seeking to expand its control everywhere in the world can be seen as both interactional and systemic sources of explanation for not recognizing and in fact ignoring—as far as that was possible—the PRC while giving full diplomatic, economic, and military support to Chiang's regime on what was then Formosa. Chinese intervention in the Korean conflict did not basically alter U.S. policy, because high priorities for containment of the Soviet Union in Europe imposed constraints on Washington against moving aggressively toward an all-out effort to defeat the Chinese Communists.

   Thus the need to maintain a favorable strategic balance with the Soviet Union—a systemic variable—was a primary motivation for the following policies toward the PRC:

1. Pursuit of a generally passive policy toward the PRC that would set up barriers against aggressionist designs of Beijing—for example, the American actions against Communist attempts to capture Quemoy and Matsu.
2. Opposition to China's stimulation and support of revolutionary movements in Asia and Africa.
3. Restraint of active measures to roll back the PRC forces from Korea.

   When Nixon and Kissinger introduced a radically changed policy toward the PRC, it was again the strategic U.S.-Soviet relationship with its balance-of-power implications highlighted by the widening Sino-Soviet split that was a major inducement for their historic initiatives. Of course there was also the question of how long the United States could remain oblivious to the reality of nearly a billion Chinese (about 20 percent of humanity) living under the control of the PRC. However, it was the increased leverage that a triangular Sino-Soviet-U.S. relationship might offer the United States in dealing with both Communist countries—a systemic variable—that may have had the greatest appeal to Nixon and Kissinger as well as to subsequent administrations. Additional motivations may have been economic; clearly the immense Chinese market and the needs of a country that was seeking to upgrade its industrial facilities through the import of capital goods provided potentially immense opportunities to American manufacturers. This constituted an interactional variable of significant potency.

The PRC leadership, before Mao's death in 1976 and thereafter, as well as the Chinese people welcomed the new relationship. This was reflected not only by the stream of official visitors to the United States that was mentioned earlier, but also by the very warm reception the Chinese people accorded to the many American tourists flocking to China. However, the unsettled Taiwan situation, aggravated by the Reagan administration's recent statements and dealings with Taipei, may produce interactional variables that could undermine what has been achieved by Nixon, Ford, and Carter. The efforts by the two Communist giants to find accommodations in their troubled relations could be ominous, but for the Chinese these efforts may also be signals to the United States not to take progress in the new U.S.-PRC relationship for granted.

In terms of idiosyncratic variables, Truman's inclination toward communist containment may have been one motivation to break off all contacts with the Chinese mainland, but most likely a much more important reason was his concern, stimulated in part by institutional and societal factors, to counter and deflate the accusations of conservative Republicans and southern Democrats that the State Department had been "soft on communism," and that by not giving the necessary support to Chiang Kai-shek his administration had contributed to the loss of China to the Communists.[27] The continuation of the policy of "no contact" with the PRC was readily understandable under the Eisenhower administration whose foreign policy was dominated by the intense anticommunist sentiments of John Foster Dulles.[28] Moreover, Eisenhower and Dulles believed that communism in China was a passing phenomenon.

John Kennedy, who considered the state of U.S.-PRC relations "irrational," was fearful, however, of the uproar that any change in the policy toward the Chinese Communists would generate in the United States.[29] No new initiatives toward policy alterations were made by Johnson who, like his predecessor, seemed to be concerned about the domestic political consequences, especially with the Vietnam War in full swing.

It was finally the *Realpolitik* espoused by Nixon, combined with his impeccable anticommunist credentials, that made the policy changes possible, Obviously, Kissinger's views on the advantages and disadvantages of playing the balance-of-power game in foreign policy played a significant role. Once the basic changes had been made, no idiosyncratic obstacles to the continuation on the path of normalization of relations were posed by Ford and Carter, who fleshed out the policies initiated by Nixon. What influence the visceral anticommunism of Ronald Reagan and many of his close advisors will have on the future development of this policy is hard to predict. There is an underlying pragmatism in Reagan's psychological profile, as demonstrated during his tenure as governor in California, which may well make him see the benefits for the American national interests that are likely to flow from the continuation of the policies toward China conducted by the three preceding administrations.

In terms of institutional variables, two points can be made. The attacks by

Senator Joseph McCarthy on the State Department during the early 1950s asserting that it was permeated by communists and fellow travelers had a lasting effect. Hence the policies of nonrecognition of the PRC were generally supported, although some doubt about their merit most likely existed; yet proposals for change were frowned on. In 1963, following Kennedy's death, an initiative for change was launched by Roger Hilsman, then assistant secretary of state, when he declared in a speech that the United States was prepared to negotiate with any country including "Red China" if the regime in that country were to modify its hostility toward the United States.[30]

The second institutional variable having a bearing on policy toward China has been the emergence of vociferous, well-financed interest groups. The influence of the China lobby, discussed earlier, has been and indeed remains pervasive in Congress. This lobby and the "Committee of One Million" rejected the Hilsman proposal, accusing the administration of being "soft on communism" and urging the American public to reject any change in the policy toward the PRC.[31]

In terms of societal variables, it is evident that the nonrecognition and the no-contact policies with respect to the mainland of China were highly acceptable to the anticommunist mood of Americans. A public opinion poll taken in 1949 indicated that only 25 percent of the respondents wanted to recognize diplomatically the regime in Peking. Fifteen years later, this percentage had increased somewhat and stood at 36 percent.[32] However, when Nixon engineered the opening to the PRC, there was no significant opposition by public opinion to this step; indeed, more than half the respondents in 1969 were prepared to accept the PRC in the United Nations, and the majority of Americans now seems to have a sympathetic feeling toward the mainland Chinese. Indeed, whereas only 11 percent of the public would have approved the PRC's admission to the United Nations in 1950, by 1971 a plurality of 45 percent gave its approval.[33]

VIETNAM

Fateful Prelude

The Vietnam War, in which nearly 60,000 Americans lost their lives, was the result of an uncertain American foreign policy as to how far the United States should help France after World War II to reestablish a measure of colonial control over Indochina. After the years of Japanese occupation in Southeast Asia had ended, Ho Chi Minh, a Moscow-trained Communist and leader of the Viet Minh, who were a coalition of Vietnamese revolutionaries, proclaimed in 1946 the independence of Vietnam. Although France was prepared to recognize Ho's "Democratic Republic of Vietnam" as a free state within the French Union, an organization to reestablish French influence over its pre-

World War II colonial empire, and although France was permitted by Ho to maintain garrisons for 5 years, conflicts arose quickly between the French government and the Viet Minh.

Conducting carefully planned guerrilla operations against the French forces and meeting considerable success in this type of warfare, the Viet Minh began to place serious difficulties in the way of reestablishing French colonial control over Indochina, and France suffered heavy costs in personnel and material.

The gradual deterioration of the French position in Indochina, coupled with the loss of mainland China and the stalemate armistice in Korea, evoked U.S. concern that the containment of communism in Asia was faltering. These concerns increased when the PRC commenced to increase its assistance to the Viet Minh despite American warnings against such actions with threats of massive nuclear retaliation.[34] The low point of France's fortunes in the hostilities came in March 1954 at Dien Bien Phu, a French fortress, which was unable to hold out against ferocious attacks by Viet Minh forces. For the United States, a crucial foreign policy decision had to be made. Should the Eisenhower administration involve American military contingents directly in support of the French in order to save a situation that was seen as having grave consequences for American security?

The chairman of the Joint Chiefs of Staff, Admiral Radford, suggested an air strike, if necessary with nuclear weapons, on the Viet Minh positions around Dien Bien Phu.[35] However, Eisenhower felt that popular support for another military involvement in Asia so soon after the end of the Korean conflict was lacking and that domestic political considerations dictated another course. Therefore, although the United States had been already assisting France with economic and military aid that reached 75 percent of the costs of the war in 1954, military intervention was ruled out.

With French casualties running to over 200,000 dead and wounded and the 15,000-soldier garrison surrounded at Dien Bien Phu early in 1954, the French were anxious to negotiate an end to the Vietnam conflict. The means was a conference at Geneva that began May 7, 1954, one day after the French commander at Dien Bien Phu had surrendered his troops. The participants were the foreign ministers of the Soviet Union, France, Great Britain, and the PRC. The United States, though invited, declined to participate; indeed, it wanted to impede any progress toward a settlement in Geneva in order to prevent any gains for the communist side. The Eisenhower administration conceived this conference as the start of "falling dominos," where the fall of one domino (one country) would lead to knocking over the next domino, producing a chain reaction of other dominoes to fall until finally the whole world would be under communist control.

Although the Geneva conference was initially stalemated, in part because Washington continued to hold out the possibility of U.S. intervention including the use of nuclear weapons, the election of French Prime Minister Pierre

Mendez-France by the end of June 1954, replacing George Bidault, moved negotiations forward rapidly and ended in agreement that concluded the military conflict and partitioned Vietnam at the seventeenth parallel. Elections in 1956 in both parts of Vietnam were to determine the future of the country. Meanwhile, French forces were to evacuate south of the seventeenth parallel, and the communist troops under Ho were to move north of the line. In addition to North and South Vietnam, the Geneva agreements also created Cambodia and Laos as independent states. Although the United States did not sign the agreements, it made a unilateral declaration promising to abide by them. At the same time, it warned that any new aggression in Indochina would be viewed with grave concern and as a threat to global peace.[36]

In order to prevent the loss of North Vietnam from triggering additional losses in Southeast Asia and the Southeast Pacific, the Eisenhower administration moved rapidly to convene a conference of representatives of Britain, France, Australia, New Zealand, Pakistan, Thailand, and the Philippines for the purpose of setting up a regional security IGO named the Southeast Asia Treaty Organization (SEATO). Dulles hoped to make SEATO the counterpart of NATO with similar commitments of the member states. However, such commitments were refused by the charter members of the new IGO; what was agreed consisted of promises by the members to meet the common danger in accordance with their constitutional processes and to consult in the event of subversion, guerrilla attacks, and other similar kinds of activity.[37] A protocol to the SEATO Treaty extended its protection to Vietnam, Laos, and Cambodia.

Growing Involvement

The first president of the Republic of Vietnam, South Vietnam's official name, was Ngo Dinh Diem, Western-trained and educated, who endeavored to eliminate pervasive existing corruption and institute a system of modern administration. At the same time, Diem had to deal with hundreds of thousands of refugees streaming into the country from Communist North Vietnam, officially called the Democratic Republic of Vietnam. These refugees made it possible for North Vietnam to serve as a means of infiltrating subversive elements who later became the nucleus for the communist-led Viet Cong forces.

The United States provided Diem with more than $325 million in economic and military aid to solidify his regime. He declined to hold elections in 1956 as specified in the 1954 Geneva agreements, because he was not a signatory and in this position reflected the stand of the Eisenhower administration, which did not consider that the appropriate conditions for free elections prevailed in North Vietnam.[28] More realistically, the administration seemed to fear that Ho Chi Minh might win such an election.

Subversion of the Diem government increased in 1959 when material aid to the Viet Cong by North Vietnam and the PRC was substantially expanded. In spite of growing assistance by the United States to South Vietnam, the Viet Cong became stronger and it seemed that many South Vietnamese shifted their allegiance to the Viet Cong. An important reason for this shift was Diem's repression of and his isolation from the Vietnamese people. Moreover, his regime had become increasingly corrupt. Meanwhile, the United States had established a large military advisory group (MAG) in South Vietnam by the late 1950s, and, toward the end of 1962, 4000 American troops were stationed in that country. At the same time, the United States tried to persuade Diem to improve his administration, strengthen village security in the countryside, and make stronger efforts to defeat the Viet Cong and its followers. However, the Diem regime did not live up to this challenge. At the end of 1963, this regime was overthrown by a military-led coup d'état and Diem was killed reportedly with the blessing of the highest level of the U.S. government, and South Vietnam was ruled until 1967 by military governments.

The Kennedy administration continued U.S. involvement in Vietnam and, by the end of 1963, the number of U.S. forces in that country had risen to 15,000. For Kennedy, the "falling domino" theory was valid; South Vietnam could not be abandoned, and in terms of American security, he believed that the PRC sought to dominate Southeast Asia and exclude American influence from that region. However, he felt that it was primarily up to the South Vietnamese leadership and people to win the struggle against the Viet Cong; all the United States could do was to send equipment and advisors.[39]

Under President Johnson, U.S. involvement in Vietnam accelerated rapidly. Following an alleged attack by North Vietnamese naval vessels on U.S. destroyers in mid-1964 in the Gulf of Tonkin, Congress passed the Tonkin Gulf Resolution authorizing the president to "take all necessary measures to repel any armed attack against the forces of the United States and prevent further aggression."[40] The consequences of this resolution were continuous bombing raids in North Vietnam beginning in 1965 and a sustained buildup of American forces in South Vietnam reaching over 540,000 by 1968. Meanwhile, in that country a new constitution was adopted in 1967 and, as the result of elections, General Nguyen Van Thieu became president and air marshall Nguyen Cao Ky assumed the office of vice-president.

The increasing commitment of U.S. forces to the Vietnam War under the Johnson administration was based on two factors. First, the president seemed to believe fully in the domino theory and thought that withdrawal would enhance the appetite of the communists for more aggression, especially because Hanoi was urged on in its war efforts by the leadership of the PRC.[41] Second, the administration accepted more or less whatever additional troops General Westmoreland, the U.S. commander in South Vietnam, requested. These requests totaled 443,000 men by the end of 1966 and nearly 543,000 by the end of 1967. When Secretary of Defense Robert McNamara began to oppose these requests, Johnson also resisted the last request, which was then scaled down by Westmoreland to less than 500,000 soldiers. A new request for an additional 206,000 troops made by Westmoreland in early 1968 was not approved by Clark Clifford, who had replaced McNamara as secretary of defense.[42] The president sided with Clifford and rejected the request. Westmoreland was recalled from Vietnam and moved up to the post of army chief of staff.

The bombing efforts of the U.S. Air Force in support of the ground war were enormous. It has been estimated that by the end of 1968 more bombs had been dropped on Vietnam than on all of Europe during World War II. Nevertheless, this did not prevent the communist forces from launching the Tet (Vietnamese New Year) offensive on January 31, 1968, which allowed them to capture many towns in South Vietnam and to penetrate into Saigon and some of the provincial capitals. Clearly, many of the optimistic predictions by the Pentagon of an early end of the war through an American victory proved to be illusions.

Policy Changes and Disengagement

With public opinion support for the Vietnam War plummeting from 61 percent in August 1965 to 40 percent in March 1968 and opposition rising from 24 to 48 percent during the same period,[43] President Johnson decided to de-escalate the war and to reduce the bombing effort. At the same time he announced that he would not seek a second term as president.

In the summer of 1968, limited informal talks were begun between Washington and Hanoi. The Thieu regime in Saigon advocated a tough position in these talks and pressured the U.S. government not to make any concessions to the North. In order to make progress in raising the informal talks to the level of full negotiations, Johnson halted the bombing completely and accepted the South Vietnamese Communists, who had assumed the name of National Liberation Front (NLF), as full partners in the negotiations that were to start in Paris and in which also the Saigon government was to participate.* However, the latter refused to sit down with the NLF, and the start of the negotiations was held in abeyance until 1969.

It was the Nixon administration that succeeded in persuading the Saigon regime to enter the negotiations, which finally began on January 24, 1969. The negotiations were protracted however; they aimed at a cease-fire, the return of American prisoners of war, and settling the conditions for the political system that was to prevail in the southern part of Vietnam. It was only toward the end

---

* Hanoi had agreed not to violate the Demilitarized Zone (DMZ) nor to launch indiscriminate attacks on major cities in the south.

of January 1973, more than 4 years after the negotiations began, that the war was finally terminated.

Nixon perceived the forthcoming negotiations in terms of settling the war on the basis of the self-respect and honor of all parties involved.[44] However, before the negotiations could get under way, the North Vietnamese launched a countrywide offensive inflicting high casualties on American and South Vietnamese troops. These attacks evoked American retaliatory air strikes against North Vietnamese sanctuaries along the Vietnamese-Kampuchean border. Nevertheless, private talks began in Paris on March 22, 1969.[45] The U.S. position included cease-fire under international supervision, offering to set a precise timetable for withdrawal, and commitment to free elections under international supervision. American troop withdrawals, however, depended on the ability of the South Vietnamese to defend themselves, and South Vietnamese forces therefore had to be strengthened. This meant that the war had to undergo "Vietnamization," with a phased U.S. withdrawal schedule spanning several years.[46] For Hanoi, this was not satisfactory; rather, it insisted on early complete withdrawal of U.S. forces and troops contributed by allied countries as well as on a political solution requiring the removal of Thieu and Ky and establishment of a coalition government composed of the NLF and remnants of the current Saigon regime.[47]

In spite of recurring attacks by communist forces, 115,000 American troops had been withdrawn by the middle of April 1970. An additional 150,000 were to be withdrawn by the spring of 1971. Meanwhile, the Paris talks stagnated while the North Vietnamese and the Viet Cong made forays into Kampuchea. Yet, public opinion opposition to the war grew to 56 percent.[48] To eliminate the Kampuchean sanctuaries, American and South Vietnamese forces pushed forward into these areas on May 1, 1970. Large quantities of weapons and materiel were captured, but after 2 months the attacks were broken off without lasting success. The incursion into Kampuchea aroused a storm of domestic protest in the United States, and Nixon was accused of not consulting Congress before launching the campaign.

In Paris, during the 1971–1972 period, the United States softened its position toward a negotiated settlement, but Hanoi continued to insist on unilateral U.S. withdrawal and nonparticipation of the Thieu leadership in a forthcoming coalition government that obviously had to be controlled by the Communists.[49] In the meantime, military operations had not stopped; U.S. bombings of the North were carried out intermittently, and in the spring of 1972 the North Vietnamese launched powerful attacks across the DMZ with modern arms supplied by the Soviet Union. Nevertheless, by early 1972, the United States had withdrawn 410,000 troops, Finally, in late October of that year, Kissinger pronounced his belief that "peace is at hand,"[50] but the anticipated agreement collapsed. This prompted the Nixon administration to resort again to intensive bombing of North Vietnam during the 1972 Christmas season, which included as targets Hanoi and the port of Haiphong. The purpose was to force a conclusion of the negotiations, but it was an action arousing moral indignation and strong protests in the United States. Yet, negotiations were resumed in January 1973, and agreement was reached to end the war—an agreement that paved the way for Vietnamese reunification under a Communist government.[51]

The settlement included an internationally supervised cease-fire, halting all bombing and port mining operations, an exchange of prisoners of war, withdrawal of U.S. forces within 2 months, and separate future cease-fires in Laos and Kampuchea. A series of mixed commissions, which were to include elements of the Viet Cong and the Saigon government, were to restructure the South Vietnamese political system; a new constitution was to be framed and elections were to be held.

This settlement clearly was a great disappointment to the Thieu regime, but it was the best the U.S. government could obtain under the enormous pressure of public opinion to extricate the Americans from the quagmire of Vietnam. Vietnamization of the war generally was a failure, and the South Vietnamese forces were increasingly in disarray. During 1974 and 1975, the cease-fire between South and North Vietnam was frequently violated, and the fighting escalated. North Vietnamese and Viet Cong forces seized major cities, including Saigon, after Thieu had resigned. The South Vietnam government unconditionally surrendered to the Viet Cong in April 1975, and a provisional revolutionary government took formal control in June.

Hanoi also faced pressure to settle the war from its supporters and suppliers of arms and equipment—the PRC and the Soviet Union—which caused resentment in the capital of North Vietnam. Indeed, the relationship between that country and the other two Communist states began to change. While the Soviet Union remained a staunch protector of Hanoi and provided substantial economic and military assistance in the years following the Paris agreement, the PRC, reflecting the historical enmity between the Vietnamese and Chinese people as well as its detente with the United States, became increasingly hostile toward the Hanoi regime, vehemently opposing the latter's attempt to control Kampuchea and perhaps Laos. In fact, the imposition of a Hanoi-controlled government in Kampuchea in 1978 replacing a regime friendly toward Beijing was one of the reasons for the PRC's punitive invasion of Vietnam's northern region in 1979, an invasion that, however, did not last long, nor did it have an enduring effect.

Although some efforts were made in the second half of the 1970s to establish diplomatic relations between Vietnam and the United States, the conditions were not ripe for such a step. Meanwhile, the United States has given its full support to endeavors of the Association of Southeast Asian Nations (ASEAN) to end the Vietnamese occupation of Kampuchea and to maintain a measure of military strength in the area that could help to counter the growing Soviet military pressure in northeast Asia and Vietnam. American consultations with the PRC on Kampuchea have been held regularly to complement U.S. cooperation with ASEAN in an attempt to turn back or at least contain Vietnamese aggression in the region.[52]

Explanatory Variables

As in the policy areas examined earlier, international variables played important roles in the formulation of policies leading to and during the Vietnam War. American support given to France in its struggle to maintain control over Indochina was evoked by the fear that the Viet Minh were seeking to expand the sphere of communist influence in the world. In other words, the *need to contain the conspiracy of international communism* in Asia as it had to be contained in Europe was a major motivation for the U.S. assistance extended to the French. Although the United States opted against participation in the Geneva agreements, once the seventeenth parallel had become the line between communists and noncommunists, successive U.S. administrations became engaged in holding this line, especially because both the PRC and the Soviet Union actively aided the North Vietnamese. Hence Washington devised policies to defeat the communist forces within South Vietnam and to inflict heavy punishment on North Vietnam as the driving power of the Viet Cong and other guerrillas, and these policies engendered growing U.S. military involvement. The inability of the combined U.S. and South Vietnamese forces to obtain these policy goals led to Nixon's change of policy and the eventual withdrawal of the United States from Vietnam. It is thus clearly the international situation as evolved from 1954 to 1975, mainly in Asia, which provided the various stimuli (interactional variables) for American policy in Vietnam, Kampuchea, and Laos during that period.

Idiosyncratic variables played a minor part in the formulation of the policies toward Indochina. In spite of Dulles' usual belligerent rhetoric, he moved cautiously with respect to the French debacle before and during Dien Bien Phu. For Eisenhower, caution was a normal characteristic. Underlying anticommunist sentiments in Kennedy's and Johnson's images of the world prompted them to seek an increasingly costly campaign to attain the policy goals of communist containment and the assurance of South Vietnam's non-Communist government. Only overwhelming domestic pressures changed Johnson's course of deploying ever more U.S. troops. As in the case of the recognition of the PRC and the conclusion of the SALT I agreement, it was the already mentioned impeccable anticommunist credentials that enabled Nixon, a man of considerable experience in international politics and skilled in understanding the intricacies of international balances of power, to extricate the United States from the quagmire of Vietnam, although whether it was peace with honor, as frequently claimed by Nixon,[53] is another question.

In institutional terms, the inability of U.S. ground and tactical air support forces to employ *effective* counterinsurgency tactics against the Viet Cong and to cope with the recurring North Vietnamese incursions into South Vietnam in spite of the rapidly increasing number of American troops from 1965 to 1968 and of repeated bombing of the North was a major factor in the American failure to obtain U.S. policy goals. In the long run, search-and-destroy missions did not succeed in defeating the Viet Cong. Although at least part of the U.S. Army had been trained in counterinsurgency tactics, the fighting under generals accustomed to operations in World War II seemed to retain its conventional and traditional modes.

Whether more troops as requested by General Westmoreland in 1968 would have altered the fortunes of war is an open question for which there is no answer. How many ground forces would have been needed to carry the war into North Vietnam to "win" rather than merely make South Vietnam secure for the South Vietnamese government and people with the forces committed by 1968 cannot be judged with any accuracy. However, it seems that, considering the high fighting spirit displayed by the North Vietnamese, grounded in nationalism as well as communist ideology, the number of Americans that would have had to be committed for such a mission would have been enormous. Some estimates have suggested over 1 million. With American patience always an uncertain commodity, yet a needed virtue to fight as difficult a basically unconventional war as Vietnam was, it is most doubtful that in view of an increasingly negative public opinion Americans would have had the fortitude to accept the extensive casualties that an enlarged war would certainly have produced. What was not foreseen when the Vietnam policies were formulated and reformulated was the insufficiency of psychological resources within the American society that were needed to sustain the war over an extended period of time. If it had been decided to engage in a full-scale war against North Vietnam in 1964, there might have been a chance for the United States to prevail, but even then the difficulty of terrain and climate as well as the particular style of the North Vietnamese conduct of military operations would most likely have led to a protracted war difficult to win. Clearly by 1967–1968 it was too late for a successful extension of the ground war to North Vietnam, which would have required stepping up the draft, a most difficult and divisive step given the growing protests against the war as it was conducted at that time.

For the above reasons, President Reagan's statement that American troops were denied permission to win[54] ignores the political and psychological realities of the late 1960s. Defeat may have been self-inflicted, as Reagan claims, but it is doubtful that the United States could have been victorious in the Vietnam struggle. One reason sometimes given for not extending the ground war with North Vietnam and, if possible, bringing Hanoi to its knees, may have been apprehension that it might have brought the PRC or the Soviet Union into the war on the side of North Vietnam. Such a consequence was not likely, since the PRC was occupied with internal struggles and the Soviet Union was interested in maintaining its detente posture with the West.

Another institutional factor bringing the Vietnam war to an end was congressional pressure that limited Nixon's freedom of action. In June 1970 the Senate voted to terminate the Tonkin Gulf Resolution of 1964, and the Cooper-Church Amendment was passed by the Senate, which cut off funds for military operations in Cambodia. Although the House did not give its approval to this amendment, the mood in Congress toward ending the war was clear. In June 1973, Congress voted to require the president to cease military actions in any part of Indochina. Although Nixon vetoed this measure, he agreed to a compromise setting August 15 as the deadline for such actions. In November of that year, the War Powers Act was passed.

Finally, societal variables had an appreciable impact on the formulation of U.S. policies in Vietnam and Indochina in general. During the 1950s, the generally anticommunist sentiments of the American people were supportive of the efforts by Eisenhower and Dulles to contain communist expansion in East Asia and the assistance given for the newly formed state of South Vietnam. However, beginning with 1965, opposition to the growing Vietnam involvement by the United States became increasingly vociferous. The main starting point was the Washington teach-in in 1965, which spawned other teach-ins on Vietnam, mostly on university campuses throughout the United States. On October 15, 1969, a quarter of a million people peacefully marched in Washington, calling for a moratorium on the war. When the president called on the "great silent majority" of Americans[55] to help him in his efforts to "win the peace," there was a brief reversal in the downward trend of public opinion support for the war,[56] but it did not last. Indeed, public opinion regarding Vietnam had become so emotional, with powerful influences in Congress and on the president, that it developed into an extremely potent variable in ending U.S. involvement in Indochina. It also influenced subsequent foreign policies not only in Indochina but with respect to U.S. overt and covert intervention in other parts of the Third World.

SUMMARY

In spite of strong U.S. support for Chiang Kai-shek in his post-World War II struggle against the Communists under Mao Zedong, the latter prevailed and, in 1949, Mao established on the Chinese mainland the People's Republic of China (PRC). The initial U.S. policy toward the PRC was one of *diplomatic nonrecognition*.

During the early stages of the Korean War in the fall of 1950, U.S. troops reached the Yalu River, the border between the PRC and North Korea. Although the American field commander, General Douglas MacArthur, believed that he could invade and defeat the PRC, Truman wanted to keep the Chinese Communists and the Soviet Union out of the Korean War, because his top priority was to prevent a Soviet attack in Western Europe. The issue was solved by the PRC forces, which attacked in strength the American troops that had reached the Yalu and inflicted a heavy defeat on the Americans.

MacArthur was relieved of his command in April 1951, and the war ended inconclusively in 1953. Following the war, U.S. policy concentrated on giving powerful military and economic support to the Chiang regime on Taiwan, where he had fled after his vanquishment on the mainland and set up the "Republic of China."

American policy changed dramatically in 1971, when Kissinger initiated the opening of a new relationship with the PRC in a trip to Peking. The deterioration of the Sino-Soviet links during the 1960s was an important motivation for this change in both Washington and Peking. The policy change also brought immediate modification of American policy in the United Nations: Washington accepted PRC representation in all U.N. bodies. In the Shanghai Communique of 1972, the United States and the PRC renounced the use of force for the settlement of disputes.

Full diplomatic relations were assumed in January 1979. The Reagan Administration has maintained the friendly relations with the PRC established by Carter, but because Reagan was also anxious not to forsake the regime in Taiwan and wants to continue the sale of advanced military aircraft to Taiwan, a fully harmonious relationship does not exist at present.

Another very complex foreign policy issue in Asia has been *U.S. involvement in Vietnam.* During the French struggle in Indochina in the middle 1950s, the United States ruled out military intervention but provided generous economic and military aid to France.

After the French defeat and the division of Vietnam into a communist North and a South that was officially called the Republic of Vietnam, the United States provided the South with large amounts of military and economic aid. However, the South Vietnamese were not able to establish a viable regime and had great difficulty in preventing the Viet Cong, a communist guerrilla force, from taking over rural areas. Beginning in 1963, U.S. involvement grew steadily until by 1968, over 500,000 U.S. troops were in Vietnam. When, despite large-scale bombings, the North Vietnamese and Viet Cong could not be defeated, American policy was changed. The war began to be de-escalated, and talks were inititated between Washington and Hanoi, the North Vietnamese capital. The negotiations, begun in 1969, were difficult and protracted. American troops were withdrawn until in 1973 they amounted to less than 100,000. In 1973 agreement was reached to end the war, which paved the way for *Vietnamese reunification under a Communist government.* This event took place in June 1975. The United States has not established diplomatic relations with North Vietnam.

NOTES

1. For details see John K. Fairbank, *The United States and China,* 3rd ed. (Cambridge, Mass.: Harvard University Press, 1971), pp. 306–317.

2. U.S., Department of State, *United States Relations with China with Special Reference to the Period 1944–1947* (Washington, D.C., Department of State 1949), pp. 358–359.

3. Thomas A. Bailey, *A Diplomatic History of the American People*, 6th ed. (New York: Appleton-Century-Crofts, 1958), pp. 817–818.

4. Dean Acheson, *Present at the Creation* (New York: W. W. Norton, 1969), pp. 429–430.

5. U.S., Department of State, *United States Relations with China*, p. xvi.

6. Agency for International Aid, *U.S. Overseas Loans and Grants and Assistance for International Organizations, July 1, 1945–September 30, 1980* (1981).

7. Harry S. Truman, *Memoirs*, Vol. 2 (Garden City, N.Y.: Doubleday, 1956), p. 362.

8. See Joseph deRivera, *The Psychological Dimensions of Foreign Policy* (New York: Charles E. Merrill, 1968), pp. 245–297.

9. For details of the controversy, see Richard H. Revere and Arthur M. Schlesinger, Jr., *The General and the President* (New York: Farrar, Straus & Young, 1951); and William Manchester, *American Caesar: Douglas MacArthur* (New York: Dell, 1979).

10. James A. Nathan and James K. Oliver, *United States Foreign Policy and World Order*, 2nd ed. (Boston: Little, Brown, 1981), p. 173.

11. John W. Spanier, *The Truman-MacArthur Controversy and the Korean War* (Cambridge Mass.: Belknap Press of Harvard University, 1959), p. 222.

12. John Spanier, *American Foreign Policy since World War II*, 7th ed. (New York: Praeger, 1977), p. 114.

13. Henry Kissinger, *White House Years* (Boston: Little, Brown, 1979), p. 714.

14. For details, see ibid., pp. 745–755.

15. Ibid., pp. 759–760.

16. Details are found in ibid., pp. 684–718.

17. For details of the voting strategies in the U.N. General Assembly and the reaction in Congress, see ibid., pp. 784–785.

18. Ibid., p. 1076.

19. Ibid., p. 1080.

20. U.S., Department of State, Bureau of Public Affairs, *Two Years of U.S.-China Relations* (January 1981).

21. Ibid.

21. Zbigniew Brzezinski, "Soviet Aim: Normalize with China, Isolate U.S.," *Times-Picayune* (New Orleans), November 24, 1982, p. 9.

22. U.S., Department of State, "Two Years of U.S.-China Relations."

23. This commitment was later included in a new PRC constitution that authorized "special administrative regions." *Times-Picayune* (New Orleans), November 26, 1982.

24. The full text can be found in U.S., Department of State, Bureau of Public Affairs, *U.S. China Joint Communique*, Current Policy No. 143 (August 1982).

25. Ibid.

26. *Times-Picayune* (New Orleans), February 26, 1983.

27. See also Acheson, *Present at the Creation*, pp. 462–471.

28. See Ole Holsti, "The Belief System and National Images: A Case Study," *Journal of Conflict Resolution* 6, 3 (September 1962), pp. 244–252.

29. Arthur M. Schlesinger, Jr., *A Thousand Days* (Boston: Houghton Mifflin, 1965), p. 479.

30. Cecil V. Crabb, Jr., *American Foreign Policy in the Nuclear Age*, 3rd ed. (New York: Harper & Row, 1972), p. 160.

31. Ibid.

32. Ibid., p. 157.

33. John E. Mueller, *War, Presidents, and Public Opinion* (New York: John Wiley & Sons, 1973), p. 15.

34. John Spanier, *American Foreign Policy since World War II*, 9th ed. (New York: Holt, Rinehart & Winston, 1981), p. 80.

35. Nathan and Oliver, *United States Foreign Policy and World Order*, p. 182.

36. Crabb, *American Foreign Policy in the Nuclear Age*, p. 376.

37. Article IV, SEATO Treaty.

38. Nathan and Oliver, *United States Foreign Policy and World Order*, p. 186.
39. Theodore C. Sorensen, *Kennedy* (New York: Harper & Row, 1965), pp. 648–659.
40. *Document on American Foreign Relations: 1964* (New York: Harper & Row, 1965), pp. 216–217.
41. See Lyndon B. Johnson, "Patterns for Peace in South East Asia," *Department of State Bulletin* 41, 1348 (April 26, 1965), pp. 606–608.
42. Nathan and Oliver, *United States Foreign Policy and World Order*, pp. 334–337.
43. John E. Mueller, "Trends in Popular Support for the Wars in Korea and Vietnam," American Political Science Review (June 1971), pp. 358–375, on p. 363.
44. Kissinger, *White House Years*, p. 242.
45. Ibid., p. 250.
46. Ibid., pp. 270–272.
47. Ibid., p. 281.
48. Mueller, "Trends in Popular Support," p. 363.
49. Kissinger, *White House Years*, p. 979. For details of the negotiations, see pp. 967–1046.
50. Ibid., p. 1399.
51. For details, see ibid., pp. 1457–1476.
52. U.S., Department of State, Bureau of Public Affairs, *Update of International Developments*, Current Policy No. 373 (March 2, 1982); and *Developing Lasting U.S.-China Relations*, Current Policy No. 398 (June 1, 1982).
53. See, in this respect also, Kissinger, *White House Years*, pp. 1412 and 1473–1475.
54. Thomas G. Paterson, *American Foreign Policy*, 2nd ed. (Lexington, Mass.: D.C. Heath, 1983), p. 610.
55. Ibid., p. 600.
56. Mueller, "Trends in Popular Support," p. 363.

11

Policies toward the Western Advanced Countries

The major concern of U.S. policies toward the Western advanced countries has been the American relationships with Western Europe and Japan. Rather than dealing with individual countries in Western Europe, our examination of U.S. policies will focus on the region as a whole, in particular, American goals vis-à-vis the possibility of West European unification and its implications for the United States, as well as the evolution of the Atlantic Alliance and its impact on NATO. As far as Japan is concerned, our discussion will encompass both security and economic policies. Since there are certain similarities in the problems American foreign policies have encountered in both Western Europe and Japan, the discussion of explanatory variables will cover both areas and therefore will be presented together at the end of this chapter.

WESTERN EUROPE

The Economic and Political Dimensions

United States post-World War II policy toward Western Europe had its origin during that war. At the request of the State Department, the Council on Foreign Relations, a nongovernmental, prestigious study group, prepared a report entitled "American Interests in the Economic Unification of Europe with respect to Trade Barriers," which was dated September 14, 1942.[1] Its conclusions stated:

> The United States would favor economic unification of Europe only if steps are taken to avoid the creation of an autarkic continental economy. Positive American policy should aim at the interpenetration of Europe's economy with that of the world, as well as a lowering of economic barriers throughout the world.[2]

At the same time, some officials in the State Department appeared to favor European unification, but in the top echelon of the department this line of thinking was frowned on, because President Roosevelt's postwar plans were based on cooperation with the Soviet Union, which was suspicious of any kind of West European unification.[3] Another pillar of the American global vista following the conclusion of World War II was a firm commitment to the United Nations, and such a commitment might also clash with support for a united Western Europe.

Congress, however, may have taken a somewhat different view in 1943 and 1944 of what might be best for U.S. policy to pursue after the end of the war. A study prepared by the Legislative Reference Service of the Library of Congress suggested that a European federation or confederation might provide the key to the difficult question of what to do about Germany. Some measure of European unification may offer Germany equal treatment with other European countries and "at the same time make her subject to restrictions."[4]

In spite of the policy recommendations emanating from the Library of Congress, whose reports were widely circulated among members of Congress, no definitive policy changes occurred in the United States until the end of 1945 or early 1946 when the existence of a definitive Soviet challenge was recognized by President Truman. Undoubtedly, the rejection of Secretary of State Byrnes' plan for the neutralization of Germany and the Soviet exclusive backing of the Polish government in Lublin played important roles in the change of policy.

It has been reported that as early as December 1945 President Truman was on record as favoring a United States of Europe and that during 1946 the State Department began to favor some measure of economic integration for Western Europe.[5] However, the clear signal for a policy supporting such integration came in 1947 with Secretary of State George C. Marshall's famous speech at Harvard University advocating economic aid to Europe and Congress' adoption of the Marshall Plan in 1948.

The OEEC

The OEEC (Organization for European Economic Cooperation) had the mission to liberalize trade among the seventeen countries receiving aid from the Marshall Plan funds, technically the European Recovery Program (ERP), and was to make proposals for the distribution of these funds based on the needs of the recipient countries. In addition, it was to liberalize international payments and promote vigorously the productivity in these countries through the efficient use of the resources at their command.[6]

The actual determination of the funds to be utilized was made by the Economic Cooperation Administration (ECA), which was established by Congress in April 1948 and was headed by an administrator of cabinet rank.[7] In addition, the position of U.S. special representative in Europe was created, whose task it was to serve as liaison and communications link between ECA and OEEC. Averill Harriman, an old hand in American foreign policy, assumed this post and set up his headquarters in Paris.

In 1949, the ECA was believed to have achieved the basic objective of the ERP, namely preventing a European economic collapse. In September of that year, Paul Hoffman, the administrator of ECA, informed the OEEC that from that point funds would no longer be distributed according to the needs of the recipient countries, but in accordance with the performance of individual countries directed at liberalizing European trade and payments.[8]

Although there was some resistance to the establishment of an organization to facilitate international payments among the OEEC states, especially by the British government, a European Payments Union was set up in July 1950. Meanwhile a sharp reduction of import quotas had been achieved, and the major aims of U.S. policy for the OEEC were in the process of being implemented. By the time the ERP was completed in 1952, the amount spent by the United States in assistance to Western Europe was slightly above $12 billion, nearly $5 billion less than was anticipated in 1948.[9]

A prime U.S. policy objective to be carried out through ERP and ECA was the regional economic integration of Western Europe. It was feared that otherwise narrow nationalistic economic interests might again lead to hostilities among the region's states. Indeed, according to a speech given toward the end of 1949 by ECA Administrator Paul Hoffman, the integration of Western Europe's economy was necessary to provide a steady improvement in the conditions for all of its people in the region.[10]

The proper treatment of Germany also was seen as important in this connection. After West Germany had become officially the Federal Republic of Germany in September 1949, it was granted the status of full partnership in the OEEC.

It is interesting to note that many members of Congress felt in 1950 that the U.S. government should put more pressure on the Europeans not only to integrate their economies but also to unite politically. However, Dean Acheson, then secretary of state, declared that while the United States looked with favor on the political unification of Western Europe, it was neither a prerequisite for economic integration nor could it be compelled by the United States against the judgment of the Europeans.[11]

However, there were also some concerns expressed in Congress and elsewhere *against* strong U.S. support for European economic and perhaps political integration. It was feared that European economic integration (1) would obviate the possibility of a world without economic discrimination and (2) might undermine the prospect of establishing a North Atlantic Federal Union, favored by a number of Americans. The administration, however, defended its policy in support of European economic integration against the first criticism as a likely step toward full multilateralism, and against the second criticism as a pragmatic means to reach a desirable North Atlantic community.[12]

Suggestions were also made to strengthen the authority of the OEEC by insisting on participation by cabinet-rank representatives in top-level meetings that were to be held more frequently and by appointing an outstanding political figure as its permanent head. But these suggestions came at a time when the idea of a French economic association with Italy and the Benelux countries (Belgium, the Netherlands, Luxembourg) was being considered in Europe, and the U.S. government became convinced that German recovery could not and should not be held down. All these concepts were under active consideration when French Foreign Minister Robert Schuman offered on May 9, 1950, his well-known proposals about the establishment of a European Coal and Steel Community (ECSC). These proposals undercut any further thoughts about strengthening the authority of the OEEC.

The Schuman Plan and the ECSC   The Schuman proposals aimed basically at the creation of a customs union for coal and steel products by France, West Germany, Italy, and the Benelux countries. Great Britain had declined to become a charter member of the ECSC as it feared that membership in the proposed Community would impair its economic relations with the Commonwealth countries, an attitude sharply criticized by the U.S. Congress.

A special and innovative feature of the ECSC was the endowment of the chief executive and administrative organ of the Community, the "High Authority," with supranational powers, which meant that this organ could issue binding rules and decisions on individual residents and enterprises in the member states without special authorization by the national legislative or administrative institutions of the ECSC member states.

President Truman expressed his approval of the Schuman scheme within days of the news conference. Dean Acheson and other high State Department officials also gave their blessing to the proposed ECSC, but regret was expressed at Britain's refusal to join the new venture. Congress also declared its support for the initial economic integration proposed by the French government, especially because it implied the future conciliation of France and West Germany. Indeed, the termination of the policy of economic restrictions on Germany that appeared to be part of the Schuman plan was considered by the U.S. government as an important step forward in the rebuilding of the West European economy.[13]

In the drafting of the ECSC Treaty, a number of American lawyers furnished their expertise, especially with respect to its antitrust provisions. At the same time, Americans in high positions with the Office of the U.S. High Commissioner in Germany helped in blunting some of the West German criticism regarding the proposed ECSC—fears were expressed that the Community structure would be used to impose constraints on German economic developments—and finally obtained German agreement for the treaty in March 1951.

The ECSC became operational on January 1, 1953. Reflecting the great importance attributed to this IGO by the United States, the first American ambassador assigned to the ECSC was a very experienced and skillful diplomat, David Bruce. Indeed, during the first few years, the hopes of the United States that the ECSC would turn out to be a successful departure for economic integration in Western Europe were fulfilled. Coal and steel production within the confines of the six members expanded, and the supranational features of the ECSC seemed to work. Jean Monnet, a zealot for European unification and a very capable business executive, had been appointed the first president of the high authority, and under his leadership the ECSC made good initial progress.[14]

The European Defense Community   The war in Korea and the fear that communist expansionism might rear its ugly head against Western Europe while U.S. military forces were heavily engaged in East Asia prompted Washington to clamor increasingly for German rearmament. It was in response to such urgings that French Prime Minister René Pleven offered in October 1950 his plan for an integrated European army that was to include German contingents. In such a scheme, national units might be integrated at either the regimental or the divisional level into "European" units, thereby assuring multinational control over the newly armed German troops, a development on which many Europeans looked with apprehension but that conceivably could be overcome by the above or similar arrangements. Although the Germans were not enthusiastic about any rearmament, negotiations, in which American representatives participated, eventually resulted in a treaty through which Pleven's plan was transformed into the European Defense Community (EDC). The core of the community was to consist of a European army, whose army corps could not be composed of more than two divisions of the same nationality. Participating states were to be the members of the ECSC (Great Britain again refused to associate itself with regional ventures within Europe).

The EDC Treaty, signed on May 27, 1952, made the Germans basically equal partners in the Defense Community, restored most sovereign powers to the West German state, and was to become the vehicle for West German membership in NATO. At the same time, the treaty emerged as a crucial ingredient of U.S. foreign policy aimed toward achieving West European unity.[15] This became very clear when, late in 1953, it appeared that the French Assembly might not ratify the EDC Treaty. John Foster Dulles, who had become President Eisenhower's secretary of state earlier in that year, threatened an "agonizing reappraisal" of American foreign policy in Europe if

France were to reject the EDC Treaty. He also instructed the U.S. ambassadors in the capitals of the Six not only to refuse possible alternatives to EDC but not even to admit that such alternatives existed.[16] Nevertheless, the French Assembly rejected the treaty on August 30, 1954. With it, the prospect of another step toward European unity, the creation of a European Political Community (EPC), also died.

With the demise of the EDC, the U.S. policy goal of bringing West Germany into NATO had to be attained by other means. This was accomplished by setting up still another IGO, the Western European Union (WEU). This organization was an expansion of the Brussels Treaty of 1948 whose signatories had been Great Britain, France, and the Benelux countries; it was basically a British initiative and added France and the Federal Republic of Germany to the original defense arrangement. Accordingly, within the framework of the WEU, in October 1954 most of the wartime restrictions imposed on West Germany were lifted and the occupation of that country by the Western powers was ended. However, the Federal Republic was prohibited from manufacturing nuclear, chemical, and biological weapons, long-range bombers and missiles, as well as large naval vessels. An agency for the control of armaments was established within the WEU to ensure compliance with the above provisions.

The EEC and Euratom   New opportunities for U.S. policy toward Western Europe to promote the unification process opened up when, in the middle of the 1950s, negotiations were initiated to create the European Economic Community (EEC) and the European Atomic Community (Euratom). However, the level of U.S. participation in these negotiations was lower than during the talks aimed at setting up the ECSC. The reason may well have been that the strong pressure exerted by the United States to obtain the ratification of the EDC proved to be counterproductive to the outcome desired.[17] In the final analysis, the Europeans had to be convinced of the desirability of unification and had to pursue it with the intensity and speed their judgment dictated. There was hope that, once the economic integration process had been initiated, the benefits derived by the people in Western Europe from cross-national collaboration would induce them and their political leaders to expand economic integration into some kind of political unification. This view of regional integration, known as "functionalism," anticipated gradual progress from economic to political integration.[18]

The progress made by the ECSC during the early years of its existence was not matched in the second half of the 1950s, in part because the economic conditions deteriorated during that period, but in part also because of some problems in the implementation of the ECSC Treaty. Hence 1955 was an opportune time to consider the extension of the integration process from one sector (coal and steel) to a full common market encompassing all sectors of the economy that the EEC was to represent. This quantum jump in economic integration came also at the right time to assuage somewhat the hurt feelings on both sides of the Atlantic caused by the failure of the EDC.

For the U.S. government and its goal to move unification forward in Western Europe, the Euratom Treaty was also very attractive. It was believed, not only in Washington but also in many European circles, that the novelty of the atomic field made it especially suitable to erect new institutions with supranational powers, since few vested interests existed in that field that would be disturbed. Washington also regarded Euratom as contributing to the economic strength of Western Europe and was prepared to allocate fuel for sale or lease to Euratom and to provide technical and financial aid.

Both the EEC and the Euratom treaties were signed early in 1957 and came into force on January 1, 1958. Although most Americans welcomed these developments as significant steps toward a United States of Europe, there was some criticism about the likely future economic effects on the United States. Some critics were concerned that the customs union—on which the EEC's common market was based and which exempted the six member states from the general GATT requirement of nondiscrimination in international trade—would, in the long run, harm American exports to Western Europe and elsewhere. Another criticism was directed against the treatment of agriculture in the treaty, for which a common market organization with preferences for Community farm products was stipulated, a development that might greatly reduce U.S. exports of agricultural commodities to the Six.[19]

Just as the U.S. government was anxious to see Great Britain as a charter member of the ECSC and EDC, Washington had hoped that this might be the case with the EEC and Euratom. However, Britain again declined, instead proposing the establishment of a European free-trade area that would include the customs union of the Six. Initially in early 1957 the United States welcomed the concept of the free-trade area and the customs union of the Six, but for Washington it was essential that the EEC Treaty not be endangered, because it provided the starting point for genuine political integration. This was seen in the various articles of that treaty that envisaged the harmonization of policies in many sectors and thereby laid out the blueprint of gradually moving toward political unification. The extensive institutional framework of the EEC and Euratom Treaties was also considered politically important inasmuch as some of their institutions, such as the Court of Justice and the Assembly, seemed to lend themselves to an easy transformation to a federal framework. The upshot of it all was that both the EEC and a European Free Trade Association (EFTA)* existed in 1960; however, in terms of U.S. policy support, it was

---

*EFTA members were Great Britain, Sweden, Denmark, Norway, Austria, Switzerland, and Portugal. Agriculture was not included in EFTA arrangements. The EFTA Treaty was signed in November 1959.

intensive with respect to the former but noncommittal regarding the latter. Nevertheless, it should be noted that the supranational features of both the EEC and Euratom were less pronounced than those of the ECSC, which clearly was and remains the high-water mark of supranationalism and which, from the legal or constitutional point of view, represented the greatest progress toward a political union.

Another factor significant for the evaluation of U.S. policy toward Western Europe was Washington's attitude regarding French insistence that the overseas territories of the prospective member states should be associated with the EEC and through this association should be granted substantial tariff preference for the importation of their (mostly tropical) commodities into all EEC member states. The United States objected that such an association would discriminate against other suppliers of tropical products. However, when France stated that without this association it would not sign the EEC Treaty, President Eisenhower and the State Department top echelon apparently overruled the objections because of the political importance attached to the success of the negotiations for the EEC and Euratom.[20]

Interim Summary   By the end of the 1950s, the economic and political dimensions of U.S. policy toward Western Europe could be fairly well identified. Its main features were the following:

1.   A major goal was the political unification of Western Europe to be achieved through regional economic integration. The attainment of this political goal would (a) prevent future intra-West European hostilities, (b) assure some control over future German behavior and prevent Germany from exercising excessive power while at the same time giving West Germany equal opportunity to participate in a prospective political federation or confederation, (c) increase the military and financial contributions of the Six to NATO as the economic well-being of the EEC rises, and (d) enhance the security of Western Europe *and* the United States against the threat of a Soviet attack in Europe.

2.   For the attainment of the above political goal, certain economic costs were acceptable. These costs included possible diversion of international trade as the result of the establishment of the customs union underlying the EEC, the reduction of U.S. agricultural exports to the EEC member states, and possibly lowered exports of tropical commodities by friendly Third World countries as a consequence of the EEC association with the former colonial possessions of the member states.

3.   To minimize possible damage flowing from the three Communities to the economies of the United States and other non-EEC countries, damage control measures were taken whenever appropriate in the form of protests as well as friendly persuasion to Community institutions and the capitals of the Six.

British Entry into the Communities and U.S. Policy Evolution   As indicated earlier, the United States has been anxious since the establishment of the ECSC to have Great Britain be a member of the three Communities. It was also hoped that some of the Scandinavian countries would join.

The major reason for Britain's refusal to become a member of the Communities had been, as mentioned already, concern that this membership would adversely affect its relations with the Commonwealth, although by the beginning of the 1960s British trade with the Commonwealth countries was declining, while that with the Six was increasing rapidly. Another more recent concern was the impact that membership may have on the "special relationship" between Britain and the United States.

Nevertheless, a change of heart in Britain became visible in early 1961, partly perhaps as the result of American pressure, but more definitely as the consequence of the realization that President Kennedy was as committed to the success of the integration experiment of the Six as his predecessors. In fact, when Prime Minister Harold MacMillan asked Kennedy during a visit to the United States whether Britain's entry into the Communities would threaten the "special relationship," he received assurances that prompted the British government to proceed with the formal application for membership.[21]

For Washington, British membership in the Communities appeared to have a number of specific advantages. On the very important issue of East-West relations, it was felt that the British position might be closer to the United States than that of France or West Germany. American policy toward building an "Atlantic community" might also be more successful with Britain in the Communities than outside. Finally, it was hoped that Britain could counter any protectionist and inward-looking tendencies that might arise among the Six. Thus U.S. aspirations for increased liberalization of world trade would not be hampered.

The negotiations between Great Britain and the Six regarding the modalities of British entry into the Communities, though often difficult and protracted, made substantial progress in 1962. However, the whole enterprise collapsed when on January 13, 1963, General de Gaulle, who had assumed the leadership of France in 1958, vetoed British entry during a famous news conference in Paris. Although the main professed reason for the veto was that Britain was not as yet ready for membership in the Communities, a prime concern for de Gaulle was the "special relationship" between that country and the United States. De Gaulle's real fear was that the United States would indirectly dominate the Communities.[22] Although France's partners initially wanted to fight the French decision through retaliatory measures against French objectives within the context of the Communities, they eventually accepted defeat. Obviously, the U.S. government was outraged and disappointed about de Gaulle's veto, which was indeed a severe defeat for U.S. policy.

Nevertheless, neither France's partners nor the United States and Great Britain gave up on their goal of British membership. High-ranking U.S. officials in the State Department continued to believe that the Communities were destined to evolve into a broader European organization that would contribute in the long run to the creation of an Atlantic community, and therefore they persisted in urging the British government not to abandon the pursuit of membership.

Although some segments of British public opinion began to waver in their support for joining the Communities in the mid-1960s, the British government renewed its application for membership in 1967.

Informal contacts in early 1969 between the British ambassador in Paris and de Gaulle seemed to indicate a softening of the latter's position toward the British application.[23] However, de Gaulle later reiterated his opposition, and it was only after his retirement in the fall of that year that new impetus was given by London to the application. With the election of a Conservative government in Britain in June 1970, negotiations with the representatives of the Communities and their member states were pursued energetically. Major difficulties such as the weakness of the British pound, the future relations with the Commonwealth, and what would constitute a reasonable transition period to phase the British economy into the common market were overcome, and on January 1, 1973, Great Britain became a full member of the Communities. On the same date, Ireland and Denmark also joined as full members, expanding the "Six" into the "Nine."

Progress and Problems

During the 1960s, the EEC evolved into a full-fledged customs union, ahead of schedule. Whereas the treaty had stipulated a 12-year transition period for this purpose, ending on January 1, 1970, the tariffs between the members had been eliminated and the common external tariff put in place against imports from third countries by July 1, 1968. Not surprisingly, this period of gestation and development produced a number of political and economic problems that sometimes affected American foreign policy and occasionally required rethinking the appropriateness of current policy goals in terms of U.S. national interests. Two examples of political problems may illustrate that perhaps a need had existed to reevaluate American policy.

De Gaulle's rejection of British membership in the Communities in 1963 not only reflected French preoccupation with the grandeur of France; it also began to rekindle gradually the fires of nationalism in other member states. In other words, it set into motion a renationalizing trend within the Communities that was again highlighted during the second half of 1965 when de Gaulle, anxious to increase the financial return for French farmers from the Common Agricultural Policy (CAP) instituted by the EEC, instructed French civil servants not to participate any more in the meetings of the Community until his demand had been met. Underlying this demand was a much more ominous objective; de Gaulle wanted to stop all movement of the Communities toward a real European union. A compromise was accepted by all EEC members in January 1966 that brought France back as full participant in the institutions of the Community but that also included a provision in effect halting any progress in the EEC decision-making progress toward greater supranationalism.[24] In other words, the political dynamics of economic integration were being seriously undermined by both the French actions and the fact that other member states acquiesced. However, it was precisely these political dynamics on which the United States counted to bring about the anxiously desired political unification of Western Europe, a prime goal of American foreign policy.

In the economic sphere, the most serious issue for U.S. policymakers was the development of the CAP by the EEC. The Common Agricultural Policy consisted of a framework of fixed prices. A target price was set up to determine the sales price of major agricultural commodities. If actual prices fell below the target price, an intervention price system triggered purchase of the commodity by one of the EEC institutions, the Commission, which was the main administrative organ. To protect the agricultural producers within the EEC, a sluice-gate price was established and a variable levy imposed on imported farm products that covers the difference between the cost of the product and the sluice-gate price. This meant that no matter how low the price of the product, it is prevented from competing with the EEC-produced item. Imports thus become possible only if a particular commodity is not produced within the Community or is produced in insufficient quantities. In addition, the CAP provides export subsidies for EEC farm products if they cannot be sold within the Community countries. The consequences of the CAP have been steadily increasing prices for food as the market prices were fixed higher each year, a tremendous surplus of some products such as butter, and the subsidization of certain exported commodities such as wheat.

Other American concerns were nontariff barriers (NTBs) employed by the EEC member states. Particularly objectionable were those NTBs that seemed to be directed especially against U.S. imports, such as the very high domestic taxes imposed on the kinds of large engines typically found in American cars.

These were some of the reasons President Kennedy recommended and Congress passed the Trade Expansion Act of 1962, which became the basis for an intensive round of negotiations under the auspices of GATT aimed at reducing tariffs and NTBs on a global level. These negotiations, which became known as the "Kennedy Round," were to accomplish for U.S. policymakers the following objectives:

1. A substantial reduction of tariffs on industrial goods, which under the Trade Expansion Act could be lowered to zero on goods produced 80 percent in the United States and the EEC. The lower the tariffs agreed

during the negotiations, the less would be the discrimination against U.S. exports that had been institutionalized by the EEC customs union and by preferential association agreements in Africa and elsewhere.

2. Persuasion of the EEC institutions and member states to pursue liberal "outward-looking" trade policies.
3. Assurance that U.S. agricultural exports to the EEC retain their "fair share" or perhaps increase their proportion in the EEC market.[25]

The main actors in the Kennedy Round were the United States and the EEC. The negotiations were prolonged, often quite difficult, and toward the end assumed the character of an immense poker game with all the bluffs and theatrics associated with such a game. Although agreement was reached finally in the spring of 1967 among all parties, the results were not fully satisfactory to Washington. Tariffs on industrial goods were lowered by between 30 and 50 percent, but little progress was made on eliminating or softening most NTBs. On the agricultural front, few concessions were made by the EEC to accommodate the U.S. demands. Washington was very disappointed about not obtaining an assured "fair share" of the agricultural market in the EEC countries. Indeed, the agricultural relations between the United States and the EEC provided a continuous source of often acrimonious controversy across the Atlantic, which at times led to serious frictions.

The adamant stance taken by the EEC representative on some issues and the general toughness of the negotiations in the Kennedy Round was a surprise to American officials. It contrasted with the climate of a preceding round of tariff-reducing negotiations in the early 1960s—the so-called Dillon Round—which was more consensual and friendly. It became obvious in the Kennedy Round that the interests of the main negotiating parties, the United States and the EEC, were diverging on a number of issues, with agriculture being the prime example. Some State Department officers in the Bureau of Economic Affairs began to wonder whether the main thrust of U.S. policy toward Western Europe—European unification—should be sustained. Indeed, as early as 1964 questions were raised whether political integration in Western Europe was a realistic goal.[26] However, no basic course changes were undertaken, and support of West European unification remained the primary U.S. objective.

Frictions and U.S. Policy Actions   Although Presidents Nixon, Ford, and Carter continued the professed support of West European unification during the 1970s, frictions and changing conditions ate away at the underpinning of this policy. Yet many Europeans looked on this policy with favor in spite of its clearly unrealistic basis. However, some U.S. policies caused considerable transatlantic tension, some with political implications.

In August 1971, President Nixon closed the so-called gold window, making it from then on impossible to exchange paper dollars into gold, and at the same time the U.S. dollar was devaluated by 10 percent. In addition, a surcharge was imposed on foreign imports into the United States, but in response to many protests from abroad this surcharge was lifted in a relatively short time.

A few years later, the United States imposed an embargo on the exports of certain farm commodities such as soybeans and cotton seed, because they were in short supply in America. This aroused shock and anger in the EEC member states, especially because Washington had been preaching free trade for so many years. Although the embargo was lifted quickly, it generated new demands for European self-sufficiency and discouraged those in Western Europe who were prepared to work for the modification of the CAP along lines suggested by American officials.[27]

A major strain placed on the U.S.-EEC relationship has been the growing American realization that the Community has become a serious competitor in international trade and investment. This has given the latter growing economic and political influence in the world, sometimes at the expense of the United States. In addition, tensions have been caused by differing perceptions of the respective benefits of transatlantic trade.

A general analysis of U.S-EEC trade from 1958 to the beginning of 1973, when the Communities were enlarged to nine members, is instructive. It reveals that U.S. exports during that period almost tripled, but shipments from the Community to the United States more than quintupled. Although the United States had a surplus during the years from 1958 to 1971, it suffered its first deficit in 1972. Looking over this surplus, we see that it ranged from a high of $2.3 billion in 1963 to a low of $413 million in 1968. Whereas this continued surplus may have been a source of satisfaction to the United States, a more thorough analysis of how American exports to the Community fared compared with those of other countries presents a somewhat different picture. When we compare the share of United States exports with those of other *nonmember* countries, we find that the American portion was 17.57 percent in 1958 and fell only slightly to 16.55 percent in 1972. However, if we compare the percentage of U.S. exports with all exports including those of European Community countries to each other, the U.S. share dropped from 12.37 to 8 percent. The reason for this is the tremendous increase in intra-EC trade from 1958 to 1972—an expected result of the creation of the Common Market. During that period, this trade increased more than eight times, while exports from third countries increased only slightly more than three times.

Since the export of agricultural commodities has been a continuing concern of the United States, it is useful to focus on the export figures from July 1, 1957, to June 30, 1973. Commodities subject to variable levies under CAP shipped to EEC countries reached a high point in the fiscal year 1965-1966 and then declined. The likely explanation for this trend is the full implementation of the variable-levy system by the end of 1964. In contrast, the exports for non-variable-levy commodities continued to remain at a relatively high level until 1969 and in fact increased beginning with the 1969-1970 fiscal year. However, it is essential to keep in mind that during the period from 1958 to 1972 the level of consumption in the Community rose steeply and that not only were American exports of agricultural commodities unable to retain their proper share of supplying this rising demand, but their net volume dropped between 1965 and 1970.[28]

When in 1973 Great Britain, Ireland, and Denmark (all former EFTA countries) joined the Communities, other EFTA countries were given the opportunity of concluding free-trade area arrangements with the EEC on industrial goods. The consequence was that most of Western Europe by the end of 1978 , after a 5-year transition period, had become a huge trading bloc. In 1982, Greece became the tenth full member of the Communities and, in spite of some current controversies, Spain and Portugal may become EEC members by the middle of the 1980s.

EC Relations with the Third World

In the Third World, U.S. and EEC interests also diverged. Indeed, in the past, American foreign policymakers were irritated by certain aspects of the Community's association policies in Africa and the preferential arrangements made with countries rimming the Mediterranean basin for which the Community claimed to have an historical special responsibility.[29]

The primary bone of contention regarding the Community's policy of concluding "association" agreements with former colonies of the member states in Africa and elsewhere, which was greatly expanded after British entry, was the granting of "reverse preferences." This means that the associate country is granted not only reduction or elimination of tariffs for goods shipped to the Community, but that it offers certain tariff preferences for the import of Community products. The United States and other nonmember states considered reverse preferences by the associated countries to Community exports of manufactured goods as discriminatory against third-country manufacturers. The Lomé Convention, tying over fifty developing countries in Africa (south of the Sahara), the Caribbean, and the Western Pacific to the Community in 1975, dispensed with the need for reciprocal preferences. It gives the associated countries the option of granting special trade concessions to the EEC countries but also allows them to make the preferences available to third countries. Thus this source of friction between the United States and the EEC was eliminated.

The Community's Mediterranean policy during the last few years has established a network of preferential agreements or associations with all Mediterranean states except Libya and Albania. Yugoslavia also has a trade agreement with the Community, but it is nonpreferential.

The United States always deplored any kind of preferential treatment by the EEC outside Europe proper. It opposed the Community's Mediterranean policy because of concern about the adverse effects on American exports of citrus fruits and other goods to the area, although the amounts involved are relatively small. As a matter of principle, the United States has proclaimed again and again that the preferential agreements are violations of GATT, which only permits full-fledged customs unions and free-trade areas to be exempted from the most-favored-nation clause. The Community has admitted a possible violation but continues to claim its special responsibility for the countries of the area.

While at this time the U.S. government appears to be quite relaxed about the potential rise of Community influence in the Lomé territories, the Mediterranean, and perhaps in the Third World generally, pressures by American business interests may give rise to different attitudes among American foreign policymakers. The quest for critical raw materials in Africa and other Third World countries needed to keep domestic industries running smoothly may spur competitive action and perhaps preemption of such materials, for which the Community could be in a better position than the United States. Although there is a clear economic imperative for economic cooperation between America and the Community, the perceived priority for national solutions to remedy adverse economic and political situations may prevent the formation of rational cooperation policies and thereby constitute a major challenge to U.S. foreign policy.

What Price Collaboration?

The increasingly serious worldwide economic crisis during the late 1970s and early 1980s has spawned national policies of the "beggar thy neighbor" kind, accompanied by growing protectionist tendencies, even *within* the EEC. The upward trend in international trade reversed itself in 1981 for the first time since the end of World War II, in spite of the successful conclusion of the "Tokyo Round" of negotiations, which aimed again at tariff reductions but concentrated more than in the Kennedy Round on the dismantlement of NTBs, on setting up special codes of behavior with respect to NTBs, and on instituting safeguard clauses. As already mentioned, these negotiations were based on the U.S. Trade Reform Act of 1974.

During the second half of the 1970s the trade deficit of the United States assumed enormous proportions, reaching over $30 billion. How did American trade with Western Europe fare in this disastrous situation? Table 11.1 provides the relevant figures, from which we can see that U.S. exports to the ten members of the EEC (Greece, the tenth member, is included in the table), always exceeded imports from these countries except for 1972. In 1980, the U.S. surplus was nearly $18 billion and in 1981 nearly $11 billion, although the global U.S. trade deficit exceeded $27 billion. In terms of the share of total U.S. exports, the exports to the EEC accounted throughout the 1960s for more than 25 percent, whereas in 1981 they were only 22.4 percent.

Table 11.1   U.S. Agricultural and Nonagricultural Trade with the European Community of Ten, 1958–1981
($Millions)

Year	Total Trade, from or to EC of Ten[a]	Breakdown of Total Trade Agriculture	Nonagriculture[a]	As Percentage of Total Agriculture	Nonagriculture[a]
Imports					
1958	2,668.5	306.9	2,361.6	11.5	88.5
1960	3,415.7	342.5	3,073.2	10.0	90.0
1968	8,333.8	595.4	7,738.4	7.1	92.9
1969	8,357.3	601.5	7,755.8	7.2	92.8
1972	12,578.9	836.8	11,742.8	6.7	93.3
1973	15,697.4	1,144.7	14,552.7	7.3	92.7
1974	19,363.8	1,193.3	18,170.5	6.2	93.8
1975	16,483.5	1,107.5	15,376.0	6.7	93.3
1976	18,213.1	1,264.6	16,948.5	6.9	93.1
1977	22,678.6	1,419.5	21,259.1	6.3	93.7
1978	29,597.0	1,922.3	27,674.7	6.5	93.5
1979	34,070.1	1,950.1	32,120.0	5.7	94.3
1980	36,742.2	2,130.2	34,612.0	5.8	94.2
1981	41,647.1	2,262.7	39,384.4	5.4	94.6
Exports					
1958	4,099.5	1,312.9	2,786.6	32.0	68.0
1960	5,752.4	1,703.8	4,048.6	29.6	70.4
1968	8,851.9	1,872.6	6,979.3	21.2	78.8
1969	9,916.5	1,736.3	8,180.2	17.5	82.5
1972	12,150.6	2,748.6	9,402.0	22.6	77.4
1973	17,120.2	4,667.7	12,452.5	27.3	72.7
1974	22,554.9	5,624.3	16,930.6	24.9	75.1
1975	23,315.0	5,705.8	17,609.2	24.5	75.5
1976	25,999.5	6,564.4	19,435.1	25.3	74.7
1977	27,630.9	6,785.0	20,845.9	24.6	75.4
1978	32,746.6	7,339.6	25,407.0	22.4	77.6
1979	43,403.1	7,847.5	35,555.6	18.1	81.9
1980	54,600.9	9,236.3	45,364.6	16.9	83.1
1981	52,363.1	9,058.8	43,304.3	17.3	82.7

Note: Some commodities formerly classified as nonagricultural (such as fur skins) have been included in agricultural trade beginning with 1970, according to the U.S. Department of Agriculture.

[a]Starting in 1978, data include shipments of nonmonetary gold.

Source: U.S., Department of State, Bureau of Intelligence and Research, *U.S. Trade With the European Community, 1958–1981* (Report 387-AR, May 14, 1982), Table III.

The story of U.S. agricultural exports to the Ten is different. The U.S. share declined from 32 percent in 1958 to a low of 17.5 percent in 1969. In the 1970s it increased temporarily as a result of a high world prices for grains and soybeans, but started to decline again in 1979 and stood at 17.3 percent in 1981. In terms of total U.S. agricultural exports, the share of those going to the Ten declined from 35.3 percent in 1960 to 20.9 percent in 1981.[30]

The transatlantic irritations caused by trade and monetary matters—during the first half of the 1970s the U.S. dollar was considered too weak, whereas at the end of the 1970s it was considered too strong, the result of very high U.S. interest rates—raised the question of what policies should be formulated to reduce friction and encourage greater cooperation between the United States and the EEC. One possibility was the closer coordination of economic policies based on studies and recommendations made by the OECD, which had been the OEEC until transformed in 1961 and whose membership then was expanded to include the United States, Canada, Japan, and most other Western economically advanced countries. Washington has worked closely with the OECD, but the latter's excellent economic analyses and suggestions were frequently not followed and, for domestic political reasons, even within the Communities, national policies were developed that ignored the OECD recommendations for policy coordination.

Summit Meetings

While the use of the OECD as an instrument of bringing about greater collaboration between Washington and the EEC was considerably less than a success, another tool to achieve this purpose and to include Japan was the annual convening of the leaders of the major Western industrial democracies in "summit" meetings. The first of these summits took place in Rambouillet, France, in 1975, and they have been held every year since then. The participants at Rambouillet were the heads of government of France, the Federal Republic of Germany, Great Britain, Italy, Japan, and the United States. Later Canada was brought into the summit process; the president of the Commission of the European Communities was authorized to attend summit sessions on topics involving Community responsibilities.

The summits of the 1970s focused primarily on the pressing issues of inflation, energy, trade, North-South relations, financial disorder, and unemployment. During the early 1980s East-West relations came to the fore, triggered by the Soviet Union's occupation of Afghanistan; the security of oil supplies from the Middle East assumed a larger role; and the Polish political and economic problems became important subjects of summit discussions, especially at the 1982 Versailles summit.

Topics and effects of the summits varied from year to year. Clearly, the expectations raised among the public were often not met after the rhetoric during and after the summits had died down. Promises made during summits were or could not be kept afterward in the face of political and economic realities. Apparent misunderstandings added to the difficulty of implementing summit objectives. A good example is the 1982 summit held at Versailles, where President Reagan believed he had obtained agreement on how the summit participants were to handle their economic and financial relations with the Soviet Union and other East Bloc countries. However, the imposition of sanctions on suppliers of materials to the construction of the Soviet gas pipeline to Western Europe following the summit highlighted the fact that full agreement had not been reached on this sensitive subject. The result was serious acrimony among the Western industrialized countries that might have caused lasting damage to the NATO alliance. Fortunately, Washington lifted the sanctions later in the year in return for an agreement by the European allies to strengthen controls over West-East trade on strategic items. During the 1983 summit at Williamsburg, Virginia, every effort was made to avoid misunderstandings of the kind that occurred in Versailles, although differences of opinion on economic matters existed between the main participants.

From a domestic political perspective, the summit process, as an Atlantic Council policy paper points out, has been personally useful to political leaders:

> In some cases it put them in a better public position within their own countries to defend painful economic policies. It has helped in controlling internal pressures by using external commitments, and by pointing out that internal policies would be questioned by leaders of other countries if such policies were not internationally defensible.[31]

For Presidents Ford and Carter, some of the summits were used for presidential politics by projecting the image of a president being deeply involved in international diplomacy. President Reagan expanded the public relations aspects of the Versailles summit by addresses to members of Parliament in Britain, and the West German Bundestag, all carefully recorded by U.S. television.

Although arguments have been put forth against the use of summitry as a policy instrument—it may endanger existing international decision-making systems such as GATT or IMF and tends to undermine the effectiveness of bilateral diplomacy—summits are likely here to stay. The imperative of coordinating and harmonizing national policies and cross-national cooperation in general can be satisfied, at least to some degree, by the summit meetings where leaders become familiar with each other and gain a common perception of the problem facing a group of states, and decisions may be forced to a head on issues that otherwise might be allowed to drift. Some summits provide a high sense of drama and political opportunity to reach decisions; they generate political support for these decisions, which otherwise may be difficult to reach in one or more countries. However, to accomplish this in the economically and politically turbulent 1980s, a higher degree of effective collective leadership will be needed than has been the case so far. The Atlantic Council policy paper quoted earlier states that this will require:

1. The early and clear identification of key policy issues;
2. An intensive focus on mutual compatibility of the principal goals of policy, both domestic and international, of the key nations;
3. Clear and early consultation among the key nations with adequate involvement of other affected nations; and
4. Where necessary, steps to move beyond consultation toward collective decision making and action.[32]

In spite of these well-meaning words, it is far from certain whether the coordination and harmonization of policies among the Western industrialized countries will be much more successful in the future than it was in the past. American leverage on West European states to adopt policies desired by Washington, very potent in the 1950s, has nearly vanished in the 1980s. The most obvious example is meaningful change in the CAP. Overall, economic interests between the United States and the member states of the European Communities are often in conflict, which is compounded by diverging perceptions about East-West relations and what should be the appropriate attitudes and behavior of the Atlantic Alliance toward the Soviet Union and its East European satellites.

The Military-Political Dimension

With the war raging in Korea during the early 1950s, Washington was apprehensive that the Soviet Union might take advantage of U.S. involvement in East Asia to launch an attack on Western Europe. Therefore, it was deemed essential to flesh out the newly created NATO. The Mutual Defense Assistance Program of 1950 became the vehicle for a vast increase in Western Europe's defense efforts, and by 1957 the West European NATO allies had spent $13 billion in their own defense. Meanwhile, an appropriate command structure was established for NATO: General Eisenhower was appointed as supreme allied commander in Europe, and a strategy was formulated for the defense of Western Europe on the ground that became known as the "forward strategy." Essentially it was and remains a defense line along the Elbe River, which separates West and East Germany.

To carry out the defensive task, three NATO commands were set up: a Central Europe Command, perhaps the most important one; as well as the Northern Europe Command and the Southern Europe Command for flank protection.* The ground forces, both American (five divisions) and European, were to act as a trip wire that would ensure nuclear retaliation if necessary. The NATO ground forces, supported by tactical air squadrons, were to serve as the "shield," while, if needed, U.S. nuclear long-range missiles would furnish "the sword" to destroy military support facilities in the Soviet homeland as well as Soviet forces on the ground.

To counter NATO, the Soviet Union created the Warsaw Treaty Organization (WTO) to which Poland, the German Democratic Republic (East Germany), Czechoslovakia, Hungary, Romania, and Bulgaria belong. Albania, initially a member of the WTO, has withdrawn completely, and Romania resists Soviet attempts at greater integration.

Doubts and Tensions The "shield and sword" doctrine was a natural complement to the doctrine of "massive retaliation." However, toward the end of the 1950s, Europeans raised the question whether in the event of a limited Soviet attack on a secondary or tertiary target in Western Europe (e.g., smaller towns), the United States would engage in massive nuclear retaliation that would open U.S. cities to Soviet counterretaliation. These questions were all the more relevant, since the Soviet Union had by that time made remarkable progress in acquiring nuclear technology and in fact surpassed the United States in the power of delivery vehicles for nuclear weapons.** Also contributing to the uncertainty of the Europeans about U.S. resolve to use nuclear weapons was, and still is, the wording of Article 5 of the NATO treaty, which, while obligating the United States to come to the assistance of a victim of Soviet aggression, leaves the modalities of assistance to U.S. discretion. Although successive secretaries of state beginning with John Foster Dulles have tried to reassure the Europeans on U.S. readiness to employ strategic nuclear weapons in the event of Soviet attacks that could not be contained otherwise, the doubts linger on.

The early 1960s saw a fundamental change in U.S. and NATO defense strategies. Instead of "massive retaliation," a new doctrine known as "flexible response" was adopted first by President Kennedy and his Defense Secretary Robert McNamara, and became official NATO doctrine in 1967. It stressed credible deterrence through a well-balanced mixture of conventional as well as tactical and strategic nuclear weapons. In case of a Soviet attack, aggression will first be met by conventional NATO forces, with the possibility of escalation first through the employment of tactical nuclear weapons, and ultimately with strategic nuclear weapons.[33] A larger number of U.S. tactical

---

*In addition, two naval commands were established; one responsible for defending the waters from the eastern shores of the United States to Western Europe and North Africa, the other covering the English Channel.

**The Soviets put "Sputnik" into orbit in 1957, before the United States had an orbiting space capsule.

weapons, ranging from artillery shells with atomic warheads to rocketry and other launchers of relatively short-range missiles, were stationed in Western Europe to make the new doctrine workable and credible.

It was assumed that the possibility of escalation would hold down the level of violence, but it was also recognized that in the end a Soviet attack in Europe might lead to a full-fledged nuclear war by the superpowers. Nevertheless, the new doctrine permitted several options before such a calamity would ensue and therefore was an improvement over the doctrine of "massive retaliation." However, since ultimately the U.S. government still had to make the decision whether under particular circumstances it would or would not resort to strategic nuclear weapons, many Europeans were still not fully reassured. Some felt more comfortable with "massive retaliation" because it would assure a prompter U.S. response, and therefore they wanted to return NATO to that doctrine.

Shared Responsibilities   A major problem regarding shared responsibilities, which arose in the 1960s, grew out of the exclusive authority of the U.S. president, anchored in federal law, to determine when nuclear weapons are to be used. Hence such weapons had to be kept under the strict control of American officials, and in order to safeguard nuclear secrets, congressionally imposed restrictions made it impossible to give nuclear weapons to NATO allies.

Some of the European allies resented this situation, because it undercut the responsibility of their leaders to assure fully the security of their countries. Having to depend on decisions regarding the possible survival of their people that would be made in Washington or by American officials in the field whose perceptions of the common interest might be quite different from those of their own leaders was viewed as unfair, if not intolerable.

The United States recognized the dilemma within NATO created by U.S. nuclear near-monopoly; only Great Britain and France of all the NATO members had acquired limited nuclear weapons. Consequently, several policies were developed to ameliorate the situation.

1.   One policy initiative was the "two-key" proposal under which an American officer and an officer from another NATO country would each have a key necessary to fire a nuclear weapon. Thus NATO partners could exercise a veto over the use of nuclear weapons but could not force the United States to employ such weapons. It was not a successful scheme to satisfy the allies, because all strategic and even some tactical nuclear weapons were in the United States under Washington's exclusive control.

2.   A second policy initiative was the creation of a "multilateral force" (MLF), which would consist of naval vessels, including five American submarines carrying nuclear missiles, all manned by multinational crews. The two-key mechanism would apply to these naval units, assuring that ultimate control would rest with the president of the United States. The MLF idea did not

generate much support from the European allies, because it was not clear that even a major portion of the U.S. nuclear stockpile would pass under MLF control. With only West Germany fully backing MLF, it was quietly abandoned by Washington.

3.   A third U.S. policy approach was to bring all NATO allies into the task of selecting targets for nuclear weapons. For this purpose, a Nuclear Planning Group was established at NATO headquarters in which thirteen member states participate. This committee meets twice a year at the level of ministers of defense and more frequently at lower levels. This arrangement was generally acceptable to all NATO members and has contributed to raising the morale of the European allies, although obvious inequalities of power and influence continue to exist within NATO.

A second major problem of shared responsibilities within NATO has been the allocation of cost for the common defense among the member states. This problem, often called "burden sharing," has plagued NATO since the 1960s and lingers on today. The following comments, which were made in 1972 by President Kennedy's National Security Advisor McGeorge Bundy, are still cogent at this time and serve as a good introduction to this problem.

> It is a fact of life for both Europe and the United States that [Western Europe's] "resolutely amilitary" population depends for its peace of mind, at least in part, upon the fact that [the U.S.] population is prepared to pay twice as much of its national income for the common defense. I do not lament this expense. I think that in the main it is essential for our own security, and that we should save very few dollars if there were no Europe for us to help defend. Moreover I recognize that much has already been done, and that more can reasonably be predicted, in the way of burden-sharing. Nonetheless, I think it would be asking a great deal of my fellow citizens, and even more of their elected representatives, to expect them to neglect entirely, in the reconstruction of the economic and financial foundations that are indispensable to all of us, the fact that among the open societies of the North Atlantic and Pacific, there is one which does much more than the others to provide for a defense which is still common.[34]

Congress reflected this mood and, led by Senator Mike Mansfield of Montana, attempted to reduce American forces in Western Europe in order to cut costs. The Johnson, Nixon, Ford, and Carter administrations always opposed these moves, because the curtailment of these forces would diminish U.S. influence in Western Europe and might destabilize the military situation in Europe by suggesting a waning American interest in the region. It should be noted that West Germany made, during the 1970s, offset payments for the U.S. expenses to maintain troops in that country amounting to several billions of dollars. The payments were used to purchase American military equipment and thereby helped to reduce the balance-of-payments deficits of the United States.

In May 1977, all NATO allies decided to increase their annual expenditures for NATO personnel and equipment by 3 percent in constant dollars. However, some of the European NATO members (e.g., Denmark and the Netherlands) have failed to fulfill this obligation, and, in view of the economic malaise gripping most of Western Europe with a 10 percent unemployment rate pervasive, it is doubtful that this pledge will be carried out.[*,35] Thus the burden-sharing problem is likely to continue, meaning that the responsibilities of the NATO members are not shared equally, which may have adverse implications for the future.

Consultation   The NATO treaty requires the member governments to engage in consultation regarding actions and policies they may want to undertake that might affect NATO interests or missions. This, however, is easier said than done, as the history of NATO has demonstrated. One reason is that the concept of "consultation" is ambiguous. Does it mean simply for a member state to inform the other members, or must it take into consideration the advice it receives from the others regarding a proposed action or policy? The latter implies a "give-and-take" examination and discussion of the problems associated with action or policy contemplated, but it does not require that the advice must be taken. Thus the requirement of consultation even under the second interpretation does not impose any serious limitation on the freedom of action of the NATO member states.

Nevertheless, even this mild constraint has often been ignored, especially by the United States. It did not consult the allies in the Korean action in 1950 nor regarding details of the Vietnam War, although in both cases NATO's defensive capabilities were likely to be affected. During the U.S.-Cuban missile crisis in 1962, potentially a most dangerous confrontation between the two superpowers, the allies were informed only after the final decision was reached by President Kennedy.

In 1969, President Nixon declared that the United States intended "to undertake deep and genuine consultation with its allies, both before and during any negotiations directly affecting their interests."[36] However, when the United States placed its armed forces on a worldwide alert during the 1973 Arab-Israeli war to deter a unilateral Soviet intervention, again no prior consultation of NATO allies took place. Not surprisingly, all except Portugal refused to grant landing rights to U.S. planes engaged in resupplying Israel with arms and equipment.

It would be erroneous, however, to conclude from the cases cited that consultation is the exception rather than the rule. In more slow-moving situations there has been intensive and comprehensive consultation. For example, with respect to the negotiations leading to the Helsinki Act on European Security and Cooperation in 1975, the allies consulted each other on every

---

*The average increases in the defense expenditures of the European NATO allies by May 1983 were only 1 percent.

position taken by them, and similar consultation sessions have been taking place regularly on the follow-up review conferences in Belgrade and Madrid. Extensive consultations also occurred about Soviet actions in Afghanistan and Poland. Thus we find a general recognition for the need to consult in the future, but whether this will be actually done in very critical circumstances that require rapid decisions is difficult to predict. Nevertheless, American policymakers should keep in mind that recurring instances of nonconsultation are likely to cause resentment among the NATO allies, since they may be regarded as a harsh reflection of the dependency relationship perceived to prevail between the allies and the much more powerful United States. Therefore, in the long run, the cohesion of NATO may be seriously endangered by nonconsultation and enhanced by conscientious consultations, as seems to have been and continues to be the basic policy of Presidents Carter and Reagan.

NATO in Decline?

French Withdrawal   In 1965, President de Gaulle pulled France out of NATO's organizational structure but remained a member of the alliance. This meant that France ceased to participate in council meetings and in various organs and committees that dealt with such subjects as defense planning and other forms of cooperation. French military forces were withdrawn from the different NATO commands, although it must be kept in mind that all military forces of the allies, with only a few exceptions, remain under national control and would only be fully integrated in the event of hostilities. De Gaulle also requested that NATO headquarters, located then in Paris, be moved out of France by 1967.

De Gaulle's action was motivated by his concern for maintaining French independence, which, he feared, was being endangered by U.S. domination of NATO. To underscore his commitment to the alliance, he stressed on several occasions that French forces would cooperate with NATO in the event of an attack against Western Europe.

Many in Europe and America believed that de Gaulle's action would lead to a gradual unraveling of NATO. However, this calamity did not materialize. The NATO Council was moved to Brussels and the military command head-quarters to Mons in Belgium. France continued to maintain several links with NATO including a French military liaison group in Mons. French forces also cooperated with NATO during military maneuvers, and a close relationship developed between French and German military staffs. Thus France's withdrawal from the NATO organization was far from fatal.

The Problem of Detente   An increasingly divisive issue in NATO has been the pursuit of detente or "relaxation of tensions." In the mid-1960s, the Europeans perceived the threat of a Soviet attack on Western Europe receding and, at the same time, they saw growing opportunities for trade with Eastern

Europe. Hence a policy of detente toward the Soviet Union made good sense to them.

Washington, however, was relatively cool to a policy of detente. It was felt that changes in Soviet behavior could only be brought about by containment, and economic interaction via trade and Western credits would only serve to strengthen an ailing Soviet economy.

The ensuing controversy sapped the vigor of NATO, and efforts were made to find new or changed rationales for NATO's continued viable existence. The result was the Harmel Report (discussed in detail in Chapter 9), which was adopted in December 1967 by all members of the alliance, including France.

This report acknowledged the need for a policy of detente toward the Soviet Union and stressed that NATO should therefore use its collective influence to bring about more amenable relations between Washington and Moscow. For this purpose and others, a climate of political solidarity was to be created through frank and timely consultations before the member governments reached major national policy decisions. The result would be enhanced cohesion among NATO members and a broader view of world events outside the NATO area.[37]

While the policy of detente remained for many Americans a political liability at home—we mentioned already President Ford's banning the use of the word in his election campaign—and the wrong approach for dealing with the Soviet Union, it brought major benefits to the Europeans. Politically, the relationship between West and East Germany improved materially, and the issue of Berlin, the object of recurring crises from 1948 to the late 1960s, was stabilized through an agreement among the United States, Britain, France, and the Soviet Union. Economically, trade between Western and Eastern Europe expanded materially, and a number of joint ventures of West and East European enterprises began to develop.

In the late 1970s, two events cast serious doubts on the validity of any detente policy: the Soviet invasion of Afghanistan and the Soviet buildup of medium-range SS-20 missiles in Europe. President Carter imposed a partial economic boycott on the Soviet Union and tried to rally Western Europe and other countries to join in a boycott of the 1980 Olympic Games to be held in Moscow. Western Europe was not enthused about these measures; French and German leaders journeyed to Moscow to save detente. Eventually, the United States also weakened the boycott by resuming grain shipments to the Soviet Union and, in fact, soliciting new Soviet grain purchases. By 1982, with a few U.S. exceptions, it was obvious that the Afghanistan adventure really had not hurt the Soviet Union economically; it was business as usual for Western Europe.

The Soviet SS-20 Deployment   A much more complex problem for U.S.-West European relations, with implications for detente, is the extensive Soviet deployment of the SS-20 missile and the NATO response to this development. In December 1979, the NATO member governments decided to upgrade and strengthen their arsenals of tactical nuclear weapons in Western Europe by deploying, beginning in 1983, Pershing II missiles and cruise missiles to counter the rapid expansion of SS-20 Soviet missiles, which are capable of hitting any target in Western Europe. Together with the increase in Backfire bombers and a new generation of Soviet long-range fighter bomber aircraft, the theater balance in Europe had been shifted heavily in favor of the Warsaw Pact organization.[38] It is important to remember that the NATO decision for the deployment of advanced LRTNF weapons designed to restore the theater nuclear balance was linked to the initiation of arms control negotiations on theater nuclear forces in Europe and, thereby, constituted a "dual-track" policy. For the Europeans, the commitment to the pursuit of meaningful arms control negotiations is an indispensable concomitant to measures of defense.

The new U.S. missiles are scheduled to be installed in the United Kingdom, West Germany, and Italy, whose governments agreed to this move. Belgium and the Netherlands, which were also to be candidates for the initial deployment of the missiles, while endorsing the decision to upgrade and modernize tactical nuclear weapons in Europe, expressed reservations. Belgium finally gave qualified approval in September 1980, but the Netherlands wanted to wait longer before making a definite commitment. Both countries were anxious to see how the arms control negotiations were going to evolve.[39]

Public opinion has expressed itself negatively regarding the installation of the LRTNF weapons in all countries earmarked for deployment. In some of these countries, especially West Germany but also the Netherlands and Great Britain, impressive demonstrations took place to protest as strongly as possible the stationing of these weapons on home soil. Many adherents of the Social Democratic Party (SPD) in Germany, mostly those leaning to the left, joined the opposition against the nuclear weapons. The issue caused political difficulties for former Chancellor Helmut Schmidt, who, with his foreign minister Hans-Dietrich Genscher, had steadfastly supported the NATO policy on the deployment of the LRTNFs. Nevertheless, large elements of the SPD, particularly those whose avowed creed is detente, continue to rebel against the NATO policy and have joined ideologically the forces identified with the renascent pacifism of the churches, youth organizations, and environmentalist movements. In countries that have held or are going to hold elections, domestic politics also play a role, since deploying the new American nuclear weapons is a highly emotion-laden issue that in some instances has generated anti-American and anticapitalist sentiments. Much depends on the arms control negotiations regarding LRTNF weapons underway currently in Geneva, which, in turn, may be influenced by the START negotiations for the reduction of strategic nuclear weapons between the United States and the Soviet Union.

The initial U.S. position in the theater nuclear weapons negotiations was the "zero option": plans for the deployment of Pershings and cruise missiles would be abandoned only if the Soviets agreed to dismantle their SS-20s. The Soviet government suggested in December 1982 a compromise under which it would reduce the number of SS-20s in exchange for U.S. nondeployment, but rejected the zero option, in part because 162 medium-range French and British nuclear weapons were not included.[40]

Significantly, early in 1983, West German polls indicated that 61 percent of the respondents favored the postponement of American deployment even if the negotiations on LRTNF should fail.[41] Nevertheless, in the elections in March 1983, the coalition of Christian Democrats (CDU/CSU) and the Free Democrats (FDP) retained its majority and Helmut Kohl remained the chancellor. At the same time, however, the "Greens," a party composed of ecologists and assorted left-wingers strongly opposed to the deployment of American theater nuclear weapons on German soil, polled more than 5 percent of the votes cast and thus was able to have twenty-seven deputies in the Bundestag. Meanwhile, in the Reagan administration disagreement over the future negotiating stance was reflected in the dismissal of the director of the U.S. Arms Control and Disarmament Agency, Eugene Rostow, who, although a "hard-liner," was perceived as not sufficiently tough. This, in turn, generated warnings from West European political leaders that the uncertainty about the U.S. negotiating policy was politically costly not only to the United States but also to friendly governments in West Germany and Great Britain.[42] The outcome of the negotiations may have been affected favorably when Soviet leader Andropov and Reagan appeared to agree that warheads rather than missiles should be counted.

These developments as well as a bourgeoning peace movement in Western Europe portend a serious danger for NATO cohesion. The United States, as the foremost power of the alliance, must make carefully designed efforts to halt the disintegration of NATO. It is quite obvious that such a development is a high-priority goal of the Soviet government, which it attempts to attain by portraying itself as being interested only in disarmament and genuine peace while it accuses the United States of seeking military superiority. For the Reagan administration, this requires a much greater understanding of West European sensitivities. Hence it is important that the military buildup of U.S. forces be seen by the world not as simply a tool of the United States to regain overwhelming influence in global affairs. Nor should the production of the neutron warhead be viewed as an attempt to limit nuclear war to Europe or to weaken the U.S. commitment to the employment of strategic nuclear weapons. Rather, it must be pointed out to the Europeans that this is an effort to strengthen both *their* and the U.S. defense against Soviet aggression or political encroachment and should deepen their confidence and trust in U.S. capabilities and resolve. If these notions can be successfully portrayed to NATO Europe, it may well be the means to counteract the obvious attractiveness of the promises made by the peace movement and produce in the Europeans the kind of balanced self-confidence, which in turn can reestablish the mutual trust so necessary for a viable NATO.

POLICY TOWARD JAPAN

Despite the fact that Japan during World War II was a main adversary of the United States, American policy toward that country following the end of the war never assumed the significance attributed to policy toward Western Europe. A basic reason for this difference is that during the postwar years it has always been the Soviet Union that presented the chief challenge to American security and well-being, and that, for geographical reasons, Western Europe was always regarded as the key element in the protection of U.S. security and the American way of life. Nevertheless, from a strategic as well as an economic perspective, Japan is a significant cog in the totality of American foreign policy. Therefore, some attention must be devoted to the evolution and implementation of U.S. policies toward Japan.

The Politicomilitary Dimension

After Japan's defeat in August 1945, the supreme commander for the Allied Powers, General Douglas MacArthur, assumed full control over all aspects of Japanese public life. Although U.S. officials first attempted to create a "reformed" Japan, they gradually followed the American example in Germany and embarked on an economic and political revitalization program. Communists were prevented from holding government and university positions, while former Japanese leaders were reinstated.[43]

In September 1951 the United States signed a peace treaty with Japan that restored Japanese sovereignty, authorized the United States to maintain a military base on Okinawa, and permitted the retention of foreign troops in Japan. A separate Treaty of Mutual Cooperation and Security was also concluded, which came into effect in 1952. The treaties officially terminated U.S. occupation.

The Treaty of Mutual Cooperation and Security has become the basic instrument for Japan's defense and security. It was reaffirmed after certain revisions in 1960 despite strong opposition that manifested itself in the Japanese Diet and through extensive turmoil and violence in the streets. In 1970 and 1980 the Security Treaty was renewed again but without much protest. Nevertheless, tensions have arisen from time to time between the United States and Japan regarding security issues, particularly as to the military role Japan is to play in the international arena, and how far and with what weapons Japan should rearm itself. Beyond that, just as in Western Europe, the question has been raised by the public whether in the event of an emergency the United

States would risk nuclear annihilation in order to defend Japan. Public opinion polls during the early 1970s suggested considerable doubt that the United States would defend Japan and that perhaps the adoption of a neutral policy might be the best choice. However, a substantial increase of Japan's own military strength is frowned on by many Japanese because of antimilitary sentiments and the cost involved.[44] Nevertheless, since 1958 the Japanese Self-Defense Forces have been built up in order to fill the gap left by the 1957 withdrawal of all American ground combat forces.

The United States has not been satisfied with this increase, which until now has not exceeded 1 percent of Japan's GNP and thus has been the lowest defense budget in relation to GNP of any major power. Washington, therefore, has urged the Japanese government to increase its defense budget materially, and Tokyo has indicated its willingness to raise defense spending by 4.3 percent after inflation and gradually approach defense expenditures (over several years) amounting to 5 percent of GNP. At the same time, Prime Minister Yasuhiro Nakasone declared in January 1983 that Japan had no intention to become a "military power."[45] This slow increase in Japanese defense capabilities may not satisfy U.S. officials.

Although Japan had always favored better relations with the People's Republic of China than the United States had during the 1950s and 1960s, and had successfully developed economic exchanges with Peking without straining relations with the United States, the sudden shift of American policy toward China in 1971 caused serious shocks, especially because no advance consultation took place as required by the security treaty. Public opinion polls taken during the latter half of 1971 in Japan suggested the likelihood of deterioration of U.S.-Japanese relations,[46] but the surprise shift in American policy did not seem to have a long-run effect. On the contrary, this relationship benefited from the return of Okinawa to Japan in 1972. Indeed, in a recent poll, public opinion favored the mutual security treaty with the United States by 63 percent.[47]

The strategic American-Japanese relationship in the 1980s will be influenced to a large degree by Japan's policies toward and relations with China and the Soviet Union. Basically underlying the U.S. foreign policy initiatives and responses will be the Nixon Doctrine. Under this doctrine, America's obligations toward the allies in Asia are maintained, but primary responsibility for supplying military personnel needs is placed on the allied country while the United States plays the major role in air and sea warfare.

American policy initiatives seeking to strengthen Japan's defensive capabilities and to link Japanese security interests with those of the NATO member states must take into consideration a number of factors[48]:

1.   The existing, albeit somewhat uneasy triangular balance-of-power relationship among the United States, the PRC, and the Soviet Union may be disturbed either by a Sino-Soviet rapprochement—which is always possible, though not probable—or by the eruption of the Sino-Soviet feud into a major

military confrontation. Since in either event Japan may not want to upset its present policy of equidistant neutrality to either the Soviet Union or China, its anxiety would rise rapidly if either of these situations should occur, and only appropriate policy responses by the United States—such as strengthening American forces in the region—could mitigate such understandable anxieties and assure Japan's full confidence in the alliance.

2.   American foreign policymakers must keep in mind that the normalization of Sino-American relations is important to Japan. The adoption by the United States of the Japanese formula for the break of diplomatic relations with Taiwan, which continued these relations on an "unofficial" basis, has broken the long impasse in U.S.-PRC relations.

3.   Korea will remain a difficult problem for U.S. policy toward Japan during the 1980s, because the Japanese consider the security of the Republic of Korea essential to their own security. The Carter administration's proposed gradual withdrawal of U.S. ground forces from South Korea caused considerable apprehension in Japan, because it could undermine not only military but also psychological stability in the region. Nevertheless, many Japanese may be prepared to accept the principle of an eventual withdrawal of American ground forces if, with the help of U.S. policy, the defensive capabilities of South Korean military force could be upgraded, and a vigorous effort were made to reduce tensions between South and North Korea.[49]

4.   Challenges to America's alliance policy with Japan in the 1980s may come from domestic politics in that country. Since its formation, the Liberal Democratic Party (LDP) has been the ruling force in Japan, and it has consistently supported the security treaty. The leading opposition party, the Japanese Socialist Party (JSP), has constantly advocated the abrogation of the security treaty, but recently it has acknowledged that this would have to be done through diplomatic negotiations. A similar attitude is held by Komeito, the Buddhist party. Even the Japanese Communist Party (JCP), which used to urge immediate abrogation, seems to accept a more gradual approach. Nevertheless, a coalition government under JSP leadership may place the security treaty in jeopardy, and Japan may assume a more neutralist stance, seeking to escape the strategic tutelage of the United States.

The Economic-Political Dimension

The economic issue that has caused increasingly serious friction between the United States and Japan has been the growing trade deficit, which in 1982 approached $20 billion. Table 11.2 shows the evolution of U.S. and Japanese exports in their mutual trade. Since 1965, Japanese exports to the United States have been consistently higher than the reverse flow of American goods to Japan; furthermore, with the exception of 1969, the gap in favor of Japan has been widening. At the same time, the expansion of trade between the two countries since 1965 has been enormous. Indeed, for Japan, the United States

Table 11.2   U.S. Trade with Japan
(\$ Millions)

	1965	1970	1976	1977	1978	1979	1980	1981
Imports from Japan	2.4	5.9	15.5	18.6	24.5	26.3	30.7	37.6
Exports to Japan	2.8	4.7	10.2	10.6	13.0	17.6	20.8	21.8
Merchandise trade balance	+0.4	−1.2	−5.3	−8.0	−11.5	−8.7	−9.9	−15.8

Source: Adapted from U.S., Department of Commerce, *Survey of Current Business*, September−November 1982.

has become the largest customer (25.7 percent in 1981) and supplier of goods and commodities (17.7 percent in 1981), except for oil (38.4 percent), which is imported from OPEC (Organization of Petroleum-Exporting Countries).[50]

One of the reasons for the rapidly growing exports by Japan (expansion between 1955 and 1976 was nearly thirtyfold) is the high productivity of its workers, which compensates for rising wage levels during the last few years. In such industries as steel, automobiles, light electric products, chemical products, synthetic fibers, and sewing machines, Japanese productivity tops that of the United States, the United Kingdom, and Germany by a wide margin.

Another reason for the continuing increase in Japanese exports has been the fact that rising exports often are perceived by the Japanese government as an essential ingredient for the continuing expansion of Japan's economic growth in general. Thus when the domestic economy shows signs of slack, greater emphasis is placed on Japanese exports. Indeed, during 1977, two important elements of overall growth, consumer demand and capital spending, were sluggish, but with the support of export business Japan reached a 6.7 percent GNP growth rate in 1977. This was a remarkable achievement.

However, additional factors have helped Japanese exports and created the wide trade gap vis-à-vis the United States and other countries. The Japanese government has on occasion provided promotional subsidies and from time to time has authorized dual pricing on various products, whereby export prices were set below domestic wholesale prices, if not below manufacturing cost. Examples are sewing machines, steel, and chemical fertilizers.[51]

In some cases, the Japanese government seems to have resorted to clear and unjustified (in terms of GATT) protectionism. For example, U.S. computers enjoy a comparative advantage, but although Japan has removed quantitative restrictions, it levies tariffs on hardware and peripheral equipment at three times the rate charged by other advanced countries.[52] It has also been accused of introducing hidden nontariff barriers to foreign consumer products, effectively impeding the importation of such goods. The upshot of all this is the enormous trade deficit for the United States, which has become intolerable for the U.S. economy.

Although the United States has been committed to continuing, reciprocal tariff reductions, as evidenced in the Kennedy and Tokyo rounds, and claims that it wants to avoid protectionist measures, it cannot ignore the layoff of workers in such industries as steel, automobiles, and TV. In order to halt the sales of Japanese steel below production cost, the United States imposed antidumping duties, which the Japanese are claiming to be unfair protectionism. Later it proposed to set up a system of reference prices for steel in the United States that would be used as a base for computing duties and that would stop sales below cost by Japanese firms. The danger of this plan, which was basically accepted by the steel companies, labor unions, and interested members of Congress, was that other industries affected by competitive imports would seek similar protection. If these demands were accommodated, it would undermine the U.S. credibility regarding its commitment to trade liberalization in the Tokyo Round.

To curb Japanese shipments of TV sets in the future, the Japanese government has accepted voluntary restrictions on such shipments by signing a so-called orderly marketing agreement (OMA). OMAs have become a popular device for curbing imports into the United States that threaten particular American industries or firms and their employees, and have also been used for the protection of the American automobile industry in 1981. They avoid the disturbance of basic tariff systems and are less onerous than the unilateral imposition of quantitative restrictions or other NTBs (nontariff barriers).

As the Japanese trade surplus rose and Japan amassed foreign currency reserves, the U.S. government urged revaluation of the yen. Beginning with the devaluation of the U.S. dollar in 1971, the value of the yen has risen gradually from 360 to 190 yen to the dollar. However, the revaluation of the yen has not perceptibly narrowed the trade gap between Japan and the United States. Moreover, the Japanese government continues to resist pressures for upward change of the yen,[53] although the stronger the yen, the lower the cost of imported raw materials and thus the production cost of industrial goods in Japan.

Increasing pressures in Congress to curb the imports of Japanese automobiles through "domestic content" legislation, which could reduce such imports by 75 percent,[54] and continuing U.S. demands for Japan to reduce official and concealed barriers to American imports have been met by recurring promises over the years but relatively little action. In late 1982, preceding Prime Minister Nakasone's visit to Washington, Japan eased tariffs on tobacco, chocolates, and other items and streamlined import testing procedures. Imports of some U.S. agricultural products were also liberalized, although Japan is already the largest market for American farm commodities, with exports amounting to about $7 billion.[55]

Faced with economic malaise in the United States and protectionist pressures, U.S. foreign trade officials do not consider the Japanese measures as adequate. They point out that every billion dollars in trade deficits means the loss of 25,000 jobs in the United States. The U.S. ambassador to Japan, Mike Mansfield, former leader of the Senate and an experienced hand in U.S. political affairs, cautioned Japan that a real "buildup" in protectionist legislation with the labor unions in the forefront could come before the 1984 elections if America's trade deficit with Japan is not narrowed. American policymakers must realize, however, that in the face of a domestic business slump and high unemployment in Japan, powerful political forces in that country place limits on the options that the Japanese government can exercise. For this reason, American policies must retain a measure of flexibility and take into account the particular vulnerabilities of the Japanese economic and political situation.

While the foregoing discussion has made it obvious that U.S.-Japanese trade carries with it the seeds for serious controversy, Japanese trade with Southeast Asia may also become a source of conflict. Beginning with the latter half of the 1960s, many developing countries, and especially Southeast Asia, have come to rely to a very large degree on goods imported from Japan; conversely, Japan has become the best customer of the region for raw materials. While the dependence on these and other products may not last because of indigenous industrialization in some of the Asian countries, it provides Japan with enormous political leverage and influence. In the meantime, U.S. exports to Southeast Asia may be impaired as the result of the economic hegemony established by Japan.[56]

The aim of U.S. foreign policy toward Japan must be the achievement of an optimal harmonious relationship, which may require compromises when the interests of the United States and its allies significantly diverge. In this connection it should be kept in mind that critical problems between allied nations usually do not appear suddenly or dramatically, but develop slowly from small misunderstandings or misjudgments.

With respect to redressing the large trade deficit, it may be essential for the U.S. government to resort to internal measures in addition to external steps. In a study conducted by the Hudson Institute, entitled *Implications of Japanese Industrial Development Policies in the 1980's for U.S. Trade and Investment*, several recommendations make these points:

- Improve U.S. conditions that determine the competitiveness of high-tech firms, such as loosening antitrust standards on collaborative research.
- In hard-hit areas of the U.S. economy, link government financial assistance with mandatory industrial adjustment.
- Create a U.S. organization capable of assuming some . . . coordinating functions . . .—something comparable to the NSC in the White House.
- In negotiations:
- Apply greatest leverage to those remaining barriers that offer long-term gains.
- Take advantage of favorable cyclical and structural trends likely to emerge in the next few years.
- Minimize or avoid efforts that are primarily a political response to adverse cyclical economic conditions.

- On market access, concentrate on U.S. sectors that have a clear comparative advantage and can follow through.
- Make proposals that have built-in concrete incentives and disincentives for the Japanese.[57]

EXPLANATORY VARIABLES

For the discussion of explanatory variables regarding American foreign policies toward Western Europe as well as Japan, it must be kept in mind that these policies toward Europe often have a multilateral character because all West European states belong to a number of IGOs, especially the EC and NATO, while policies toward Japan are mostly bilateral, although Japan participates in the economic summits and is a member of the OECD. Nevertheless, the sources of explanation for these policies do show basic similarities. One of the most potent explanations for their formulation flows from international variables. A major stimulus for these policies was and continues to be systemic in nature, namely, the bipolar system between the two superpowers with its emphasis on mutual deterrence. American apprehension about a Soviet threat of upsetting the bipolar balance of power has been the motivation for U.S. policy initiatives in both the economic-political and military-political spheres toward Western Europe, and has also been at the base of the Mutual Security Treaty with Japan and recent American pressure on Tokyo to increase its defensive capabilities.

As we have pointed out, American support for a united Western Europe was founded on the perceived need for a stronger common defense through some kind of European union. This was seen as a sound collateral to NATO, creating a more powerful barrier to possible Soviet expansionism toward the West and serving to enhance U.S. containment policy. However, since these expectations were not quite fulfilled and various tensions between the United States and its European allies arose during the period generally beginning with the 1970s, American foreign policy had to respond to different disagreements with Western Europe and adjust to changing economic and political conditions in that region. Explanation of these policy responses and new initiatives are found in a number of interactional variables stemming from actions by EC and NATO member states, and new circumstances that arose in different countries.

Similarly, actions by the Japanese government and changing conditions and moods in Japan have produced stimuli for U.S. policy formulation that fell into the category of interactional variables and that became determinants for American policy. Clearly, one of the most complex situations for U.S. policymakers has been the growing imbalance in U.S.-Japanese trade. Not only did this imbalance affect domestic policymaking, especially in the 1970s and early 1980s, but it also had an impact on the credibility of the American commitment to open trade. Moreover, since Japan is becoming increasingly important for U.S. security interests, American trade and security interests had to be meshed properly for the attainment of U.S. foreign policy goals on a global basis.

Institutional variables also played their roles in the formulation of U.S. policies toward Western Europe and Japan. The State Department was in the forefront in promoting American support for West European integration, although beginning with the late 1960s officials in the Bureau of Economic and Business Affairs became doubtful about this policy as the EC assumed greater and greater economic power and became a tough competitor in international trade.

During the early 1960s, the Department of Agriculture sought to influence trade policy toward the Communities when it warned about agricultural surpluses that would be created by the CAP. However, these warnings, which were fully justified, as later events demonstrated, fell on deaf ears in the Community institutions and member governments.

American economic interest groups also played their part in influencing the formulation of policy, especially in connection with the Kennedy and Tokyo rounds. Certain groups such as the steel producers made strong demands to stop or reduce the growing influx into the United States of West European-produced steel. Congress has been responsive to these demands and has involved itself in trade policy development, because it had to pass the various pieces of trade legislation underlying the Kennedy and Tokyo rounds of tariff and NTB reductions.

With respect to policy in NATO affairs, it was the Defense Department that furnished the largest input into policy regarding changing strategic doctrines as well as the problem of theater nuclear forces and the need for the common defense by the European allies. Since the talks on weapon reductions are formally coordinated by the secretary of state and ACDA, the State Department had an important voice in policy on these matters as well. Differences of views between State and Defense complicate policy formulation on arms control and weapons reduction.

In trade policy toward Japan, the State Department, in cooperation with the Departments of Commerce and Agriculture, furnished coordination and input in the formulation of policy. Various economic interest groups affected by trade with Japan, such as TV, steel, and automobile manufacturers, effectively influenced the evolution of this policy, which for most Americans and especially for Congress remains unsatisfactory. In the military sphere, the Defense Department has been the major proponent of a stronger Japanese defense posture.

Idiosyncratic variables of American leaders were important indirectly in the formulation of policy toward Western Europe and Japan. All presidents from Truman to Reagan generally supported the sympathetic approach reflected in these policies and thereby created an appropriate climate of opinion for the development of these policies, even if in some instances—for example support for a United States of Europe—President Johnson and others may have had doubts about the realization and benefits of individual policies. In some cases, however, idiosyncratic variables may have been counterproductive. One such case is Secretary of State Dulles' strong insistence on policy reappraisal if EDC were to fail. Another instance is President Reagan's very tough anticommunism, which most likely was a major factor in the imposition of sanctions against European suppliers of materials for the Soviet gas pipeline to Western Europe. His decision created considerable unhappiness in the region and disarray among the NATO allies.

Societal variables played a very minor role in influencing or explaining U.S. policies toward Western Europe and Japan. The extensive demonstration against the deployment of U.S. Pershing II and cruise missiles in Europe, which were held in several West European countries with anti-American overtones, may have produced a measure of disenchantment in American public opinion about the willingness of West Europeans to defend themselves against possible Soviet aggression. Nevertheless, they neither led to strong demands for extracting U.S. forces from Europe, nor did they create any widespread anti-Europeanism. However, these demonstrations may have contributed to the development of the peace movement in the United States, whose configuration and extent remains unclear at this time.

With respect to Japan, it is uncertain how much the public at large shares the concerns of management and labor in industries severely affected by Japanese imports. For the public, these concerns may be balanced by the lower prices of imported consumer articles. Nor does it appear that the issue of strengthened Japanese defense forces has meant much to the general public in the United States.

SUMMARY

After it had become clear in 1946 that the World War II collaboration between the United States and the Soviet Union could not continue in peacetime, U.S. policymakers began to concentrate on the *economic and political integration of Western Europe* as a major American foreign policy goal. Washington supported all European efforts that could contribute to the realization of this goal: the *establishment of the ECSC*, the *promotion of the EDC*, and the *creation of the EEC and Euratom*. When it appeared doubtful that the EDC would materialize, the U.S. government mobilized every resource and spared no efforts to save the EDC. Not only general security considerations were at play; Washington was anxious to see West Germany become a member of NATO, and its accession to NATO was tied to the establishment of EDC.

The American wish to have Great Britain as a charter member of the three Communities was not realized. At first Britain declined and, when the British government was prepared to accede, de Gaulle objected. Finally in *1973,*

Britain, as well as *Ireland* and *Denmark*, joined France, West Germany, Italy, and the Benelux countries as members of the *Communities*.

Progress toward the U.S. goal of European unification slowed down during the 1960s. At the same time, U.S. concerns were voiced about the effects of the *Common Agricultural Policy (CAP)*, which Washington feared would reduce American exports to Western Europe. The *subsidies* paid by Community institutions *to farmers* for sales within and outside the EEC might harm shipments of American agricultural commodities worldwide. Apart from a slowdown of agricultural exports, *sales of U.S. products to Western Europe* have shown a substantial *surplus over imports from the EEC* at all times except in 1972.

The United States has also been apprehensive about the *preferential trade agreements* concluded by the EEC with countries in *Africa, the Caribbean*, the *Mediterranean area*, and the *EFTA states*. These agreements were likely to affect unfavorably the competitive position of American exporters. Recurring trade negotiations under the auspices of GATT such as the *Kennedy* and *Tokyo rounds* to lower tariffs and dismantle NTBs have successfully reduced tariffs on many products and thereby softened the impact of preferential EEC agreements. *Summit meetings* have helped on many occasions to overcome frictions between the United States and the Communities. The original U.S. goal of European union has remained elusive, although the pro-unification rhetoric persists.

In the military-political arena NATO holds the center stage, but the transatlantic partnership had its share of troubles. They include questions of *nuclear strategy* (massive retaliation or flexible response), the *sharing of responsibility and authority for squeezing the nuclear trigger*, the *sharing of financial burdens*, the issue of *proper consultation* among the allies, *French withdrawal* from NATO's military structure, the *usefulness or dangers of detente*, and judiciousness of *deploying American theater nuclear weapons* in response to the Soviet Union's installation of the SS-20 missiles. In spite of the problems, NATO remains a cornerstone of American defense and foreign policy.

For U.S. policy toward Japan, a *military-political* and *economic dimension* can be distinguished. The basic instrument for Japan's defense and security is the *Treaty of Mutual Cooperation and Security* with the United States. This treaty is also an important cog in U.S. security. To raise Japan's defensive capabilities, Washington has urged Tokyo to increase the expenditures for its armed forces.

U.S.-Japanese economic relations are characterized by a *growing American deficit*. U.S. policy has attempted to slow the flood of Japanese imports, especially in electronics and automobiles. *Increasing protectionist pressures* in Congress have prompted some Japanese accommodations: some barriers to American imports have been dismantled, a number of tariffs lowered, and imports of certain agricultural commodities were liberalized.

NOTES

1. Max Beloff, *The United States and the Unity of Europe* (New York: Vantage Books, 1963), p. 4.
2. Quoted in ibid., pp. 4–5.
3. Ibid., p. 5.
4. Quoted in ibid., p. 7.
5. Ibid., p. 11.
6. Thomas G. Paterson, *American Foreign Policy*, 2nd ed. (Lexington, Mass.: D.C. Heath, 1983), p. 39.
7. Details about the ECA are found in Title I of the Foreign Assistance Act of 1948.
8. Beloff, *United States and the Unity of Europe*, p. 54.
9. Paterson, *American Foreign Policy*, p. 39.
10. Beloff, *United States and the Unity of Europe*, p. 61.
11. Ibid., p. 65.
12. Ibid., pp. 66–67.
13. Ibid., pp. 78–82.
14. For a thorough analysis of the ECSC, see Ernst B. Haas, *The Uniting of Europe* (Stanford, Calif.: Stanford University Press, 1958); and Walter Hallstein, *United Europe* (Cambridge, Mass.: Harvard University Press, 1963).
15. For a broader discussion of these issues, see F.C.S. Northrop, *European Union and United States Foreign Policy* (New York: Macmillan, 1954).
16. Beloff, *United States and the Unity of Europe*, pp. 114–115.
17. Ibid., p. 125.
18. For details on the theory of functionalism and other integration theories, see Charles C. Pentland, *International Theory and European Integration* (New York: Free Press, 1973).
19. For a detailed analysis of these factors, see Isaiah Frank, *The European Common Market: An Analysis of Commercial Policy* (New York: Praeger, 1961).
20. Beloff, *United States and the Unity of Europe*, p. 128.
21. Ibid., pp. 140–141.
22. For a detailed analysis of de Gaulle's reasons for the veto, see Werner Feld, *The European Common Market and the World* (Englewood Cliffs, N.J.: Prentice-Hall, 1967), pp. 75–76.
23. *Le Monde*, February 21 and March 11, 1969.
24. For details, see Feld, *European Common Market and the World*, p. 19.
25. For more details, see ibid., pp. 101–103.
26. This information was gleaned from the author's conversation with State Department officials.
27. For details, see Werner J. Feld, *The European Community in World Affairs* (Port Washington, N.Y.: Alfred Publishers, 1976), p. 192.
28. Ibid., pp. 185–187.
29. For a more detailed discussion see ibid., pp. 131–154.
30. U.S., Department of State, Bureau of Intelligence and Research, *U.S. Trade with the European Community, 1958–1981* (Report 387-AR, May 14, 1982), pp. 1–2.
31. The Atlantic Council of the United States, *Summit Meetings and Collective Leadership in the 1980s,* (Washington, D.C., 1980), p. 30. This publication is one of the occasional policy papers of the council and provides a useful summation of the 1970 summits and interesting conclusions.
32. Ibid., p. 10.
33. For details, see NATO Information Service, *Aspects of NATO Defense Policy* (Brussels, Belgium, 1969).
34. *Europe Documents*, No. 710, December 14, 1972.
35. For details, see Werner J. Feld and John K. Wildgen, *NATO and the Atlantic Defense* (New York: Praeger, 1982), p. 128.

36. *Department of State Bulletin*, April 28, 1969, p. 353.

37. For details of the Harmel Report, see *NATO Handbook* (March 1977), pp. 67–69.

38. For an up-to-date discussion of the balance of strategic and tactical nuclear weapons in East-West relations, see the Atlantic Council of the United States, *The Credibility of the NATO Deterrent* (Washington, D.C., 1981).

39. Committee on Foreign Affairs, U.S. House of Representatives, *NATO after Afghanistan*, report prepared for the Subcommittee on Europe and the Middle East, October 27, 1980, p. 19.

40. *Time*, January 24, 1983, p. 16.

41. *Times-Picayune* (New Orleans), January 14, 1983.

42. Ibid.

43. Paterson, *American Foreign Policy*, p. 458.

44. Robert Scalopino, *American-Japanese Relations in a Changing Era* (New York: Library Press, 1971), pp. 101–103.

45. Interview on ABC "This Week with David Brinkley," January 16, 1983. See also *Times-Picayune* (New Orleans), January 17, 1983.

46. Scalopino, *American-Japanese Relations*, p. 65. See also K. Muraoka, *Japanese Security and the United States* (London: International Institute for Strategic Studies, 1973), pp. 38–39.

47. The Atlantic Council of the United States, *The Common Security Interests of Japan, the United States, and NATO* (Washington, D.C., December 1983), p. 26.

48. Ibid., p. 28.

49. K. Wakaizumi, "Consensus in Japan," *Foreign Policy* (Summer 1971), pp. 158–179, esp. pp. 173–174.

50. U.S., Department of State, Bureau of Intelligence and Research, *Trade Patterns of the West, 1981* (Report 443-AR, August 6, 1982).

51. For a comprehensive analysis of these "growth" factors, see S. Tsuru, *The Mainsprings of Japanese Growth: A Turning Point?* (Paris: Atlantic Institute, 1976), pp. 22–27.

52. *Wall Street Journal*, November 15, 1977, p. 48.

53. *Wall Street Journal*, November 18, 1977, p. 20.

54. *Business Week*, October 4, 1982, p. 64.

55. *Wall Street Journal*, January 13, 1983; and *The Washington Post*, January 14, 1983.

56. For details see Werner J. Feld, "Global Allies or Competitors: U.S. Policy toward an Ascendant European Community and Japan," in *Challenge to America: United States Foreign Policy in the 1980s*, edited by Charles W. Kegley and Patrick McGowan (Beverly Hills, Calif.: Sage Publications, 1977), pp. 171–200.

57. *Business America*, November 1, 1982.

12

Policies toward
the Third World

THE CHARACTERISTICS OF
THIRD WORLD COUNTRIES

Decolonization after World War II rapidly changed the political configuration of the world. Vast areas in Africa, Asia, the Caribbean, and the Western Pacific that had been possessions or otherwise under the control of Great Britain, France, Italy, Belgium, the Netherlands, Portugal, Spain, and South Africa were transformed into independent states from 1945 to the end of the 1970s. As a consequence, the number of United Nations members, originally 51, had more than tripled by 1983.

The newly independent states, as well as all countries in Latin America and a few states in Asia that had been already independent before World War II are characterized by low per capita incomes, although the levels of income for individual states vary considerably. These countries can be divided into low-income and middle-income countries, based on GNP per person: the average annual income of the former in 1980 was $250, while that of the latter was $1580.* The breaking point between the two categories of countries is $360 annual income. We should note that this figure represents a substantial im-

---

*Defining per capita income by per capita GNP is generally used in World Bank and U.N. statistics, for example, the annual *World Development Report* published by the World Bank, although this definition may produce distortion.

provement over the 1950 and 1960 figures, as can be seen from Table 12.1. The annual growth of income from 1950 to 1980 has been slowest in the low-income countries.

The basic reason for the low per capita incomes in these states is the inadequate level of their economic development, which is substantially inferior to development in the economically advanced countries of Europe, North America, Australia, and New Zealand. In these states, per capita GNP in 1980 was $10,660, and growth in income was almost double that of the low-income countries (Table 12.1). Because of their low level of economic development, these countries have been called "underdeveloped," "less-developed" (LDCs), or "developing" (a term reflecting hope for the future). All are part of the so-called Third World, with the term "First World" denoting the group of Western economically advanced countries and the "Second World" referring to the Communist states, often referred to as the "centrally planned econo-mies," with widely differing per captia GNPs.[1] Third World countries that were members of the United Nations by 1979 (most of them) are shown in Table 12.2, which also provides the year of entry into the United Nations.

The differences in per capita GNP within the categories of both low-income and middle-income countries are enormous. In the first category of countries located primarily in sub-Saharan Africa and in a few areas of Asia, Bangladesh has a $90 per capita GNP, while Indonesia has $370. In the second category, Kenya is lowest with $380 and Israel highest with a $4150 per capita GNP. A special category is labeled "capital-surplus" (oil exporters) countries, which have many of the characteristics of the Third World but whose per capita GNP reaches $17,100 in Kuwait and $7280 in Saudi Arabia, although the actual income of many inhabitants in these countries may be substantially lower.[2]

Indeed, *within* most LDCs, per capita incomes also vary widely from region to region.[3] In the majority of Third World countries, the economy is concen-trated on traditional agriculture and the production of raw materials such as

Table 12.1   Income Based on GNP per Person

	1950	1960	1980
GNP per Person[a] *(1980 U.S. dollars)*			
Industrialized countries	$4,130	$5,580	$10,660
Middle-income countries	640	820	1,580
Low-income countries	170	180	250
	1950–1960		*1960–1980*
Average Annual Growth (%)			
Industrialized countries	3.1		3.2
Middle-income countries	2.5		3.3
Low-income countries	0.6		1.7

[a]Excludes all centrally planned economies.

Source: The World Bank, *World Development Report, 1980* (Washington, D.C., 1981), p. 6.

Table 12.2   Membership of Developing Countries in the United Nations and Year of Entry

Year of Entry	Developing Country
1945	Argentina, Bolivia, Brazil, Chile, Colombia, Costa Rica, Cuba, Dominican Republic, Ecuador, Egypt, El Salvador, Ethiopia, Guatemala, Haiti, Honduras, India, Iran, Iraq, Lebanon, Liberia, Mexico, Nicaragua, Panama, Paraguay, Peru, Philippines, Saudi Arabia, Syrian Arab Republic, Uruguay, Venezuela, Yugoslavia
1946	Afghanistan, Thailand
1947	Pakistan, Yemen
1948	Burma
1950	Indonesia
1955	Democratic Kampuchea, Jordan, Laos People's Democratic Republic, Libyan Arab Republic, Nepal, Romania, Sri Lanka
1956	Morocco, Sudan, Tunisia
1957	Ghana, Malaysia
1958	Guinea
1960	Benin, Central African Empire, Chad, Congo, Cyprus, Gabon, Ivory Coast, Madagascar, Mali, Niger, Nigeria, Senegal, Somalia, Togo, United Republic of Cameroon, Upper Volta, Zaire
1961	Mauritania, Sierra Leone, United Republic of Tanzania
1962	Algeria, Burundi, Jamaica, Rwanda, Trinidad and Tobago, Uganda
1963	Kenya, Kuwait
1964	Malawi, Malta, Zambia
1965	Gambia, Maldives, Singapore
1966	Barbados, Botswana, Guyana, Lesotho
1967	Democratic Yemen
1968	Equatorial Guinea, Mauritius, Swaziland
1970	Fiji
1971	Bahrain, Bhutan, Oman, Qatar, United Arab Emirates
1973	Bahamas
1974	Bangladesh, Grenada, Guinea-Bissau
1975	Cape Verde, Comoro, Mozambique, Papua New Guinea, São Tomé and Prińcipe, Surinam
1976	Angola, Samoa, Seychelles
1977	Djibouti, Vietnam
1978	Dominica, Solomon Islands
1979	Saint Lucia

Source: Karl P. Sauvant, "The Origins of the NIEO Discussions," in *Changing Priorities on the International Agenda*, edited by Karl P. Sauvant (New York: Pergamon Press, 1981), pp. 7–40.

minerals. A few, such as Nigeria, also produce oil. Industrialization is seen as a high-priority goal, but only in some of the middle-income Third World states has the establishment of viable industries made progress. Eleven of the developing countries falling into this category had more than 50 percent of total LDC production and more than 75 percent of LDC manufacturing exports. They are called the newly industrializing countries (NICs) and had very high GNP growth rates, large increases in exports, and high rates in domestic investment. Mostly recognized as NICs are Yugoslavia, Mexico, Brazil, Taiwan, Singapore, Hong Kong, and Korea, and a few others may join this category.[4] However, it should be kept in mind that the economics of the NICs are not characteristic of the bulk of Third World countries.

Most LDCs must rely on the export of primary products to earn foreign currency needed for purchases abroad, and these earnings are subject to violent fluctuations depending on world market conditions and prices. This situation has created much economic and political instability in the Third World and has contributed to very high rates of unemployment and underemployment. For example, the rate of unemployment in the Republic of Djibouti on the east coast of Africa was 85 percent in 1982, and many of the LDCs have unemployment and underemployment rates exceeding 40 percent.[5]

These difficult conditions are compounded by a huge increase in population, which in the Third World is likely to climb from 3.4 billion in 1980 to 5 billion in 2000, while in the developed countries the population during that period will rise only from 1 billion to 1.2 billion.[6] While improved health care in the Third World has contributed to the population explosion, the level of health care in the low-income LDCs remains very limited, with one physician for every 10,300 people compared with one for every 630 in the industrialized countries. At the same time, undernourishment is widespread, affecting 22 percent of the people in the LDCs in 1976.[7] Added to the difficulties of raising development levels is the low rate of literacy, which in the low-income Third World countries was 39 percent in 1976.[8]

The rapid population increase in the Third World, averaging 2.5 percent annually from 1960 to 1980, combined with the other conditions mentioned above, has a most important effect on the future economic development of low-income countries. It has been estimated that the growth of low-income countries that must import all their oil and that had an average annual income of only $168 in 1980 (in 1977 dollars) would at best have an average income of $261 and in the worst case $215 in the year 2000. In the latter case, the total rise is about 25 percent. In contrast, the middle-income oil-importing countries would be doing much better. Their increase would be close to 100 percent in 2000. Details are found in Table 12.3.

Finally, in many Third World countries and especially in Africa, traditional social structures including tribal organizations persist as they have existed for centuries. In some of these countries, the political systems consist of long-standing monarchies; Saudi Arabia and Bhutan are examples. In other coun-

Table 12.3   Developing Countries' GNP per Person, 1980–2000
(1977 Dollars)

		1985		1990		2000	
		Low	High	Low	High	Low	High
Country Group	1980	Case	Case	Case	Case	Case	Case
Low-income oil importers	168	177	183	188	206	215	261
Middle-income oil importers	1275	1408	1448	1585	1719	2009	2423
Oil exporters	753	873	896	1012	1058	1360	1475
All developing countries	615	679	702	761	825	955	1139

Source: Adapted from World Bank, World Development Report, 1980, p. 13.

tries the political and governmental leadership is made up of individuals who received their education in Great Britain, France, the United States, or the Soviet Union. In some cases the military have assumed the top governmental positions. Few genuine democracies exist in the Third World.

There is often a conceptual gap between the masses living in the countryside or in rapidly expanding urban slums and the governmental leadership; a viable middle class that could bridge this gap is usually very small or nonexistent, although in the more developed Third World countries a professional and business middle class is slowly emerging.

Leaders in Third World countries frequently resort to the instrument of nationalism to mobilize popular support for their domestic and foreign policies. To enhance the legitimacy of these policies among the indigenous audience, their tone is often anti-Western and anticapitalistic, a factor U.S. policymakers must take into account when dealing with the formulation of American policy responses to the Third World.

U.S. ECONOMIC AID POLICIES IN THE 1950s

Following his victory in the 1948 election, President Truman stressed, in his inaugural address in January, four themes in future U.S. policy: (1) endorsement of the United Nations, (2) support for the European Recovery Program, (3) the development of a North Atlantic defense organization, and (4) a bold new program of technical assistance for the newly independent countries beset by the problems of underdevelopment.[9] The latter theme became the "Point 4" program, which began to operate in 1950 under the Technical Cooperation Administration, especially established for this purpose. This organization was replaced in 1951 by the Mutual Security Agency, which provided both economic and military aid, to be in turn superseded in 1955 by the International Cooperation Administration, set up within the State Department to supervise economic aid, while military assistance programs were assigned to the Defense Department.

Several objectives characterized U.S. foreign aid programs during the 1950s: (1) the promotion of economic development in general so that in due time the LDCs could reach a takeoff point on their own to enhance their levels of development, (2) assurance that the emerging LDCs would assume some kind of democratic system or at least have governments friendly toward the United States rather than the Soviet Union, and (3) strengthening some of the developing countries especially vulnerable to Soviet threats (e.g., Iran, Pakistan, Thailand, and South Vietnam) by economic *and* military measures. For the Eisenhower administration, it was considered equally essential to follow the maxim of containing the Soviet Union and communism in general in the application of foreign aid policies.

In contrast to the Soviet Union, which was and in fact remains quite selective regarding beneficiaries of its foreign aid, the United States tended to distribute its aid broadly to a large number of recipient countries. The purpose of this policy was to avoid criticism by individual LDCs of being neglected, but the result was that grants and loans to most countries were often quite small. However, in percentage of GNP, the initial total aid to LDCs was substantial and was nearly 1 percent of GNP. Supplementing development grants since 1954 has been the Food for Peace program, which sprang from the Agricultural Trade Development and Assistance Act of 1954, better known as Public Law (PL) 480. Although expenditures for economic development grants per se accounted for only a small amount of the total (about 15 percent), they played an important role in foreign aid and at times were reinforced by donations to volunteer relief agencies and sales of agricultural products in local currency.*

Most of the aid given during the 1950s was bilateral, perhaps to solicit some measure of gratitude on the part of the recipient states and exert a maximum of influence on their governments. It is doubtful that these hopes were realized to any great extent; few LDCs were able to install viable democratic governments, because their societies were simply not ready for such a system. Few recipient countries fully committed themselves to support the United States in international politics; most preferred to assume a nonaligned or neutral status in the competition between superpowers.

THIRD WORLD CHALLENGES IN THE 1960s

In the 1960s, a fundamental change took place in aid policy toward the Third World. Increasing selectivity was applied in the dispensation of foreign aid, and new criteria established under President Kennedy emphasized carefully conceived long-range development projects, greater self-help by recipient countries, and increasing preference for loans over outright grants. A new instrument for aid was established by Kennedy: the Peace Corps. Volunteers of the

---

*Title I of PL 480 provides food sales in cases of natural disasters; Title II furnishes food on a grant basis to food deficit countries and for humanitarian purposes; Title III provides support for longer-term programs in agricultural and rural development.

Peace Corps were sent to a number of LDCs in Africa, Asia, and Latin America engaging in grass roots community projects and providing technical assistance in a number of fields. By the end of the 1960s, several thousand Peace Corps volunteers were active, and most them performed their functions in an exemplary fashion.

As the result of Kennedy's new criteria, some 8 percent of the overall U.S. foreign aid budget was allocated to only twenty LDCs by 1963.[10] At the same time, this budget began to shrink, and aid was discontinued to some states (e.g., Israel and Iran) that made impressive progress in raising their level of development. The result was that only a few countries in Africa and Asia received appreciable amounts of aid, although smaller amounts were spread among a number of states. In Asia, the main recipients of aid were Thailand, South Vietnam, the Philippines, South Korea, and India; in Latin America, aid was given primarily for regional development programs, and in the early 1960s the far-reaching Alliance for Progress was launched, which was designed to improve Latin America's economic and social conditions.

The Alliance for Progress

The Alliance for Progress policy was motivated by a number of factors: increasingly serious economic problems in Latin America, the likelihood of political upheaval, and deteriorating inter-American relations. It was assumed that if economic conditions in the Latin American countries could be substantially improved, political unrest would cease and U.S. relations with its southern neighbor could be improved.

The concept of the alliance was innovative. It was based not only on direct grants for which an initial allocation of $500 million was earmarked, but also on maximum self-help and mutual collaboration between Washington and the recipient countries. Regional planning and cooperation within Latin America were seen as crucial, and attempts were to be made to arrest the wide price fluctuations of Latin America export commodities.

A significant part of the alliance program stressed social, economic, and administrative changes in Latin America that had to be carried out by the South American governments themselves. They included changes in tax structures, traditional systems of land tenure, and improvement of production, which really amounted to restructuring of a society that had been based for centuries on oligarchies controlling vast land holdings and privileges of a small elite in most countries. It was not anticipated that these changes could be made overnight, and therefore a 10-year transition period was included in the alliance program.

To initiate this ambitious scheme, President Kennedy pledged that the United States would provide $10 billion in governmental funds, which would be supplemented by another $10 billion from other public and private funds.

Hence, from the beginning, the private sector was to be involved in providing means for improvement of the Latin American economy. In addition, South and Central American governments and private resources were expected to raise an additional $80 billion to complete the enormous task set by the Alliance for Progress.[11]

In spite of the high hopes placed in this program, it soon became clear that it was condemned to failure. Opposition by vested interests (mostly conservative elites), unwillingness of most governments to upset the traditional administrative procedures and social systems, and continued political unrest and coups sapped whatever advance the alliance might make toward the final goals. The private sector did not really rise to the challenge, partly because there was uncertainty about the profitability of investments in Latin America and partly because of the fear of the nationalization of plants built in certain countries. The alliance program demonstrated that administrative and social "engineering" is a very problematic undertaking regardless of how rational the measures suggested appear in terms of long-range improvement of the economic conditions.

Nevertheless, in spite of the failure of the overall program, some economic advances were made. The growth rate of GNP rose 2.5 to 5 percent in 1969, the infrastructure in a number of Latin American countries improved through better transportation and communication networks and through new electricity-generating facilities, and in some countries (e.g., Brazil) industrialization made impressive strides forward. Latin American funds were committed to expanding the economy and exports began to earn higher prices, although it should be remembered that the 1960s were, in general, an era of economic expansion worldwide. It should also be noted that GNP growth rates may be somewhat misleading. In Brazil, for example, the share of income received by the poorest 40 percent of the population declined from 10 percent in 1960 to 8 percent in 1970. During the same period, the share of the richest 5 percent increased from 29 to 38 percent.[12]

The Alliance for Progress program was carried out under the auspices of a new organization established by President Kennedy in 1961: the Agency for International Development (AID) replaced the Mutual Security Agency. The AID is semiautonomous but must follow policy directives from the State Department. It cooperates with multilateral institutions such as the World Bank (The International Bank for Reconstruction and Development) and regional banks such as the Inter-American Development Bank, which, like the World Bank, received substantial U.S. contributions and played an important role in the Alliance for Progress. In 1960 the United States was instrumental in establishing another multilateral institution for development purposes: the International Development Association (IDA). Closely integrated with the World Bank, IDA makes long-term "soft" loans at low interest rates to enhance development in the Third World. The emphasis on greater multilateralism, as reflected by U.S. support for the various international financial institutions, represented a policy shift away from the almost exclusive bilateralism practiced by the United States in the early years of foreign aid.

The Group of "77" Demands and UNCTAD

Rejecting the pressures by the two superpowers through the dispensation of foreign aid to affiliate with either of them, LCDs began in the middle 1950s to ally themselves in a nonaligned movement that had its first meetings in Bandung in 1955 and in Belgrade in 1961. Although this movement was essentially political, it also had economic ambitions. Indeed, the declaration of the Belgrade conference was that all countries concerned with economic development problems should convene an international economic conference. Working through the United Nations and especially its Economic and Social Council, it was decided in 1962 to convene a U.N. Conference on Trade and Development (UNCTAD) in Geneva in 1964. To establish a common front, the LDCs organized a formal grouping, known as the "Group of 77." These seventy-seven countries cosponsored the Joint Declaration of the Developing Countries to the U.N. General Assembly in 1963, which became the basis for a series of goals of the UNCTAD meeting in 1964. These goals were as follows:

1. The expansion of markets for exports of manufactured and semimanufactured products from LDCs and the elimination of all tariffs and NTBs impeding such exports;
2. Increased exports of LDC primary products, both raw and processed, to the developed countries and stabilization of prices for these products at fair and remunerative levels;
3. More adequate financial resources at favorable terms to enable LDCs to increase the import of capital goods and industrial raw materials essential for development;
4. Better coordination of trade and aid policies; and
5. Reduction of shipping and insurance costs.[13]

The goals articulated by UNCTAD received a mixed response by the developed countries. The preference proposals for LDC exports were rejected by the United States, which argued that these preferences would have little positive effect on narrowing the trade gap while at the same time undermining the GATT principle of nondiscrimination among trading partners. However, as far as reciprocity was concerned, an accord was reached in GATT to add new provisions to the existing agreement (Part IV) in 1965, which eliminated this principle for trade negotiations in which LDCs were involved. In addition, they made possible the establishment of commodity agreements to stabilize and assure more equitable prices.

Meanwhile, UNCTAD developed into a permanent organization with a secretariat and a secretary-general. The Group of 77 retained its name, although by now its membership exceeds 135 LCDs. Furthermore, the UNCTAD meeting in 1964, a huge affair with more than 1500 delegates and lasting several weeks, was and continues to be followed by UNCTAD II, III, and so on every 3 or 4 years, all large meetings spanning several weeks.

UNCTAD II was held in New Delhi, India, in 1968, and just before this conference Washington changed its attitude on general preferences for LDC exports. The reason was growing isolation from other developed countries in the OECD that were more sympathetic to the preference scheme as well as increased pressures from Latin American countries. As a consequence, agreement on the principle of establishing a general preference scheme was reached during UNCTAD II, and the United States implemented this scheme in 1975 under the provisions of the Trade Reform Act of 1974.

POLICY FLUCTUATIONS IN THE 1970s

From the second half of the 1960s to the early 1970s, the amount of U.S. economic assistance to the Third World declined. It was $3.5 billion in 1967 and $3.0 billion in 1973. However, in real value (constant 1967 dollars), the decline was to $2 billion.[14]

Looking at Table 12.4, we see that in contemporary dollars, the amount of aid from 1975 to 1980 showed a generally rising trend, but considering inflation, it actually decreased, although the percentage of aid in relation to GNP remained steady though very low.

In addition to the reduction in aid in real dollars, assistance was increasingly tied to purchases from the United States and to the use of American shipping and insurance. These considerations reduced the value of the aid, because in many cases the cost of goods from the United States and other costs were above world market prices.

New UNCTAD Priorities

During the 1970s, the U.N. Second Development Decade was launched. UNCTAD III, IV, and V were held during this decade in Santiago, Chile, Nairobi, Kenya, and Manila, Philippines, respectively. The basic program of the Group of 77 was not formulated during these conferences but by the Algiers summit of nonaligned countries in 1973. The main economic demands crystal-

Table 12.4   U.S. Economic Aid from 1969 to 1980
(\$ Billions and Percentage of GNP)

	1969	1975	1976	1977	1978	1979	1980
Dollars	3.1	4.2	4.4	4.7	5.7	4.6	7.1
% of GNP	0.51	0.27	0.26	0.25	0.27	0.19	0.27

Source: Adapted from World Bank, *World Development Report 1980*, Table 16, p. 140.

lized during that summit formed the foundation of the New International Economic Order (NIEO), adopted by the U.N. General Assembly in 1974. The NIEO proposal expanded on the earlier UNCTAD demands and included the following:

1. Increased low-cost or free transfer of technology to LDCs without restrictive conditions imposed by suppliers regarding the use of the technology;
2. Efforts to restructure the existing industrial property system and to revise the Paris Convention for the Protection of Industrial Property of 1883, primarily the legal rules on patents and licenses;
3. A binding code of conduct for multinational corporations curbing their economic and political power and vesting extensive control over their subsidiaries in LDC host governments;
4. An international agency and a common fund of $10 to $12 billion to support the price of commodities exported by LDCs;
5. An extension of the General Preference System (GPS) for LDC exports to the developed countries, including the elimination of quantitative restrictions imposed by some importing countries;
6. A commitment by the developed countries to the transfer of 0.7 percent of GNP in outright grants to the Third World; and
7. A moratorium on the repayment of interest and principal of loans made by Western financial institutions to LDCs and rescheduling of payments, with complete cancellation of debts incurred by the poorest LDCs.*,[15]

These and other demands of the Third World embodied in the NIEO have required and continue to require responses by the developed countries. The ensuing dialogue on finding solutions for Third World problems is generally referred to as the "North-South Dialogue," because most of the developed countries are located in the Northern Hemisphere and the bulk of the LDCs in the Southern Hemisphere.

The United States has put in place a general preference system for imports from LDCs, but this system has not fully met the expectations of the LDCs. However, other developed countries such as the Ten of the European Communities also have restrictions in the GPS installed by them. As for technology transfers and the code of conduct for multinational corporations, the United States participates in negotiations in the United Nations that have been under way under the auspices of UNCTAD and ECOSOC since the middle of the 1970s. So far, these negotiations have not met with success, partly because the United States, in concert with other Western countries, insists on certain principles such as the voluntary nature of the codes and safeguards on the

---

*It should be noted that the amount of debt owed by LDCs to international financial institutions and banks in the Western developed countries exceeded $600 billion in 1982.[16]

nationalization of subsidiaries by host countries. Otherwise, however, considerable progress has been made in the negotiations.[17]

Much of what was recommended in 1976 by UNCTAD IV in Nairobi with respect to technology transfer had become American foreign policy before the conference. In his speech at the opening session of the conference, Secretary of State Kissinger declared:

> First, to adapt technology to the needs of developing countries, the United States supports the establishment of a network of research and development institutions at the local, regional, and international levels. We need to strengthen global research capacities for development and to expand intergovernmental cooperation. . . .
>
> The second element of our program is to improve the amount and quality of technological information available to developing countries and to improve their selection of technology relevant to their needs. . . . For its part, the United States will inventory its national technological information resources and make available . . . consultants and other services to improve access to our National Library of Medicine, the Division of Scientific Information of the National Science Foundation, the National Agricultural Library, and the Smithsonian Information Service. . . .
>
> Third, to nurture new generations of technologists and technology managers, the United States proposes a priority effort to train individuals who can develop, identify, and apply technology suited to the needs of developing countries. . . .
>
> The fourth element of our approach is to make the process of transferring existing technology more effective and equitable.

The United States also supported the creation of an UNCTAD Advisory Service to strengthen the ability of Third World countries to identify, select, and negotiate for the technology most appropriate to their requirements. The Nairobi conference decided to set up such an organization from the regular budget of UNCTAD.[18]

During the conference, the United States also proposed a multibillion-dollar International Resources Bank that could assist the Third World in obtaining needed technology, but this proposal was rejected. The likely reason for the rejection was the private-investor orientation of the proposed bank, under which the funds of the bank would be used by private corporations for natural resources developments and at the same time aid in the improvement of technological, managerial, and marketing capabilities in the host country. The bias against private enterprise and concomitant fear of outside domination, so frequently found in Third World motivation, appeared to carry the day.

One Third World demand that has remained unfulfilled is a system that would prevent wide fluctuations in prices for LDC exports of primary materials. Such a system, which would include the accumulation of buffer stocks, a common fund for financing such stocks, multilateral purchase and supply agreements for particular commodities, and compensatory finance measures, is obviously highly complex. During UNCTAD IV in Nairobi, there appeared to be the possibility of finding the necessary finances for a common fund for *all* commodities in which Washington was prepared to participate. However, disagreement between the developed countries and the Group of 77 as to how the system and especially the fund would be managed prevented a successful outcome. Nevertheless, U.S. policy supports the negotiation of stabilization agreements for individual commodities such as sugar and natural rubber; moreover, such agreements were concluded during the 1970s, and this policy remains in force.

Another demand unfulfilled by the United States is economic assistance grants that were to amount to 0.7 percent of GNP. As we have seen, the United States public aid is far below this figure, although Sweden, Norway, and the Netherlands exceeded 0.9 percent in 1980.[19]

Although the Ford and Carter administrations were sympathetic to the plight of the Third World as reflected, for example, by the statements of Henry Kissinger quoted earlier and the appointment of Andrew Young as the U.S. ambassador to the United Nations by President Carter, they did not embrace the principles of the NIEO in their totality and insisted on the retention of the free-market forces as the underlying foundation of the global economy. In particular, the requested use of individual commodity agreements and debt relief as instruments of resource transfer was rejected.

During the 1970s there was increased emphasis in U.S. foreign economic assistance to allocate funds to multilateral financial institutions and programs. At the end of the decade, these institutions included the World Bank, the IDA for long-term soft loans to the poorest countries, the International Finance Corporation (IFC) for the encouragement of private sector financing with risk-sharing on development projects otherwise difficult to finance, and the Inter-American, Asian, and African Development Banks or Funds. American support was also provided to the U.N. Development Program (UNDP), UNICEF, the U.N. Relief and Works Agency (UNRWA), the International Atomic Energy Agency (IAEA), the U.N. Environmental Programs, and economic programs of the OAS.[20]

Foreign economic assistance is of course not only an exercise in humanitarianism but an instrument to meet the enlightened economic interests of the American people. Secretary of State Cyrus Vance made this point in a talk in July 1979:

> Around 800,000 jobs in manufacturing alone depend directly or indirectly on exports to developing countries. . . .
> Developing countries mean critical markets for farmers. They now buy approximately a third of all the wheat, cotton, and rice we produce in the United States. And for American business, developing countries not only supply essential raw materials and energy that our industrial society needs to function, they also

mean growing markets for our manufactured goods. Indeed, the 12 fastest growing major markets for the United States are developing countries.[21]

In the same speech, Vance emphasized that the United States was focusing attention and resources on practical solutions to concrete development problems such as food, energy, health, and education.

> We now devote over half of our bilateral economic assistance to agriculture and rural development and one out of every seven of our bilateral aid dollars is used in support of family planning programs. . . . (T)hrough our consistent support of human rights, including economic rights, we are seeking to help other governments cope with the growing demand by people around the world to share fully in the political affairs and economic growth of these nations.[22]

Changing Policy Emphasis in the Reagan Administration

During the Reagan administration, a major shift in the emphasis of U.S. policy toward the Third World took place. In a statement by the AID director in March 1981, the commitment was stressed to provide increased opportunities for the private sector to participate in AID programs.

> Incorporating opportunities for growth of the private commerical sector in developing countries, and in related ways increasing avenues for our own private sector to expand its associations and business, has not previously received the attention it deserves in AID. I have already initiated work in AID to find important and significant programs to involve American financial and manufacturing sectors in investment and advisory activities. We must be careful here to facilitate business involvement and not to substitute for private capital. Ultimately the most significant economic development will come from vigorous free markets in goods and services. I am convinced AID can play a significant catalytic role and will be back to you for advice and counsel as our ideas develop.[23]

The concept of increased private sector involvement was echoed by President Reagan himself in an address to the annual meeting of the IMF, World Bank, IDA, and IFC in the fall of 1981, in which he urged these institutions to "play a more active role in generating private sources and stimulating individual initiation in the development effort."[24] Later in 1981 he said:

> Investment is the lifeblood of development. Private capital flows, commercial lending, and private investment can account for almost 70% of total financial flows to developing countries. It's impractical, not to mention foolish, to attack these flows for ideological reasons.[25]

He also struck a theme to be repeated later, namely that "unless a nation puts its own financial and economic house in order, no amount of aid will produce progress."[26]

This theme and the role of the private sector were reflected in a major development program proposed in 1982 by the Reagan administration, the Caribbean Basin Initiative. Responding to perceived political and perhaps military threats emanating from Cuba, it is designed to help the economies of large and small Caribbean islands and rim countries to overcome structural underdevelopment and strengthen democratically oriented governments in the Basin to resist violent, externally supported insurgents aiming to impose totalitarian regimes hostile to the United States. The proposed economic aid package of trade, investment, and financial assistance has as its centerpiece a U.S. offer of one-way free trade for exports from the region to the United States. It also seeks authority to offer American firms significant tax incentives for new investment and to increase direct financial assistance for both urgent balance-of-payments problems and longer-term structural imbalances. Finally, it favors land reform where needed and more equitable financing of government services.[27]

The Caribbean Basin Initiative aroused some concern in business circles and Congress that it would damage production and employment opportunities in the United States. However, the imports affected by the free-trade proposals were estimated to be less than 0.5 percent, and some safeguard measures were included in the underlying legislation to deal with any serious injury that might be sustained by American producers.

The budget authority request for fiscal year 1983 included a substantial amount of funds for the Caribbean Basin Initiative. While the increase of funds requested for AID was slight, the amount requested for multilateral development banks rose by nearly 20 percent over the 1982 actual budget. Table 12.5 shows the 1983 amounts requested for all items, but it should be noted that supplementary requests for F.Y. 83 were made subsequently.

The important role of the private sector as seen by Reagan was also a major motivation for the administration to oppose the seabed regime as envisioned by the draft treaty on the law of the sea, the result of drawn-out negotiations in the U.N. Conference on the Law of the Sea (UNCLOS III), which spanned more than a decade. The regime was to be an elaborate institutional structure under which United Nations-directed operations were to undertake the task of mining the seabed for manganese and other minerals. The United States, and some Western governments, feared the emergence of a vast new U.N. bureaucracy subsidized to a substantial degree by the Western World—a bureaucracy that by itself could not mine the first module of seabed materials. Hence the United States voted against the adoption of the draft treaty. However, the draft treaty received sufficient favorable votes (under its own requirements) to enter into force for the countries that voted for it. Whether the seabed regime can become operable is very doubtful, however, because the necessary technology for

Table 12.5   Foreign Economic and Financial Assistance Request for Fiscal Year 1983 and 1982 Actual Budget ($ Millions)

Source	FY 1982 (Actual)	FY 1983 (Request)
Multilateral development banks	1261.7	1537.0
International Fund for Agricultural Development	—	65.4
International organizations	215.4	173.3
AID	1771.3	1815.5
PL 480 (Food for Peace)	1000.0	1028.0
Peace Corps	105.0	97.5
Refugee assistance	503.0	419.0
Offsetting receipts and other	−327.0	−371.7
Total	4529.4	4764.0

Source: Adapted from U.S., Department of State, Bureau of Public Affairs, *International Security and Economic Cooperation FY 1983*, March 1982, p. 2.

seabed mining is in the exclusive hands of private American and West European corporations, and the U.S. government has refused to pay any funds toward establishing the regime.[28]

The Security Dimension

Since the problems of the Third World flow basically from economic underdevelopment, we have concentrated so far on the economic aspects of U.S. policy toward the LDCs. However, there is also a significant security dimension in foreign aid as an instrument of policy. Former Secretary of State Vance succinctly stated in 1978 the objectives of U.S. security assistance programs:

> *First*, they are designed to assist our friends and allies to provide for their legitimate defense needs.
> *Second*, these programs support our strategic and political objectives of reducing tensions and promoting stability in areas of potential confrontation and conflict.
> *Third*, they provide economic assistance to countries which are experiencing political and economic stresses and where U.S. security interests are involved.[29]

Except for the years before the Marshall Plan, military assistance has always been a substantial part of U.S. assistance programs, as was already pointed out in Chapter 8. During the 4 years following the institution of the Marshall Plan, the military share of all assistance resources committed by the United States grew from less than 4 percent to about 35 percent, mainly to contribute to the containment of Soviet expansionism. During the Eisenhower administration, the military share of the assistance programs reached 44 percent and then has fluctuated widely, as can be seen from Figure 12.1, depending on military-strategic needs as the Vietnam War expanded and wound down from 1965 to 1975. New requirements emerged in the Middle East and Persian Gulf regions, beginning with the replenishment of Israeli military stocks during and after the October 1973 Israeli-Arab War, the increasingly close economic military relationship with Egypt subsequent to President Sadat's expulsion of the Soviet advisors, and the possible expansionist designs of the Soviet Union following the Iran debacle and the invasion of Afghanistan in 1979. Other needs may come from activities of Soviet allies such as the East Germans and Cubans in Ethiopia and the latter in Angola. Central America and especially El Salvador are the latest places where military and economic aid have been dispensed to stem a guerrilla movement that receives support from Cuba and indirectly from the Soviet Union.

An appreciation of the current military assistance scope can be gained from analysis of the fiscal year 1983 International Security Program displayed in Table 12.6. The requested funds are about 1.5 billion higher than for F.Y. 1982. Significantly, 87 percent ($3.4 billion) of the FMS guaranteed financing is to go to seven countries—Egypt, Greece, Israel, Korea, Pakistan, Spain, and Turkey—all countries critical to the U.S. defense effort considering perceived Soviet threats. Although direct credits for FMS are planned for twenty countries including the eastern Caribbean, the bulk goes to Egypt, Israel, Sudan, Portugal, and Turkey, with repayment for the first three countries ($950 million) forgiven.

Economic support funds provide economic assistance on a grant or loan basis to countries of special political and security interest to Washington. The five countries listed in the preceding paragraph receive the bulk of the $2.8 billion requested, but $50 million is reserved for the Caribbean Basin Initiative.

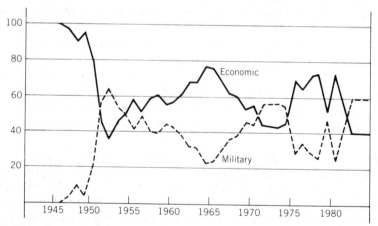

Figure 12.1   Economic and military assistance as percentage of total assistance.

Source: U.S., Loans and Grants (AID); U.S., Department of Commerce, Bureau of Economic Analysis; National Income and Product Accounts (DRI Data Base).

Table 12.6   Fiscal Year 1983 International Security Program
($ millions)

	Budget Authority	
	FY 1982 *(Actual)*	FY 1983 *(Request)*
Foreign military sales credits (FMS)		
Credits	750.0[a]	1739.0[b]
Guaranteed loan commitments	(3083.5)	(3928.8)
Economic support funds	2564.0	2886.0
Military assistance program (MAP)	176.5	107.5
International military education and training	38.5	53.7
Peacekeeping operations	151.0	43.5
Antiterrorism assistance	—	5.0
Offsetting receipts and other	−194.0	−171.7
Total	3486.0	4663.0

[a]Forgiven credits.
[b]Of which $950 million is forgiven.

Source: U.S., Department of State, Bureau of Public Affairs, *International Security and Economic Cooperation Program FY 1983*, March 1982, p. 2.

The military assistance program, providing defense articles, services, and training to eligible foreign governments on a grant basis, is minor compared to the other items. Peacekeeping operations shown in Table 12.6 refer to the observer force in the Sinai, the U.N. force in Cyprus, and the Chad peace-keeping force sponsored by the Organization of African Unity (OAU). Again, the amount that was requested for F.Y. 1983 was relatively small.

All in all, it is obvious that U.S. military assistance programs are carefully targeted in order to achieve the maximum effect for funds expended. In this connection, it should be pointed out again that inflation had a considerable negative impact on the expenditures of resources not only on military assistance but also on economic aid programs. Figure 12.2 portrays graphically how much the real resources have fallen for nearly three decades. Food shipments under PL 480 provide a good example. In 1960, $1.1 billion bought shipments of 14.3 million metric tons of foodstuffs, whereas in 1981 it cost $1.4 billion to ship only 5.2 million tons.[30]

Global Negotiations

American policies toward the Third World over nearly three decades were motivated by a mixture of enlightened economic self-interest, national security concerns, and humanitarianism, and aimed at raising development levels and improving defense capabilities with priorities given to countries considered especially vulnerable to external pressures. These policies have not generally satisfied the leadership of the Group of 77. With the various UNCTAD

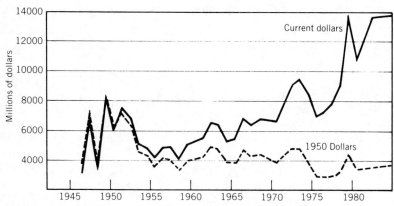

Figure 12.2 Total military and economic assistance: the ravages of inflation.
Sources: U.S., Loans and Grants (AID); U.S., Department of Commerce, Bureau of Economic Analysis; National Income and Product Accounts (DRI Data Base).

meetings having been unsuccessful in attaining to an appreciable degree the aims of the group articulated and pressed over 20 years and the full implementation of the NIEO still being elusive, the Group of 77 has resorted to a strategy of global negotiations mainly in the U.N. General Assembly and perhaps other U.N. bodies to achieve the goals of the NIEO.

The Group of 77 prefers a single global forum for the negotiations of all issues, regardless of existing mandates and competences of specialized agencies. The United States, generally somewhat cool to the idea of these negotiations, believed under the Carter administration that priority attention and actual negotiations should focus on a few paramount and urgent issues such as food, energy in energy-deficient countries, protectionism, and the recycling of payment surplus. The United States favored decentralizing the negotiations to multilateral forums such as the IMF, World Bank, GATT, and the Food and Agricultural Organization (FAO).

The issue of global negotiation was a prime topic during the summit talks at Cancun, Mexico, in October 1981, which were held to discuss economic cooperation between the developed and developing countries within the context of the North-South dialogue. The United States objected to any suggestion that it would consider negotiating a massive transfer of resources from "North" to "South," which many saw as the objective of the negotiations. President Reagan expressed opposition to such an idea, which, he said, "would mean some gigantic new international bureaucracy to be in charge. . . . If global negotiations means that we continue negotiations as to how all of us can help resolve these problems, we're perfectly willing to."[31] The summit also addressed the question of in which forum or forums the global negotiations should be held. The United States insisted on its earlier stand developed by the

Carter administration that various forums other than the Assembly should be used, with emphasis on specific issues rather than dealing with broad notions of a new international economic order. Moreover, the negotiations should not be used as a platform for political rhetoric.

During the summit, Reagan returned to his theme: the virtues of private enterprise. He stated: "History demonstrates that time and time again, in place after place, economic growth and human progress make their greatest strides in countries that encourage economic freedom."[32]

The LDC leaders present at Cancun, not surprisingly, questioned the merit of Reagan's emphasis on private enterprise as being able to solve the difficult problems of raising the levels of development. They also wanted to give the United Nations a larger voice in the global negotiations. However, they did not engage in serious recriminations, and the next step in the negotiations was left, perhaps purposively, quite vague in the final summary of the summit.

It is interesting to point out that three NICs (Yugoslavia, Brazil, and Mexico) participated in the Cancun summit. Although the Brazilian and Mexican representatives seemed to take something of an intermediate position between the United States and the Group of 77 stands, in principle they were in favor of global negotiations on NIEO demands although Mexico seemed to prefer specialized forums rather than the General Assembly.[33] In general, despite the impressive industrial growth of the NICs that might shatter the perception of common interests between them and the rest of the LDCs, the Third World has demonstrated a surprising degree of cohesion on all NIEO demands in whatever U.N. forum these demands are discussed and negotiated, and as a consequence, the LDCs generally have been effective and unified bargainers.[35] At the same time, the NICs have resisted "graduation" into developed-country status, partly because they do not want to lose preferential access to the markets of the developed countries and want to remain eligible for special status in intra-LDC trade. Hence, efforts of the developed countries to split the NICs away from other developing countries are not likely to succeed in the near future.

Meanwhile, the issue of global negotiations stagnated during 1982. Proposals and counterproposals were made between the Group of 77 and the industrialized countries on how these negotiations were to be conducted, but no agreement had been reached by early 1983. However, while no decision had been reached on the global negotiations, individual U.N. agencies continued their work in the development field. For example, in September 1982, thirty-one countries other than the United States provided $2 billion extra funds to the World Bank to preserve the support levels of IDA for interest-free loans to very poor countries.[36] In addition, attempts were under way to alleviate manifestations of hunger by making the international agricultural and food organizations operating within the framework of the United Nations use available resources more effectively and avoid duplication of work.

OPEC and the Middle East

Although most members of the Organization of Petroleum-Exporting Countries (OPEC) exhibit the characteristics of the Third World (even though per capita GNPs are generally at the upper levels of middle-income countries and in few cases substantially higher—Libya, Saudi Arabia, and Kuwait), U.S. policy formulation with respect to these countries and especially those located in the Middle East has marched to a different drummer. The reasons are obvious. Oil became a scarce commodity after the selective embargo had been imposed by OPEC following the Israeli-Arab War of 1973, and it was generally perceived that the petroleum reserves would be gradually exhausted. Assurance of the *continual* supply of this valuable resource that is essential for the effective performance of the Western industrialized economies became the prime objective of U.S. policies. Since a large amount of the petroleum reserves were concentrated in several Middle East countries, and because the Soviet Union, following the invasion of Afghanistan, constituted a potential threat to such oil-rich countries as Saudi Arabia and Kuwait, the security of the region and the protection of these countries assumed paramount importance.

Thirteen oil-producing and oil-exporting countries formed OPEC in 1960.* Beginning in 1970, the OPEC countries called for an increase in the pooled price of oil and for the nationalization of the Western, mostly American, oil-producing and processing facilities in the member states. Rapidly rising demand and shortage of supply meant that the developed market economies were highly vulnerable to supply interruption and in a weak bargaining position. Hence, since the fall of 1973, OPEC as a producer cartel has determined oil prices; OPEC raised the price unilaterally from about $2.48 in 1972 to $11.65 for a barrel of oil in January 1, 1974. By January 1981, the official price for crude oil was allowed to go as high as $41 a barrel,[37] but the average price paid during 1981 and 1982 was $35; by 1983, as a result of an abundance of oil in the world market, the actual price had dropped to $30 and less.[38]

The Assurance of Oil Supplies   In the face of the unilateral power of OPEC to raise crude oil prices and in order to assure the continued flow of petroleum to the United States whose daily oil imports were beginning to rise rapidly from the 1973 level of 3.3 million barrels, as well as to other Western countries, the U.S. government convened a thirteen-nation energy conference in Washington in February 1974. The purpose was to work out a common program for easing the energy crisis. In the end, it was agreed to set up a coordinating group to decide how to organize most efficiently the coordination program. In particular, the Energy Coordinating Group (ECG) was charged with the following tasks: (1) conservation of energy and restraint of demand, (2) setting up a system for

---

*Current members are Iran, Iraq, Kuwait, Libya, Saudi Arabia, Venezuela, Ecuador, Indonesia, United Arab Emirates, Algeria, Nigeria, Quatar, and Gabon.

allocating oil supplies in times of emergency or severe shortage, (3) acceleration of the development of additional energy sources in order to diversify energy supplies, and (4) acceleration of energy R&D programs through international cooperative efforts.

France declined participation in this coordinating group, and perhaps because of this, no agreement was reached on a proposed "code of conduct," which was to regulate the efforts several governments were making to work out special deals with Mideastern oil producers. France, for example, was negotiating pacts with Saudi Arabia, Kuwait, and Libya that would guarantee it millions of barrels of oil in return for stepped-up deliveries of French weapons and technology to the producers. These efforts later obtained results and set an example that other participants in the Washington conference were to follow.

Despite U.S. opposition to bilateral agreements with Arab oil-producing countries (because such agreements appeared to signal defection from existing alliance systems), Washington itself concluded a series of bilateral accords on trade, investment, and technology.[39] The first of the American agreements was signed with Saudi Arabia. American justification for this and other bilateral accords was their link to a Middle East settlement and an eventual moderation of oil prices.[40]

French suspicions that the Washington conference had been called to reassert U.S. leadership over disintegrating alliance affairs and to create some new interlocking machinery to tie European energy plans and activities to American resources were not entirely unfounded. Not only were American science and technology used to solve energy problems per se, they were also to be a means of achieving diplomatic ends. Commercial gains from the supply of American nuclear generating equipment and enriched uranium may also have been motivating factors. To reinforce the proposed technological ties in the energy field, President Nixon reminded European leaders, during a White House dinner held on the occasion of the Washington conference, that they could not be independent of the United States in economic and political affairs and at the same time expect to rely on American support in security areas. Nixon declared that "security and economic considerations are inevitably linked, and energy cannot be separated from either."[41] As Henry Nau points out, the energy crisis was to supply practical proof to the Europeans that they could not do without U.S. leadership in alliance affairs and that U.S. leadership could not be accepted exclusively in security areas.[42]

A major result of the Washington conference was the establishment of the International Energy Agency (IEA), now operating under the auspices of the OECD. Although the French government was urged strongly to join the IEA, it declined official participation. Paris wanted to avoid the impression that the oil-consuming countries were forming a cartel, but perhaps more important, it wished to preserve its freedom for dealing with the oil producers.[43] Norway, initially interested in full participation, had a change of heart and became only an "associate" of the IEA. Other IEA members, besides the nine EC countries and the United States, today include Austria, Canada, Japan, New Zealand, Spain, Sweden, Switzerland, and Turkey.

The IEA remains the principal vehicle both for energy cooperation among the industrialized countries and for the coordination of national programs of energy conservation, development, and reduced dependence. Specific IEA tasks are wide-ranging and include (a) the organization of international cooperation in the field of enriched uranium production, (b) the creation of economic and monetary coordination measures, to be implemented when needed to cope with the multiple effects of price rises, and (c) relations with the non-energy-producing developing countries (hard hit by the oil price increases).[44]

In order to find a solution to the problems facing the petroleum consumers and producers, a preparatory meeting for an international energy conference was convened in April 1975. The consumer participants were the United States, members of the European Communities, and Japan. The producers were represented by Algeria (as leader) and by Iran, Venezuela, and Saudi Arabia. Since the Third World would be affected by any conference of this type, India, Brazil, and Zaire were invited. The IEA, OPEC, and the United Nations were represented by observers.

The formulation of an agenda for the preparatory meeting proved to be troublesome. The United States wanted the conference to be limited strictly to petroleum issues (prices, harmonization of supply and demand, petrodollars), whereas the developing countries wanted to extend it to other raw materials and to "North-South" relations in general. Fruitless disputes on the title, scope, and procedures of the planned conference marked the preparatory meeting from the beginning. The rigid attitude of the oil-producing and other developing countries could not be overcome by any of the compromises offered by the consumer states, and the emerging deadlock killed the meeting.

Despite this failure to initiate a useful dialogue between the oil consumer and producer countries, an IEA ministerial meeting at the end of May 1975 suggested new initiatives for the resumption of the preparatory meeting. Secretary of State Kissinger proposed that a number of committees be established for such a new meeting. These would explore problems related to raw materials other than petroleum, noted Kissinger, but substantive negotiations would have to be conducted in other forums.

In December 1975 a Ministerial Conference on International Economic Cooperation (CIEC) was convened in Paris at the invitation of France. Delegates from twenty-seven countries participated, of which nineteen were Third World countries. Canada and Venezuela furnished the cochairs for the conference. Following Kissinger's suggestion, commissions were set up on the following topics: energy and raw materials, development problems, and financial affairs. Each commission had fifteen members—ten from the developing countries and five from the industrialized world.

During 1976, eight meetings of these four commissions were held, but progress in reaching agreement was very slow and often impossible. The

European Community, either on its own or with other industrialized countries, submitted position papers to the four commissions on nearly all topics. Despite the opposing positions of the industrialized and developing countries, there had been some hope that before the end of 1976 a meeting at the ministerial level might wind up the North-South negotiations successfully. However, the positions not having moved much closer together, it was decided to postpone such a meeting to 1977.

The results of the spring CIEC meeting were very disappointing. Clearly, the strategies of the industrialized countries failed. For the Third World representatives, the problem of technology transfers appeared to be most important, and insofar as oil prices were concerned, OPEC's autonomy was not to be touched.

The industrialized oil-consuming countries' hope of obtaining a measure of control over oil prices, in exchange for the "goodies" they were offering, was unrealistic. It was a mistaken calculation, because the main priorities of the Third World representatives were in quite different areas, and they seemed to be convinced that they could obtain satisfaction of their interests and demands in due time through the U.N. forums—without making concessions. The Third World countries, however, may have underestimated the permanence of the oil crisis and its impact on the industrialized countries, which can make generosity onerous; for in the view of the latter, the increases in the prices of oil and gas have already led to a redistribution of global wealth and are a major cause of the sluggish world economy.

It was evident in the negotiations that the solidarity of the developing countries was very high despite differences in particular interests. Clearly, they did not want to give up the "oil weapon," regardless of the adverse implications for their economic development that are likely to flow from even higher oil prices. One of these implications may be greater reliance by the industrialized world on substitutes for raw materials traditionally imported from developing countries in order to save foreign currency. Synthetic fibers instead of rubber or cotton products are an example. Indeed, the representatives of the Third World asked the industrialized countries to impose limits on the production of substitutes, at the same time demanding the transfer of technologies that would enable them to manufacture oil-base synthetic products.

Undoubtedly the most potent weapon of the industrialized countries including the United States was conservation. Legally mandated reduction in the use of gasoline in automobiles, the more efficient use of energy by industries and individuals, and a deteriorating world economy were the major causes of the oil glut that is currently forcing oil prices downward and placing OPEC into disarray—making it difficult, if not impossible, for the members to agree on production quotas and prices.[45]

The Consequences of OPEC Wealth   The new-found wealth of the OPEC countries led to ambitious indigenous economic development programs. Spending at a high rate for these programs, their current account surpluses in fact declined from 1974 to 1978.[46] For this reason, they were interested in keeping production and earnings at a high level, but some countries such as Saudi Arabia were also aware that irresponsible management of prices and supply would result in severe damage to the Western economies, in which a growing number of OPEC nationals had begun to invest heavily both indirectly in portfolio placements and directly in industrial firms, banks, and other media. This set the stage for recycling the immense earnings of the OPEC countries, especially those in the Middle East. Some of the surpluses were recycled through private banks, which accepted OPEC funds for deposits and loaned them to oil-importing countries. Similar roles were and are played by the World Bank and the IMF.

Oil-producing countries also have made direct commitments to both developed and developing countries for loans and grants. The vast majority of loans and grants to the latter have gone to Arab and Moslem states. This means that these financial transfers do not go necessarily to the neediest countries. As for the developed countries, OPEC investments in industry and banking have raised fears of economic control and political influence. This is especially the case when investments are made in important sectors of the economy, and this has raised questions about U.S. policy vis-à-vis these investments. In addition, the decline in the oil price during 1983 has generated apprehension about the impact that lower OPEC earnings will have on the banking system in the United States, including loans extended to consuming countries by American banks, and on American firms that have become dependent on large OPEC inflows of funds for their operations and sales. Of course, the profit picture of U.S. oil companies may also be affected adversely by lower petroleum prices, and so will be the budgets of oil-producing states in the United States. Louisiana is a good example. Every one-dollar drop in the world price of oil reduces Louisiana's revenues by $30 million.[47]

The foregoing discussion points up the tremendous significance of U.S. political and economic relations with the OPEC countries, particularly those located in the Middle East that might be threatened by Soviet expansionism. Iran is a prime example of the volatility in the Middle East. Iran, a major oil producer, was a long-time close friend and ally of the United States under the shah. The Islamic Revolution, organized by the Ayatollah Khomeini in 1979, deposed the shah and ushered in a period of hostility between the United States and Iran highlighted by the capture of U.S. diplomatic and military personnel in late 1979, who remained as hostages until January 1981. The war between Iraq and Iran also poses problems for the United States and enhances the volatility of the region. Both actions affected Saudi Arabia, whose leaders were concerned about U.S. attempts to keep the shah in power and later to gain the freedom of the hostages. All this may have undermined the political stability in Saudi Arabia, which has become a major U.S. ally in the Arab world. The sale of AWACS (Airborne Warning and Control System) planes in 1981 by the Reagan administration in spite of major opposition in Congress may have strengthened American relations with the Saudis, which had cooled as the result of the U.S.-sponsored Camp David agreement between Israel and Egypt.

The Soviet invasion of Afghanistan put into stark relief the fragility of secure oil supplies from the Middle East to the industrialized democracies. It motivated President Carter to enunciate in January the so-called Carter Doctrine, which committed the United States to the defense of the Persian Gulf area through which the oil flow from a number of gulf oil producers had to pass on their way to Western Europe, Japan, and the United States and other consuming countries. The doctrine stated that an attempt by any outside force to gain control of the Persian Gulf region would be regarded as an assault on the vital interests of the United States and that such an assault would be repelled by any means necessary including military force. To implement the new policy, American warships with U.S. Marine contingents were stationed near the Persian Gulf, and a Rapid Deployment Force amounting to 100,000 to 200,000 soldiers was created. Egypt and Oman offered facilities for U.S. forces, and later the United States began to build new facilities along the Horn of Africa (Somalia) reaching as far as Kenya. The Reagan administration has basically adopted the Carter Doctrine and seeks to strengthen further the defense of the region and the military capabilities of selected countries such as Saudi Arabia and Egypt to deter any Soviet aggression.

If U.S. policy had to contend only with the fragility of the oil supply from the Arab producers in the Middle East in the face of possible Soviet expansionist designs toward the Persian Gulf, it would have to cope with a difficult task. But this complex situation has been compounded by problems caused American policymakers by Israel, basically perceived as a staunch ally, albeit with very much a mind of its own.

The Impact of Israel　　Israel has always received a large amount of aid from the United States; in the Reagan administration budget request for 1983, it was the largest aid recipient, with total economic and military assistance amounting to nearly $2.5 billion.[48] Both the various administrations and Congress have always been sensitive to the power and influence of the Jewish lobby and to the fact that a high percentage of the Jewish electorate turns out on election days.

Although the United States has over the years generally given Israel very strong support in the international arena and for the wars fought against Arab countries, the U.S. government must consider in its foreign policy formulation the totality of its Middle East interests. The foremost goal is enduring peace among the states of the region, and the Carter administration saw the Camp David agreement between Israel and Egypt as an important step in this direction. However, the peace process has stalled because of the continuing controversy over some kind of autonomy for the Palestinians on the West Bank. The main problem is the continued construction of Israeli settlements on the occupied West Bank, which the government of Prime Minister Menachem Begin insists are necessary for Israeli security and which has increased anti-

Jewish sentiment by the Arab population claiming that these lands have been in Arab hands for a very long time. On the other hand, Israel contends that it has made substantial concessions in the peace process by withdrawing from the Sinai peninsula, inlcuding the oil fields located there, and will not make additional concessions until a fundamental change in Arab enmity occurs, meaning recognition of the Jewish state. Egyptian President Anwar Sadat's assassination in October 1981 has greatly reduced the prospects of finding a compromise solution for Arab autonomy on the West Bank, an objective of the Camp David accords.

The question of recognition brings up possible negotiations between the Israeli government and the Palestine Liberation Organization (PLO) headed by Yasir Arafat. The Israeli government has asserted that it cannot negotiate with the PLO because of the latter's frequent terrorist acts against Israeli citizens and property. The United States has basically supported this position, although some officials under the Carter administration did engage in informal contacts with the PLO; the former U.S. ambassador to the United Nations, Andrew Young, was among these officials, and as a result he was forced to resign. Nevertheless, there is widespread sentiment in the United States and especially in Western Europe that without direct negotiations between Israel and the PLO a peace settlement will remain elusive.

Another issue beclouding the peace process is the question of Arab refugees, many of whom live in stark misery in Lebanese camps. Israel claims that the refugees could have been resettled long ago in Arab countries with lots of space and with Arab oil money. The continuation of the camps had the primary purpose of fanning Arab emotions and soliciting Western support for a return to what used to be Palestine and for the establishment of a sovereign Palestinian state. The Arabs demand that Israel take the refugees back and compensate them for the land seized by Israel since 1948. The Israelis reject this demand, although a limited number of the refugees may be readmitted within the context of an overall peace settlement.

The prospect of such a settlement has been pushed back further into the future by the Israeli invasion of southern Lebanon in June 1982, justified by the Begin government as a necessary means to assure the security of Israeli territory from recurring attacks by PLO guerrillas well equipped with modern weapons. Israeli forces captured part of Beirut, and they cut the main highway between that city and Damascus in Syria.

The Reagan administration worked hard to find a solution to the new situation in Lebanon. Its first goal was to reestablish the full sovereignty of the Lebanese government. In pursuit of this goal, the United States succeeded in inducing the withdrawal of the PLO military forces from southern Lebanon, including Beirut, and agreed to putting in place a multinational military force in that city in which American marines participated. The next step was to be the withdrawal of all foreign military forces from Lebanon: the Israelis, Syrians, and the remaining PLO guerrillas.[49] This action was to be carried out within the context of a U.S. proposal for peace in the region made by President Reagan on September 1, 1982, which contained the following specific points:

1. An immediate halt to further settlements in the West Bank and Gaza;
2. Free elections for a self-governing Palestinian authority followed by a 5-year transition period;
3. The peaceful and orderly transfer of authority from Israel to the Palestinian inhabitants of the West Bank and Gaza during the transition period;
4. The self-government of the Palestinians to be conducted in association with Jordan;
5. Jerusalem should remain undivided but its final status should be decided by negotiation.[50]

Reagan did not think that the formation of an independent Palestinian state was possible and stressed that Israel's right to a secure future had to be recognized. He said: "America's commitment to the security of Israel is ironclad."[51] Nevertheless, Israel immediately rejected the Reagan proposals, calling them a violation of the Camp David peace process.[52] The proposal received a better reception from the Arab states and the PLO, who offered qualified approval. Meanwhile, U.S. efforts to rebuild a peaceful Lebanon, free of all foreign forces and sovereign over all its territory, continue through complex and protracted negotiations. Secretary of State Shultz involved himself personally in achieving the withdrawal of Israeli, Syrian, and PLO forces from Lebanon. Shuttling between Lebanon and Israel for nearly 2 weeks and at the same time keeping Egyptian, Saudi, and Jordanian leaders informed of the progress of the negotiations, Shultz succeeded in obtaining an agreement by Israel and Lebanon about the conditions of the withdrawal of Israeli forces. However, a precondition for that withdrawal was similar and simultaneous action by the Syrian and PLO troops. The agreement, however, is violently opposed by Syria, whose position is strongly backed by Moscow and which has received large amounts of Soviet tanks, anti-aircraft weapons, and other equipment. As a consequence, the outcome of this struggle is uncertain at this writing.

The frictions between the United States and Israel have been generally dissipated as a result of the cooperative behavior of the Israeli negotiators, but these frictions may arise again whenever talks should begin on the conditions in the West Bank area. The central issue remains Israel's perception of insecurity and of threats from its neighbors. With the climate of peace with Egypt eroding, the perceptions of Israeli insecurity will increase, and the settlement policy will continue. The prospects of cutting this Gordian knot are still far in the future, and it will require new U.S. policy initiatives to bring about a solution.

EXPLANATORY VARIABLES

Perhaps more than in any other policy area, international variables have been responsible for the economic and military assistance policies of the United States toward the Third World. These variables are mostly of the "interactional" type; situations and conditions in a particular country or groups of countries were the stimuli for specific policies. However, systemic variables have also exerted some influence on policy formulation. The prevailing free-market economic system has been held responsible by many Third World leaders for the economic development problems in their countries and has led the Group of 77 to demand changes in the form of the NIEO. These demands required policy responses by the United States. They were rejected as far as they aimed at a complete restructuring of the global economic system. However, some individual demands such as the general preference system for LDC-manufactured and semi-manufactured goods received not only a sympathetic hearing but became U.S. policy, although perhaps not to the extent desired by the Group of 77. Other demands are still in various stages of negotiations in U.N. forums in which Washington plays an active role.

Another systemic variable influential on policy formulation has been the East-West relationship. This includes the perceived threat by the United States of Soviet expansionist designs and the actual Soviet interventions in Africa and Asia to exert control over selected countries such as Ethiopia and more recently Vietnam. Third World countries considered vulnerable to these threats and to possible interventions received military and economic assistance depending on interactional variables flowing from individual situations and from the ability of the countries involved to contribute to the U.S. policy of containing the Soviet Union and Soviet-supported Communist satellites and surrogates. Cuba is a prime example of the latter.

A third systemic variable that has influenced U.S. policy toward Third World countries is found in the global physical system, namely, the gradual exhaustion of petroleum reserves. Policies toward the OPEC countries were shaped by the concern about protecting this valuable resource for the Western industrialized countries from outside interference and assuring the continued flow of oil. These concerns also influenced policies toward non-oil producers. Examples are Israel and Pakistan (a neighbor of Soviet-invaded Afghanistan). American military and economic aid was offered to Pakistan in much greater amounts after the Soviet invasion of Afghanistan.

In institutional terms, the basic input for economic assistance has come from the various foreign aid organizations, the most recent of whom has been AID. The Department of Agriculture also had an indirect input into economic assistance through the administration of PL 480, the sale of agricultural commodities to LDCs (which for wheat, cotton, and rice are considerable), and technical assistance programs to Third World countries for the more efficient production of farm commodities. The provision of food to feed hungry mouths has always been a high U.S. priority. The Commerce Department also had an interest in LDCs, and during the 1970s exports to developing countries grew faster than to the developed states, even if OPEC is excluded. This trend is likely to continue, and therefore, the LDC market is considered to be the most dynamic export market of the United States.[53]

Of course, given the linkage between North-South and East-West relations in U.S. policy formulation, with the latter usually predominating, the Defense Department has a major voice where military assistance programs are to be put in place. Over the years as U.S. aid programs to the Third World have shifted from a broad, often undifferentiated approach to a more selective one with the bulk of assistance given to what were considered strategically important countries, the institutional influence of the Pentagon has increased among the executive departments and agencies of the U.S. government.

As far as the overall level of foreign aid is concerned, congressional approvals have lagged behind the requests made by the executive branch, and as time has passed since the 1950s, congressional appropriations have been declining in terms of percentage of GNP. One of the reasons is the lack of a powerful constituency in support of aid, especially economic assistance, despite the economic benefits that flow from requirements to spend most or all of the funds in the United States. The situation is quite different with respect to military sales, even if payments are guaranteed by the United States. A very powerful lobby, with the help of constituents in many states where weapons and equipment are produced, ensures that the MAPs are approved by Congress.

As far as societal variables are concerned, a permissive consensus exists, especially for aid that contributes to the containment of communist expansionism. Otherwise, interest in assistance to the Third World is low, as is illustrated by the difficulty of the United Nations Association of the United States to retain the few members it has nationwide.

In terms of idiosyncratic variables, the influence of four presidents on economic aid programs should be mentioned. President Eisenhower was largely responsible for the Food for Peace program; President Kennedy assumed the leadership in putting the Alliance for Progress in place, which was less than a success; and President Carter injected his human rights concern into aid policy and appeared to be particularly sensitive to African problems as reflected by the appointment of a black, Andrew Young, to the post of U.S. ambassador to the United Nations. President Reagan injected his profound belief in private enterprise into the aid policies, which changed their character, but it is far from certain whether this new thrust will be successful.

Both Carter and Reagan became intimately involved in the formulation of Middle East policies. Carter, through remarkable persistence against many odds, succeeded in bringing about the 1979 Camp David Accord between Begin and Sadat. However, whether this accomplishment will ultimately produce a lasting peace in the Middle East is becoming increasingly uncertain.

Perhaps the underlying assumptions of the accord were not quite realistic. The same can be said about President Reagan's peace proposals made in September 1982. Although well-meaning and comprehensive, the proposals ignored Israel's frantic concern about security after having been the victims of recurring PLO attacks for many years. In that respect, no matter how offensive Prime Minister Begin might be to some Israelis and especially to the outside world, he has overwhelmingly high emotional support, and therefore, unless the Reagan proposals are susceptible to modification, they are likely to be doomed.

SUMMARY

American policies toward the Third World must take account of the general characteristics of the developing countries. They include low per capita income, low level of industrialization, reliance on exports of primary products (agricultural and minerals), high unemployment, low levels of literacy, high rates of disease and famine, rapidly increasing population, frequently traditional social systems, and authoritarian or one-party political systems.

Initial U.S. policy goals in the 1950s stressed the *upgrading of economic levels*, the *promotion of democracy*, and *strengthening developing countries* perceived to be vulnerable to Soviet threats. Foreign aid in terms of percentage of GNP was close 1 percent; most aid was given bilaterally to engender gratitude from recipients.

In the 1960s, greater emphasis in U.S. policy was placed on *self-help*, increased *use of loans instead of outright grants*, and a *higher concentration* of aid on a *small number* of developing countries. A major project was the *Alliance for Progress* in Latin America, which by and large turned out to be a failure.

The Third World challenged American policymakers with the creation of the *United Nations Conference on Trade and Development (UNCTAD)* in 1964, and its political arm, the *nonaligned movement*, established in the mid-1950s. UNCTAD's objectives included *expanded exports* of Third World-manufactured and semimanufactured goods to the advanced countries, the *stabilization* of Third World export commodity prices, and *increased financial resources*. The United States accommodated to a large extent the demand for expanded exports by eliminating most tariffs for Third World goods. Greater financial resources were made available from public and private sources as well as international institutions such as the IMF and World Bank. However, no comprehensive agreement has been reached on price stabilization for commodity export prices. Washington also *rejected* the *free transfer of technology and patent rights* demanded by UNCTAD.

In terms of percentage of GNP, American public economic aid to the Third World *declined* during the 1970s and 1980s to about 0.27 percent, while the Third World wanted 0.70 percent. Under the Reagan administration, the assistance emphasis changed and the *private sector* was called on to provide aid through *investments and trade*. The model for this kind of foreign aid is the *Caribbean Basin Initiative*, under which private firms are offered tax incentives for new investment in that area.

Another significant development in U.S. policy toward the Third World has been increasing concern with the *security dimension*. Most aid, economic and military, since the 1960s was made available on the basis of security considerations, especially with respect to communist-related threats or expansionist designs.

American policy toward OPEC and the Middle East had two main objectives: the *assurance of adequate oil supplies* to America and Western Europe and the *restoration of peace* in the region. The principal vehicle for the first objective is the *International Energy Agency* located in Paris. A second instrument to be used in the event of Soviet moves toward the Persian Gulf, possibly from Afghanistan, would be the *Rapid Deployment Force* in order to deny Soviet access to oil-rich Saudi Arabia and other gulf states. Although energy conservation in the consumer countries has produced a substantial *oil surplus* at present that has materially lowered oil prices, this situation may be reversed as the world economy expands again.

In spite of energetic efforts on the part of the United States to bring peace to the Middle East by first seeking the *withdrawal of foreign troops from Lebanon* and later *finding a modus vivendi for the Palestinians* on the West Bank of the Jordan, the outlook for success remains bleak. Syria opposes a withdrawal agreement reached between Lebanon and Israel, and the Israeli government is so obsessed with security that the Palestinian issue has little prospect of being solved in the near future.

NOTES

1. The People's Republic of China's per capita GNP was $230 in 1980, while that of the German Democratic Republic (East Germany) was $5710 [The World Bank, *World Development Report* (Washington, D.C., 1981), Table 1, pp. 134–135].
2. Ibid.
3. See Albert Fishlow, Carlos F. Diaz-Alejandro, Richard R. Fagen, and Roger D. Hansen, *Rich and Poor Nations in the World Economy* (New York: McGraw-Hill, 1978), pp. 174–180.
4. For additional details, see Robert L. Rothstein, *The Third World and U.S. Foreign Policy* (Boulder, Colo.: Westview Press, 1981), pp. 147–154.
5. Karl P. Sauvant, "The Origins of the NIEO Discussions," in *Changing Priorities on the International Agenda*, edited by Karl P. Sauvant (New York: Pergamon Press, 1981), pp. 7–40, on p. 14.
6. World Bank, *World Development Report*, 1980, p. 34.
7. Sauvant, "Origins of the NIEO Discussions," p. 12.
8. World Bank, *World Development Report*, 1981, p. 6.
9. Thomas G. Paterson, *American Foreign Policy*, 2nd ed. (Lexington, Mass.: D.C. Heath, 1983), p. 455.
10. Cecil V. Crabb, Jr., *American Foreign Policy in the Nuclear Age*, 3rd ed. (New York: Harper & Row, 1972), p. 408.

11. Ibid., pp. 340–341.
12. Joan Edelman Spero, *The Politics of International Economic Relations* (New York: St. Martin's Press, 1981), pp. 158–159.
13. Ibid., pp. 191–192.
14. Ibid., p. 162.
15. For details see Odette Jankowitsch and Karl P. Sauvant, "The Initiating Role of the Non-Aligned Countries," in Sauvant (ed.), *Changing Priorities*, p. 41–72.
16. *Time*, January 10, 1983, p. 43.
17. For details, see Werner J. Feld, *Multinational Corporations and U.N. Politics* (New York: Pergamon Press, 1980), esp. Chapters 5–8.
18. U.S., Department of State, Bureau of Public Affairs, *UNCTAD IV: Expanding Cooperation for Global Development*, May 6, 1976, pp. 9–11.
19. World Bank, *World Development Report*, 1980, p. 140.
20. U.S., Department of State, Bureau of Public Affairs, *U.S. Foreign Assistance Programs for Fiscal Year 1979*, March 2, 1978, pp. 8–10.
21. U.S., Department of State, Bureau of Public Affairs, *America and the Developing World*, July 23, 1979.
22. Ibid.
23. U.S., Department of State, Bureau of Public Affairs, *Development Assistance for the Third World*, March 19, 1981, pp. 3–4.
24. U.S., Department of State, Bureau of Public Affairs, *Challenges of World Development*, September 29, 1981.
25. U.S., Department of State, Bureau of Public Affairs, *Cooperative Strategy for Global Growth*, October 15, 1981.
26. U.S., Department of State, *Challenges of World Development*.
27. U.S., Department of State, Bureau of Public Affairs, *U.S. Interests in the Caribbean Basin*, GIST, May 1982.
28. For details, see Werner J. Feld and Robert S. Jordan, *International Organizations* (New York: Praeger, 1983), pp. 245–256.
29. U.S., Department of State, Bureau of Public Affairs, *Foreign Assistance and U.S. Foreign Policy*, May 1, 1978, pp. 5–6.
30. U.S., Department of State, Bureau of Public Affairs, *International Security and Economic Cooperation FY 1983*, March 1982, p. 10.
31. *Facts on File*, 1981, p. 787. See also U.S., Department of State *Bulletin* 81, 2057 (December 1981), pp. 1–9 for details.
32. *Facts on File*, 1981, p. 787.
33. Ibid., p. 788.
34. Spero, *Politics of International Economic Relations*, p. 204.
35. Rothstein, *Third World and U.S. Foreign Policy*, pp. 153–154.
36. *Times-Picayune* (New Orleans), September 13, 1982.
37. Arthur S. Banks and William Overstreet (eds.), *Political Handbook of the World 1981* (New York: McGraw-Hill, 1981), p. 587.
38. *Times-Picayune* (New Orleans), February 2, 1983.
39. For a summary review of these agreements, see Treasury Secretary William Simon's testimony before the Subcommittee on Multinational Corporations, Committee on Foreign Relations, U.S. Senate, August 12, 1974.
40. See Henry R. Nau, "Diplomatic Uses of Technology in U.S. Energy Policy," paper presented at the convention of the International Studies Association/South, Lexington, Kentucky, October 22–25, 1974; also Nau's *National Politics and International Technology: Nuclear Reactor Development in Western Europe* (Baltimore: Johns Hopkins University Press, 1974).
41. U.S., Department of State *Bulletin*, March 4, 1974.
42. See Nau, "Diplomatic Uses of Technology."

43. See Carl A. Ehrhardt, "Europe and Energy Policy at Top Level," *Aussenpolitik* 26, 1 (1975), p. 6.
44. *Agence Europe Bulletin*, July 11, 1974.
45. For a more detailed account of the OPEC activities, see Spero, *Politics of International Economic Relations*, pp. 114–133.
46. Ibid., p. 265.
47. *Times-Picayune* (New Orleans), March 8, 1983.
48. U.S., Department of State, *International Security and Economic Cooperation*, Appendix A, p. A-6.
49. For details see U.S., Department of State, Bureau of Public Affairs, *Securing a Peaceful Future for Lebanon*, December 2, 1982.
50. *Facts on File*, September 3, 1982, pp. 143–144, which reproduced Reagan's address on Mideast policy verbatim.
51. Ibid.
52. Ibid.
53. U.S., Department of State, Bureau of Public Affairs, *U.S. Trade and Foreign Policy*, October 29, 1981, p. 3.

CHAPTER 13

American Foreign Policy Aspirations and Results: A Summary Assessment

The basic purpose of any state's foreign policy is the promotion of its national interests, and U.S. foreign policy is no exception. Policymakers hope to achieve this purpose by effectively influencing the behavior of other states, IGOs, and powerful nongovernmental actors in such a way as to assure U.S. territorial integrity and security, enhance the economic well-being of the American people, and allow them to maintain their traditional way of life.

As we have seen in the preceding chapters, to achieve these ends requires policy formulation that takes into careful account the comparative capabilities of other international actors, the opportunities and limitations flowing from the global physical environment, and selected relevant domestic needs. To implement the policies thus formulated, the choice of appropriate instruments is crucial. Unless government leaders devise their policies diligently and realistically, and select their implementing instruments with great circumspection, they may not attain their policy objectives, and the outcome of the whole policy process may be quite different from what they intended.

How have major U.S. foreign policies fared with respect to their intended objectives? How have the aspirations of the policymakers been treated by the harsh realities of the world? What were some of the reasons that aspirations and realities could not be matched? This chapter will present a brief catalogue of policy successes, failures, and mixed results, and seek to answer some of the above questions.

SUCCESSES

Considering the volatility of the international situation and frequent changes in the distribution of power in the world, *unqualified* successes in the foreign policies of any state are rare, especially if one evaluates outcomes from a historical perspective over a protracted period. For the United States since World War II the most clear-cut and comprehensive success, considering the particular aims of the policy, has been the European Recovery Program, better known as the Marshall Plan. Western Europe's recovery during the 1950s was solid and greatly added to the economic and political stability of the EC member states during the 1960s and 1970s. The instruments employed for the transfer of the massive funds from the United States to Western Europe and for their distribution in that region—the ECA and OEEC—performed generally well, and thus the outcome of the policy coincided with its intended goal.

In spite of recurring frictions among the members of the Atlantic Alliance, NATO must also be marked up as a success of American foreign policy. NATO has fulfilled the basic objectives of U.S., Canadian, and West European policymakers to serve as a barrier to possible Soviet aggression against the European alliance members. American steadfast support of the NATO goals has been a significant factor in this outcome. However, the future relations among the NATO members may be clouded; a major reason is the prospective deployment of U.S. theater nuclear weapons and the concurrent arms control negotiations on these weapons between the two superpowers, to which we will return later.

Both NATO and the Marshall Plan have contributed significantly to the success of another U.S. policy, the containment of Soviet expansionism, *at least as far as Western Europe is concerned.* In this respect, the intended policy goal became the actual outcome as of this time. Of course, this outcome was to a large degree also a result of a successful nuclear deterrence policy, based first on the strategy of massive retaliation and later on the doctrine of flexible responses. Indeed, without a powerful nuclear "sword," American security policy would have had a much weaker foundation, and Soviet containment in Western Europe may have failed.

Trying to stop continued escalation of nuclear weapons and their underlying technology, which eventually might undermine the MAD principle of the deterrence strategy, was the aim of the SALT negotiations during the early 1970s. The Nixon-Kissinger team achieved an initial breakthrough toward this goal with the signature and ratification of the SALT I agreement and the conclusion of the Vladivostok accord. This must be seen as a success of U.S. policy, although there was no follow-up through SALT II and the START negotiations. Meanwhile, the two superpowers, for the present at least, comply with the unratified provisions of SALT II.

Finally, another policy venture devised and carried out during the Nixon-Kissinger era must be recorded as a success of U.S. foreign policy. This is the opening of relations between the United States and the PRC, which, under the Ford and Carter administrations, bloomed into full diplomatic and economic intercourse. After two decades of ignoring the PRC, which failed to produce any fundamental change in the Communist regime of China or to influence its international behavior, the new relationship with Beijing enhanced American flexibility to deal with the Soviet threat by being able to take advantage of balance-of-power realities that emerged from the U.S. policy moves. The continued success of this policy, however, depends on the level of commitment on the part of the Reagan and succeeding administrations to the relationship with the PRC and their skill of implementation. It also is contingent on what directions PRC interests and goals will take in the future and on its international behavior.

FAILURES

Undoubtedly, the greatest failure of U.S. policy since World War II has been in Vietnam. Whatever the particular reasons for the defeats on the battlefield, the policies formulated especially by the Johnson administration both disregarded societal realities in the United States and misunderstood the nature and fervor of the motivations driving the communist leadership in Hanoi and the Viet Cong guerrillas in what was then South Vietnam. In the United States the psychological resources for fighting as difficult and protracted a war as Vietnam were lacking, but only a few policymakers were aware of this problem in 1964 or 1965. Moreover, the various U.S. administrations were unable to offer fully convincing justifications for being in Vietnam. The fighting spirit and the resilience of the Vietnamese and Viet Cong were underestimated, and the tactics employed by U.S. armed forces to gain victory were either inappropriate or poorly applied.

The consequences of the Vietnam debacle were far-reaching but most likely were not foreseen by policymakers when the pertinent policies were framed in the middle 1960s. Because of the debacle, Congress was anxious to place constraints on the Executive and there has been considerable reluctance to get America involved again in foreign adventures. This gave Moscow opportunities to expand its influence in Africa, Asia, and Latin America. The Soviet instrument for this expansion was the deployment of Soviet military and political advisors to Ethiopia, Angola, and Mozambique, reinforced by East German and Cuban soldiers. In Asia, the Vietnamese, supported by Soviet arms and money, play Moscow's game and have subjugated most of Indochina. In Central America, although it is not quite clear how intimate the relationship is between Moscow and the Sandanistas or the Salvadoran guerrillas, the Soviet Union has increased its influence during the early 1980s, even though this influence is exercised mostly through Moscow's client, Cuba.

Another consequence of Vietnam is primarily psychological in nature, but nevertheless, it constitutes a significant reality in international politics. This is the perception that the military power of the United States is declining while that of the Soviet Union is growing. Public opinion polls in Western Europe bear this out,[1] and similar perceptions may prevail elsewhere. The rearmament efforts by the Reagan administration may change these perceptions, but it is too early to say what the long-term perceptual trends will be. They may well depend on the support the American people give to continued, steep upgrading of the U.S. defense posture. Public opinion polls taken in November 1982 by the Gallup organization suggest that support for increased defense spending has dropped substantially and that peace and arms control have become higher priorities.[2] Indeed, the House of Representatives appears to have many members who are sympathetic to the nuclear freeze movement, which may augur badly for the continued strengthening of the U.S. military. The same polls indicate that both the general public and elites are wary of direct intervention in Central America.[3] Additional funds for the El Salvador military and economic support missions, requested by President Reagan, are opposed by many members of Congress. Certainly until now, this mission, started in earnest in 1981, has not been successful in spite of the elections held in the spring of 1982, and, unless the State Department and diplomatic changes made in June 1983 produce better results than achieved so far, this policy may also fall into the category of failures.

All this brings us back to the basic U.S. policy of containing not only Soviet expansionism but communism in general. We have pointed out that in Western Europe this policy has been eminently successful. In Asia, however, this policy did not prevent the Soviet invasion of Afghanistan, which clearly extended Soviet military direct influence beyond the areas Moscow has dominated since 1948 (i.e., the East European satellites Poland, Czechoslovakia, Hungary, Romania, Bulgaria, and East Germany). Moreover, as mentioned earlier, Soviet influence grew in some countries in the Third World as well.

In the economic-political sphere, the sanctions imposed on Poland failed to change significantly the behavior of the Polish government. Indeed, the U.S. attempt to prevent the delivery of high-technology items, produced under U.S. patents, for the construction of the Soviet gas pipeline in order to punish Moscow for the part it played in the imposition of martial law in Poland, backfired. It generated such opposition by the European NATO allies, especially France, West Germany, Great Britain, and Italy, that the sanctions had to be dropped in order to reduce the enormous tensions that the U.S. policy had created within the NATO family.

Finally, the Alliance for Progress was a U.S. policy that turned out to be largely a failure. Aiming to give Latin America a sustained economic uplift, its various implementation instruments such as administrative reforms and changes in the traditional patterns of land ownership flew head on in the face of political and social realities that had been ignored by otherwise well-meaning policymakers. Moreover, the expectation that large-scale contributions for investment would be forthcoming from private sources reflected too much confidence in the profit motive of large corporations, which did not see the investment opportunities throughout Latin America that were envisioned by the policy planners. Even the charisma of President Kennedy could not overcome the gaps between policy objective and the perceived realities of the situation.

MIXED RESULTS

A prime case in which American foreign policy aspirations were fulfilled initially but where the outcomes later diverged considerably is Washington's policy toward the political unification of Western Europe. This policy's aim and rationale were to create a strong "two-pillar" Atlantic Community based in Western Europe on a politically unified entity, whereby the common defense against Soviet aggressive designs would be strengthened. The United States was prepared to accept major economic costs to achieve this policy. As shown in Chapter 11, progress toward unification was indeed made by the EC member states until the early 1960s.

However, while for some Europeans political union remains a pleasant vista and some political leaders support it with equally pleasant rhetoric, the reality of revived nationalism in all the member states has reduced the Community institutions into nothing more than an intergovernmental structure that is operated in accordance with the utilitarian interests of the current ten EC members. In part, this outcome may have been due to unwise implementation of the American policy. Too much pressure was exerted during the 1950s by the Eisenhower administration to push unification forward. At the same time, the EC has grown into a powerful competitor of the United States in international trade and has created trading blocs in Europe, the Mediterranean, and Africa harmful to U.S. export interests. The resulting, sometimes severe, frictions across the Atlantic have not only left their scars on the economic relationship between the United States and Western Europe, but have also spilled over into the military-strategic sphere. Although the strong opposition to the deployment of U.S. nuclear theater weapons (Pershing II and cruise missiles) by various groups in Western Europe has as its principal sources the plain fear of nuclear devastation and the desire to extract Western Europe from the struggle between the superpowers, the transatlantic competition for economic advantages has aggravated the existing tensions. American policy implementation, in turn, has not always displayed the necessary sensitivity to and empathy with European concerns, which from the American perspective may appear as weak-kneed neutralism and moves toward "Finlandization," but which nevertheless represent political realities that are difficult to tackle by U.S. policymakers.

Another example of mixed foreign policy results is the Camp David accord among Presidents Carter and Sadat and Prime Minister Begin. Hailed by

Carter as an outstanding success, it initially produced some of the anticipated results when Israel evacuated the Sinai peninsula to return this territory to Egypt. However, the autonomy talks for the Palestinians on the West Bank and the Gaza Strip have not made any material progress, and the peace in the region desired by both Carter and Reagan remains elusive.

The reality is that Prime Minister Begin, with the support of many Israelis, persists in the continuation of his settlements policy on the West Bank for perceived security needs and for the "reincorporation of Judea and Samaria" into the state of Israel. Hence the realistic prospects for a solution of the Palestinian problem on anything but Israeli terms are bleak, and this should have been taken into consideration by U.S. policymakers when Reagan's peace proposals were made in September 1982. Their rejection by the Israeli government was predictable.

Without question, the Israel-Palestinian issue is the key to peace in the Middle East regardless of American policies toward other states in the region, such as Saudi Arabia, Egypt, and Jordan. Large-scale arms deliveries to these countries, whether purchased with cash or provided under various grants, may enhance the security of the region; but how, for example, a country like Saudi Arabia could use the very sophisticated weapons systems delivered by Washington effectively against a Soviet onslaught remains highly problematic. A possible rationale may have been that in case of need these systems could be employed by American forces. However, there is always the danger of an internal upheaval as the case of Iran has so dramatically shown, and the possibility always exists that these weapons systems might fall into enemy hands. Extreme religious movements and left-wing revolutionary groups may find fertile ground in countries ruled by tradition-laden wealthy dynasties as exist not only in Saudi Arabia but also other Persian Gulf states. These are realities policymakers must keep in mind if they want to avoid outcomes like the Iranian revolution, which resulted in a loss of American weapons and equipment that had been counted on as an important ingredient of U.S. security in the region.

Similar considerations also apply to arms deliveries to other Third World countries undertaken to bolster local and regional security in different parts of the world and expected ultimately to benefit U.S. policies of containing the spread of communist power. In spite of the clear risks in large-scale deliveries of weapons to Third World countries—they may be employed against neighbors or fall into the hands of countries hostile to the United States—it is not likely that the trend of these deliveries will be altered, especially as long as the Soviet Union follows the same policies, which reduce the LDCs' ability to improve their already poor economies.

The ultimate test for the congruence of policy goals and outcomes is likely to be the U.S. policy on arms control and disarmament as it evolves during the next few years. This policy will be closely related to the issue of continued buildup of the American defense posture, and, in fact, considerable intermeshing will and must occur between the formulation and implementation of the two policies. Moreover, Congress will involve itself much more than previously in what directions these policies will take, because the level of interest in these issues on the part of the American public has been rising rapidly. With increasing concerns about survival of a nuclear exchange between the superpowers on the minds of many Americans, as reflected by the growing nuclear freeze movement and many members of Congress responding to the demands of these movements sympathetically, the stage is set for the "politics of the unthinkable" inside and outside of Congress.

What are the military realities underlying the decisions to be made on these crucial issues for the United States and the world? To give answers to these questions is extremely difficult. The Reagan administration, alleging to give "straight facts" on an unflagging Soviet buildup to military superiority, claimed in 1983 that America must be rearmed to the tune of a record $1.6 trillion.[4] To prove the need for this rearmament, the administration released a multicolored brochure with photographs, illustrations, and charts. Henry Kissinger asks in *Years of Upheaval*: "What in the name of God is strategic superiority?" and then states that until we answer that question, "arms control will be threatened by demagoguery and the strategic buildup by the absence of a rationale."[5]

A third, very recent view by a well-known international relations specialist, Stanley Hoffmann of Harvard University, suggests the negotiation of an agreement between the superpowers that would leave each with only the kind and number of weapons needed for assured destruction and for the limited counterforce capacity against civilian populations (but not counter-silo capacity) that makes the threat of assured destruction credible.

> This entails getting rid of as many vulnerable systems as possible, giving up as many weapons that threaten the other side's weapons as possible, and, while there is still time, controlling those weapons whose proliferation could become unverifiable. It would mean both decreasing reliance on the land-based leg of the nuclear triad (which is the thickest leg on the Soviet side), and also avoiding or sharply limiting the deployment of Trident 2 submarines and sea-based cruise missiles in exchange for extensive reductions of Soviet land-based intercontinental missiles. It would of course mean abandoning the MX and the B-1.[6]

With respect to the deployment of the U.S. Pershing II and the ground-launched cruise missiles, Hoffmann believes that they are going to make only a marginal contribution to deterrence. Nevertheless, the Pershing is especially feared by the Soviet Union, because it can reach its territory within only 6 minutes of flight time. This provides a powerful incentive for Moscow to find a compromise in the LRINF talks. The incentive for Washington is its difficulty in holding the NATO allies to the deployment schedule agreed on in 1979. According to Hoffmann, the compromise must include a drastic reduction of SS-20 missiles, the elimination of the Pershing deployment, and a reduction of the cruise missiles.[7]

While Hoffmann's views present an attractive solution to difficult problems, it is far from sure that they take into account realistically the accommodation that would be needed to be made by the Soviet government. That government is not subject top the same kind of public opinion and legislative pressures to which the U.S. administration is exposed. Only a concentrated effort to mobilize world public opinion in support of a truly mutual reduction of superpower nuclear weapons *might* have enough of an impact on the Soviet leadership to make them take the appropriate steps for nuclear disarmament, and even that is far from certain.

Perhaps a less confrontational stance than that adopted by the Reagan administration might serve as an inducement for accommodation to a true reduction of nuclear weapons. Whatever U.S. policies may emerge, their *outcomes* may not be fully assessable until the end of the decade. Hopefully, the world can be spared a nuclear holocaust. In this respect, it is unfortunate that few of the current American leaders have had an opportunity to witnesss the awesome sight of a nuclear mushroom cloud and the accompanying destruction.

Attitude surveys of the general public and leaders taken in late 1982 suggest a declining concern about the military balance between the superpowers. These surveys also show a continuing erosion of the consensus that the national interest requires active American participation in world affairs.[8] Coupled with the concern about nuclear devastation, which, as we have noted earlier in this chapter, is reflected in the nuclear freeze movement and has struck a responsive chord in Congress, public opinion may well place definite constraints on arms control policy formulation regardless of Pentagon endeavors to counter the spread of dovish attitudes among the public. Hence American policymakers may well be faced with a very serious dilemma flowing from both domestic and international sources when they seek to develop the appropriate policies in this most critical area.

NOTES

1. Werner J. Feld and John K. Wildgen, *NATO and the Atlantic Defense* (New York: Praeger, 1982), p. 121.
2. *New York Times*, March 7, 1983, p. A15.
3. Ibid.
4. *Times Picayune* (New Orleans), March 10, 1983.
5. Henry Kissinger, *Years of Upheaval* (Boston: Little, Brown, 1982), p. 1029.
6. Stanley Hoffmann, "Detente without Illusions," *New York Times*, March 7, 1983, p. A15.
7. Ibid.
8. John E. Rielly, "America's World Role," *New York Times*, March 7, 1983, p. A15.

APPENDIX A

Acronyms

ABMs   antiballistic missiles

ACDA   Arms Control and Disarmament Agencies

AFL-CIO   American Federation of Labor and Congress of Industrial
            Organizations

AID   Agency for International Development

ALCM   air-launched cruise missile

ASEAN   Association of Southeast Asian Nations

AWACS   airborne warning and control system

BTO   Brussels Treaty Organization

CAP   Common Agricultural Policy

CDU/CSU   Christian Democrats (Germany)

CCNAA   Coordination Council for North American Affairs

CIA	Central Intelligence Agency
CIEC	Conference on International Economic Cooperation
CIPEC	Intergovernmental Council for Copper-Exporting Countries
CSCE	Conference on Security and Cooperation in Europe
DIA	Defense Intelligence Agency
DMZ	demilitarized zone
DOD	Department of Defense
DPRC	Defense Programs Review Committee
EC	European Communities
ECG	Energy Coordinating Group
ECA	Economic Cooperation Administration
ECSC	European Coal and Steel Community
EDC	European Defense Community
EEC	European Economic Community
EFTA	European Free Trade Association
EPC	European Political Community
ERP	European Recovery Program (Marshall Plan)
ESF	Economic Support Fund
Euratom	European Atomic Community
FAA	Foreign Assistance Act
FAO	Food and Agricultural Organization (United Nations)
FAS	Foreign Agricultural Service

FBI   Federal Bureau of Investigation

FDP   Free Democrats

FMS   foreign military sales

FSO   foreign service officer

GATT   General Agreement on Tariffs and Trade

GLCM   ground-launched cruise missiles

GNP   gross national product

GPS   general preference system

IAEA   International Atomic Energy Agency

ICA   International Commodity Agreements

ICA   International Communications Agency

ICBM   intercontinental ballistic missile

IDA   International Development Association

IDCA   International Development Cooperation Agency

IEA   International Energy Agency

IFC   International Finance Corporation

IG   interdepartmental groups

IGO   intergovernmental organization

ILO   International Labor Organization

IMF   International Monetary Fund

IMRB   intermediate-range ballistic missile

IRG   interdepartmental regional group

ISA	International Security Affairs
JCP	Japanese Communist Party
JCS	Joint Chiefs of Staff
JSP	Japanese Socialist Party
LDC	less-developed country
LPD	Liberal Democratic Party (Japan)
LRTNF	long-range theater nuclear force
LWV	League of Women Voters
MAAG	military assistance advisory group
MAD	mutually assured destruction
MAG	military advisory group
MAP	military assistance program
MBFR	Mutual Balance Force Reductions
MFN	most-favored nation
MIRV	multiple independently targetable reentry vehicle
MIT	Massachusetts Institute of Technology
MLF	multilateral force
MNC	multinational corporation
MNE	multinational enterprise
MRB	medium-range ballistic missile
MTN	multilateral trade negotiations
NATO	North Atlantic Treaty Organization

NGO   international nongovernmental organizations

NICs   newly industrialized countries

NIE   National Intelligence Estimate

NIEO   New International Economic Order

NLF   National Liberation Front

NPT   Non-Proliferation Treaty

NRO   National Reconnaisance Office

NSA   National Security Agency

NSC   National Security Council

NTB   nontariff barriers

OAS   Organization of American States

OCB   Operations Coordinating Board

OECD   Organization for Economic Cooperation and Development

OEEC   Organization of European Economic Cooperation

OMA   orderly marketing agreement

OPEC   Organization of Petroleum-Exporting Countries

PRC   People's Republic of China

RDF   Rapid Deployment Force

RIAS   Radio Information in the American Sector (of Berlin)

SACEUR   supreme allied commander—Europe

SALT   Strategic Arms Limitation Talks

SAM   surface-to-air missile

SEATO	Southeast Asia Treaty Organization
SIG	senior interdepartmental group
SLBM	submarine-launched ballistic missile
SOP	standard operating procedure
SPD	Social Democratic Party (Germany)
SRG	senior review group
START	Strategic Arms Reduction Talks
TNC	transnational corporations
UAW	United International Union of Automobile, Aerospace, and Agricultural Implements Workers of America
UNCLOS	United Nations Conference on the Law of the Sea
UNCTAD	United Nations Conference on Trade and Development
UNDP	United Nations Development Program
UNICEF	United Nations International Children's Educational Fund
UNRWA	United Nations Relief and Works Agency
USG	undersecretaries group
USIA	United States Information Agency
USIS	United States Information Service
USW	Unted Steel Workers
WEU	Western European Union
WSAG	Washington Special Actions Group
WTO	Warsaw Treaty Organization

Index